"Joseph Foresi's book is likely to produce future investment legends like those referenced within its pages. If I could turn back time, I would prioritize reading and re-reading this book and then implementing its Five-Factor Analysis on as many companies as I could. This book is certain to produce outstanding stock pickers in the years ahead that know how to select one career defining stock after another. It is the perfect book for aspiring investors and the CIOs, Directors of Research, and Professors who are looking to train them."

Colin Williams, *retired investment analyst, mutual fund manager and partner at William Blair, USA*

"Joseph Foresi has written a clear, useful guide to fundamental analysis, the cornerstone of business evaluation. Investors in publicly traded stocks, private equity, private debt, and venture capital can all use this book to help them make better decisions."

Ann C. Logue, *CFA, author of* Hedge Funds for Dummies

"This book focuses on a key foundation in equity markets – what ultimately drives valuation of a stock, which is critical for all investors. Joseph's work experience in equity analysis coupled with the clear writing provides a knowledgeable and easy-to-understand explanation of the topic. This book will help readers gain fundamental insights into their investment decisions."

Dave Kale, *professor, University of Rhode Island, USA*

Anatomy of a Stock

Calling aspiring financial analysts and serious professional investors! Written by a #1-ranked Wall Street analyst, this book will help you navigate the consistently unpredictable nature of financial markets through a sound, value-based investment approach.

Wall Street routinely cycles through different investment paradigms that often fail over the long term, because they don't take into account the only consistent thing about markets: their inconsistency. This book examines the positives and negatives of those paradigms to develop a fundamental, research-backed investing approach. Tools include the five-factor analysis method, step-by-step guidance for building financial models, and strategies for identifying market cycles, accompanied by clear explanations, real-world examples, and a structured ten-step investment process to successfully navigate the markets.

This book will be an essential resource for aspiring financial analysts, individual investors seeking professional-level insights, early-career investment professionals, and finance students at undergraduate and MBA levels. Let *Anatomy of a Stock* help you learn to invest like a pro!

Joseph D. Foresi is a finance professional with over two decades of experience. He was ranked the #1 analyst of the decade in 2020 based on stock picking performance out of thousands of analysts. He graduated magna cum laude from the University of Massachusetts, Amherst, and holds an MBA from Northeastern University and a doctoral degree from the University of Rhode Island.

Anatomy of a Stock

A Guide to Fundamental Equity Analysis for Aspiring Investors

Joseph D. Foresi

Routledge
Taylor & Francis Group
NEW YORK AND LONDON

Designed cover image: Tuadesk / © Getty Images

First published 2026
by Routledge
605 Third Avenue, New York, NY 10158

and by Routledge
4 Park Square, Milton Park, Abingdon, Oxon, OX14 4RN

Routledge is an imprint of the Taylor & Francis Group, an informa business

ISBN: 978-1-041-16845-4 (hbk)
ISBN: 978-1-041-16843-0 (pbk)
ISBN: 978-1-003-68664-4 (ebk)

DOI: 10.4324/9781003686644

Typeset in Times New Roman
by codeMantra

To my family

"An investment in knowledge pays the best interest."

– Benjamin Franklin

Contents

Figures

Tables

About the Author

Joseph D. Foresi is a finance professional with over 20 years of experience.

Over his career, Joseph has developed a robust financial skill set in understanding, analyzing, and leading public and private companies focused on identifying, creating, and capturing shareholder value.

He has applied his skill set to his work in the investment industry and corporate finance. In the investment industry, he has worked in private wealth and asset management. As a Wall Street equity analyst, he was ranked the #1 Analyst of the Decade in 2020 out of thousands of analysts based on his stock-picking performance. He has built domain expertise in the technology sector and areas like fintech and digital services. Joseph has been quoted in many financial publications, including *Barrons* and the *Wall Street Journal*, and made numerous public appearances including on CNBC.

Joseph has been part of the corporate finance leadership team for a Fortune 50 company where he utilized his expertise to drive shareholder value through the investor relations program. Before joining the IR team, he built and led an M&A origination team responsible for driving acquisitions for one of the world's most acquisitive companies.

Joseph graduated magna cum laude from the University of Massachusetts at Amherst. He has an MBA from Northeastern University and a doctorate from the University of Rhode Island. His thesis focused on valuation's role in the investment process. He has published academic papers, taught at the undergraduate and graduate level, given invited talks, and has had faculty appointments with various New England based college and universities. He and his family live in Boston, Massachusetts, where he works and serves on the board of several local organizations.

Acknowledgments

I would like to thank my wife, Sarah. I am sure she questioned my sanity in writing a book. I want to thank my children Julietta and Joseph for their patience. They are amazing and someday this book will sit on one of their shelves collecting dust like my father's does on mine.

I would like to acknowledge my immediate family. Dr. Joseph Foresi, Jr., who passed away during the writing of this book. He would often say he was proud of me, but never as much as I was to be his son. My mother Isabella for her constant encouragement and optimism. My brother Mark Foresi. Thank you for listening to me. My sister Sabrina, the creative sibling.

There are several colleagues who I have had the pleasure of working with throughout my career. Wall Street is filled with very talented people. Thank you to all of you! Dave Mackey and Colin Williams are two I want to particularly mention. They listened while I talked, which must have been a tough thing to do. I also want to acknowledge the associates who on my team: Jeffrey Rossetti, Michael Reid, Drew Kootman, Steven Chang, and Dan Reagan. I appreciate your hard work.

I believe knowledge is accumulated. I encourage the reader to take look at the bibliography or reading list on pages 279–282. I am an avid reader, who learned a little bit from all these books. They are great resources. I want to specifically acknowledge a few of the works. If you haven't read Peter L. Bernstein, you should. He has guided generations of finance professionals through his four masterpieces: *Capital Ideas*, *Against the Gods*, *The Power of Gold*, and *Capital Ideas Evolving*. I was and am a novice when it comes to stock screening. *Your Next Great Stock: How to Screen the Market for Tomorrow's Top Performers* by Jack Hough helped tremendously and *Business & Competitive Analysis: Effective Application of New and Classic Methods* by Craig Fleisher and Babette Bensoussan. I had the pleasure of coming across Wiley's *The Little Book Series*, which was very helpful, including the works by Pat Dorsey, Aswath Damodaran, and James Montier. If their great work is any indication of how good the rest of the series is, you should probably take a look.

A book like this takes several people to get it into the market. I would like to start by thanking Zick Rubin, who I came to as a first-time author. He guided me through the whole process. I would like to thank those who helped improve and edit this manuscript including Annie Logue and Dave Kale.

Introduction

> If you are ready to give up everything else and study the whole history and background of the market and all principal companies whose stocks are on the board **as carefully as a medical student studies anatomy**---if you can do all that and in addition you have the cool nerves of a gambler, the sixth sense of a clairvoyant and the courage of a lion, you have a ghost of a chance.
>
> -Bernard Baruch

The quote above is by the famous investor Bernard Baruch as part of his introduction to Charles Mackay's 1932 classic *Extraordinary Popular Delusion and the Madness of Crowds*. The book you are about to read provides you, the aspiring analyst or professional investor, with the tools to address one of the key characteristics Baruch believes is important to being a successful investor, studying the anatomy of a stock.

My book provides step-by-step instructions on "how to" perform fundamental equity research. The *Charter Financial Analyst (CFA)* program describes fundamental equity research as involving the analysis of a company's financial statements, business strategies, and macroeconomic factors to determine its intrinsic value and make investment recommendations.

I suggest the reader think of fundamental research as the foundation from which you can build or use different investment styles. I believe fundamental research works best when combined with a value investing approach. The combination of the two if practiced properly should result in superior, long-term stock picking success. This book provides the reader with equity research tools and examples of how to use those tools. My investment philosophy builds off the investment approaches set by some of the greatest investors of our generation. My contribution is this book, which should be thought of as a starting, not an ending point.

I designed this book for aspiring professional investors but believe it delivers value to a wide audience. The reader should be willing to take from it what you find interesting and works for you and leave the rest. I have read many investment books and academic journal articles over the decades leading me to believe this book is unique in it creates a hybrid between the high-level practitioner books, investor biographies, and academic textbooks taking practical elements from all three.

I believe humans are constantly looking for a way to understand the world around them. The previous is a simple sentence, but the phrase is far reaching. Think about it. We are constantly striving toward a better understanding of our surroundings. These understandings, laws, and science itself, whose process is like the investment process, are manmade. They are human creations.

The author is no different. He has a desire to understand the world around him, especially the chaotic world of investing, particularly in public equities. Why equities? Jeremy Siegel in his

DOI: 10.4324/9781003686644-1

popular book *Stocks for the Long Run* does perhaps the best job of making the case for investing in equities. According to Siegel, equities have provided the best return of any asset class over the long run. The total real (inflation adjusted) and nominal returns from 1802 to 2012 continue to favor stocks over the other asset classes. Total returns are the reinvestment of capital gains, interest, and dividends back into the business. Siegel 2014 5th edition of the book shows the return from investing $1 after inflation on a logarithmic scale. Annualized total returns for the different asset classes from 1802 to 2012 were 6.6% real (8.1% nominal) for stocks, 3.6% real (5.1% nominal) for bonds, 2.7% real (4.2% nominal) for bills, 0.7% real (2.1% nominal) for gold, and −1.4% real (1.4% nominal) for the US Dollar. Siegel notes stocks may fluctuate but eventually revert to the mean. I can only surmise given the market is at an all-time high in 2021 at the time of the initial writing of this introduction that stocks continue to outpace all other asset classes.

The irony is that we are very quick to forget the usefulness of fundamental analysis particularly value investing in bull markets. Benjamin Graham considered the "father of value investing" defined value investing as identifying and investing in companies trading below their intrinsic value based on a fundamental analysis. A fundamental, value-based approach to investing looks archaic when markets hit all-time highs. What could go wrong? Value investing, which continues to evolve, sometimes feels like insurance, you wonder why you have it sometimes, until you need it. I believe you need to have insurance all the time! As a quick reminder, the same inertia driving the market today drove it down in March 2020 due to fears regarding the pandemic, when a value-based approach to the market would have resulted in taking advantage of that buying opportunity.

If you believe in Jeremy Siegel, then developing the ability to pick the optimal or best portfolio of stocks would be a financially rewarding skill set. In fact, the discovery of a method to find the "optimal portfolio" is the goal of every investor. The search for the optimal stock portfolio often feels like Alchemy, the attempt to use chemistry and mix medals to create gold. As we will see, the investment community is constantly creating and retiring new market "beating" investment approaches or paradigms.

Siegel's book, which was first published in 1994, shed light on the strength of the historical returns in equities reigniting at the time an interest in equities as an asset class, which continues today. The key question in our opinion is, "What specific characteristics are necessary for a stock to outperform the market?" We believe in an in-depth knowledge of these characteristics, which we identify as the *Foresi Five Factors*, and their practical application currently puts the aspiring analyst in the best position to succeed. The truth is in stock picking and in life you can only put yourself in the best position to be successful.

We should start by accepting the element of luck in both life and stock picking, especially for the novice investor. Our efforts are constantly improving our understanding and processes to avoid the probabilistic contribution from luck.

The reader should be fair warned. They are about to embark on a difficult adventure. The deck is stacked against them from the beginning with a less than a 10% chance of even a mutual fund manager, someone who is considered an informed or professional investor, beating the market over a long period of time, a discouraging stat for the rest of us.

Typically, we can reduce our dependency on things like luck through hard work. The popular *10,000 Hour Rule* is the theory that if a person devotes 10,000 hours to learning a skill, they will master it. The 10,000-hour rule is helpful for rules-based games like chess and structured occupations. However, the problem with applying the same idea to investing is that financial markets are dynamic and always changing, so no matter how much you work at it, you will always run into something you have never seen before. It could be a new situation or a potential Black Swan, which is an unforeseen event with typically extreme circumstances.

One of the very few "laws" of the market is, "The only thing predictable about markets is they are unpredictable." Knowing this law and having a "healthy" paranoia toward it is a positive, which can be used to the investor's advantage. It is the reason no one specific investment approach or paradigm outside of a fundamental, value-based investment approach has worked in perpetuity to date. The more detailed the investment approach, especially the approaches primarily based on stock price movement, typically the more challenging it is for the approach to succeed over time. The good news is **all** market participants face this challenge.

Despite the challenges, I believe it is possible for individuals to deliver better than market returns over the long-term. These investors are going to need more than just hard work. I believe it is possible to beat the market by creating, focusing, and refining an investment process and analytical framework. I stress a heavy focus on improving the investment process over the results.

My book primarily teaches the reader how to perform fundamental equity research. I look at both the top down, which begins at the macro level like GDP and then narrows, and bottoms up approach, which starts with the micro or the company's financials and builds from there. My preference is for the bottoms up approach. Fundamental research can be paired with several different investment styles. I believe fundamental equity research is most successful when combined with value-based investing. Both my investment process and five factor analysis build off the value-based investing approach. My approach is grounded in fundamentals, yet flexible enough to adjust to the ever-changing market dynamics.

I view my work as a starting point for the aspiring investor, not an ending point. The information contained in my book should be thought of as a jumping-off point to be built on and adjusted based on the user's observations and to an extent the evolution of the markets. Investment approaches must evolve. We have seen this over the years with value investing, as future generations of "value" investors have adjusted the parameters around their approach to company characteristics and valuation. Similarly, my work in this book has evolved over time to include newer aspects of investing like psychology. I expect my investment process to continue to evolve.

I am NOT an expert, given the very nature of markets, there can be no experts, but I am experienced, which is an important factor to success. Markets are unpredictable, dynamic, and ever changing and evolving. They are constantly evolving in the short term in both a positive and negative manner with healthy fundamentals driving long-term success. We will hear more about the difference between expertise among analysts and those in other rules-based subjects from Daniel Kahneman in our psychology section.

Through trial and error associated with investing, we can begin to form good habits. If we work hard and accept markets are dynamic, we can layer in lessons learned (Rules) increasing our probability of success. Forming good investing habits, such as being disciplined in your investing approach, will help compensate for the unpredictable nature of markets and the psychological flaws of human beings. Good investing habits reduce our overall dependency on talent and luck.

If all of this sounds overwhelming, it is because it is. I would recommend indexing as the primary and best option for the average investor, especially those who don't have the time. However, the information in this book would be beneficial for the brave of heart. The ones who want to learn how to pick their own stocks like a professional. As we will see, indexing is a viable option for the average investor, but active management if conducted in the manner I am suggesting using the proper characteristics to locate the best investment opportunities and revisions can beat the market over the long term for those willing to take on the task.

I want to stress that it is extremely important to be flexible in our thought process or approach. As we will see, markets are cyclical and dynamic. One particular investment approach or paradigm shift may be suitable for a particular type of market environment, but not suitable for another. The history of Wall Street is littered with different investment approaches or paradigms like technical analysis, mutual funds, hedge funds, and quants. None of these approaches are in and of themselves at their core "bad" approaches. They just have design flaws, which allow them to work for a period but then fall out of favor. My research has found that among all the many different investment approaches throughout history, a fundamentally grounded, value-based investment approach is currently the best approach to long-term success and more importantly survival! A fundamental, value-based approach does the best job of accounting for the wild, unpredictable market swings and protects capital. It is important to note I came to my conclusion after years of practice, experience, and research. My conclusion is not my starting point and is probably not an end point.

There are numerous books written by a wide range of investment professionals and unfortunately nonprofessionals professing to provide a successful formula or methodology for stock picking success. Unfortunately, you can probably discard most of them. A standard, set formula does not exist in my opinion. The unpredictable, dynamic nature of markets makes all "trading" strategies obsolete over the long run. Remember my overriding theme, which I will repeat throughout this book, "The only thing consistent about the market is they are consistently unpredictable." As humans, our desire for mental shortcuts and need for a logical understanding pulls us toward this one size fits all "successful" investment approaches. We encourage the reader to, "Resist the Draw!"

My book does not provide a set formula. Instead, I focus on a establishing a successful fundamentally focused framework, a process driven approach to investing, and loose "rules" allowing the reader to begin with a much better starting point than if they were to just buy a stock "blindly" with no understand of the market or without doing any fundamental research, which happens almost all of the time, and actually serves as an advantage for those who are doing their homework. Although by no means perfect, I believe by shifting the focus to the process; rather than just the outcome, it will provide the investor with added flexibility, which is crucial in an unpredictable market.

I can't tell you how many times I have had a friend or relative ask me why the stock they bought is going up or down. Most of these conversations are one-sided as the individual hasn't even done the work to understand the company. The decision to purchase or sell the stock is based on a recommendation or a hunch. A small number of fortunes have been won in this speculative manner, but a much larger number of fortunes have been lost. The success stories get all the attention, while the losses get way too little. It astounds me to hear speculative investment stories. If someone buys a car or a house, they devote the time to understand what they are purchasing, but when it comes to investing, they seem to be willing to just, "Throw the money away." There are psychological reasons for this. It is amazing and an opportunity for an informed investor.

The last piece of the equation is values. I personally believe in being ethical in all endeavors. The challenge facing many investors is attempting to win at a game where winning is incredibly difficult and perhaps not sustainable, but extremely lucrative. The natural tendency is to try to gain an advantage in any way you can, particularly because there is money at risk. We cannot stress more empathically to stick to your ethical principles. Ethics is all we have at the end of the day making them incredibly important. Plus, if you cheat, you may lose with penalties being fines, jail, disbarment, etc. There have been many examples of this throughout time on both the company and investor side. I have unfortunately had a front row seat to witness some of these events.

The foundation of all investing is a cautious approach to risk. Investing at its core is about managing risk. I believe this type of approach is best reflected in a value-based investment approach. Value investing focuses on building and preserving long-term wealth, rather than getting rich quickly. My book focuses on stock picking, which is just one piece of a larger financial picture, where the real goal is to maximize your reward while managing your risk. Perhaps the most important rule of investing is:

Golden Rule: Investing is risky, so buy great companies with great prospects at great prices.

It sounds simple enough, but we will see as we progress through our journey how complicated it can get, especially when you include our innate, human psychological flaws.

The book you are about to read follows a logical progression. The first part of this book asks two very important questions, "Can you beat the market?" I believe the answer to this question is, "Yes." The next logical question then is, "How do you beat the market?" I attempt to answer the second question by looking at the positives and negatives associated with the different investment approaches: speculating vs. fundamentals, weighing the pros and cons, and examining the investors who have been successful at beating the market over the long term and their approaches. My conclusion is that a flexible, fundamental, value-based investment approach currently provides the best opportunity to succeed over the long term, because it accounts for the inevitability of market fluctuations and protects capital.

The second part of this book shows you how to perform fundamental research. It begins with the crucial understanding of the business cycle. Bringing us to another rule:

Golden Rule: Market movements combine psychology and fundamentals, two separate things.

Please re-read the prior sentence. Market volatility is **separate** from the fundamentals providing a savvy, patient investor with a true opportunity when they converge. A simple way to remember this is the market as well as stock price movement is based on psychology or investor sentiment; while fundamentals, which do exist, are altogether different. It is the convergence of these two areas that provides the best opportunities to invest. Investors can never count on anything, but true capitalism produces fluctuations in the business cycles consistently producing market volatility. Investor psychology works in much the same way as excitement and/or fear causes stock prices to appreciate or depreciate well ahead of any change in fundamentals. We will see the savvy investor uses the volatile nature of Mr. Market to their advantage.

The second half of this book walks the reader through our step-by-step approach to conducting fundamental equity research from a top down and bottoms up perspective. From a top-down perspective, I walk the reader through how to conduct an industry analysis and develop a "circle of competence" to identify stock opportunities.

My primary focus is the *bottoms up* approach to equity research, which is the method I recommend. I will introduce the reader to my ten step *Investment Process*. My investment process shows you where to find and how to aggregate qualitative and quantitative information on a specific company as you develop a basic understanding. My investment process walks the reader through the essential skill sets associated with being a successful investor including such things as creating a model, coming up with an intrinsic value and margin of safety, developing an investment thesis, and building a portfolio.

The most important step in my investment process is my *Five Factor* analysis, which is rooted in value investing. I propose a five factor analysis as a framework for identifying the investment opportunities with the characteristics or proper anatomy necessary to outperform the market over the long term.

I complement my investment process and five factor analysis with a set of *Golden Rules*, which are lessons learned from years of experience to guide us on our way. The goal is to learn and continue to improve our investment process and analysis over time, so that it helps us in our search for the next set of what we like to call "Forever" stocks or the best set of stocks you can own over the long term (five to ten years). If you can find enough of these stocks and buy them at the right price, you will be able to achieve the goal of all investors, which is constructing the optimal equity portfolio.

Think of your investment portfolio as your financial work of art. I begin by teaching you how to paint or conduct fundamental equity research through my bottoms up step-by-step investment process of looking at equities. I then focus on the most important factors, think of this as choosing your subjects for the painting through my five factor analysis. We belong to the value investing school of artists. Finally, my rules will serve as instructions for how to and how not to paint. The market itself will supply the paint through your different equity opportunities and price movements!

It is important to remember nothing is static. The information and analysis provided in this book was updated in 2024. Although the high-level takeaways have a perpetual shelf life, I expect the examples and even the processes can and will change and hopefully improve over time. I am reminded of all the examples of long-extinct investment approaches, industries, and companies we read about in all those old investment books. Today, there are exciting advancements in the areas of macro-economic modeling, data analytics, behavioral finance, and quantitative and socially responsible investing, which I expect will influence the next generation of investors and continue to build on the practice of fundamental analysis just like I have tried to do in my book.

Reading the book is not enough. It is only a starting point to success. The reader will then need to absorb the material and most importantly try investing for themselves. It is only through these real-life experiences where the lessons, which we call rules, are learned. The reader should use this book as a foundation for developing their own process and rules to become their own investment artist.

Happy Investing!

Dr. Joseph D. Foresi

Bibliography

CFA Institute. (2020, September). Advance Your Career with CFA Certification. www.cfainstitute.com

Mackay, C. (1981). *Extraordinary Popular Delusions and the Madness of Crowds.* Bonanza Books.

Siegel, J. J. (2014). *Stocks for the Long Run* (5th ed.). McGraw-Hill Education.

Part I

The Argument for Fundamental Research

Chapter 1

Why Fundamental Equity Research Matters

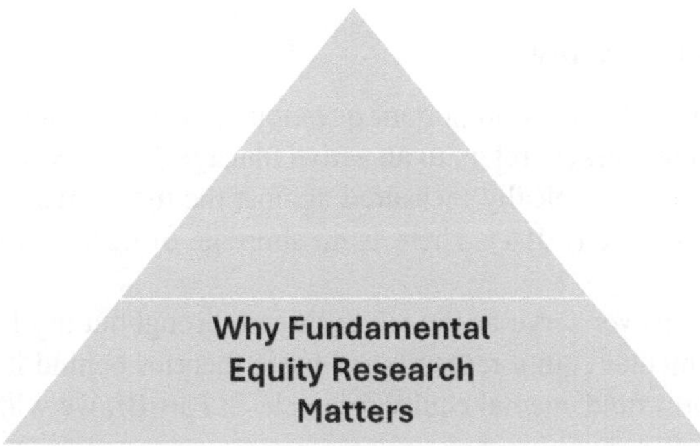

A Fitting Tribute

On January 17, 2019, the legendary Jack Bogle the founder of Vanguard passed away. It was a sad day in the investment community, which lost a revolutionary. Jack Bogle was a founder of the index investing, which is a common form of *passive investing* where the investor typically purchases a representative market benchmark and holds it for a long period of time. *Passive investing* tries to maximize returns by minimizing buying and selling activity, thus the use of the term passive. One of the first investment books I ever read was Bogle's (1999) *Common Sense on Mutual Funds*. Although I could never confirm it, I swear I once ran into the legendary Jack Bogle having breakfast at the Ritz Hotel in Philadelphia.

Bogle's passing received many tributes throughout the investment world. Perhaps one of the most touching tributes to Bogle came from a somewhat unusual source. A *CNBC* article at the time reminded its readers of Warren Buffett's tribute to Bogle at his 2017 annual Berkshire conference. Warren Buffett is perhaps the most famous *active* manager in history. *Active managers* make buy, hold, and sell decisions on their portfolio on a regular basis to outperform the market, which is in stark contrast to passive investing.

At the shareholder meeting, Warren Buffett did not hold back. He said, "Jack Bogle has probably done more for the American investor than any man in the country." Buffett went on to say,

> Many years ago, he (Jack) wasn't the only one that was talking about an index fund, but it wouldn't have happened without him. I mean, Paul Samuelson talked about it. Ben Graham even talked about it. But the truth is, it was not in the interest of the investment industry of Wall Street. It was not in their interest to develop index funds because it dramatically brought down

DOI: 10.4324/9781003686644-3

> fees. And, as we've talked about some in the reports, and other people have commented, index funds, overall, have delivered for shareholders a result that has been better than Wall Street professionals as a whole.

How big an impact have index funds had on shareholders, you may ask? Well, no surprise, Buffett tried to provide an answer. He concluded, "And I estimate that Jack, at a minimum, has saved (investors).... tens and tens and tens of billions...And those numbers are going to be hundreds and hundreds of billions over time." Bogle attended the 2017 meeting and was able to hear this glowing tribute in person just days before his 88th birthday.

Why would an active investing legend like Warren Buffett pay such tribute to Jack Bogle, one of the founders of the passive investing movement, especially when the growth in passive investing has negative implications for active managers? Let's see if we can find out.

Passive vs. Active Investing

We begin our journey with the most important question for any aspiring investor, "Can you beat the market?" "Beating the market" refers to an active manager's ability to outperform the market. An investor's performance is typically measured against the major market indices, S&P500 and Dow Jones Industrial Average (DJIA). There is no shortage of debate around the answer to this crucial question.

The question and its answer serve as the silver thread throughout my book. In Part I, we look at the validity of fundamental equity research and basic theories behind it. In Part II, I will show the reader how to perform fundamental equity research. In Part III, we will look at some different applications.

I begin by weighing in on the debate around the validity of active management. The move to passive management is the latest Wall Street paradigm. We look at a number of these different paradigms throughout the book through the lens of their luminaries and the luminaries' contributions. A common theme throughout the history of Wall Street is the multitude of different potentially successful investment approaches presented to investors. Each approach or shift challenges the validity of commonly accepted practices, but only a few including indexing and fundamental research have survived (Figure 1.1).

Two significant challenges to active management and fundamental equity research have come from the passive investment movement and the efficient market hypothesis (EMH). I believe passive investing, particularly low-cost indexing, has natural attributes like mirroring the market and a low fee structure, which provides it with long-term staying power, ahead of other paradigm shifts. The recent short term performance statistics favor passive investing over active investment

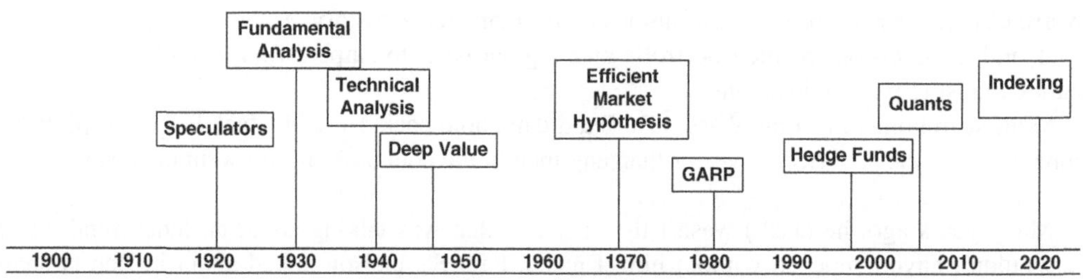

Figure 1.1 Wall Street's Changing Investment Landscape.

management, driving an impressive flow of funds into the indices and out of active management over the last two decades.

Although the recent trends toward passive investing are impressive, there is a need for active management. Indices are manmade implying a person can create a new portfolio of stocks with the potential to outperform the current indices. Passive and active management can co-exist. The active managers who adopt certain characteristics like low fees, low turnover (trading) structure will have the best opportunity to compete against the indexers. We need to remember one of the few market laws: The only predictable thing about the stock market is its unpredictability. Indexing has benefitted from a strong US domestic market, which will change over time. Ultimately, the dynamic nature of markets implies only humans making active decisions can outmaneuver it, at least at this point and time.

The foundation for indexing was set by the emergence of the EMH, a seismic paradigm shift coming from the academic community in the 1970s. Although passive investing (indexing) has potentially long-term staying power, the EMH essentially looks at stock prices as being efficient and representative of the company's intrinsic value. The validity of the EMH would have rendered fundamental equity research useless. The objections to the EMH have come from several different sources including investors and academics. I would argue that technology has increased market efficiency to an extent but has not eliminated it.

I currently agree with the consensus, which includes great fundamental investors like Warren Buffett himself, who believe the average investor should choose indexes. There are various reasons given for this, including my opinion, which is that, given the amount of effort and challenges associated with active, fundamental analysis, it is probably best for the average investor to stick with a low-cost indexing approach. However, there is room for the aspiring investor to succeed if given the right tools, which I present in this book.

I believe fundamental equity analysis still matters. The beauty of fundamental analysis is its flexibility. If practiced correctly, fundamental analysis theoretically takes advantage of market inefficiency and accounts for their inevitable, unpredictable nature. Other often price-based approaches like technical or quantitative analysis do not account for these seismic moves in the markets or the underlining fundamentals of a business. Fundamental analysis is a necessity not a nice to have.

I am a fundamentalist who believes it is possible to beat the market. However, it has been my experience that with the correct approach (process) and hard work, you can put yourself in the best position to identify significant equity investment opportunities on your own, which can deliver better than market, long-term returns.

Types of Investment Vehicles

Let's learn a little bit more about the various types of active and passive investment vehicles. Two of the more common active investment vehicles are mutual and hedge funds. According to the *Oxford Dictionary*, a mutual fund is an investment program funded by shareholders that trades in diversified holdings and is professionally managed. The concept of a mutual fund is to essentially pool assets for a professional manager to use to investment in assets like stocks, bonds, and others to drive a return for a fee. The advantages to a mutual fund is the fund pools capital from several investors, is professionally managed, and invests in a diversified group of assets.

There are different types of mutual funds. Mutual funds can be *closed* or *open ended*. A closed-end fund issues shares traded on a stock exchange. Open-ended funds, about 90% of all funds, issue shares redeemable by the investment company. Mutual fund shares typically reflect the Net Asset Value (NAV) of the portfolio, which is the value of the fund minus the liabilities divided by the outstanding shares typically calculated at the end of the day. Funds can be *load* or *no-load* funds. A load fund charges a fee when shares are purchased. A no-load fund does not.

The fee structure of mutual funds is controversial because it is large and sometimes hidden. Mutual funds charge numerous different fees. They charge a fee based on their assets with the average fee between 0.5% and 1.0%. Other potential fees include contingent deferred sales load, a 1–6% charge paid when withdrawing funds, or a 12b-1 fee, a fee charged to offset the costs of advertising and marketing. An expense ratio is the total management fees displayed as a percentage of the fund's assets. The average expense ratio for active mutual funds is 0.5–1.0%.

A second type of active management is a hedge fund. A hedge fund is a private investment vehicle available only to *accredited investors*. An accredited investor is an investor with a special status under the financial regulation laws of a country. For example, a person with an annual income exceeding $200,000 in the US is considered an accredited investor. Hedge funds are unregulated and tend to be riskier than mutual funds through their use of things like leverage. A hedge fund's standard fee structure is known in the industry as "2 and 20." The "2 and 20" fee structure includes a 2% fee for Asset Under Management, **and** a 20% fee for the profits being generated over a specific benchmark, known as a hurdle rate. Hedge fund fees are controversial because of their size. Hedge funds charge a standard management fee like mutual funds and share in the profit.

A combination of the high fee structure and mediocre performance has led to the emergence of indexing. Indexing is essentially the creation of a portfolio of assets, typically equities, which mirrors an index like the S&P500 or DJIA for a low fee. The expense ratio for indexing is 0.5% or lower. Indexes are traded as Exchange-Traded Funds or ETFs, which are financial instruments replicating the performance of the broader market, specific sector, and/or trend. ETF investment vehicles can be active or passive.

Passive Investing

John C. Bogle-Bogleheads

Don't Look for the Needle in the Haystack. Just Buy the Haystack

The story of passive investing begins with the John C. Bogle, the "father of index investing." As a college student at Princeton, Bogle, wrote his 130-page thesis based on an examination of the mutual fund industry entitled "The Economic Role of the Investment Company," which was published in 1951. The thesis itself was a remarkable achievement as Bogle was a C student struggling to pass an economics course taught by Princeton Professor Paul Samuelson, who was awarded a Nobel Prize in economist. Bogle put his efforts into his Senior Thesis to keep his scholarship and finish his college career on a positive note. The inspiration for the thesis came from a Fortune Magazine article titled "Big Money in Boston," which talked about the emerging mutual fund industry and a company called Massachusetts Investors Trust. Bogle found the topic fascinating and began working on his thesis. His hard work paid off. Bogle graduated magna cum laude. Walter Morgan, founder of Wellington funds and a Princeton graduate, read Bogle's thesis and later agreed to give him a job. Bogle would go on to write 13 books with his first book earning him a foreword from none other than Professor Samuelson. The thesis would go on to change the investment landscape forever!

Bogle's examination of the mutual fund industry led him to set up the first index mutual fund at Vanguard in 1975. Bogle's theory was instead of paying an investment company high fees to "professionals" to beat or outperform the market through active management, investors were better off mirroring the markets performance through a lower-cost index fund. Bogle's approach can best be described as "if you can't beat them, join them" in our opinion. He believed it is foolish to think high-fee active management can outperform indexing over the long run. In his 1999 book, *Common Sense on Mutual Funds*, Bogle lays out his investment philosophy, recommending investors take a common sense approach to investing based on eight basic principles: (1) Select low-cost funds, (2) Consider carefully the added cost of advice, (3) Do not overrate past fund performance, (4) Use past performance to determine consistency and risk, (5) Be aware of star or star mutual fund performers, (6) Be aware of asset size, (7) Don't own to many funds, and (8) Buy your fund portfolio and own it.

Jack Bogle would go on to become an investing legend. He and his investment principles developed a following among investors who call themselves *Bogleheads*, who subscribe to his principles on low-cost investing. They even have their own website, *Bogleheads Investing Advice and Info.*

Passive vs. Active Scorecard

The natural question is, "What do the statistics say about being able to 'beat' or outperform the market?" The answer to the question is an important one, as it serves as the foundation for active management. Beating the market is no small task. There are common barriers to beating the market including investment fees, taxes, and investor psychology. Unfortunately, the recent data is not encouraging for active managers and the average investor.

We look at the passive vs. active scorecard from several perspectives by time frame (short vs. long term), performance, and investment vehicle (mutual fund vs. hedge fund). The S&P500 Dow Jones regularly researches the performance of active managers vs. the market (S&P500 index). It is important to note that the S&P500 Dow Jones has a vested interest in the results as they are the indexers themselves.

The S&P500's recent findings indicate the chances of active managers beating the market over the long term are not attractive. The latest S&P Dow Jones report SPIVA US Scorecard Year-End 2024 noted 65% of all active US-based equity funds underperformed the S&P500 in 2024, vs. 60% in 2023, and slightly above the 64% average annual rate reported over the 24-year history of SPIVA Scorecard. The 2024 average US Equity Fund Performance (Asset-Weighted) for all large-cap funds was 24% vs. 25% for S&P500 in Yr. 1, 7% vs. 9% for S&P500 in Yr. 3, 13% vs. 15% for S&P500 in Yr. 5, 12% vs. 13% for S&P500 in Yr. 10, and 9% vs. 10% for S&P500 in Yr. 20.

Hedge Funds

Well maybe the problem with the active manager's inability to outperform the market is with the sample set. Surely, well-compensated hedge fund managers outperform the market "earning," pun intended, their lucrative compensation packages and their above industry, unusually high fees ("2 and 20").

Unfortunately, we again run into the reality of how difficult it is to outperform the market, which is even harder given a high fee structure. Despite their salaries and fame, hedge funds have failed to outperform the index like other types of active managers. Warren Buffett picked up on the connection between the high management fees and lack of performance. He famously placed a $1 million bet with Protégé Partners LLC, a NY-based investment Management Company, in 2007. Buffett wagered an unmanaged, low-cost S&P500 index fund would outperform an actively managed group of high-cost hedge funds (picked by Protégé) based on the hedge funds' performance net of fees, costs, and expenses over a ten-year period. The winnings would go to charity.

Buffett was trying to make a point by placing the bet against active managers. He believes over the long run speculative trading and high fees negatively impact performance. Buffett won his bet. However, the bet was not a sure thing. It took four years for Buffett's index to outpace the hedge funds, which seemed to outperform the market during market contractions. Still, over the long term, the buy-and-hold strategy associated with indexing won. The trend seems to have continued. If we look at the returns of hedge funds as measured by the Barclay Hedge Fund Index based on 1,000 hedge funds (out of possible 3,000), the hedge funds average return underperformed the S&P500 ever year from 2010 to 2020. The returns for the S&P500 were 2x or 3x better in certain year. The S&P500 average annual return averaged 14% almost 3x higher than the 5% average for hedge funds over the time frame. Buffett's bet was a good one.

Movement to Passive Investing

The growth in assets moving to passive investing has been incredible over the last couple of decades. According to Morningstar's US Fund Flows, more than half of the US long-term funds 53% were in passive investing. The active to passive investing trend passed the milestone 50% mark in 2023. To put it in perspective, the trend has grown from roughly 20% market share for passive investing in the early 2010s. I followed two indexing companies, MSCI and S&P Global, during my time as an equity analyst and was able to track these trends firsthand.

Passive Investing-Short-Term vs. Long-Term Outlook

The short-term evidence provided above appears to be decidedly against active management, but let's examine it a little further. As we mentioned before and will throughout the book, Wall Street is littered with failed paradigms. We encourage the reader to personally, mentally weigh in on these debates around the validity of these different shifts and form their own belief system, which can be tested over time, as we have ours.

Passive investing appears to have unique characteristics, making it a viable long-term investment strategy. Passive investing is like "betting on the House (Casino)" in our opinion, which is a gambling phrase, essentially meaning betting on the Casino to win vs. the gambler. The reason you would want to bet on the "House" is because it has a statistical "edge" over the gambler. The longer you stay in a casino, the better your chances of losing. Your probability of winning individual games is often below 50/50. As we will see, there are many similarities between gambling, particularly poker and bridge, and investing.

Indexing by mirroring the benchmarks allows you to place your investment directly with the stock market (or "House") increasing your odds of long-term success. Most US active managers compare their annual returns to these benchmarks, S&P500 or DJIA. If you mirror the benchmarks through indexing, you ensure at least in-line performance. Your decision to invest in indices, essentially becomes a one-decision investment in the long-term prospects of the US stock market, which has historically risen over time and outpaced all other asset classes. It is a, "If you can't beat them, join them" type investment, which when combined with the instant diversification and low fees and trading is a powerful long-term proposition.

Active Management Matters

There is a case to be made for active management over passive. Warren Buffett makes the case for us in our earlier examples. At their core, indices are manmade portfolios, which means a person or people could construct a new or better portfolio over the long term that would outperform the present benchmarks. Remember Buffett alluded to Paul Samuelson and Ben Graham, whom we will both meet later, also having the idea behind the possible creation of indices. In fact, we have seen a shift over time between the popularity of the two major indices to the S&P500 as the standard benchmark away from the DJIA, as the S&P500 has proven to be comparatively more useful.

Active and passive management approaches are not mutually exclusive and can co-exist. Buffett is again instrumental in separating out a few of the characteristics, which would help level the playing field between active and passive. The active managers taking a low-fee, buy-and-hold strategy like indices are best positioned to directly compete against them over the long term. The active managers charging high fees and aggressively trading are putting themselves at a disadvantage vs. indices, because those managers are potentially hurting their own aggregate performance, setting a higher hurdle for their long-term survival.

The investment firm Dodge & Cox lays out the case for active management in their October 2016 white paper, "Understanding the Case for Active Management." Dodge & Cox is a fundamentally driven, long-term oriented investment firm. They have a vested interest in proving active management matters much in the same way the indexers' statistics supported passive investing. Dodge & Cox points out for the reader that when you look at a 20-year performance, a larger number of US large-cap firms 107 out of 305 outperformed their indices, according to Morningstar. The survivorship bias of these results is offset by the power of compounding in their opinion. The investment firm went on to point out the six attributes they believe are necessary for a modern investment firm to compete over the long-term including high active shares, low fees and expenses, low turnover, risk-avoidance, firm-wide focus on a core competency, and close alignment of interest. They back up their attributes with third-party research. High active shares are the percentage of your portfolio different than the indices. The higher the percentage the better, which contrasts with "closet indexers," who try to mirror the index with only slight changes to the holdings vs. the index in the hopes of generating outperformance. The six attributes seem to be aligned with Buffett's thinking.

The dynamic, unpredictable nature of the stock market favors active management. Although passive investing has dominated over the last decade and has characteristics, which provide it with long-term staying power vs. other paradigm shifts, the pendulum will swing back. We are only looking at a decade of results, which have been bolstered by a Bull market or a market where securities prices have only been primarily increasing when reviewing the impact of passive investing. We know things will change. Bear markets or stock markets when securities prices are primarily declining will return. Other asset classes and perhaps even other international markets have the potential to outperform the US markets over the short and the long term. To use our earlier analogy, there may be better Casino's! The unpredictability of the markets makes it impossible for one formula or approach to succeed over the long term, at least to this point. Remember: Markets are part rational and irrational just like humans, which makes humans (themselves) best equipped to navigate them. At the very least, we will need to occasionally turn off the auto-pilot investing!

Random Walk Hypothesis

The origins of passive investing can be traced back to the academic work in finance of the 1960s–1970s. The decade saw the advancement in key areas like financial theory with the development of William Sharpe's Capital Asset Pricing Model or CAPM and computational power. Professor Paul Samuelson (remember him from earlier-John Bogle's Professor) and Eugene Fama took advantage of these advancements to run advanced statistical analysis on a large amount of stock prices to see if there were any discernible patterns. The result of their efforts was the development of the Random Walk Hypothesis, which essentially described stock prices as random in the short term. At first, the theory seemed to hold up, but eventually, academics began to recognize patterns like the January effect, which is when stock prices experience an uptick in the month of January as investors reset their portfolios for the upcoming year.

Efficient Market Hypothesis

Evidence of discernable stock market patterns led to a revision in the Random Walk Hypothesis to the EMH. Efficient market supporters believe the stock market is efficient and stock prices reflect all the currently available information. An efficient market theorist believes it is impossible to outperform or "beat" the stock market as all available information is already in the market stock prices. The EMH, if true, would render stock picking useless. Indexing is a natural, logical extension of the hypothesis. If markets are efficient, then to fully benefit from their upward trajectory, it would only make sense to own a synthetic version of the market itself. The efficient market theory contradicts the use of fundamental and technical analysis. We provide the formula for the EMH.

There are different forms of the efficient market theory including *strong*, *semi-strong*, and *weak*. The strong form of efficient market theory suggests stock prices fully reflect all information in the public and private markets, even investors with inside information cannot benefit. The semi-strong form advocates security prices instantly adjust to new public information. The strong and semi-strong forms imply a fundamental analyst will not be able to achieve better than market returns. The weak form stresses the current stock prices fully reflect available security market information. The weak form contradicts technical analysis, which is based on historical price movements.

Eugene F. Fama-Efficient Market Hypothesis

I'd Compare Stock Pickers to Astrologers, But I Don't Want to Bad Mouth Astrologers

The EMH was the invention of Eugene Fama, a third-generation Italian American from Boston. Fama attended Tufts as an undergraduate. He continued his studies at the University of Chicago where he received his doctorate degree. The University of Chicago emphasizes a quantitative approach compared to the theoretical work being done at MIT. Professor Fama was looking for a subject to teach a class at the University. He decided to base the class on the work of Professor Harry Markowitz, whom we will meet in Chapter 7. Professor Fama published his doctoral thesis in January 1965 in *The Journal of Business* entitled, "The Behavior of Stock Market Prices," a simplified version called "Random Walks In Stock Prices" appeared in the *Financial Analyst Journal* (1966). Fama's conclusion was consistent with other academics at the time, which is stock prices are not predictable. Fama believed stocks have a 50/50 chance of going up and down but avoids stating security analysis is a waste of time. According to Fama, security analysts, including yours truly, add a level of order to the market.

Fama followed up his earlier work on stock price movement by publishing an article in the May 1970 *Journal of Finance* entitled "Efficient Capital Markets: A Review of Theory and Empirical Work." The article was building on Markowitz's "Efficiency" (portfolio) theory applying it to the overall market; thus, we have the EMH. We will learn more about efficient portfolios when we look at modern portfolio theory in Chapter 7. Like Paul Samuelson, Fama believed stock prices reflect all relevant information. Fama notes you must reject the idea of market equilibrium if you reject the EMH, which we will find out is exactly what successful investors like George Soros do.

Burton G. Malkiel-Enter the Random Walk

> Tip of the Week if you bought $1,000 worth of Nortel stock one year ago, it would now be worth $49. If you bought $1,000 worth of Budweiser (the beer, not the stock) one year ago, drank all the beer, and traded in the cans for the nickel deposit, you would have $79. The advice to you... start drinking heavily.

Burton G. Malkiel published his 1973 classic, *A Random Walk Down Wall Street*, focusing on the random walk and the efficient market thesis. Like Fama, Malkiel believes asset prices (stock prices and the stock market) exhibit signs of a random walk or are unpredictable making it impossible to consistently outperform the market, which supports the indexing approach. Malkiel believes there are two key investment premises: *firm-foundation* and *castle-in-the-air theory*. The *firm-foundation theory* is like fundamental analysis. The firm-foundation theory involves deriving an intrinsic value for an asset. The *castle-in-the-air* or *greater fool's theory* is based on predicting crowd's moods making an asset worth anything the crowd will pay for it, which relates to technical analysis. History has shown us asset prices can be well above or below their intrinsic value, especially given the booms (manias) and busts (panics), more on this later. The randomness of historical stock price movements contradicts the technical analysis of them. Here is a fun list of investment strategies cited in Malkiel's book, which he would argue **do not** work: Filters, Dow Theory, Relative Strength, Price-Volume, Chart Patterns, Hemline Indicator, Super Bowl Indicator, Odd-Lot Theory, Dog of the Dow, Weekend Effect, and Momentum Investing.

The firm foundation theory and consequently fundamental analysis are believed to be flawed for many reasons according to Malkiel. It is extremely difficult if not impossible to predict the future performance of a company based on data or the past. "Expert" analysts make mistakes and are susceptible to human flaws. Random, unexpected events ranging anywhere from changes in raw material prices to natural disasters take place. Accounting can be manipulated or even fraudulent. There can be corruption or conflict of interests amongst the "expert" analyst ranks impacting their judgment. These challenges make fundamental analysis difficult for the experts and potentially impossible for the average person.

Malkiel suggests the best way for the average person to participate in the market is through diversity and efficiency. There is a high correlation between risk and reward, meaning the higher the risk, the higher the reward. Modern portfolio theory suggests you can diversify away the risk by spreading it across several assets. The greater the diversity across asset classes, geography, the better. If we combine diversity with the EMH, we end up with an indexing approach, which is a low-cost way to gain diversification through passive investments. As we have seen, indexing has gained significant momentum as potentially the best approach for the average investor. Malkiel's book was published around the time Bogle was starting Vanguard. Malkiel went on to serve on Vanguard's board of directors.

Markets Are Inefficient

There have been objections from the investment community and contradictory evidence from the academia to the validity of the EMH. The objections range from simple examples to various types of academic evidence of stock price patterns. They are too numerous to mention all of them individually, so we provide select highlights from a few below.

There are everyday examples of stock market inefficiency. The easiest examples are rapid movements either up (bubbles, manias) or down (crashes), which are separate from economic fundamentals. For example, the global pandemic negatively impacted the global economic community driving up the number of unemployed workers into the millions of people in countries like the US as Gross Domestic Product or GDP went negative, yet the US stock market produced solid performance during this period despite these challenges. At the opposite end of the spectrum, there are numerous cases of market crashes like in 1987 or the financial crisis in 2007, which should not happen in efficient markets. On a more micro level, there have been and will be documented instances where investors have benefitted from arbitrage, like taking advantage of mispriced options or buying a company that trades at a discount to its acquisition price even though the acquisition has already been announced.

Leaders in the investment community have rejected the EMH. Warren Buffett was among the objectors. He defended fundamental analysis vs. the random walk theory in his 1984 Columbia article entitled *The Superinvestor of Graham-and-Doddsville* where he cited the impressive record of a number of fundamental analysts who beat the market over a long period of time. Peter Lynch, a successful Fidelity mutual fund manager, who like Buffett outperformed the market for an extended period, has argued the random walk theory and EMH contradict each other. Lynch argues if the market is truly efficient, then market prices should reflect the efficiency and cannot also be random. Numerous other investment professionals have filed their objections to the EMH as well.

There are academics who also refute the EMH. Yale economist Robert Shiller has made a "chicken or the egg" argument. He argued if markets were efficient, then no one would trade them. If there is no reason to enter the market, then there is no way they can become efficient. The academic objections are supported by numerous studies pointing out different market anomalies, which refute the EMH. For example, a 1995 paper in the *Financial Analyst Journal* by David Dremen and Michael Barry entitled "Overreaction, Underreaction, and the Low P/E effect," pointed out the fact that low P/E (Price to Earnings) stocks have greater returns. Even Malkiel himself admits in his 1973 book that there is enough "gremlins lurking about" in the data to prevent EMH from being conclusively proven. Behavioral economists argue cognitive biases are the ones that create market opportunities and inefficiencies.

Robert Shiller-Noise Trader Model

> The error with the EMH is it overlooks the fact that the statistical tests have not shown returns are not forecastable, only that returns are not very forecastable.

Unsatisfied by the Random and EMH explanation of the stock market, several academics in the 1980s including Sanford Grossman, Joseph Stiglitz, Robert Shiller, and Fischer Black contributed to the formation of a new stock market theory known as the Noise Trader Model, which would support the pursuit of active management. The Noise Trader Model hypothesized that the stock price represented two things intrinsic value and noise. The market has two participants informed or professional investors who have access to sophisticated information. The uninformed investor is everyone else who creates the noise. The informed investor will take advantage of their asymmetric information to arbitrage the difference between the stock price and intrinsic value, essentially adding efficiency to the market. This book was designed to help teach the reader to think like an informed investor. Table 1.1 compares the EMH to the Noise Trader Model across key categories including stock price representation, information, and overall market view.

Table 1.1 Efficient Market Hypothesis vs. Noise Trader Model

	Efficient Market Hypothesis (EMH)	*Noise Trader Model (NTM)*
Stock price representation	Intrinsic value	Intrinsic value + noise
Information	Strong, semi-strong, weak	Asymmetric
Market view	Efficient	Inefficiency (sophisticated-adds efficiency)
Investment style	Passive	Active

We now come across the golden rule below. I provide golden rules throughout the book. Think of them as a proposed explanation of a phenomenon to guide your stock picking efforts. They are there for your own further investigation. This golden rule is more a law like gravity.

Golden Rule: The only consistent thing about markets is that they are consistently unpredictable.

Fundamental Equity Analysis

Fundamental equity analysis is the analysis of a business using quantitative and qualitative factors. Quantitative factors focus on practices like financial statement analysis. Qualitative factors include elements like company, industry, and economic analysis. There are two ways of performing fundamental equity analysis: *top down* and *bottoms up*. The *top-down* approach starts with the major global trends and then focuses on the best businesses. The *bottom-up* method begins with a specific company and then moves into the industry and economic analysis.

Why Fundamental Equity Research Matters

The fundamental equity research's unique, flexible approach has withstood the test of time. The core tenants of fundamental equity research, which we will discuss in the next section, are loose enough that they can, with some adjustments, be applied throughout the different market cycles to identify equity opportunities. Theoretically, if practiced correctly, fundamental analysts would be poised to buy when markets are under pressure and sell when intrinsic values are achieved. The benefit to fundamental analysis is it considers changes in a company's industry, or economic outlook, going beyond just price movements, whereas other investment methodologies are sometimes based on the erratic price movements themselves!

Most of Wall Street's paradigm shifts have proven to be limited compared to fundamental analysis. They tend to falter during unpredictable market movements. Technical and quantitative analysis have run into significant challenges when the market behaves unpredictably. Technical analysis is a financial analysis using historical patterns in market data to identify trends. We know markets are unpredictable and believe stock prices are "semi-efficient." Technical analysis not only doesn't account for a rapid movement in prices because it is historically based but also does not protect against externalities like a company losing market share or going bankrupt.

Quantitative analysis runs into similar challenges as technical analysis. Quantitative analysis uses mathematical and/or statistics to understand market behavior. Quantitative modeling is perhaps more forward looking than technical analysis. However, it still runs into the challenges associated with irrational market behavior and particularly price movements. These sharp moves can be potentially catastrophic as we have seen with Long-Term Capital Management and during

2007 crash. Quantitative analysis does not account for changes in competitive dynamics or other fundamentally centric business challenges. I am speaking in generalities and not suggesting fundamental analysis can outrun significant moves in the market. However, we are suggesting it is better equipped to predict or handle these changes.

One of the reasons fundamental analyses fail is because it is not properly followed. The process is a difficult one. It involves things like hard work, patience, and discipline. The process is methodical and fights against several of our cognitive biases. It is about managing risk. Potential investors often forget to implement necessary steps like building a margin of safety. These are just some of the challenges associated with fundamental equity research.

Golden Rule: Investing is hard work requiring discipline and patience.

Fundamental equity research is not without its limitations. We think it is foolish to believe fundamental equity analysis will outperform the market in the short term. Markets are way too erratic for that to be true. However, we do believe if practiced properly, it will outperform the market over the long term. At its core, fundamental analysis when practiced properly still works. However, the paradigm must continue to progress. We have attempted to add to the field of fundamental equity research by unifying some of the tenants and providing a starting point or framework and process for evaluating companies known as the *Foresi Five Factors*.

You Can Beat the Market

We have throughout the chapter tried to answer for ourselves the most important question, "Can you beat the market?" The conclusion we have come up with is, "Yes." However, our answer comes with stipulations. Market outperformance is not easy, should not be attempted by everyone, and most likely won't happen on an annual basis. The fact is that passive indexing is a viable option for a portion of investors. The aspiring investors and investment managers, who want to compete, must have certain attributes, giving them the best opportunity to do so. They must utilize the right combination of investment approaches. The use of fundamental equity research is crucial because it is unique in that it theoretically provides for and capitalizes on the market's inefficiency and unpredictability.

It may be time to review how we evaluate active management performance. We certainly see value in using three-, five-, and ten-year performance metrics vs. the benchmark. However, the practice of measuring performance every year leads to bad behavior. Investment professionals end up chasing short-term performance and market movements, instead of focusing on long-term wealth creation. Perhaps the focus needs to shift toward factors like putting an emphasis on the quality of the investment process being used and trustworthiness of the investment manager.

Bibliography

Bogle, J. C. (1951). *The Economic Role of the Investment Company.* Princeton University.

Bogle, J. C. (1999). *Common Sense on Mutual Funds.* John Wiley & Sons, Inc.

Bogle, J. C. (2017). *The Little Book of Common Sense Investing: The Only Way to Guarantee Your Fair Share of Stock Market Returns.* Wiley.

Buffett, W. E. (1984). The superinvestors of Graham-and-Doddsville. *Columbia Business School Magazine*, 13.

Dodge & Cox. (2016). *Understanding the case for active management* [White paper] https://higherlogicdownload.s3.amazonaws.com/INVESTMENTADVISER/4d240ae3-bc9b-4155-8bd1-14cbac904146/UploadedImages/amc/docs/Understanding-the-case-for-active-management-Dodge-Cox.pdf.

Dreman, D. N., & Berry, M. A. (1995). Overreaction, underreaction, and the low-P/E effect. *Financial Analysts Journal, 51*(4), 19–30.

Fama, E. F. (1965a). Random walks in stock prices. *Financial Analyst Journal, 21*(5), 55–59.

Fama, E. F. (1965b). The behavior of stock-market prices. *The Journal of Business, 38*(1), 34–105.

Fama, E. F. (1970). Efficient capital markets: A review of theory and empirical work. *The Journal of Finance, 25*(2), 383–417.

Ganti, A. R., Edwards, T., Di Gioia, D., Chapman, F., & Didio, N. (2024). *SPIVA U.S. scorecard year-end 2024.* S&P Down Jones Indices.

Malkiel, B. G. (1973). *A Random Walk Down Wall Street.* W. W. Norton & Company.

Moyer, L. (2019, January 17). *Warren Buffett once gave a touching tribute to his friend Jack Bogle at Berkshire's annual meeting.* Retrieved from CNBC: www.cnbc.com

Oxford English Dictionary. (n.d.). Oxford English dictionary. Retrieved March 27, 2026, from https://www.oed.com

Shiller, R. J. (2003). From efficient markets theory to behavioral finance. *Journal of Economic Perspectives, 17*(1), 83–104.

Shiller, R. J. (2014). Speculative asset prices (Nobel Prize Lecture). *American Economic Review, 104*(6), 1483–1527.

Staff, F. (2018, March 25). An audience with Nobel prize-winning economist Eugene Fama. *Financial News.*

Chapter 2

The Graham School of Fundamental Research

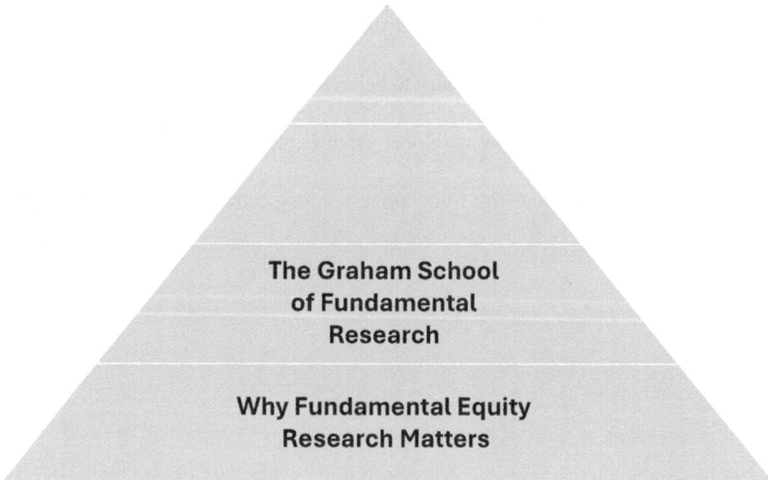

Market Lessons

Each of the investment approaches I will present in this book has an individual who is considered its "founder" or originator. As we saw in the last section, Eugene Fama is considered the originator of the Efficient Market Hypothesis and Jack Bogle for indexing. These visionaries establish paradigms, which are then adopted by other promoters.

The visionary behind fundamental equity research is Ben Graham. Graham ran the investment firm Graham-Newman Partnership and taught investment classes at Columbia University. Warren Buffett, among others, was one of his pupils. Graham helped shape fundamental equity research and its response to the market's unpredictable movements due in part because he lived through one of the worst-performing markets in history. The Dow Jones Industrial Average lost an incredible 80% from 1929 to 1932! To make matters worse, Graham was levered during this period. That's right, one of the greatest investors in history and Warren Buffett's mentor suffered massive losses at the hands of the market. Graham survived, but his experience shaped him. The harsh lessons of market unpredictability and risk left an indelible imprint on him, his work, and the beginnings of what would become fundamental equity research.

DOI: 10.4324/9781003686644-4

Graham School of Fundamental Equity Research

I begin the chapter by presenting a few key finance concepts, which will help us on our journey. The first is the concept of wealth and its creation. The path to becoming wealthy is not a mystery; it is just hard to do. Wealth is created by thoughtfully using capital to drive shareholder equity over time. Being wealthy is very different than being rich. The good news is we have the powerful concept of compounding interest to help us on our way. It is quite the human achievement that an individual can become wealthy not by increasing their own individual labor output, but rather by taking their capital and allocating it to an investment vehicle with a steady annual return and letting the power of compounding do the rest. It's downright magical!

After establishing a foundational understanding of some important concepts, we then turn our attention to taking an in-depth look at fundamental equity research. I begin with a look at the difference between speculating vs. investing. Speculators use technical analysis to identify patterns to beat the market. Speculating is about finding trends, betting small, riding the winners, and quickly cutting your losses. Investing is different than speculating. Investors utilize fundamental analysis to identify and buy great companies trading below their intrinsic value when the opportunity presents itself. We provide a thorough understanding of fundamental equity research and its cornerstone attributes. We suggest the best approach to the market is a fundamentally based flexible process as opposed to the current approaches, which tend to be too focused or ridge on our opinion. It is this type of approach that allows the investor the best opportunity to account for their inherently irrational environment.

We see an evolution in the approach to fundamental equity analysis over the years. The successful investors utilizing fundamental analysis have expanded their thinking around the cornerstone attributes. Ben Graham, the father of fundamental analysis, was focused on "deep value" or companies trading below their intrinsic value. Warren Buffett's approach concentrated on the search for great companies at "reasonable" prices. Peter Lynch expanded the valuation parameters to include Growth at a Reasonable Price (GARP). Our *Foresi Five Factors* approach attempts to compliment the current approach to fundamental analysis by focusing attention on the process and measuring the common characteristics of companies that outperform.

Investing at its core is risk management. The key is to minimize your risk and maximize your return. There are no such things as safe investment opportunities. We will touch on this more in upcoming sections. As a preview, the reason we are looking to buy great companies with good free cash flow at great prices is because it puts us in the best position to succeed. A reminder of our golden rule from the introduction.

Golden Rule: Purchasing great companies at good prices reduces risk.

Foundations of Finance

Wealth Creation Formula

I believe the objective of investing is to build wealth over time. It is very important to understand the difference between creating wealth and getting rich. Rich people will spend their money until it is gone. Wealthy people will save and make investments to grow their wealth. If you are looking to get rich, you are more than likely to fail while speculating on the stock market over the long run. If you are looking to become wealthy, then you will need to dedicate yourself to the process of building wealth over time. Fundamental equity analysis is designed for those who are looking to build long-term wealth through investing.

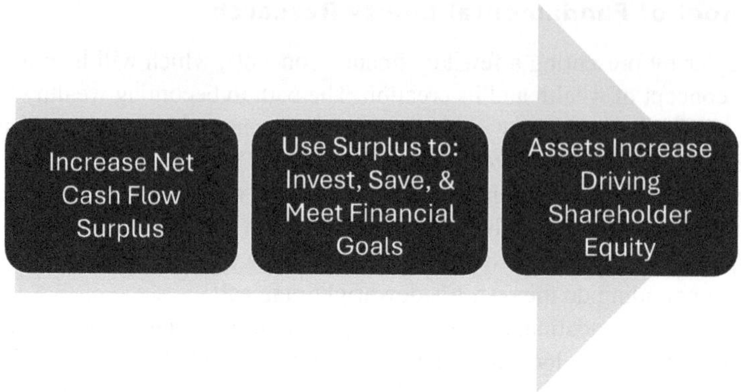

Figure 2.1 Wealth Creation Formula.

The formula for measuring wealth is simple: assets minus liabilities. Individuals call this their *Net Worth* statement. Corporations call it *Shareholder's Equity*. Simply put it is what you own or assets minus what you owe or liabilities. Assets can be liquid or easily convertible into cash or less liquid like Real Estate, which may take time to sell. Liabilities can be current liabilities, which are things owed in less than one year, or long-term liabilities, which are over one year in duration, like mortgages.

Golden Rule: Ca$h is King.

We quickly come to a key Golden Rule of investing: Ca$h is King. The reason why you may hear investors use this common phrase is because as you can see in any cash flow statement: a corporation can create positive momentum by increasing their net cash flow generation. The way it works is the greater the free cash flow generation, the bigger the surplus, the more capital the company will be able to accumulate and allocate to expenditures and/or return it to shareholders. The higher the capital accumulation and investments, the greater the assets, and the higher your shareholder equity! We call this the wealth creation formula. It is the bedrock of true wealth creation (Figure 2.1).

Golden Rule: Thoughtful capital (cash) allocation creates wealth.

Cash is considered king because the use of it generates wealth, or, said in a more formal manner, thoughtful capital allocation generates wealth. Financial Capital is defined as an economic resource measured in terms of money used by entities (businesses) to buy what they need to make their products or provide their services to the sector of the economy upon which their operation is based, i.e., retail, corporate, investment banking, etc. We will learn more about capital when we begin to understand businesses. The best allocation of capital in a wealth-building exercise would be investing in areas with high returns while protecting your principal, especially when there is inflation, which eats away at the impact of cash balances. Corporations deploy their capital as it is called in the corporate world through several different methods including investments, acquisitions, and returning it to shareholders through dividends and/or stock buyback.

Interest Takes on Different Forms

Golden Rule: Follow the power of compound interest.

We quickly come across another golden rule of investing: the power of compounding interest. The power of capital accumulation goes well beyond purchasing power. We will need to understand the time value of money to really understand the power of compounding interest. To do so, we will need to introduce a simple but powerful formula. The formula for Future Value (FV) is the present value multiplied by the accumulation function or one plus the interest rate to the square root of time.

The formula is so powerful, we felt we needed to provide an example. Here is how the formula works and why compounding interest is so important. Let's take a $1,000 investment as an example. We can put the investment into a short-term Treasury bill or T-Bill paying a 5% dividend. Here is what the investment would be worth over time:

Yr. 1-$1,050
Yr. 5-$1,276
Yr. 10-$1,628
Yr. 20-$2,653

You can see in this example how you make over 100% return over 20 years without having to put in one ounce of labor! You just let the money compound. An investor would need to move to a long-term instrument like a bond instead of a T-Bill as the duration increased. As you can see in this example, the power of compounding interest is a modern marvel. As a side note, the paying of interest on debt is just the opposite, a negative. Interest is extremely unique in that it can be positive, negative, and/or necessity.

The example above is what Warren Buffett and others mean when they talk about the power of compounding interest. As a side note, financial interest is not the only thing Buffett believes compounds. Buffett also feels knowledge compounds. He believes you should read 500 pages a day. The power of compounding may apply to all skill sets or knowledge bases.

Golden Rule: Protect principle while seeking the best return for as little risk as possible.

We come to another golden rule: protect principle while seeking the best returns. How do you magically turn one hundred dollars ($100) into one hundred and five dollars ($105) or maybe even one hundred and ten dollars ($110)? You can do it by finding an asset, which provides a yield or interest. Ideally, a person or entity would like to protect the principle or the original dollar value, while finding the greatest rate of return or yield. The rate of return for $100, which becomes $105, is 5%, $110 is 10%, and so on. Rate of return or yield is found by dividing the interest or return by the original principal value.

There are many different assets, which can provide a return. Asset categories include equities, bonds, mutual funds and indexing, and real estate. We focus here specifically on equities. We provided a preview of the historical returns from an assortment of asset classes in our introduction and found equities to be the asset class providing the highest return over the "long run." We will look more closely at asset allocation in part two of the book. We will look at the use of fundamental analysis for some of the other asset classes outside of equities in part three of our book. As a rule, the opportunity for returns is often consistent with the risk to principle. Institutions typically pay a higher interest rate to have access to funds for a longer period.

Equities

Let's dive a little deeper into developing an in-depth understanding of equities, the focus of this book. Portions of this section may be a review, but even the author has found value in periodically reviewing the topic.

There are different long and short-term approaches to investing in equities. Long-term strategies include buy and hold, dollar cost averaging, and direct investment or dividend investment plans. Short-term strategies include the use of margin or borrowing a portion of the money to purchase stock, short selling, or borrowing the company shares from the brokerage firm and betting the stock goes down, and options or the right to buy (Call Option) or sell (Put Option) the stock at a specific price.

We will take a more detailed look into these strategies as we go on, but let's first develop a basic understanding of equities. There are various types of equity. Equity typically refers to shareholder equity, which represents the amount of money that would be returned to a company's shareholders if all assets were liquidated and debts paid off. A stock (also known as equity) is a security representing the ownership of a portion of a corporation. Stock entitles the owner to a proportion of the corporate assets and profits equal to the amount of stock or shares they own. Corporations issue stock to raise funds. There are multiple benefits to owning stock including their appreciation in value, dividends, and potential stock splits.

One of the potential benefits of owning stock is the opportunity to be paid a *dividend*. The owners of the stock or stockholders are entitled to dividends, which can be paid in the form of money, stock, or other property. An investor must own the stock on its record date to receive the dividend. Dividends remain with the stock up to two business days before the record date. Dividend-paying companies typically pay out 30–70% of their earnings to stockholders. The range of corporate approaches to paying a potential dividend can fluctuate from a growth company that pays out no dividends but rather reinvests its earnings to grow the business to a Real Estate Investment Trust (REIT), which is required to pay out 90% of its earnings. Dividends are an amazing benefit of investing, adding to your total return and fitting nicely with the power of compound interest.

There are typically two types of stock, *common* and *preferred*. The difference between common and preferred stock can be found in their names: Common vs. preferred. The owners of "common" stock do not own any particular asset, but instead all the assets of the corporation are shared or the "common" property of all investors. A common stockholder has a right to the corporation's dividend. A preferred shareholder gets preference of payment of the dividend over the common

Table 2.1 Stock Classification

Type of Company	*Definitions*
Blue-chip	A group of well-established co. with a great track record
Income	Higher than average paying dividend stocks
Growth	Corporations that can earn above industry average profits
Business Cycle	
Cyclical	Stocks moving in conjunction with the business cycle
Defensive	Stocks remaining stable during declines in the business cycle
Market Capitalization	
Large cap	Over $10 billion in market cap
Mid cap	$2 to $10 billion in market cap
Small cap	$300 million to $2 billion in market cap
Penny stocks	Stocks selling for less than $1 per share

shareholder. The amount of dividend paid to the preferred shareholder is known in either a stated amount, percentage of the stock's par value, or assigned value of the stock certificate, before the stock is purchased. Preferred stock is generally callable meaning the corporation may exchange the stock at its option for a specific amount of money. Investors may purchase cumulative preferred stock whose unpaid dividends accumulate and have priority over the payment of dividends to common shareholders. Preferred stock can sometimes be convertible or exchangeable for a specified number of common shares at the stockholder's option.

Stocks can be classified into different categories. These categories include the characteristics of the company, how they react to business cycles, and market capitalization. Stocks can be purchased because they display specific characteristics investors are looking for like steadiness (Blue Chip), ability to grow, and/or income. Companies can mature from growth stocks to income over time, which may change the way you decide to value them, more on this later. Investors may look at different types of stocks based on the business cycle. Stocks can be characterized by their market capitalization or the value of the company, typically measured by multiplying the present share price by the number of shares outstanding. Small-cap stocks have traditionally outperformed medium and large-cap stocks over a long period of time (Table 2.1).

Raising Capital, Going Public, and Trading on Exchanges

I talked about the importance of capital, which is the life blood of the economy and its participants. Companies need capital throughout the life cycle of the business. There are a variety of ways a company can raise capital. The three primary ways of raising capital include issuing equity, generating capital from operations, and taking on debt. The simplest and perhaps most popular example of raising capital through the issuance of equity is the television show "Shark Tank," where potential investors ("Sharks") offer to fund or provide capital to a "new" business in exchange for a stake or percentage of the ownership or equity. I hesitated to use this example because there may be future generations who read this book and wonder "What is 'Shark Tank'?" They may have the same thought about our case study, Mastercard, as a company, if it doesn't exist. Unfortunately, these references are unavoidable and common for finance books. I remember reading about textile and railroad company examples in our old finance books.

There are two markets for purchasing securities: the *primary* and *secondary* markets. The primary market involves purchasing securities from an investment bank, a representative of the issuer, or the issuer of the security themselves. Most investors are familiar with *Initial Public Offerings* or IPOs, which are sold in the primary markets. An IPO is when owners of a company initially offer a part of their ownership to be sold in the public market typically through an investment bank, which is known as "going public." There are several reasons for doing an IPO including raising capital for expansion, paying off debt, creating a liquidity event for the owners, and putting a brand into the public market, which will allow you to use stock options to attract talent.

The standard IPO process involves picking an investment bank, performing due diligence, pricing the offering, stabilizing the shares, and transitioning to a public company. The process starts with a private company picking an investment bank or banks known as a syndicate. These banks are called *underwriters* as they underwrite the offering through the submission of a proposal including items like the size of the offering, the number of shares to be sold, and the fees. The second step is the due diligence performed on the company, which is done by several entities including the Security and Exchange Commission (SEC). The company typically files a prospectus registration statement or S-1 with the SEC, which contains all the company's relevant information. The third step is pricing the offer. Here, a company puts together a prospectus, travels to see investors known as a "road show," joins a stock exchange, and prices the public offering. Once the company is public, the underwriter will look to stabilize the share price by creating a market for roughly 25 days after, known as a quiet period. The quiet period ends, and the sell-side analysts issue all their initiation reports and estimates. Congratulations! You are a public company.

Wall Street has recently seen the emergence of a new trend in primary market activity known as *SPAC*, which stands for *Special Purpose Acquisition Companies*. A SPAC also known as a "blank check company" is a public company created to acquire a private asset. The process starts with the forming of a management team and corporate structure, depositing funds in a trust, and filing of an S-1. The SPAC management team then does a roadshow meeting with investors to raise interest and funds. The SPAC then lists on an exchange. The SPAC then looks to acquire a private company or assets through either a cash purchase, share issuance, and/or special financing. The private company is now bought through a reverse merger, called "de-SPACing." SPAC investors have a window to redeem shares if they don't like the deal. SPACs often come with warrants that can be exercised as well.

There are positives and negatives associated with SPACs vs. standard IPOs. SPAC fees are typically lower at 2–5% vs. traditional IPOs at 7%. There is a redemption of shares option for investors associated with SPACs. SPACs can be quicker to market and potentially provide more financial information. However, investors in SPACs need to "trust" management to pick the right business to merger with. The vetting practice of these target businesses can be questionable. The volume of capital markets activity like IPO and SPACs tends to be most active during strong stock markets and vice versa. For example, 2020 was an incredibly strong year for capital markets with IPOs up to 209 in 2020 up from 151 in 2019 bringing in $85 billion, a roughly 70% annual increase; while the popularity of SPACs exploded with 248 in 2020 up from 59 in 2019 bringing in $82 billion, an amazing 500% annual increase, according to SIFMA. The strength of the IPO market tends to be a good indicator of the overall strength of the economy. The two go hand in hand.

There are different ways for a company to raise capital after "going public." The owners of existing shares may look to sell those shares in a *secondary offering*. A secondary offering does not dilute the share count, and the proceeds don't go to the company but rather the current shareholder sells the shares. However, the company can raise capital by doing a *follow on offering* in the secondary market. A follow-on offer is when a company issues new shares in the secondary market, diluting the shareholder and raising capital for the company itself.

The *secondary market* is where existing securities are sold. The NYSE or NASDAQ stock exchanges are examples of secondary markets. Each exchange has requirements for being able to list with the exchange and remain in good standing. There are normally three types of orders placed for equity trades: *Market*, *limit*, and *stop*. Market orders are buy or sell orders being placed while the market is open with immediate best execution in mind. A limit order is a request to buy or sell a stock; however, orders by other investors can be placed ahead of a limit order. A stop order or a stop-loss order guarantees the sell order will be executed at a specific price. Orders can be either *discretionary* or *non-discretionary*. A discretionary order gives the broker or account executive the discretion on when to execute the order. A non-discretionary order or account means the customer needs to request the trade.

Different types of market orders can be effectively used in different circumstances. Market orders are the least effective from a strategic investing standpoint. A market order can be combined with a stop order to limit or mitigate losses. A limit order used to buy or sell stocks is comparatively more strategic than a market order from an investment standpoint in our opinion. Investors can use limit orders to purchase equity investments at a price below the market price building in a crucial margin of safety. They can set a limit order to sell the stock when it hits the long-term intrinsic value. We will see market and stop orders can be effectively used for speculation purposes, while limit orders can be used to invest with a bonus of helping the investor avoid inherent psychological flaws.

Golden Rule: Stocks represent ownership, but they don't know you own them.

Once you have made a stock purchase. You should track your performance by understanding your cost basis, dividends, and total return. One way to do this is by calculating your Holding Period Return (HPR). We look at an example of HPR in the Appendix.

Different Approaches to Investing

After developing a solid, basic understanding of equities, we can now confidently move forward by looking at the various approaches to investing in the stock market and their famous promoters. As we discussed in my introduction to the book, there is no shortage of methodologies or get rich quick money-making schemes professing they are designed to "beat the market." Wall Street's history is littered with the rise and eventual failure of these different approaches, ranging from technical analysis to deep value investing and most recently quantitative analysis. The problem with these different approaches and all approaches in general is not their authors, lack of thoroughness, or inconsistency, although certain approaches are comparatively more thoughtful, thorough than others. The flaw with all market approaches lies with the markets themselves. The only consistent thing about markets is that they are inconsistent and irrational. They reflect the mental makeup of their participants. Investors are human part logical, part psychological. As we will see in future sections, it is our mental makeup, which leads us to search for potential shortcuts or methodologies for market success. Let's be clear here. I am not suggesting certain market approaches can't work. In fact, some approaches do and have worked for an extended period. The problem is if one of the only market "truths" is that it is irrational and unpredictable, then by default, there can be no one successful market approach over the long-term, especially without modifications.

However, there is hope. The following section discusses two different approaches to beating the market: speculating (technical analysis) and investing (fundamental analysis). The section examines the methods used by some of the world's greatest investors. We believe each approach has positives and negatives. After evaluating these different systems, our conclusion is that fundamental analysis is the proper investment approach.

My approach is designed to provide an adjustable framework or lenses and context to help avoid easy mistakes. I feel to be successful, any long-term investment methodology must be flexible, taking into account the positive aspects of select investment methods and the dynamic nature of the market. Successful long-term investment approaches must be subject to revisions to survive. We believe it is important to focus on a flexible, adjustable process above any specific methodology. The process-based approach is necessary to counteract the volatile nature of markets and avoid the flaws of some of the more traditional approaches.

Golden Rule: Best approach: A flexible, fundamental approach, incorporating the best of the different methodologies and focused on risk management.

Speculating vs. Investing

There are two different approaches to the market: speculating and investing. The primary difference between speculating and investing is the amount of risk. Speculating is the use of capital or cash to undertake a financial endeavor with a high probability of failure. Speculators, or traders, as we will refer to them going forward, typically hold assets for a very short periods of time. Investing is the use of capital or cash to undertake a well-researched decision on a financial endeavor based on thorough analysis. The financial endeavor is expected to generate a positive return or profit, typically in the form of asset appreciation or income generation over a long period of time. We believe the practice of thorough analysis provides superior returns over the long run vs. speculating. The two approaches to the market are not mutually exclusive in our opinion with both providing valuable takeaways.

Speculators vs. Fundamentalist

Speculators

Regardless of whether you are a trader or an investor, it has become increasingly more difficult over time to outperform the market. The challenge of outperforming the market has increased for all investment approaches as market efficiency as it pertains to the flow of information has improved over time. The improvement in market efficiency has had the biggest negative impact on speculators. To get some sense of how inefficient the stock market used to be, it may be helpful to remember the early stock market employed people to get on ladders and physically write down stock quotes on a "Big Board" and update them when they changed. The information associated with public companies was often hard to get to or delayed. We can compare the big board model with our modern-day smart phones, which bring us instant, real-time quotes and news. We have come a long way to improving market efficiency from a historical perspective.

Traders took advantage of the early market inefficiencies. The famous 1923 classic *Reminiscences of a Stock Operator* by Edwin Lefevre looks at Jesse Livermore, the original Wall Street speculator, using the fictional name Larry Livingston. Livingston (Livermore) was a trend follower trying to identify trends before the market realized and capitalized on them. The example used in the book was Livingston selling short USWTC. There are common mistakes speculators make, especially those who have little to no experience. Some common mistakes made by speculators mentioned in the 1923 classic are that early speculators had poor motivation for speculating, like greed, and lousy timing; they don't really think, their successes are made on hope; they don't know what moves the markets; they lack experience; and some of them are just ill-suited for speculation. Livingston did promote market lessons including sitting tight, being confident, studying general conditions, and trusting your senses. His market lessons focused on trusting yourself.

Perhaps the most interesting takeaway from Livingston in our opinion was his strong "ticker sense." He was famous for putting sell or buy orders into the market to tell if the stock wanted to "go up" (show him a profit) or "go down" (showed him a loss). He always wanted to buy stocks on upticks because those stocks proved there was more demand than supply and vice versa. So how did things end for the real Jesse Livermore the original "Wolf and Great Bear of Wall Street?" Unfortunately, he ended up committing suicide in 1940, after once again losing his fortune. The speculators' advantage due to market inefficiency deteriorated over time as the efficient flow of information improved. The early advantages of a Livermore-like trader are eliminated by the instantaneous, efficient flow of information and market reaction.

Gordon Gekko-"Greed Is Good"

The heroic notion of the swashbuckling Wall Street trader, which began with Livermore, continues to live on in our modern culture. The caricature peaked in popular culture in the 1980s. The essence of the image was on display in the film "Wall Street" released in 1987. In the film directed by Oliver Stone, the lead character Bud Fox (Charlie Sheen) is a stockbroker trying to gain the favor of corporate raider Gordon Gekko by providing him with insider information leading him to a moral dilemma. The movie spawned a generation of future Wall Streeter's. It is interesting to think of the impact the movie, which is fiction, had on society. These cultural shifts spawn a generation of followers. Entertainment, including books and movies, often sculpts the thoughts and culture of the general population. I believe today the model of American success has shifted from Wall Street trader to modern-day Silicon Valley entrepreneurs. It is important to remember entertainment is just that entertainment and does not reflect the true essence of a subject. They are typically misleading caricatures and story lines, but we digress.

What Makes a Good Trader? Hold on to Profits, Quickly Cut Losses, Bet Small

Market Wizards, written by Jack Schwager, attempted to answer the question of what makes a good trader by interviewing great speculators in 1989. Trading requires hard work, courage, patience, discipline, and a willingness to lose. Speculators must identify potentially profitable situations and trends. They usually rely on technical analysis or charts to identify these trends, but it can include other forms of analysis like fundamentals and "market sense." Once the opportunity or trend is identified, the speculator enters the trade. The biggest challenge is sticking with the winners and quickly selling the losers or cutting your losses. The latter is crucial! Traders typically make small bets representing a fraction of the portfolio (1%, 5%, or 10%). They work to limit their downside by using stop limit orders put in place at a specific level well before the trade is initiated. Successful traders like William O'Neill recommended cutting losses at 7%. Ed Seykota rules of trading probably sum it up the best, "Cut Losses, Ride Winners, Keep Bets Small, Follow the Rules w/o Question, and Know When to Break the Rules." As you can probably already tell, trading is exciting, but risky.

There is a psychology to trading in and of itself. Here are some examples. Traders believe the stock market is something to be listened to by developing an intuition over time. If a commodity, stock, or the market goes up or down after you enter a trade, the market is telling you something. Listen to the market. It is good to have a healthy amount of fear of the market. Risk should be respected. Never trade with a specific monetary target in mind like I need to make $1 million to buy a house. Don't bet your lifestyle. Make sure you don't let your ego impact your trading. It is important to be flexible in your approach and willing to be contrarian. Understand your limitations. "Take a day off" if the trading losses mount.

Famous Traders

Jesse Livermore-The Grandfather of Speculators

There have been many famous speculators following in the footsteps of the "grandfather" of trading, Jesse Livermore. These traders attempted to develop market-beating strategies or mental models, which are designed to bring them success. These models often involve stock screens or other technical factors. There are inherent problems with these mental, trading-based models. The models are often too restrictive or time or period sensitive. Any investor can adopt the models, rendering them ineffective over time. The models must contend with the only consistent thing about markets, their inconsistency. As we said at the beginning of the section, markets are consistently irrational and unpredictable. Market models based on trading "intuition" and technical analysis are perhaps the most exposed to potential volatile market movements. I include a summary of the speculators' approach to the market discussed at the end of the chapter.

George Soros-Reflexivity

> Markets are constantly in a state of uncertainty and flux, and money is made by discounting the obvious and betting on the unexpected.

One of the most famous traders in modern times, George Soros, provides a description of his theory on the markets known as *reflexivity* in his 1987 book *The Alchemy of Finance*. Soros and James (Jim) Rogers, Jr., ran the Quantum Fund. Reflexivity is the philosophical theory referring to an act of self-reference where examination or action "bends back on" and affects the person instigating the action. Reflexivity as it applies to markets is the theory that the market or stock prices have a "prevailing bias" driven by "underlying trends," which influence the stock prices and in turn have a reflexive relationship with "prevailing bias" and "underlying trends." These create "boom" and "bust" cycles where no real equilibrium is ever reached. In essence, the market and stocks are consistently being over or underestimated. They are constantly over and under shooting the real value.

Soros' reflexivity theory adds an additional dimension to the different schools of thought, namely, fundamental, technical, and efficient market presented in the next section. Reflexivity implies market prices are biased in one direction and can influence the events they anticipate. Soros views the understanding of reflexivity as complimentary, especially to fundamental analysis. Reflexivity sounds a lot like Graham and Buffett's version of "Mr. Market" as we will see later in this chapter.

Soros runs through examples of how he ran the Quantum fund in *The Alchemy of Finance*. He creates macro- and micro-economic models. Once those models are set up, he tries to understand the patterns on the way up and when it reverses on the way down. An example of the micro model is the rise of conglomerates like Teledyne (TDY), a stock Soros uses to exemplify reflexivity. TDY's stock price rose as the company bought other companies, then fell as those companies were consolidated. On the macro level, Soros' works to try to trade on his constantly changing assumptions regarding the relationship between monetary policy, stock market movements, currencies, and commodities. We will discuss the boom-and-bust cycles more in the next chapter entitled *Boom, Bust, and Bubbles*, which looks at the macro-economic factors.

There have been several famous traders in addition to Livermore and Soros. Below is a selective list of famous traders whose fame is derived for good and sometimes bad reasons. The list includes

Table 2.2 Famous Trader's Approaches

Trader	*Approach*
George Soros	Reflexivity-stock prices reflect positive or negative reflexive loops resulting in constant boom/bust cycles.
Jim Rogers	Flexible approach taking concentrated positions based on 3-dimensional econ model taking advantage of hysteria.
Paul Tudor Jones	Risk-controlled ("Great Defense") approach to trading looking to capture market swings.
Ed Seykota	Trend Trader picking opportunities primarily based on long-term aspects, chart patterns, and timing.
John Paulson	Contrarian bets, including against the housing market in 2007, quick reversals. Began Career in Merger Arbitrage.
Nicolas Darvas	Darvas Box Theory targets stocks using highs and volume as indicators. Drawing a box around highs and lows for entry point and stop loss.
Nick Leeson	Doubling Down Strategy-every time he loses money; he would double the amount lost to recoup the money. Caused Baring Collapse.
Simon Cawkwell	A.K.A. Evil Knievel-Famous short-seller who benefits from the underperformance of companies.
Peter Schiff	Holds long-term views on foreign stocks and commodities. He is bearish on US stocks and economy.
Edward O. Thorp	Methodical, scientific, probabilistic approach to finding and exploiting market inefficiencies through a proven trading edge (back testing).

Nicolas Darvas, Ed Seykota, Jim Rogers, Paul Tudor Jones, George Soros, Nick Leeson, Simon Cawkwell, John Paulson, Peter Schiff, and Edward O. Thorp. Thorp is credited with starting the quantitative movement (Table 2.2).

Speculation Is a Flawed Long-Term Game

If speculation in the market sounds a lot like gambling, it is because it carries similarities. Speculating is often compared to the card game, poker. You can see the resemblance in the action and mentality of traders as described above. They bet small to start, cut their losses early, sometimes fold, and leave the table if they are going cold. Sound familiar? As displayed in the table above, traders even try to beat the Street by developing specific trading strategies. The probability that a trading strategy is effective was higher during the earlier days of the stock market, when there were larger inefficiencies, but as efficiency has increased, the effectiveness and longevity of the trading strategies have declined.

Edward O. Thorp is perhaps the best representation of the gaming element associated with the stock market. His remarkable life is described in the 2017 autobiography *A Man for All Markets: From Las Vegas to Wall Street, How I Beat the Dealer and the Market.* Thorp began his career as an academic mathematician. He honed his skills by developing a method based on probabilities to win at poker. Thorp describes his poker strategy in his 1962 bestseller *Beat the Dealer.* Thorp proceeded to apply his mathematical skills to Wall Street by developing a pricing model for options, which provided arbitrage opportunities, ahead of the widespread use of the Black-Scholes model. After his first mover advantage in options deteriorated, he moved on to finding statistical arbitrage through the mispricing of assets. Thorp believed in taking a scientific method-like approach to finding a discernable edge and capitalizing on the advantage when you have tested your thesis.

Interestingly, Thorp's quantitative method crossed paths with several well-known Wall Street investors. The billionaire "Bond King" Bill Gross founder of PIMCO read Thorp's poker playing book while recovering from a terrible car accident and eventually went to Las Vegas to hone his skills at poker, which he believes would eventually translate into being a better trader. Gross eventually used Thorp's second book, *Beat the Market,* published in 1967 for his MBA thesis, which landed him a job at Pacific Mutual Life from which he started PIMCO. Thorp knew and invested with Warren Buffett, who is an accomplished bridge player, which leads one to wonder, if speculators are like poker players, then perhaps fundamental investors are similar to bridge players. Bill Gates also happens to be an avid bridge player. Either way, the similarities between card games and the market appear to exist on some level. As we will see later in the book, Thorp went on to influence Ken Griffin and the quant movement as well.

Technicals

Speculators tend to use a technical analysis approach to the market. As a result, we use the two terms speculators and technicians interchangeably throughout our books. A technician or chartist examines historical patterns associated with supply and demand forces. Technicians develop charts plotting price movements and market averages. These charts allow them to observe trends leading them to believe the stock market value or assets will either increase or decrease. There are several different technical indicators. We look at the four primary technical indicators: moving averages, Moving Average Convergence Divergence (MACD), Relative Strength Index (RSI), and On-Balance Volume (OBV).

Moving Averages

Moving averages smooth out price lines by using an average price over a period. The 50-, 100-, and 200-day moving average tends to be the most popular. There are a couple of different moving averages. Ranging (as opposed to trending) is a horizontal moving average trend line. An uptrend is a moving average line angled upward. A crossover uses a 200- and 50-day moving average with a buy signal taking place when the 50-day crosses above 200-day. A sell signal when the 50-day crosses below the 200-day. Moving averages can provide support or resistance. The relative strength indicator is an oscillator like the moving averages.

MACD is an oscillating indicator fluctuating above and below zero. An oscillator is a technical analysis tool representing a band between two extreme values. The asset is typically overbought at the upper end of the oscillator and oversold at the lower end. A MACD strategy is to buy when the line is above zero and sell when it is below zero. MACD has fast and slow signal lines. A buy signal occurs when a fast line crosses through and above a slow line. A sell signal occurs when the fast line crosses through the slow line.

The RSI is an oscillator moving between 0 and 100 providing different information than the MACD. The overbought region is typically above 70, and the oversold area is typically below 30. The uptrend remains over 70 for a sustained period. Downtrends remain below 30 for a long period of time. You can short at the top and buy at the bottom if you're a technician. Stock trades can be made above and below the 50 range.

Volumes can be a valuable technical indicator as well. OBV indicator aggregates the volume information into a single one-line indicator, which measures cumulative buying and selling pressure. A rising asset should be accompanied by a rising OBV and vice versa. A dislocation between the price and the OBV could indicate an opportunity (*Investopedia*).

Fundamentalist

Participants in the stock market can choose to take a fundamental investment approach, which is the one presented in this book, in addition to or instead of technical analysis. A fundamental equity research analyst thoroughly researches a company's prospects including its industry, positioning, product strength, and growth prospects. The analyst comes up with an intrinsic value for the company based on its prospects. The company can then be either overvalued, fully valued, or undervalued based on a comparison of the price the company is trading at vs. their intrinsic value. The price at which you buy or sell a stock is then determined by applying a margin of safety, which is essentially a risk discount to the intrinsic value. As you can see, the fundamentals of a company particularly valuation are crucial in this method.

Fundamentally Speaking

The Active Camp (Fundamental Approach)

As a reminder, the term active management refers to any investor or speculator, who is actively trying to "beat the market" by delivering a portfolio return that exceeds the stock market's return as measured by its benchmark. I addressed the speculators' approach to generating stock market returns and provided a description of fundamental analysis and the two different approaches, top down or bottom's up in the earlier sections. Fundamental analysis can be used with a variety of different investment approaches including buy and hold, contrarian investors, and quantitative analysis. We will see in Part III different applications of fundamental analysis.

We believe fundamental analysis is necessary for locating successful investment opportunities. The Noise Trader Model academic model presented earlier supports our view believing active management provides stock market efficiency by arbitraging away inefficiency.

Fundamental analysis can be applied to a variety of investment styles including buy and hold, contrarian, and growth. Although I believe fundamental analysis has a little bit of each of these styles in it when performed successfully, I believe fundamental analysis is most effective when combined with a "version" of *value investing*. Value investing is an investment approach focused on purchasing stocks below their intrinsic value. We look at the development of fundamental analysis including *value investing*, the great fundamental investors, and their approach in the upcoming section.

Value Investing

Value investors have historically applied fundamental analysis to equities to identify investment opportunities and successfully beat the market. Fundamental equity investing at its core is about finding great companies with potentially strong free cash flow and buying them at attractive prices. The father of value investing is Ben Graham, who we met in the introduction to this chapter. We will learn more about Ben Graham and other luminaries in the upcoming section but first let's look at value investing as an investment approach.

Please note I use the term value and fundamental investor interchangeably going forward. I believe the term value investor is somewhat misleading given the advancements in the value investing school of thought, especially the use of valuation and the discipline around it. I would submit that the term fundamental investor is perhaps more all-encompassing.

Successful value investors have a unique perspective. Their view differs from the generally accepted Wall Street approach. The great value investors base their approach on a couple of crucial concepts. These concepts originated with Ben Graham. I list the key cornerstones below, which we will touch on in the upcoming section.

Cornerstones of Value Investing

- **Speculating vs. Investing**. Investing is done by researching a company. Speculating is betting a stock's price will go up or down.
- **Mr. Market**. The market is erratic and unpredictable, swinging back and forth providing risk and opportunity.
- **Price vs. Value**. The stock price is the result of the supply and demand for stock in the market. Value is what the company is worth. They are two separate things.
- **Intrinsic Value**. The value of a business is the present value of future cash flows.
- **Margin of Safety**. Investors must pay a price below the intrinsic value to be successful, essentially building in a "margin of safety."
- **No one knows the future**. We cannot predict either market or stock price movements, but we do know in the end the fundamental or intrinsic value of an asset will be realized.

Three Generations of Fundamental Investors

There have been three generations of value based, fundamental investors. We categorize them into *traditional*, *first*, and *second generation*. Each of these generations adds value to the original investment paradigm. The traditional value investing school follows the cornerstones and teachings of Ben Graham. Traditionally, value investors focus heavily on stringent valuation metrics and look to

Table 2.3 Fundamental, Value-Based Equity Investing

Traditional	*First Generation*	*Second Generation*
Ben Graham Philip Carret Walter Schloss John Templeton John Neff Seth Klarman	Warren Buffett Charles Munger Bill Ruane	Peter Lynch Shelby Davis
	Contribution	
Speculating vs. investing Mr. Market Price vs. value Intrinsic value Margin of safety Deep value bias Diversification	Circle of competence Competitive moats Long-term holding periods Flexible valuation Focus on a few great names	Growth at reasonable price Inventive due diligence

diversify their portfolio with multiple holdings. Remember, Graham was writing after the horrific experience of the Great Depression, which led to a very conservative initial approach to investing.

Our list of successful fundamental investors shares a belief that value-based investing is the cornerstones of investing as established by the traditional school, but expand, alter, and update their view, when necessary, in select areas like the characteristics of good companies or valuation disciplines. The first generation of value investors includes famous investors like Warren Buffett. The first generation expand on the traditional school by expanding on the parameters used to determine valuation moving beyond "deep value" to a more flexible valuation approach while at the same time narrowing the focus to a few, high-quality companies with specific characteristics like a competitive moat. The second generation is marked by investors like Peter Lynch. The second generation again expanded the valuation parameters to account for growth, using GARP, and became more inventive around due diligence. The second generation was looking for good companies, but not necessarily "forever" stocks (Table 2.3).

My *Foresi Five Factors* approach is an attempt to add to the current investment paradigm. It suggests focusing on a process and its improvement rather than just results. The five factors competitive advantages, catalyst, valuation, quality of management, and psychology bring together the most important elements of the current schools of thought and build upon them in my opinion. I believe it is a starting point, not an ending as fundamental analysis continues to evolve.

Benjamin Graham-"Father of Value Investing"

> The intelligent investor is a realist who sells to optimists and buys from pessimists.

The story of fundamental analysis begins with Benjamin Graham, whom we mentioned in our introduction to this chapter. Ben Graham is known as the "father of value investing." Graham was born in London in 1894. His family moved to New York City when he was a year old. Graham was a bright student and won a scholarship to Columbia University. He graduated from Columbia at the age of 20 and began his Wall Street career. He set up the Graham-Newman Partnership in 1923 and began teaching investment classes at Columbia in 1928. Graham's teachings spurred a generation of fundamental analyst known as the Graham School. His most famous student is Warren Buffett, who took Graham's class in 1950, and worked at his partnership for a time. Buffett has often said, after his father, Graham is the most important influence in his life.

Graham was the first to systematize the process of investing. His approach to the markets was laid out in his two famous works *Security Analysis* (1934) and *The Intelligent Investor* (1949). These books are the cornerstone of modern fundamental analysis. Graham was a value investor. He believed in protecting your principal, while searching for an acceptable return. He promoted analysis based on strong fundamental quantitative and qualitative research in an effort to derive an intrinsic value based on earnings projections. The intrinsic value is then compared to where the stock price is trading to make investment decisions.

Security Analysis is considered one of the most influential finance books ever written. The book was based on the transcription of Graham's lectures at Columbia University by his student David Dodd. The Wall Street Crash of 1929 had a large negative financial impact on Graham. For perspective, nearly half of the banks failed with unemployment rates as high as 30% in 1929. We believe the crash influenced Graham's investment style as he took a conservative, valuation-driven approach to investing, putting an emphasis on areas like cash flow, which is related to the solvency of a company.

Security Analysis launched the concept of value investing. There are three key concepts laid out in the book: understanding the difference between speculating and investing, determining a company's cash generation, and studying a balance sheet to understand the true positioning of a company. The underlying value of a stock is the value of the business it represents, which is separate from the speculative moves up or down in stock price. Graham believed investors must quantitatively and qualitatively research the fundamentals of a company and derive a value before purchasing it. The process of researching a company increases the probability of success vs. just guessing. An investor's ability to understand the "true" cash flow of a company is crucial, especially as companies can manipulate accounting methods to inflate results. Graham believed investors should look closely at financial statements working like detectives to figure out what "normal earnings" might look like but being careful not to extrapolate future trends from the past. The analyst should have a strong understanding of the industry, company's prospects, and ability to handle change within the industry. Although the income statement gets most of the attention, the balance sheet can be a key contributor to understanding a company's true financial position, especially weaknesses.

Like *Security Analysis*, Graham's *Intelligent Investor* has had a profound impact on the investment community. An intelligent investor is patient, disciplined, and eager to learn. They can harness their emotions and think independently. It is a trait, "more of character than of the brain" according to Graham. He revisits his explanation of investment vs. speculation. Graham believes speculative ventures should never be more than 10% of investment funds. Speculative ventures (and the speculative mindset) should not be mingled with investment activities. Holding cash is typically a poor investment as the value of cash deteriorates over time due to inflation. Two ways to fight inflation are either through investing in stocks or Real Estate Investment Trusts (REITs). The stock market has historically provided the best returns, as an asset class vs. bonds and other asset classes. Investors should be aware of a couple of things regarding the market, specifically past returns do not necessarily translate into future returns, if everyone believes the market is a good investment, then it is sure to embed those expectations in higher prices, and once stock prices are inflated by higher expectations, then it will be harder to garner higher future returns. Graham believed the higher the stock price or market, the higher the risk. He does not believe returns are based just on the amount of risk an investor is willing to take.

Different Types of Investors

Graham introduces the reader to two types of investors: *defensive* or *enterprising*. He encourages an individual to look at the amount of risk they are willing to take and decide if they are a *defensive or enterprising investor.* The typical portfolio should have 50% stocks and 50% bonds. An investor should never have less than 25% or more than 75% of the portfolio in common stock. The percentage of stocks should go up in a bear market as stocks are cheaper and down in a bull market as they are more expensive. We can see Graham is trying to manage risk across asset classes: equities vs. bonds. The *defensive investor* should be focused on a portfolio of high-grade stocks and bonds. Graham's rules for the *defensive investor* include: the portfolio should have a minimum of ten and maximum of 30 stocks, companies should be large and well capitalized, there should be a long record of continuous dividend payments, and investors should not pay more than 25× the average earnings of seven years (and not more than 20× TTM). *Enterprising investors* can gain superior returns based on intelligence and skill. Graham believes the *enterprising investor* should buy when markets are low and sell when they are high. They should purchase carefully chosen growth stocks, bargains (trading 50% below value), "special situations," and/or relatively unpopular large companies. *Enterprising investors* should not: purchase high yield or "junk" bonds, foreign bonds, day trade, or participate in IPOs (Table 2.4).

Stock Selection

Graham describes his method of stock analysis and selection. There are typically five things to look for when analyzing a stock: management competency, long-term prospects of the company, financial strength, capital structure, and dividend record and rate. We believe there are key characteristics to look at as well, which are outlined in the *Foresi Five Factor* approach. Graham believes the largest source of value for a company is the future potential earnings, which can hopefully be made by making the fewest assumptions, while considering the required rate of return. He believes it is important to avoid serial acquirers, companies looking to borrow debt or sell stock, and high client

Table 2.4 Graham's Defensive vs. Enterprising Approach

Defensive Stock Selection Criteria	*Detail*
Large companies	Small Co.'s have high volatility
Financial condition	LT debt not more than net current assets
Earnings stability	Positive earnings the last ten years
Dividend record	Uninterrupted for the past 20 years
Earnings growth	+1/3 min. EPS past ten years using (three-year avg. beginning and end)
Moderate P/E	No more than 15× avg. EPS last three years
Moderate price to asset	No more than 1.5× book value; PE × PB no more 22.5×
Enterprising Stock Selection Criteria	
Financial condition	Current assets 1.5× current liabilities
Earnings stability	No deficit in the last five years
Dividend record	Currently paying a dividend
Earnings growth	Earning grew (translates into growing over three to five years)
Valuation	Price less than 120% net tangible assets

Source: Adapted from *Intelligent Investor* by Benjamin Graham, 1949.

concentration. Instead, you are looking for companies with a competitive advantage and steady organic, growers who reinvest in the business. Graham promotes a two-part appraisal process for stocks. The analyst should first look at the past performance, then project it forward and alter it based on their outlook. The more the historical analysis, the better, seven to ten years.

The Critical "Margin of Safety" Concept

Graham's discussion of the "margin of safety" is the most important section of the book. It is perhaps Graham's most important concept and contribution. The margin of safety is the difference between the intrinsic value of the company and the price we are willing to buy the stock below its intrinsic value. Investors must determine a purchase price and have the discipline to buy at or below the price. The better the "margin of safety," the more leeway the investor has if future forecasts or results differ. Diversification increases the "margin of safety" from a portfolio perspective. We touch further on approaches to valuation and the "margin of safety," which is a key component that is often overlooked, in our section on valuation.

Graham's Family Tree

Benjamin Graham's teaching at Columbia and work spawned a family tree of successful investors. His famous students included Warren Buffett, Irving Kahn, William Ruane, and Walter Schloss. Buffett and Kahn even named their sons after him. If the list wasn't impressive enough, the influence of Graham's original teachings reaches far beyond his direct students. The family tree adopted by John Szramiak for a business insider article, "Here's Ben Graham's Family Tree of Value Investing" adapted from a 2015 book by Andrew Hunt author of *Better Value Investing*. Graham's "children" according to Hunt include those who applied his work to valuation theory (Buffett, Munger), International opportunities (Templeton), special situations (Greenblatt, Klarman), and empirical research (Fama and French).

Graham's work often cited how human nature or individual psychology played into investing and the difficulties it presented. His "grandchildren" tried to explore this element of investing through the lenses of behavioral finance (Kahneman), which is covered in our section on psychology, and reflexivity (Soros), which was covered in our section on traders. The most recent version of Graham's family tree are his "great-grandchildren" focused on developing your organization or personality to overcome the behavioral, psychological challenges. The latest generation focuses on checklists (Pabrai), organizational structure, positive psychology, and intellectual development.

The Warren Buffetts of the World

Several investors believe they can outperform or "beat" the market by outsmarting it. As with most fans of low probability, highly lucrative careers, active investors have their idols. None stands taller from a popular standpoint than Warren Buffett. Idols and Heroes typically earn nicknames like the "The British Bulldog"-Winston Churchill, "Babe" Ruth-George Herman Ruth, or "The Splendid Splinter"-Ted Williams, etc. Buffett is no exception with nicknames like "Oracle of Omaha" or "Sage." Buffett does his best to live up to other aspects of being an idol including his persona of humility, practicality, and good old-fashioned American values. He lives in a "modest" house in Omaha, Nebraska. He is philanthropic pledging to give away 99% of his wealth, which was estimated to be $73 billion dollars at the time of this writing to good causes. Investors even make their "pilgrimage" to visit Buffett and his business partner Charlie Munger at the Berkshire Hathaway annual meeting, which attracts 35,000 to 40,000 investors/fans per year.

Circle of Competence

Although we compare Buffett in stature to the great baseball player Babe Ruth, it is interesting to note Buffett himself may prefer another famous baseball player Ted Williams as comparison instead, which is a lot closer to our hearts having been a lifelong Red Sox fan. In fact, Warren Buffett has a picture in his office of his head imposed on Ted Williams's body from William's book, *The Science of Hitting,* which shows the different areas of a strike zone where Ted Williams was most productive. It is a reminder to Buffett to stay with what he knows (we presume fundamental analysis) giving himself the best opportunity to succeed.

Buffett refers to your area of expertise as the "circle of competence." He recommends all investors invest based on their circle of competence, like Ted Williams' philosophy of trying to get the best pitch to hit (Stock to Buy) and understanding where he was effective and deficient. Ted Williams hitting chart highlights the importance of knowledge and discipline, which are crucial characteristics of being a successful investor. Buffett directly cites Ted Williams in a couple of his shareholder letter including 1994 where Buffett writes, "Nevertheless, we will stick with the approach that got us here and try not to relax our standards. Ted Williams, in *The Story of My Life*, explains why his argument is; to be a good hitter, you've got to get a good ball to hit. It's the first rule in the book. If I have to bite at stuff that is out of my happy zone, I'm not a .344 hitter. I might only be a .250 hitter." Charlie (Munger) and I (Warren Buffett) agree and will try to wait for opportunities that are well within our own "happy zone."

Baseball references are one of the many analogies Buffett uses to describe investing. He likes to say there are no called strikes in investing. They only occur when you swing and miss. When you are investing, you don't need to know every stock or investment opportunity, so don't worry about what you missed. Instead, do careful homework on only a couple of dozen pitches, so the few swings you take are hits. The highest probability for success comes from investing in what you know best or your "circle of competency"!

Does Buffett Deserve Such Praise?

Warren Buffet (Berkshire Hathaway) has an impressive investment record. As of 2022, Berkshire Hathaway (NYSE: BKR.A) outperformed the S&P500 39 out of 58 years or nearly 2/3rd of the time since 1965. Most of the underperformance has happened since 2007 (six out of ten years). Buffett had set a benchmark for himself of beating the market (DJIA) by 10 points a year. Overall, Berkshire Hathaway has been incredibly successful. If you had invested $10,000 in Berkshire in 1965, you would have made $355 million as of 2022, a 20% compound annual gain vs. 10% for the S&P500. Buffett's success serves as proof of the possibility and power of active management, so much so that even Edward O. Thorp, the grandfather of quantitative analysis, is a proud owner of his shares.

Buffett Isn't Alone

Warren Buffett's impact, impressive record, and status in the investment community can be compared to others who have changed their industry. To use a sports analogy, it's like Babe Ruth's impact and status on the game of baseball. Similar to how there were other great baseball players outside of Babe Ruth, there are other great investors besides Buffett. When we compare Berkshire Hathaway (Buffett) with other notable investors, we find his long-term record to be impressive. Berkshire Hathaway returns over a long period of time are outstanding. Frederick Vanhaverbeke looks at the performance of the world's greatest investors in his 2014 book *Excess Returns: A Comparative Study of the Methods of the World's Greatest Investors.* Other notable investors who posted strong returns over a sustained period include George Soros, Shelby Davis, and Walter Schloss. Investors with strong shorter-term records include Jim Rogers, Joel Greenblatt, David Tepper, and Stan Druckenmiller. These other notable investors had their own, sometimes different investment styles.

What Can We Learn from Great Fundamental Investors?

Like our look at the top traders, we continue our conversation by taking a closer look at the methodologies of a select group of famous fundamental investors. Our discussion regarding the fundamental approach began with Benjamin Graham, continues with Warren Buffett and Charlie Munger, and evolves into Peter Lynch.

Warren himself provided us with a roadmap of famous investors. As we briefly touched on in Chapter 1, Buffett defended fundamental analysis vs. the random walk theory and the Academy in his 1984 Columbia article entitled *The Superinvestors of Graham-and-Doddsville.* Buffett argues there is no magic to figuring out how the top investors historically made their money. They all came from a place called Graham-and-Doddsville. These investors used different versions of the wisdom passed down from Ben Graham (Graham School) to develop the same impressive results. Buffett sarcastically refers to this group of Superinvestors as the best coin flippers, who care more about price vs. value than beta, the capital asset pricing model, or covariance. Buffett cites the following Superinvestors in the piece: Walter Schloss (WJS Partners), Tom Knapp (Tweedy, Browne), Bill Ruane (Sequoia Funds), Charlie Munger, Rick Guerin (Pacific Partners), and Stan Perlmeter (Perlmeter Investments).

Table 2.5 Famous Fundamental Investors Approach

Investor	*Approach*
Ben Graham	Father of value investing
Warren Buffett	The cash flow king-evolved Graham's approach to include factors like competitive moat
Charles Munger	Believes in high quality, highly concentrated portfolios containing a few companies
Philip Carret	Search for value, avoid speculation, and watch business cycle. Your Portfolio is your business
Bill Ruane	Value investor-focus on good companies, strong balance sheet, healthy earnings and Berkshire owner
Walter Schloss	A straightforward, by the "book value" investor who is less interested in the underlying nature of business
Shelby Davis	Insurance sector specialist-"Davis Double Play" earnings growth complimented by multiple expansion
John Templeton	Templeton touch-discipline, research, and character build. International deep bargain hunter
John Neff	Contrarian investor looking for low PE stocks with opportunity to improve their prospects
Peter Lynch	A True Magellan-GARP investor looking for the ten baggers
Seth Klarman	Oracle of Boston-the value investors chief objective is to avoid losses

Schloss, Buffett, Knapp, and Ruane took classes from and worked with Ben at his Graham Newman fund. There are many potential fundamental investors who belong on this list. We included a look at Philip Carret, Walter Schloss, Bill Ruane, Shelby Davis, John Templeton, John Neff, Peter Lynch, and Seth Klarman acknowledging there is room for others (Table 2.5).

What Makes a Good Fundamental Investor?

Identify Stocks Trading Below Intrinsic Value, Build in a Margin of Safety

There are common themes across all investors. Investors want to protect their principal, while growing their assets through managed risk. They believe the market is irrational, which provides an opportunity. As we saw in the prior section, traders look for trends in the market they should be following compared to fundamental analysts, who look for undervalued stocks. The fundamental analyst begins by searching for and identifying potential undervalued opportunities. They research these opportunities and establish an intrinsic value preferably from a cash flow valuation. Once an intrinsic value is established, the fundamental analyst builds in a margin of safety for where they would buy the stock. The volatility in the market is expected to provide opportunities to buy these companies when the market price meets the intrinsic value. Fundamental analysts are then patient to see if the stock price will come close to the price at which they believe the stock should be bought. Fundamental analysis began with Ben Graham, who put a large focus on valuation. It has since progressed to including finding great companies like Buffett does to looking for GARP opportunities like Lynch. I include a summary of the investors' approach to the market discussed at the end of this chapter.

Golden Rule: Fundamental analysis is about finding great companies, establishing an intrinsic value (typically through a cash flow calculation), and building in a margin of safety to come up with an entry point, then being patient for the volatile market to provide an opportunity.

Warren Buffett-Focus on Fundamentals

> When we own outstanding businesses with outstanding managements, our favorite holding period is forever.

There are several great biographies about Warren Buffett. My favorite is *Buffett: The Making of an American Capitalist* by Roger Lowenstein (1995). Lowenstein follows Warren through the milestones in his life including his birth in Omaha, Nebraska in 1930, purchase of his first stock at age 11, studying under his mentor Benjamin Graham, and founding of the Buffett Partnership at the age of 25. Warren took control of Berkshire Hathaway in 1965. He turned Berkshire from a cash rich, textile company in a declining industry into a global holding company by using Berkshire's cash flow to buy other companies. Berkshire has accumulated holdings in a vast array of companies over time including Coca-Cola, See's Candy, Washington Post, and Gillette.

Buffett uses a good, old-fashioned value-based investment strategy. His philosophy is simple identify good businesses, buy them at good prices, and hold them for a long time. Buffett's philosophy builds on the foundation set by his teacher Benjamin Graham. There is an overlap in the way Buffett and Graham go about identifying opportunities, purchasing them, and the positive characteristics they look for. Buffett believes you should only buy a **select** group of stocks in good companies with strong long-term fundamentals and earnings power. He looks for simple to understand and easy to predict businesses that have franchise power. He thinks of a business' as being castles wanting to know how the business will expand its competitive moat. He likes highly transparent, innovative management teams with proven track records, preferring companies that return dividends to shareholders when the investor's returns from the capital exceed those the business can produce.

Lessons from the Letters

Berkshire Hathaway's Shareholder Letters (https://www.berkshirehathaway.com/letters/letters.html) are essential reads for any investor. These letters contain pieces of business wisdom from arguably the world's greatest investor. Professor Lawrence A. Cunningham published in 1997 *The Essays of Warren Buffett: Lessons for Corporate America*, which serves as an excellent reference for Buffett's thoughts on a wide range of business topics. Cunningham breaks B`uffett's writings into five sections: corporate governance, corporate finance and investing, common stock, mergers and acquisitions, and accounting and taxation. We provide an abbreviated review of the highlights from each of the five sections presented by Cunningham below to provide insights into Buffett's wisdom.

Corporate Governance: Buffett points out the flaws in corporate governance in his shareholder letters. Perhaps one of the largest flaws is the lack of accountability for the CEO's present governance structures vs. the relatively higher amount of accountability for the rest of a company's employees. He sees the traditional granting of stock options to corporate managers as flawed as the compounding nature of retained earnings provides positive, unearned (on the part of management) momentum. Buffett would instead recommend hiring honest, hardworking, and competent managers you can trust and linking corporate incentive with what the manager has direct control over. He believes in providing the manager with capital and incentivizing them on both out and underperformance metrics based on their ability to grow capital. Buffett notes managers can buy stock in the market if they really want to own it.

Corporate Finance and Investing: Buffett considers himself a business analyst, who takes a fundamental, long-term approach to investing. He touches on several crucial investment topics in his shareholder letters attributable to the Graham school including the crucial ideas of Mr. Market, the difference between price and value, and the margin of safety. It is important to note that Buffett has stated he is comfortable talking about Graham's investment philosophy but won't discuss individual investments in detail for proprietary reasons. Buffett routinely interjects common sense into his letters pointing out the flaws with Wall Street's "latest" money making approach, including the Academy's views. We will discuss Buffett's specific investment approach in further detail shortly.

Common Stock: Buffett has insightful views on common stock, particularly his own. He hopes Berkshire Hathaway's stock price trades "close" to its intrinsic value. The market would be truly efficient if all stock prices closely reflected their intrinsic value, but certainly harder to take advantage of and less fun, in my opinion. An alignment of the stock price and value allows Berkshire's shareholders to directly benefit from the positive (and negative) value creation. It would encourage longer-term holding based on performance. Long-term holders can fully participate in "the power of compounding" (in my opinion) and avoid transaction costs. Buffett has purposefully avoided paying dividends and/or splitting his own stock to encourage long-term holders. Berkshire's Class A stock was trading near $790,000 per share as of March 2025.

Mergers and Acquisitions: Buffett tries to buy companies with excellent economic characteristics run by trusted, competent managers. He applies his commonsense approach to buying businesses believing there are very few reasons to ever pay a premium when purchasing a business. The exceptions being companies with strong franchise characteristics or the opportunity to unlock value through successful management. Buffett believes value-creating acquisitions are very difficult to find and execute. Think about the flawed thinking in buying a company at its market price plus a premium, which typically happens, vs. buying a company at or near its intrinsic value.

Accounting and **Taxation**: Buffett is a teacher, who educates his shareholders in a few different ways. One method is to separate the "consensus" Wall Street view from those taken by fundamental investors. A good example is Buffett's separation of price from value. The world of corporate accounting provides plenty of opportunities to make helpful distinctions.

Generally Accepted Accounting Principles (GAAP) and now "Non-GAAP" are accounting measures, or a "form," as Buffett describes it, used by corporations in their financial statement reporting. Buffett believes financial statements should answer three basic questions: How much a company is worth, can it meet its future obligation, and how good the managers are doing operating the business. Instead, the goal for corporations is often to use accounting to put themselves in the best possible light with investors in my opinion. Buffett would argue there is a difference between accounting earnings, goodwill, and book value vs. economic earnings, goodwill, and intrinsic value. He has developed a range of concepts designed to make financial statements more useful for investors including examples like "look through" earnings, "Owner's Earnings," and intrinsic value, which we will walk through shortly.

Buffett's Approach to Financial Analysis

Buffett uses a method of measuring a company's contribution to his investment portfolio known as "look through" earnings. The purpose of the method is to calculate the meaningful earnings generated by an entity attributable to an investor's portion of ownership in the business. Standard accounting principles tend to skew this number as it can be misrepresented based on the percentage of ownership. The "look through" calculation is quite simple. Multiply the entities annual "true" operating income by the percentage of the company owned by the investor and subtract out the taxes attributable to the portion of the operating income. Buffett suggests individual investors take the same approach with the goal of creating a portfolio with the highest possible "look through" earnings ten years from now.

Buffett's methodology for investing in companies is very similar to his mentor Ben Graham. Buffett attempts to establish an intrinsic value for a company by forecasting the company's future cash flows and then discounting them back to present-day levels to derive an intrinsic value. Buffett is looking for a rough approximation when it comes to intrinsic value. As Buffett says in one of his many aphorisms, "It is better to be approximately right than precisely wrong." Once an intrinsic value is established, he can build in a "margin of safety" choosing a level well below the intrinsic value to purchase the stock.

Buffett's Owner's Earnings vs. Earnings Per Share (EPS)

Buffett favors an "Owner's Earnings" formula vs. the common Earnings Per Share (EPS) valuation calculation. We will touch on valuation in greater detail in an upcoming section, but Buffett's view is worth examining. "Owner's earnings" represent the cash an owner or investors can potentially derive from the business. The "Owner's earnings" formula is essentially reported earnings plus depreciation and non-cash charges minus the amount of capital expenditure needed to maintain its competitive position over the long-term. The toughest calculation to make is understanding how much capital expenditure the company needs now or in the future to run the business. Buffett's formula succeeds where standard methods fail because it shows the pathway for cash to create value vs. the typically used net income, which doesn't account for how the company is using the cash. "Owner's earnings" is normally calculated on a Trailing Twelve Month (TTM) basis. Buffett then divides the "Owner's earnings" by the difference between the discount and growth rate. Buffett's formula does not lend itself to speculation or high-flying technology companies as a higher-than-expected growth rate essentially makes the formula obsolete. The formula and methodology are designed for predictable, low-growth businesses.

Three-Step Valuation Process

Let's walk through an example of a discounted cash flow valuation using our case study, Mastercard. Below are the three steps necessary for Buffett to derive his valuation and entry point:

Step 1-Forecasting: The 1st step is to forecast out the different valuation inputs Buffett is looking to use in deriving Owner's Earnings. We will see in the section on valuation, forecasting can be effectively performed in a variety of different ways ranging from using general assumption to performing meticulously detailed estimates. There are a wide variety of options to choose from when deciding what inputs to use as well. The Buffett approach typically models out five to ten years in the future some form of cash flow.

Step 2-Intrinsic Value: The 2nd step is to derive an intrinsic value. The most common way to perform this calculation is by using a Discounted Cash Flow or DCF model. The objective of the DCF is to find the NPV of all future cash flows and discount them back to the present value. The total NPV is then divided by the share count to derive an intrinsic value. We note as you will see in the valuation section there are a wide variety of inputs to choose from including the discount and growth rate when working toward deriving an intrinsic value.

Step 3-Build in a Margin of Safety: The 3rd step would be to build a margin of safety to see at what level the prospective investor should be comfortable purchasing the stock. The additional "Margin of Safety" would add a crucial "cushion" to the investment. Remember investing is risky, so buying at a discounted level is a way of improving your risk reward. It would be similar to wanting to buy a product on sale, and who wouldn't want to do that, especially if you plan on selling it again. My 10 Year Free Cash Flow to Equity (FCFE) Valuation for Mastercard, which you can find in our valuation section. We can see my 10-year intrinsic value is $485 as of mid-2020. I would suggest building in a 35% margin of safety, which would give us a target entry point of around $360, the stock was trading at $350 at the time of the writing of this book.

Buffett's Approach to Investing

Warren Buffett is looking to buy great companies at great prices and hold them forever. He believes Mr. Market, who shows up at his house every day, is volatile, going through different moods, "ups" (Optimism-overvaluation) and "downs" (Pessimism-undervaluation), which have rough similarities to Soros' reflexivity theory described in our trading section. Both views of market volatility contradict the Efficient Market Theory. Buffett sees volatility as an opportunity, not necessarily a risk, to be diversified away as academics suggest. He takes issue with other academic theories including Beta and diversification as well. Buffett recommends investors should ignore Mr. Market and instead come up with their own value, intrinsic value, which is in opposition to the traders' (i.e.) approach of trying to ride the trends. The "downs" or "sell offs" in stock prices provides an

Table 2.6 Warren Buffett's Top 5 Investment Risks

1 The certainty with which the long-term economic characteristics of the business can be evaluated.
2 The certainty with which management can be evaluated, both as to its ability to realize the full potential of the business and to wisely employ its cash flow.
3 The certainty with which management can be counted on to channel the reward from the business to the shareholder rather than to itself.
4 The purchase price of the business.
5 The level of taxation and inflation that will be experienced will determine the degree by which an investor's purchasing power return is reduced from his gross return.

opportunity to purchase the selective few great company's well below their intrinsic value building in the aforementioned "margin of safety."

It is important to make the distinction between price and value, which are two very different things. The price is the level at which a stock trades in the market. Wall Street sell-side analysts assign "price" targets. Fundamental analysts assign a value or intrinsic value, which is not a small distinction. Wall Street is transaction oriented focused on price. Fundamental analysts, typically buy side analysts, are focused on an assets' true value, which is defined as the present value of all future cash flows. An intelligent investor will derive an intrinsic value and then build in a margin of safety. The purchase of a stock will be made when the price "roughly" intersects with the discounted intrinsic value. I think the Mr. Market analogy is extremely helpful in understanding investing. Mr. Market reflects the human condition, which is partly logical and a much bigger emotional part. Mr. Market is each of us!

Buffett believes in buying a small amount of very good companies in areas where you have expertise and holding them for a long time. He recommends investing in your "Circle of Competency" or what you know. Buffett believes good businesses "can employ large amounts of incremental capital at very high rates." Strong businesses have a few key characteristics: economic moats, economic goodwill, incremental earnings, simplicity, and skilled management. Buffett defines risk using the dictionary term, "the possibility of loss or injury." He feels risk is mitigated by holding a high concentration of well-researched businesses bought at very good prices, which is in opposition to academics, who believe risk should be diversified away. He recommends holding these businesses for a very long time (ten years). He lists five investment risks. Buffett sees the primary reasons for poor investment results being: (1) High costs (management fees, etc.), (2) Portfolio decisions made based on tips or speculation, not principles, and (3) The attempt to time the market (Table 2.6).

Charlie Munger-In, Out, and Too Tough

> Go to bed smarter than when you woke up.

Charlie Munger, who passed away in 2023, was vice chairman of Berkshire Hathaway. Buffett describes Charlie as his partner. The usefulness of a partner appears to be a common, positive theme across successful investment funds. Charlie Munger was born in Omaha, Nebraska in 1924. He worked at Buffet and Son, a grocery store owned by Warren's grandfather, as a teenager. Warren worked there as well, but at a different time than Charlie. Munger dropped out of college at the age of 19 in 1943 and joined the military where he became a Second Lieutenant. After the military, Charlie Munger received his law degree from Harvard Law School, his father's alma mater. He then began his career at a law firm as a real estate attorney. Quickly moving into the investment world where he ran investment firms/partnerships on his own. Buffett and Munger had overlapping relationships in Omaha. They first had lunch at the Omaha Club. The two men formed a mutual respect over dinner at Johnny's Dinner in 1959 beginning a multi-decade-long friendship. Munger became the vice chairman of Berkshire Hathaway in 1978. He had started his own investment practice in 1962, Wheeler Munger & Co. Munger is a voracious reader often referred to as "A Book with Legs." Interestingly, Charlie Munger is also a card player, a hobby he learned in the army. We know Buffett plays bridge along with friend Bill Gates, while Edward O. Thorp and others are poker players.

Charlie Munger's simple approach to investing involves buying and holding a concentrated portfolio of well-researched stocks. He is often credited with helping evolve Warren Buffett's style to move beyond his early "cigarette butt" (Deep Value Based) approach learned from Ben Graham. Munger's approach to life and investing is captured in his 2005 book, *Poor Charlie's Almanack: The Wit & Wisdom of Charles T. Munger*. Munger believes the world is made up of mental models, which involve multiple factors. He encourages investors to develop those mental models by keeping the models that work and discarding those that don't. Munger himself has over 100 models ranging across different subjects like history, physics, biology, etc. The combination and application of these models reinforces and amplifies the "Lollapalooza effect." Munger's approach to investing is simple, "Preparation, patience, discipline, & objectivity." He believes in a well-researched, highly concentrated (three investments per year) portfolio refuting the diversification trend. His core philosophy, which applies to investing, is based on *The Psychology of Human Misjudgment,* a 1995 Munger Speech. The idea is that the practitioner analyzes the world's driving forces rationally and how your mind forms conclusions where some are useful, but others are not. It's a two-step decision process for making effective decisions: (1) Understand the forces at play, and (2) Understand how your subconscious might be leading you astray. He believes in checklists, very much like the investment checklist or process we have developed later in this book. The value-based investment approach puts the odds in your favor and allows wiggle room for mistakes. Buying good companies with expanding competitive moats is crucial. The businesses must be easy to understand putting companies into three categories, "In," "Out," or "too tough."

Philip L. Carret-"Father of the Mutual Fund Industry"

> Trading in and out of the market is the pinnacle of stupidity. I have a very simple strategy; I buy good companies at attractive prices. Then I sit on them.

Philip Carret was a founding father of the mutual fund industry in the US Philip Lord Carret was born in 1896 passing away in 1998 at the age of 101. Carret went to Harvard graduating in 1917 with a degree in Chemistry. A former World War I aviator, although he never saw action, Carret launched the Mutual Fund Trust in 1928 after managing money for friends and family. He ran the Pioneer fund for 55 years turning a $10,000 investment into $8 million. He is famous for his long, successful track record. Buffett has said he has "the best long-term investment record of anyone I know." Carret may have even played a role in Buffett's development. The story goes Carret traveled to Omaha in the mid-1940s and met Buffett's father Howard, who recommended a stock named Grief Brother's Corporation, a barrel maker, then selling at $0.68. Carret & Company held stock until 1997 when it was trading at $36.50. Carret was a Berkshire shareholder traveling to Omaha for its annual meetings where Buffett has introduced him as "one of his heroes." As an interesting side note, Carret was interested in astronomy and traveled around the world chasing eclipses.

Philip Carret was a long-time, value investor. He believed finding a value for a security and making decisions based on the value rather than just speculating was the "right" way to invest. He wrote many books but is perhaps best known for the 1927 *The Art of Speculation*. In the book, Carret discusses his belief that every investor is speculating at some level because it is impossible to know everything about an investment. There is always an unknown element. He devotes most of the book to helping investors deal with these unknowns. Carret believes investors must look to buy investments trading below their real value. He views the market as a popularity contest, like John Maynard Keynes. The swings in the market provide opportunity. "Great prosperity affords an advantageous time for selling stocks, extreme business depression an opportunity to purchase." There is a bias to the upside in the market's given human disposition, which makes it difficult to short sell. Investors will benefit from knowing where you are in the market cycle, what stocks might benefit, which ones offer value, and understanding the language of business or accounting. The market is always forward-looking. Investors are looking to minimize your losses, maximize your profits, and do what is in the best interest of long-term "business" or portfolio.

Walter Schloss-(Book) Value Is at the Heart of the Matter

> When I buy a stock, I have kind of an idea where I want to sell it.

Walter Schloss is perhaps the most amazing story amongst the Superinvestors. Schloss was born in NYC in 1916. He never went to college or used a computer. Instead, he started working as a runner on Wall Street at the age of 18. He got his introduction to the Graham school of investing by taking Graham's course at night at the New York Stock Exchange Institute. Schloss along with Buffett worked at the Graham-Newman partnership. Schloss was a philanthropist serving as treasurer of Freedom House and patron of the Tenement Museum.

Schloss was a true Graham follower. He looked to buy undervalued stocks with solid fundamentals building in a margin of safety and holding them until they became overvalued. He emphasized the price-to-book valuation metric, as the optimal value metric, looking to buy stocks below their price-to-book. He has held over 100 stocks at one time. Schloss didn't talk to management. Schloss' approach to holding a wide number of stocks and less of a focus on business fundamentals differs from the Buffett, Munger, and Ruane approach. Below are Schloss' 16 factors for successful investing (Table 2.7).

Bill Ruane-Balance Sheet Bonanza

> We try to own common stocks of high-quality companies with good earnings growth prospects... We try to buy these companies at prices we believe underestimate their real value.

Bill Ruane is another successful value investor. Ruane was born in Chicago in 1925 attending the University of Minnesota undergraduate and Harvard Business School in 1949. He was a follower of the Graham approach to investing employing his value investing techniques. Ruane met Buffett at a value investing seminar hosted by Graham. He and Buffett were lifelong friends until his death in 2005. Ruane founded Ruane Cunniff, with Rick Cunniff in 1970 launching the Sequoia Fund. Ruane was a philanthropist adopting a block in Harlem in 1992, renovating the block and improving the community. He gave every child on the block a scholarship to a catholic school. Ruane's firm was renamed Ruane, Cunniff, and Goldfarb in

Table 2.7 Walter Schloss 16 Factors

1	Price is the most important factor to use in relation to value.
2	Try to establish the value of the company. Remember a share of a stock represents part of a business and not just a piece of paper.
3	Use book value as a starting point to try and establish the value of enterprise. Be sure that debt doesn't equal 100% of the equity.
4	Have patience. Stocks don't go up immediately.
5	Don't buy on tips for a quick move. Let the professionals do that if they can. Don't sell on bad news.
6	Don't be afraid to be a loner but be sure you are correct in your judgment. You can't be 100% certain but try to look for weakness in your thinking. Buy on a scale and sell on a scale up.
7	Have the courage of your convictions once you have made a decision.
8	Have a philosophy of investment and try to follow it.
9	Don't be in too much of a hurry to sell. If the stock reaches a price you think is a fair one, then you can sell but often because a stock goes up, say 50%, people say sell it and button up your profit. Before selling try to reevaluate the company again and see where the stock sells in relation to its book value. Be aware of the level of the stock market. Are yields low and PE ratio high?
10	When buying a stock, I find it helpful to buy near the low of the past few years. A stock may go as high as $125 and then decline to $60 and you think it's attractive. Three years before the stock sold at 20, which shows there is some vulnerability in it.
11	Try to buy assets at a discount rather than buying earnings. Earnings can change dramatically in a short time. Usually, assets change slowly. One has to know much more about a company if one buys earnings.
12	Listen to suggestions from people you respect. This doesn't mean you have to accept them. Remember, it's your money and generally, it is harder to keep the money than to make it. Once you lose a lot of money it is hard to make it back.
13	Try not to let your emotions affect your judgment. Fear and greed are probably the worst emotions to have in connection with the purchase and sale of stocks.
14	Remember the word compounding. For example, if you can make 12% a year and reinvest the money back, you will double your money in six years, taxes excluded. Remember the rule of 72. Your rate of return into 72 will tell you the number of years to double your money.
15	Prefer stocks over bonds. Bonds will limit your gains and inflation will reduce your purchasing power.
16	Be careful of leverage, it can go against you.

2004 when Robert Goldfarb became president. Sequoia fund was reopened to new investors in 2008 after being closed in 1982.

Ruane is a value investor, whose style was perhaps more Buffett than Graham. He followed the value investor mandate of buying great companies at attractive prices building in a margin of safety below their intrinsic value. Ruane put an emphasis on strong balance sheets, little or no debt and great FCF generation, and future earnings growth projections. He took large, concentrated positions. Stocks could be domestic or international. Larger market factors were taken into consideration. He was willing to hold cash in Treasury Bills when the market was overpriced. There is a second reason why Buffett liked Ruane. Ruane was one of the earliest investors in Berkshire Hathaway, which comprised 1/5th of the Sequoia fund at one point of time. In fact, Buffett even recommended investors in Buffett Partnership invest with Sequoia fund after he wound down his 1st partnership.

Shelby C. Davis-Fully Insured

You make most of your money in a bear market. You just don't realize it at the time.

Shelby Cullom Davis was a little-known successful investor. Shelby was born in Peoria, Illinois in 1909. His uncle was former Illinois governor Shelby Moore Cullom. Shelby had a very diverse background before going into investing. He was well educated receiving his bachelor from Princeton (1930), master's degree from Columbia (1931), and doctorate from the University of Geneva (1934) in political science. He held multiple jobs before embarking on his investing career. He worked in politics for Thomas E. Dewey and as European correspondent for CBS radio in Geneva. Shelby started his investment career with an investment of $100,000 when he founded and headed Shelby Cullom Davis & Company in 1947. The firm specializes in insurance securities. Shelby took $50,000 from his wife and amassed $900 million in 47 years. Shelby was notoriously frugal. He rarely wrote anything down or would use scraps of paper like the back of envelopes when he did to save money. Shelby C. Davis reportedly put his money in a charitable trust, leaving little to his children. Shelby later served as the American Ambassador to Switzerland under Presidents Nixon and Ford. He was involved with philanthropy, providing significant financial support to Princeton and funding professorships at several universities.

Shelby's investment style could be considered GARP. His specialty was the insurance sector, a similarity he shared with Buffett, where he had experience. He saw several advantages to insurance including the growth aspect, valuation in relation to book value, and dividend payment stream. Shelby had read Graham's writings and was looking to capitalize on the power of compounding. He was specifically looking for insurance companies with strong balance sheets making sure the insurer did not have risky assets. He met with management and believed in diversification with portfolios of +30 names. Shelby was able to use margin and his focus on insurance stocks becoming a millionaire by the early 1950s. He went abroad in the 1960s to find globally, attractive insurance company investment opportunities in areas like Japan, Africa, etc. Shelby liked to find what he called the "Davis Double Play" which is where there was an initial boost from better earnings and then investors bid up the valuation. He eventually moved beyond insurance companies into other sectors, but historically, his greatest successes were in the insurance industry.

Shelby C. Davis was the patriarch of what turned out to be a successful investment family. John Rothschild book *The Davis Dynasty* looks at the history of the family's progression from father to son. Shelby C. Davis' son Shelby Moore Cullom (M.C.) Davis did not work for his father. They were not close. However, Shelby M. C. Davis did learn the basics from his father including the power of compounding interest through dividends and the "Davis Double Play." Shelby M.C. Davis began his investment career at Bank of New York where he was named the youngest Vice President in the history of the company as he rose to head of the research department. He and a friend successfully ran the New York Venture Fund using margin to magnify positive performance. Shelby M.C. Davis went on to found the investment management firm, Davis Select Advisers, which managed $100 billion across several funds as of 2008. Rothschild outlines the Davis strategy: (1) Avoid cheap stocks, which are cheap for a reason, (2) Avoid expensive stocks, no stock should trade at any price, (3) Buy moderately priced stocks with good growth trajectories, (4) Wait until price is right, industries can have bear markets, companies can too, (5) Don't fight progress, (6) Invest in a theme, (7) Let your winners ride, 8) Bet on superior management, (9) Ignore the review mirror, and (10) Stay the course.

Sir John Templeton-Templeton Touch

> Bull markets are born on pessimism, grow on skepticism, mature on optimism, and die on euphoria. The time of maximum pessimism is the best time to buy, and the time of maximum optimism is the best time to sell.

Sir John Templeton is probably the only knighted investor to make the list. John M. Templeton was born in Winchester, Tennessee in 1912. He attended Yale University. Templeton was a card player, poker, which is a common theme with several of the traders and investors we have discussed. He used his prowess at poker to help put himself through college. He went on to attend Balliol College at Oxford as a Rhodes Scholar earning an M.A. in law. He was a CFA charter holder. Templeton became a billionaire though his pioneering of mutual funds, which began in 1954. He went public in 1959 with five funds and $66 million in assets under management. He was modest, practical, and spiritual. Templeton was a philanthropist giving away $1 billion.

Templeton was a Graham follower. He took advantage of market volatility to buy several stocks in the Depression and WWII. Templeton bought 100 shares of each of the NYSE-listed companies trading for less than $1 in 1930. He attributed his success to being upbeat, avoiding anxiety, and staying disciplined. Templeton is perhaps best captured in *The Templeton Touch* by William Proctor. The book covers him as an investor and person. His investment style was simple. He looked for global investment bargains trying to capitalize on investor fear as in the example above and selling when momentum was at his back. He relied heavily on the quantitative approach and diversification. He liked to find areas where the entrepreneurial spirit is thriving, and government intervention is low. He was a bargain hunter looking for companies, industries, nations at the "point of maximum pessimism." *Investing the Templeton Way* by Lauren C. Templeton, who is Sir John Templeton's great niece, provides a nice view into the Templeton style of investing as well.

John Neff-The Professional's Professional

> Successful stocks don't tell you when to sell. When you feel like bragging, it's probably time to sell.

John Neff is a value investor success story. He was born in Wauseon, Ohio in 1931. He attended the University of Toledo graduating summa cum laude in 1955. Neff worked at National City Bank of Cleveland before attending Case Western Reserve University where he graduated from in 1958. He ran the Vanguard Windsor Fund for 31 years from 1964 to 1995 where he outperformed the S&P500 with an annual return of 13.7% vs. 10.6%. Under Neff's management Windsor became the highest-returning and largest mutual fund. The Windsor Fund was eventually closed to new investors for a short period in the 1980s. He retired in 1995. Neff passed away after an illness in 2019.

Neff was a contrarian, "low P/E" investor. He described his life and investment philosophy in his autobiography, *John Neff On Investing.* Neff would scan the companies trading at 52-week lows. He would then investigate the names looking at the business prospects, managements, and balance sheets to separate those that are misunderstood from those whose longer-term prospects would continue to be challenged. Neff's contrarian style was somewhat different than David Dreman, who was more of a statistical contrarian. Dreman's book *Contrarian Investment Strategies: The Next Generation* is a must read for contrarian investors describing how a contrarian can outperform the market taking advantage of investor's overreaction. The book contains statistics supporting the contrarian approach to the market. John Neff's investment philosophy was influenced by Sidney

Robbins, a Ben Graham follower. He tended to have high turnover with average holding periods of less than three years. However, like other value investors he focused on ROE and dividend yield, while at the same time trying to predict the economy and a company's future earnings. Neff's criteria included: low P/E, fundamental growth above 7%, yield protection, superior relationships between total return to P/E, compensation for cyclical exposure, solid companies in growing fields, and strong fundamental cases. We look at one of Neff's identifying metrics in our valuation section.

Peter Lynch-Truly A Magellan

> Know what you own and know why you own it.

Peter Lynch is a well-known investor whose popularity rivals Buffett. Lynch was born in 1944 in Newton, Massachusetts. Tragedy struck the family when Lynch was little as his father was diagnosed with cancer when he was seven and died three years later. Peter graduated from Boston College (BC) in 1965. He used his savings to buy 100 shares of Flying Tiger Airlines at $8 per share. It eventually rose to $80. Peter worked as a caddie during his teens. His caddying paid off in more than one way as he was hired as an intern at Fidelity partly because he had met among others D. George Sullivan (Fidelity's President), while caddying at Brae Burn Country Club in Newton. He originally covered paper, chemical, and publishing as an equity analyst. He was hired permanently in 1969 after a two-year stint in the army with his coverage shifting to textiles, metals, mining, and chemicals. He became Director of Research also known as DOR from 1974 to 1977. Lynch took over the Magellan Fund in 1977, which had $18 million in assets. He grew the funds to more than $14 billion with more than 1,000 stocks by 1990. The Magellan fund averaged an incredible 29% annual return!

Lynch popularized the "GARP" investment strategy. The GARP approach combines growth investing with a value-based approach. There are two books describing Lynch's investment style, *One Up On Wall Street*, which looks at the theory, and *Beating the Street,* which looks at the application. Lynch was a big proponent of, "Investing in what you know" or "local knowledge." Lynch believed you could spot a good investment in your day-to-day life. He talks about going to the mall with his children or buying coffee. You can then take those data points and study the financials of the business to make an investment decision. We will go through this in more detail in our sections regarding developing industry knowledge and screening. Lynch believed the individual investor may have an advantage over the Wall Street professional. He believed in taking a long-term, fundamental approach to investing in high-quality companies. He did not believe in market timing or the academic approach. Lynch was always looking for the "ten baggers." He thought investing, if you were right 6 out of 10 times, you would be considered successful. The point was to make some of those market-leading successes.

Seth Klarman-Oracle of Boston

> A margin of safety is necessary because valuation is an imprecise art, the future is unpredictable, and investors are human and do make mistakes. It is adherence to the concept of a margin of safety that best distinguishes value investors from all others, who are not as concerned about loss.

Seth Klarman is one of the quieter investors on our list. He is known for keeping a low profile. He was born in NYC in 1957. He moved to the Baltimore area when he was 6. Klarman had various business ventures as a child including a paper route, snow shoveling business, and sold stamp-coins on the weekends. He bought his 1st stock Johnson & Johnson when he was ten years old, because he used a lot of Band-Aids. He was regularly calling his broker for quotes by the time he was 12 years old. Klarman attended Cornell University (1979) and then Harvard Business School. Klarman founded the Baupost group in Boston after graduating in 1982 with Harvard Professor's Jordan BAruch, Isaac AUerbach, William J. POorvu, and Howard H. STevenson with the BAUPOST name being an acronym. Baupost has grown to $27 billion in assets from the $27 million started with in 1982, a 20% compound return on investment. Klarman also started The Klarman Family Foundation, which is active in donating to the Jewish community. He has donated to Cornell and Harvard Business School. Klarman is known as the "Oracle of Boston" a play on location as Buffett is often referred to as the "Oracle of Omaha."

Klarman is a value-based investor. His primary means of communication is his letters to shareholders. He also wrote one book on investing, *Margin of Safety, Risk Averse Investing Strategies for the Thoughtful Investor* (1991). Klarman believes every investment needs to build in a margin of safety because valuation is imprecise, the future is unpredictable, and investors are human and make mistakes. Value investing requires a lot of hard work, unusual strict discipline, and a long-term horizon. The primary goal of every investor, especially value-oriented investors, is to avoid losses. Compounding is amazing, but one bad investment can destroy a portfolio and should be avoided. He believes large capitalization stocks do a better job of pricing in the opportunity. Essentially, Klarman is looking to "buy a bargain and wait." He is willing to hold cash when no opportunities are available. He believes holding cash or buying dividend-paying securities helps to keep cash available. His valuation methods include the Net Present Value, liquidation value, and sum-of-parts valuation. Value investing looks at a couple of niches which can be divided into three categories: selling at a discount to break up or liquidation value, rate-of-return situations, and asset conversion opportunities. Klarman's value approach applies to his book with only 5,000 copies printed. The scarcity of the book has driven the price up from $25 to $700 for used copies and newer copies going for $2,500–$4,000.

What's the Best Approach-Speculating vs. Fundamentalist?

We have looked at two approaches to the market: speculating and investing, in this chapter. Each approach has its positives and negatives.

The speculative or trading approach teaches an investor to bet in small amounts and cut their losses quickly, but the efficiencies in the market, randomness of stock movements, and availability of information make it very difficult to spot or benefit from singular or stock-specific trends. Technical analysis has been proven to be ineffective over time, especially since it relies on historical pricing data.

On the other hand, the fundamental approach appears to be a sound approach. It is the one we prescribe to and support. It promotes finding the best names, their intrinsic value, and building in a margin of safety before buying. However, it requires a lot of effort, time, and patience, so even if you find a name you are interested in, you need to wait until it gets to an attractive level building in a margin of safety. Fundamental analysis fails to account for technology investing and to some extent shorting stocks. It may be very difficult to be a fundamental investor in different types of markets, particularly perpetually "Bullish" environments (Table 2.8).

I believe perhaps the best approach to investing is a flexible, fundamentally based approach as it accounts for the inevitability of market volatility. I would use the cornerstones of value investing as building blocks for the approach with select aspects of value investing needing to evolve

Table 2.8 Different Investment Approaches

Characteristic	*Trading*	*Investing*
Type of investing	Active	Active
Belief	Follow the trend	Market volatility provide opp't
Objective	Protect principle and grow	Protect principle and grow
Working to identify	Trends	Undervalued stocks
Tools	Technical analysis	Fundamental analysis
Key metric	Moving avg., relative strength	Intrinsic value, margin of safety
Size of position	All small bets (1%–5%)	Concentrated positions (10–15 names)
Upside	Let winner's ride	Own until intrinsic value is reached
Downside	Cut loses quick/limit order	Build in margin of safety
Card game	Poker	Bridge
Founder	Jesse Livermore	Ben Graham

over time to stay relevant. We have already begun to see an evolution of the investment paradigm among the different generations of fundamental analysts primarily along the lines of the valuation parameters used and the quality and number of the companies selected. We now turn our attention to our attempt to build on the foundation through our investment process and five-factor analysis.

Bibliography

Buffett, W. E. (1984). The superinvestors of Graham-and-Doddsville. *Columbia Business School Magazine*, 13.

Buffett, W. E. (1988). *Chairman's Letter.* Berkshire Hathaway Inc.

Buffett, W. E. (1989, February 28). *Chairman's Letter*. Berkshire Hathaway Inc.

Buffett, W. E. (1995, March 7). *Chairman's Letter*. Berkshire Hathaway Inc.

Carret, P. L. (1997). *The Art of Speculation.* Wiley.

Cunningham, L. A. (1997). The essays of Warren Buffett: Lesson for corporate America. *Cadozo Law Review*, 9, 1–4.

Davis Funds. (n.d.). Wisdom of great investors – Quotes. Retrieved March 27, 2026, from https://davisfunds.com/education/wisdom-quotes

Dreman, D. (1998). *Contrarian Investment Strategies: The Psychological Edge.* Simon & Shuster.

Fox, 2. C. (Producer), & Stone, O. (Director). (1987). *Wall Street* [Motion Picture].

Franklin Templeton. (2025, November 13). *Templeton maxims*. https://www.franklintempleton.co.uk/resources-and-literature/templeton-maxims

Graham, B. (1949). *The Intelligent Investor.* Harper.

Graham, B. (Revised 2006). *The Intelligent Investor.* Harper Business.

Graham, B., & Dodd, D. L. (1934). *Security Analysis.* McGraw Hill Companies.

Kaufman, P. D. (2006). *Poor Charlie's Almanack: The Wit and Wisdom of Charles T. Munger* (Expanded ed.). Walsworth Pub.

Klarman, S. (1991). *Margin of Safety.* HarperCollins.

Lefevre, E. (1923). *Reminiscences of a Stock Operator.* George H Doran Company.

Lowenstein, R. (1995). *Buffett: The Making of an American Capitalist.* Random House.

Lynch, P., & Rothchild, J. (1989). *One Up on Wall Street.* Simon & Shuster.

Lynch, P., & Rothschild, J. (1993). *Beating the Street.* Simon & Shuster.

Martin, D. (1995, November 19). INVEST IT: Patience? This man practically invented it. *The New York Times*.

Munger, C. (2005). *Poor Charlie's Almanack.* The Donning Company.

Munger, C. T. (1995, June 1). The psychology of human misjudgment [Speech transcript]. https://singjupost.com/full-transcript-the-psychology-of-human-misjudgement-charlie-munger/.

Neff, J. (2001). *John Neff on Investing.* Wiley.

Proctor, W., & Phillips, S. (2012). *The Templeton Touch.* Templeton Press.

Rothschild, J. (2001). *The Davis Dynasty.* John Wiley & Sons, Inc.

Ruane, W. J., Cunniff, R. T., & Goldfarb, R. (2024). *Summary Prospectus.* Sequoia Fund.

Schwager, J. D. (2012). *Market Wizards.* John Wiley & Sons.

SIFMA. (2020, August 24). *2020, the year of the SPAC.* Retrieved from https://www.sifma.org/resources/research/insights/2020-the-year-of-the-spac/

Soros, G. (1987). *The Alchemy of Finance.* John Wiley & Sons.

Soros, G. (1993). Markets are constantly in a state of uncertainty and flux... *Interview in The Wall Street Journal.*

Szramiak, J. (2016, January 31). *Business Insider.* Retrieved from Vintage Value Investing: www.businessinsider.com

Templeton, L. C., & Phillips, S. (2008). *Investing the Templeton Way.* McGraw Hill.

Thorp, E. O. (2017). *A Man for All Markets from Las Vegas to Wall Street, How I Beat the Dealer and the Market.* Random House.

Vanhaverbeke, F. (2014). *Excess Returns: A Comparative Study of the Methods of the World's Greatest Investors.* Harriman House.

Williams, T., & Underwood, J. (1968). *The Science of Hitting.* Simon & Schuster.

Part II

The Investment Process

Chapter 3

Market Cycles

Boom, Bust, and Bubbles

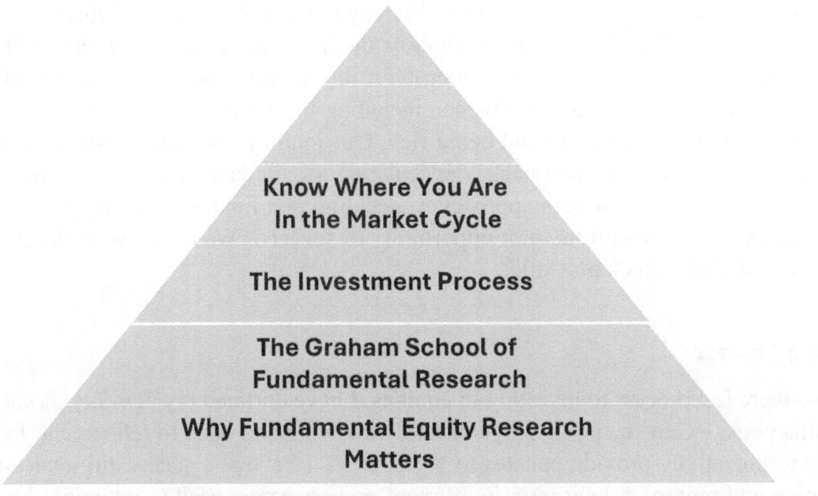

The Process

There have been countless books written about different types of paradigms outside of the investment approaches we have been focusing on in our book. The paradigms these books are focused on involve a change in focus from the outcomes to the process. A particularly compelling read is James Clear's 2018 book *Atomic Habit*, among others in the genre. The author encourages the reader to focus on habits instead of outcomes. He believes that by shifting the focus to the process, it improves your chances of reaching the outcome or goal. Clear thinks readers can run into problems when they spend too much time focused on goals and not enough time on the system because everyone starts with the same goal, achieving a goal is only a momentary change, goals restrict your happiness, and goals are at odds with long-term progress. Clear suggests we instead focus on the continuous process improvement. He believes the creation and execution of good habit compounds, which as we know, can be a very good thing. I tend to agree! Our investment process presented in this chapter and subsequent five-factor analysis is a step in this direction. The process is a starting point, not an ending. Remember the wealth creation game is a long-term one, which is not to ignore annual returns, but rather to focus us all on the process ahead of the results.

DOI: 10.4324/9781003686644-6

Table 3.1 Ten-Step Investment Process

Step 1: Understand the Overall Market Outlook
Step 2: Pick an Industry or Subsector
Step 3: Screen for the Best Stock Opportunities
Step 4: Begin Due Diligence
Step 5: Build a Basic Understanding/Shell
Step 6: Gain an Ethical Edge
Step 7: Develop an Investment Thesis
Step 8: Buy, Hold, or Sell
Step 9: Build a Portfolio
Step 10: Rinse and Repeat

We have covered a lot of ground so far. We began by looking at the debate between passive vs. active investing, deciding, although not easy, the individuals or organizations with the "right" characteristics will be able to produce long-term returns that can outpace the market. We then set a foundational understanding of finance including the *Wealth Creation Formula* and the difference between building wealth and being rich. Our journey continued with an in-depth look at the approaches to investing, particularly speculation vs. fundamental analysis. We reviewed the strengths and weaknesses of both approaches, deciding that fundamental analysis, not without its challenges, provides us with the best opportunity to succeed. We can now begin our first step to effectively building a stock portfolio.

Investing Process

I believe there is a process to investing in equities. I have outlined my *Ten-Step Process of Investing* in this book. I view the process as constantly evolving and open to refinement. I expect future editions to potentially provide updates to the process. I believe a successful investor focuses on developing and refining a long-term investment process as opposed to adopting the current successful trend, especially given the consistent unpredictable nature of markets, particularly outlier events. The investing process steps are: understand where you are in the economic cycle, pick an industry or subsector, screen for the best stock opportunities in the sector, begin due diligence on a few of the interesting companies, select a company, build a model, construct an investment thesis and intrinsic value, look to gain an **ethical** edge, set up buy, hold, or sell parameters, build a portfolio, and rinse and repeat (Table 3.1).

Business Cycles

We now turn our attention to understanding, "Where we are in the market cycle?" An in-depth understanding of the business cycle is critical to deciding how to best allocate capital. It will allow us to decide which of the five factors to emphasize. Markets behave very much like the humans who invest in them. As we said earlier, the only thing consistent about markets is that markets are consistently irrational and unpredictable. In this section, I look at the history of business cycles and their thought leaders, develop a basic understanding of the business cycle, provide an example/model of where we are in the business cycle, and finish with a look at the boom and bust cycles and black swan events. It is very important to make a distinction here. We are trying to make a rough approximation of where we are in the cycle; not a prediction on the future, which is impossible.

Different Business Cycle Approaches

Did you know capitalism is flawed? Theorists have known about three major flaws of capitalism caused by economic fluctuation known as business cycles for centuries. The overall debate regarding business cycles involves three primary areas: existence, causes, and remedies. Modern economists believe changes in the trajectory of the economy are random, similar to stock price fluctuations, but there is data confirming the statistical significance of the business cycle in economic fluctuations. The debate is framed around the causes of the economic fluctuations and whether those causes are *exogenous* or *endogenous*. There are different theories regarding the causes including credit/debt cycles, product life cycles, politics, and government intervention. The theories extend into land price fluctuation known as Georgism. Perhaps the biggest debate is how to handle these economic fluctuations including a laissez-faire approach vs. government intervention (Table 3.2).

I believe business cycles have and will always exist. Business cycle theory has evolved over time. There are many luminaries in business cycle theory including Nikolai Kondratiev, Joseph Schumpeter, John Maynard Keynes, William C. Mitchell, and Charles Kindleberger. The origins of business cycle theory go back to Jean Sismondi, who first looked at the subject in the early 1800s. Sismondi reminds us of Bachelier whom we will meet in more detail in the Academics section. Economists had denied the existence of the cycle prior to his writing. The idea of "Ups" and "Downs" or waves can be attributed to Nikolai Kondratiev and the Kondratiev wave. Joseph Schumpeter brought various business cycle theories together in his seminal two-volume work, *Business Cycles*. There have been many contributors to business cycle theory after Schumpeter's seminal work including the works of contributors like Minsky, Vernon, etc., around the causes of the cycles and especially how to handle them either through Government intervention (Keynesian) or laissez-faire (classical economic), an endless debate. We finish the section with our personal favorite, Charles Kindleberger, who, along with Minsky, maps out the steps and responses to a financial crisis (Table 3.3).

Modern economic thought regarding the business cycle has evolved over time much in the same way as modern portfolio theory in finance, which we will see in an upcoming section. I use the term business cycle interchangeably with the terms economic and trade cycle. The business cycle essentially monitors the upward and downward movements in real GDP. The time between cycles is the difference between the expansions and contractions. Rapid expansion is a "Boom," while rapid contraction is considered a "Bust."

Table 3.2 Different Business Cycle Theories

Economist	*Business Cycle Schools of Thought*
Neo Classical	Promoted Exogenous factors and little government intervention
Keynesian	Promoted Endogenous factors and government intervention
Mainstream	Believe business cycles are causes are random
Credit/Debt Cycle	Credit expansion and contraction impacts business cycles
Real Business Cycle	Product life cycles and innovations impact economic fluctuations
Political Business Cycle	Politics (Elections/Partisanship) impact cycles
Austrian Business Cycle	Low interest rates and government intervention causes booms and busts
Georgism	Land price fluctuation

Table 3.3 Notable Economist Business Cycle Contribution

Economist	*Business Cycle Contribution*
Jean Sismondi	Father/Founder of the Business Cycle
Celement Juglar	*The Juglar Cycle* added a topic (investments) and timeframe (seven to eleven years) to business cycle theory
Nikolai Kondratiev	*The Kondratiev Wave* set the foundation for long term wave and innovation theory
Joseph Schumpeter	Took a typology approach using many different waves; promoted the importance to the entrepreneur and innovation
John Maynard Keynes	Keynesian economics believes in a demand-driven economy with government intervention during difficult times
Hyman Minsky	Credit/debt cycle theorist who believes credit cycles impact economic fluctuation
Raymond Vernon	Father of Globalization – Developed the product life cycle theory serving as the basis for RBC Theory
Michal Kalecki	Focused on interaction between politics and the economy
Richard Goodwin	Endogenous model developed where the bargaining power of the worker cause the economic swings
William C. Mitchell	Empirical economist and early leader of the NBER
Charles Kindelberger	Worked with Minsky to outline the seven steps to financial crisis and conclusions

Brief History of Business Cycle Theory

The emergence of economic thought around the existence of a business cycle began in the early 1800s. Jean Charles Leonard Sismondi, a historian and political economist, published in 1819 his *Nouveaux principles d'econommie politique, our de la richesse dans ses rapports avec le population.* His work proved to be the first systematic exposition of an economic crisis. Classic economists had denied the existence of a business cycle prior to his work. Sismondi and his contemporary Robert Owen identified the causes of economic cycles as *overproduction* and *under consumption* caused by wealth inequality. They advocated for government intervention. Sismondi was vindicated by the panic of 1825.

Sismondi's theory gained momentum and refinement throughout the 1800s. Charles Dunoyer extended it to include theories on alternating cycles. In 1860, Clement Juglar, a French doctor and statistician, was one of the first to identify the length of an economic cycle. *The Juglar Cycle* was a fixed investment cycle lasting 7–11 years long. It observed the oscillation of investments into fixed capital.

Luminaries like Joseph Schumpeter continued to help sculpt Business cycle theories in the 1900s. Schumpeter, an eastern European born political economist, came to the US taking a Harvard professorship in 1932 where he remained until the end of his career. Schumpeter is perhaps best known for popularizing the term, "Creative Destruction." Schumpeter knew Paul Samuelson. In fact, he was criticized for not offering Samuelson an assistant professorship.

In 1939, Schumpeter produced his seminal two-volume work named *Business Cycles*. Schumpeter's business cycle hero is the entrepreneur who disturbs equilibrium and drives economic development, which proceeds in a cyclical fashion along several different time scales. Schumpeter tries to connect three things: Innovation, cycles, and development. He suggests a typology model with four main cycles: (Joseph) Kitchin Cycle (Inventory – 3–5 years), (Clement) Juglar Cycle (Fixed Investment – 7–11 years), (Simon) Kuznets Swing (Infrastructure – 15–25 years), and

(Nikolai) Kondratiev Wave (Technology – 45–60 years). These "cycles" start and stop at different intervals but could be added together to form a wave. Schumpeter argues *The Juglar Cycle* was marketed by four stages: expansion, crisis, recession, and recovery. His Juglar model associated recovery and prosperity with increased productivity, consumer confidence, aggregate demand, and prices. Schumpeter believed *long cycles or waves* were caused by innovation. He felt entrepreneurs would take on risk during times of "neighborhood" equilibrium spurring growth. Although interest in the typology approach has moderated with the development of modern economics, it still serves as a good starting point for basic business cycle theory.

Out of the four main cycle theories, Schumpeter favored the Kondratiev theory. Born in Galuevskaya, Russia in 1892, Nikolai Kondratiev was a soviet economist and early thought leader in wave theory. Kondratiev brought these ideas to light in his book, *The Major Economic Cycles,* published in 1925. A Kondratiev wave is a phenomenon ranging from 40 to 60 years. It is a *long wave* consisting of high and low sectorial growth. Kondratiev broke the cycle into three phases, namely, expansion, stagnation, and recession. The waves had causes like opportunity, social freedom, etc. The waves have potentially positive effects, like technological advancements, and other poor effects, like terrorism, etc. Kondratiev himself was an interesting historical figure who was condemned for his views, imprisoned, and even executed in 1938!

Kondratiev believed cycles were caused by technology and credit. His views are based on *innovation theory*, which is the aggregation or bunching of innovations which in turn become technological revolution. These innovations create leading industrial or commercial sectors. Schumpeter adopted Kondratiev's views.

Kondratiev's theories have had modern modifications. The technology cycles have been labeled: (1) Industrial Revolution (1771), (2) Railways (1829), (3) Electrical Engineering (1875), (4) Automobiles (1908), and (5) Information Technology (1971).

Kondratiev's *long-wave theory* has supporters and detractors. Supporters would point to recent research involving spectral analysis confirming the presence of Kondratiev waves in world GDP with acceptable statistical significance (Korotayev & Tsirel). Detractors believe long-wave theory recognizes patterns, which may not exist. Regardless of the position, it remains difficult to recognize the time frame and causes of these waves. We recognize the challenge, but the existence of the waves provides proof that cycles do exist. The challenge is using the clues we are given to figure out where we are in the cycle, even though we will never get the exact timing or reasoning right. Schumpeter not only adopted the Kondratiev wave but also suggested naming the cycles after "Kondratiev" in his honor. Business cycle is much easier to say or remember.

Neo-classical vs. Keynesian

There are different explanations for these economic fluctuations or business cycles. The key debate for economists is whether the fluctuations are caused by external (exogenous) vs. internal (endogenous) forces. The debate is not unlike the overproduction vs. underconsumption debate presented by Sismondi. The classical (neo-classical) school classified as "supply side" argues for exogenous causes. The Keynesian school classified as "demand side" believes the causes are endogenous. Exogenous causes include items like the rate of technological advancements and savings rate. Endogenous causes relate to capital investments, policy decisions, and expanding workforce population. For the most part, the supply-side economist believes in minimal government intervention. Classical economists took a laissez-faire approach to the economy. The Keynesian school took a different approach believing in government intervention. Today, mainstream economists view changes in the business environment as random.

John Maynard Keynes-Keynesian Economics

Markets can remain irrational longer than you can remain solvent.

Few individuals fundamentally changed their industry like John Maynard Keynes. We are reminded of Benjamin Graham from the last section. Keynes was born in 1883 in Cambridge, England. He is the son of an economist. He attended Eton College in 1897 on scholarship and then Cambridge University. Keynes wrote *The General Theory of Employment, Interest, and Money* in 1936. In the book, Keynes laid out his theory of economics known as Keynesian economics. Similar to Graham, it is important to note that Keynes was writing and developing his theories during the Great Depression. Keynesian economics believes aggregate demand impacts business cycles, not supply as had been thought up to that time. He felt the governments should utilize monetary and fiscal policy to help the people especially during times of crisis. Monetary policy is a government use of interest rates to control economic activity. Fiscal policy is government spending. Keynes felt moderate government intervention was economically beneficial. Government support could help its citizens who would in turn spend more causing demand to go up. It was believed economies would find their way back to equilibrium by themselves prior to Keynes work. Keynesian economists generally believe in free market without government intervention except in times of crisis. Keynes himself believed in balanced government budgets. A brief review of very basic economic terms and theories will be helpful for a better understanding of business cycles.

Equilibrium

The economic definition of *equilibrium* is an economic state where the market supply equals demand.

Let's look at an example. A car company is looking to produce cars. The company can sell cars for between $10,000 and $30,000. The car company will produce cars between 5,000 and 25,000 cars per year. It will produce more cars at higher prices to maximize its profits and less at lower prices because profitability is lower. The consumer will demand more cars at lower prices and less at higher prices. The supply and demand curves intersect at the $20,000 price point where the car company produces 15,000 cars and the consumer demands 15,000. This intersection is known as equilibrium.

Macroeconomic Equilibrium

The macro economy theoretically works similar to our car example, but on a larger scale. The macroeconomic equilibrium for an economy is where the supply or production from domestic and external sources equals the total demand for those goods at a general price level. Factors affecting aggregate demand in the macro economy include consumer wealth, business expectations, consumer income expectations, capacity utilization, monetary and fiscal policy (Keynesian factors), exchange rate, and global economic growth. Aggregate means the total amount of finished goods and services. The supply curve in macroeconomics can have short and long run factors. Short-run aggregate supply factors include input prices, labor productivity, expectations for output prices, taxes and subsidiaries, exchange rates, and all the things impacting long-run supply. Long-run aggregate supply factors include size of labor supply, human capital, supply of natural resources, stock of physical capital, and technology. The neo-classical economist believes in the supply-side movement through exogenous factors to disrupt and restore equilibrium. Keynesians believe the demand side impacts equilibrium through endogenous factors.

Keynesian Multiplier

The Keynesian multiplier is an economic theory asserting that endogenous factors like an increase in consumption, investment expenditures, and government spending raise Gross Domestic Product or GDP by more than the amount of the increase. There are a couple of main components to the Keynesian multiplier including the aggregate demand curve, which can be impacted by consumer spending in a positive and negative fashion, when it is negatively impacted, an increase in government spending can help offset the impact; the labor supply is often slow to adjust; and a change in consumer and government spending will increase total output. We include an example of the Keynesian multiplier in Appendix V.

Credit/Debt Cycle

There are number of different schools of thought regarding the causes of economic fluctuations in addition to the Neo-Classical vs. Keynesian debate. The credit/debt cycle theory points to the expansion of credit translating into economic expansion with a contraction in credit resulting in a recession or worse depression. Post-Keynesian economist Hyman Minsky was born in Chicago in 1919. He attended the University of Chicago and earned his Ph.D. from Harvard University under Joseph Schumpeter. Minsky was the founder of the "Financial Instability Hypothesis" proposing cycle fluctuation was attributed to fluctuations in credit, interest rates, and general fragility (credit/debt cycle). The hypothesis is lenders (banks) are willing to loan to companies to expand economic growth during healthy environments, which leads to excessive indebtedness eventually causing companies to stop investing and pushing the economy into recession. Minsky, who did not build traditional, mathematical economic models, expounded on the dangers of speculative asset bubbles. His theories received revived attention during the subprime mortgage crisis in 2007–2008 leading the *New York Times* to label it the "Minsky Moment."

Real Business Cycle

The Chicago school of economics has their view on economic fluctuations known as Real Business Cycle (RBC) Theory. RBC theory believes economic fluctuations are caused by random changes in the total productivity factors, which are in turn caused by changes in technology, legal, and regulatory environments. It explains the business cycles from the viewpoint of the life cycle of the individual goods making up the economy. RBC supporters believe economic fluctuations do not stem from monetary shocks, but rather from shocks like innovation. The theory originated with Raymond Vernon, an American economist and Harvard professor, who has been referred to as the "Father of Globalization." Vernon's wrote a groundbreaking article in 1966 entitled, "International Investment and International Trade in the Product Cycle." He identified three imperatives for success in international business in the article: innovation, responsiveness to varying local markets, and cost. The article served as the basis for Product Life Cycle theory. Vernon divided products into three categories: New, maturing, and standardizing. The product life cycle consisted of five stages: introduction, growth, maturity, saturation, and abandonment. We touch on the product life cycle in a little more depth in the strategy session. Interestingly, Vernon was a pioneer of computerized stock-market analysis. He was also an excellent rower setting records well into his 80s.

Political Business Cycle

The Political Business Cycle links economic fluctuations with politics. The theory is often associated with Polish economist Michal Kalecki. It has been claimed that Kalecki developed some of the same ideas as Keynes even before Keynes, but he is less well known to the English-speaking world. Kalecki believed industry leaders wanted political stability but rejected full employment because it provided the worker with too much bargaining power. Political Business Cycle theory contains sub-segments. The electoral business cycle theorist believes incumbent politicians encourage political prosperity before elections to ensure re-election, but the citizens pay for it after the election with recession. Newly elected officials are conservative with their economic policies initially, then become aggressive going into elections. The partisan business cycle suggests that the policies of one party result in externalities like inflation causing for the next party to get elected. The new party addresses the issue but creates another and so on.

Marxian Economics

Marxian economists believe capitalism is doomed to fail. The Marxist view is capitalism is susceptible to crisis as profit is a motivator, but profit tends to decline leading to business failure and unemployment. Keynes appears aware of the flaws within capitalism but felt the system could be supported during crisis through government intervention and should be maintained. All supporters of business cycle theory acknowledge economic fluctuations. Richard Goodwin was an American economist and mathematician who received his Ph.D. from Harvard in 1950. He described himself as, "a lifelong but wayward Marxist." He fled the US during the Marxist era. Goodwin focused on the Goodwin Model or Goodwin's class struggle model is an endogenous model where the worker increased his bargaining power for labor putting pressure on profits and leading to an economic slowdown. He provided a Marxist model of long-term institutional growth to explain the Kondratiev wave.

Austrian School

The Austrian business cycle theory believes economic fluctuations are caused by the excessive issuance of credit by banks in fractional reserve banking systems. The Austrian school believes the bank credit problem could be exacerbated by a central bank policy where interest rates are set way to low, which expands the money supply and leads to a "boom" allowing for poor capital investments to take place. These investments don't pay off, and the "boom" leads to a "bust." The global lowering of interest rates during the 2020 pandemic at the time of the writing of this book has many worried global economies are in a "boom" cycle and thus headed for a "bust." The Austrian school argues business cycles are caused by government intervention and cycles would be mild without them. After examining all the different business cycle theories, we can now expand on a golden rule.

Golden Rule: If capitalism exists, business cycles will take place regardless of when and why.

Business Cycle Basics

We turn our attention to the basics of business cycles. The standard definition of the business cycle provided by economist Arthur F Burns and Wesley C. Mitchell in 1946 in their book *Measuring Business Cycles* is,

> Business cycles is a type of fluctuation found in the aggregate economic activity of nations organizing their work mainly in business enterprises: a cycle consists of expansion occurring

> at about the same time in many economic activities, followed by similarly general recessions, contractions, and revivals which merge into the expansion phase of the next cycle; in duration, business cycles vary from more than one year to ten or twelve years; they are not divisible into shorter cycles of similar characteristics with amplitudes approximating their own.

Wesley C. Mitchell's contribution to business cycle theory goes well beyond the definition. Mitchell was an American economist who was well known for his empirical work on business cycles. He received his Ph.D. in 1899 from the University of Chicago. Samuelson named Mitchell along with others as one of several "American saints in economics" born after 1860. Mitchell's contribution to the understanding of business cycle includes two books, *Business Cycles* (1913) and *Measuring Business Cycles*. His work was more empirical than theoretical. He used his empirical work to support his endogenous work on the business cycle, which included the flaws created by capitalism. He was the leader of *The National Bureau of Economic Research* or NBER in its first couple of decades. The NBER is generally considered the final arbiter of the start and stop dates of a recession.

Step 1 of Investment Process: Understand the Overall Market Outlook

We introduce to you the first step of our process and a golden rule: know where you are in the market. It is impossible to perfectly predict where you are in economic cycles, but looking at certain metrics helps you get a better understanding.

> *Golden Rule: Know where you are in the business cycle.*

We divide our view into two categories: Macro and Market factors. The Macro factors involve GDP, Unemployment, Interest Rates, Inflation, and Consumer Spending. The Market factors are divided into two categories: valuation (fundamentals) and sentiment (psychology). The value of the market in comparison to the historical challenges and overall confidence in the future.

Bulls, Bears, and Economic Cycles

Markets can be either bullish or optimistic or bearish or pessimistic. The economy is observed to go through four phases during the economic cycle: *expansion*, *peak*, *contraction*, and *trough*. Expansion is marked by economic growth and conversely lower unemployment. Recovery/expansions usually last three to five years in length. The peak is the highest value reached by some quantity in a time frame. Contraction is a period of economic decline. A recession is a type of contraction commonly defined as a downturn in the economy with the technical definition being two consecutive quarters of declining real GDP. Recessions have averaged around ten months in length since the 1950s. Trough is the bottom of the business cycle. As we stated earlier, the National Bureau of Economic Research (NBER) is generally considered the final arbiter of the dates between peak and troughs.

Business Cycle Indicators

Business cycle indicators (BCI) help us to get a rough understanding of where we are in the cycle. It would be naive to think BCIs can lead you to an exact understanding of the business cycle and the current location in the cycle. However, we can use these and additional metrics plus the mosaic theory to draw our own assumptions about where we are in the cycle. These factors are GDP, interest rate levels, unemployment, inflation, and consumer spending. Other factors I use as BCI are consumer confidence, consumer debt levels, business confidence, stock market valuation, and real estate. I briefly touch on each indicator from a US-centric standpoint below, followed by a table, and an evaluation of where I think they are in the business cycle, which can differ from stock market movements. Remember: It is the convergence of market movements and fundamentals that begins to create buying opportunities.

Gross Domestic Product (GDP)

GDP is the primary measure of economic growth. GDP is the total market value of all the finished goods and services a country produces. The US Bureau of Economic (BEA) Analysis calculates the US GDP quarterly. There are a number of different ways as well as types of GDP calculations. GDP can be calculated using an *expenditure*, *production*, and *income* approach. The expenditure approach calculates the spending by different groups participating in the economy. The production approach calculates the total value of economic output and deducts the costs of intermediate goods consumed in the process. The income approach measures the income earned by all factors of production in the economy. We use real or adjusted for inflation GDP as a preferable measure of GDP than nominal, which does not account for inflation. Real GDP is calculated by using a *price deflator*, which compares current price levels to a base year. Nominal GDP is divided by the deflator. The Real GDP formula is consumption spending plus investment plus government spending plus net exports, which is exports minus imports. We include a GDP Example in Appendix A.

Macro Factors: GDP, Unemployment, Interest Rates, Inflation, Consumers

US Real GDP

We look at the Real US GDP changes provided by the BEA going back to 1990. The NBER has announced five changes in the business cycle since 1990. The 1st Cycle Peaked in July 1990 and Troughed in March 1991; 2nd Peaked in March 2001 and Troughed November 2001; 3rd known as the "Great Recession" Peaked in December 2007 and Troughed June 2009, and 4th Peaked in February 2020 and troughed in April 2020 during the COVID-19 pandemic recession. The February 2020 peak marked the end of a 128-month expansion beginning in June 2009. The longest expansion on record dating back to 1854. The NBER believes the dramatic decline in GDP due to COVID-19 warranted the immediate announcement of a recession in early June 2020. The 2020 recession lasted two months, making it the shortest recession on record.

Economic Forecasting

There are two primary sources for macro-economic forecasting in the US: Congressional Budget Office (CBO) and Federal Reserve (Fed). These agencies face the unenviable task of not only needing to predict the unpredictable but also considering unexpected events like the pandemic.

Unemployment

The definition of unemployment is not as simple as it seems. The average person may think unemployment is someone who simply isn't working or someone looking for work but can't find it.

The keeper of unemployment statistics in the US is the Bureau of Labor Statistics or BLS which reports these statistics monthly. There are three types of unemployment. Frictional unemployment or a time lag in matching qualified workers with job openings. Structural unemployment where an unemployed worker doesn't have the skills to match newly created jobs. Cyclical unemployment where the economy produces at less than capacity during contraction phase of a business cycle.

The BLS conducts a monthly survey called the Current Population Survey (CPS) to measure unemployment in the country. The monthly sample survey is of 60,000 households, which is 110,000 people. There are possible errors associated with the sample set, but they are considered insignificant. According to the BLS, people are considered employed if they did any work at all for pay during the reference week. They are classified as unemployed if they don't have jobs but have been **actively** looking for work in the prior four weeks and are currently available for work. Criticisms of the BLS method are it doesn't: account for discouraged or marginally attached workers, separate part- and full-time workers, account for those with low-paying jobs, and capture the long-term unemployed, who haven't been working for at least 27 weeks. Investors sometimes focus on the monthly U-6 measure, which accounts for the underemployed and marginally attached workers.

US Unemployment

We look at the US unemployment rate reported by BLS. We start with a longer-term time frame then focus more closely on recent changes. The US annual unemployment rate has averaged 5.9% from 1948 to 2020. The highest periods of unemployment came in 1975 ~8.5%, 1982–1983 ~9.5%, 2009–2010 roughly 9.5%, and early 2020 ~10%. The 2009–2010 timeframe coincides with the "Great Recession," while 2020 was the pandemic. All the periods of high unemployment are consistent with economic downturns.

Interest Rates

We turn to our 3rd Business Cycle Indicator or BCI interest rates. Remember I touched on how interest rates can be good, bad, and a necessity in our section on personal finance. The two indicators I look at are the 10-year T-Note and the 30-day T-Bill. We will look closer at these metrics in our valuation section when we look for a risk-free rate. The art of investing is finding the best risk/rewards, protecting capital, and finding the best yield. The decline in interest rates began in 1990 and continued to 2021 forcing investors to invest in the stock market as the market provides the best potential overall yield compared to different asset classes. 10-year T-Note rates have fallen from 8% in 1990, to 5.1% in 2000, to 3.30% in 2010, and eventually declined to 0.9% in 2020. Interest rates have rebounded to ~4% in 2022–2024. The CBO estimates the 10-year T-Note rate is expected to be 3.8% in 2025 and 2026.

Inflation

Inflation is an important factor in the market. It can erode the purchasing power of cash. Investors use it as a primary factor in figuring out returns. The two primary inflationary measures are: Personal Consumption Expenditure (PCE) Price Index and Consumer Price Index (CPI). The measures are presented as headline measures, which means they include everything. They are core measures which exclude things like food and energy prices. The PCE Price Index is tracked by the

Bureau of Economic Affairs and measures the component statistics for consumption in GDP, which is the actual and imputed expenditures of households including durable and non-durable goods data. The CPI Index is tracked by the BLS, who as you remember reports unemployment. The CPI index measures the changes in the price levels of a weighted average market basket of goods purchased by households. The US Federal government uses different inflationary measures for different purposes. The Federal government uses CPI to adjust benefits from programs like social security. The FOMC (Federal Open Market Committee) focuses on the PCE in its economic projections and states its long-term inflation goal in terms of PCE headline results. The FOMC made the change to PCE from CPI because the PCE: expenditure weights change as people substitute in different goods for others, include more comprehensive coverage, and revise historical PCE data.

Inflation has been an area of concern in 2022–2024 coming out of the pandemic after being "under control" over the last decade ending in 2020. Inflation has historically been a periodic problem. The 1970s and 1980s were particularly difficult from an inflationary perspective, reaching a rate of 10% in 1974 and 1980 according to the PCE Price Index. Inflation is expected to be 2%–2.5% for PCE in the short term according to the CBO.

The Consumer

The 5th core BCI is the consumer. We can measure consumer activity in several different ways. I focus on three main categories including consumption, credit, and confidence. We will tackle consumer confidence in the next section. As discussed in the prior segment, the US Bureau of Economic Analysis measures Personal Consumption Expenditures or PCE. The PCE is presented as a price index when measuring inflation, but it can also measure general consumer spending as well. The PCE is the value of goods and services purchased by or on behalf of US residents.

Consumer Spending

Let's look at real PCE spending from a monthly and annual perspective. Remember "real" means adjusted for inflation. The early 2020s saw a pickup in PCE spending to roughly 5% in 2021 and 2022. We have since seen a moderation to ~2%. The annual performance of consumer spending appears to be very similar to GDP. There have historically been periods of positive annual increases in spending of around +5% in the late 1990s with a high of +8% in 2002 and times of declines like in the early 2020s due to the pandemic.

Consumer Credit

Consumer credit is a great cross-over point between the macro and market BCI. The US Federal Reserve tracks outstanding credit for individuals, households, family, and other personal expenditures, excluding real estate loans. The Fed separates credit into two categories: revolving and nonrevolving. Revolving credit can be secured or unsecured to borrow up to a limited and repaid at any time. Credit card debt is the largest part of revolving debt. Nonrevolving is closed-end credit extended to consumers that is repaid on a prearranged repayment schedule and may or may not be secured. Car and education loans are the majority of the nonrevolving credit loans.

Consumers are willing to take on debt when they feel good about the environment and vice versa. A look at consumer monthly debt levels shows a large slow down as we enter the pandemic in 2019 (−19% in April 2019) and a rebound in 2022. If we take more of a historical view, we see consumer credit increases by about 5% per year with major double-digit increases during the periods of 1945–1950, 1963–1965, 1971–1973, 1983–1985, 1994–1995, and 2000. There were major declines in 1958 +0.66%, 1991 −1.27%, 2010 −1%, and −0.3% in 2020.

Market Factors: Valuation, Real Estate, Confidence

S&P 500 Valuation

The two primary US stock market indices are the S&P (S&P500) and Dow (Dow Jones Industrial Average (DJIA)). The S&P is a capitalization-weighted index measuring the performance of 500 large companies listed on the stock exchanges in the US. It is maintained by S&P Dow Jones, a joint venture, majority owned by S&P Global, a company I know very well as I used to follow it from an investment research perspective. MSCI, a company I used to also follow from an investment research perspective, has commanding market share in the indexing markets, internationally. The Dow is a price-weighted index measuring the stock performance of 30 large companies listed on the exchange. The value of the DJIA is the sum of the price of one share of stock for each component divided by a factor, which changes when one of the companies has a stock split or pays a dividend. I and most investors prefer the S&P as our domestic (US) index of choice vs. the DJIA, given its comparative ability to represent the market.

The S&P market index can be valued in a multitude of ways. I prefer to use a relative valuation method known as Price/Earnings or P/E ratio. The ratio can be looked at from two different viewpoints: Trailing Twelve Months (TTM) and Next Twelve Months (NTM). We can then compare it to its historical average to get a sense of where the current valuation stands vs. historical metrics. S&P's average historical P/E ratio is about 15–16×, which compares to 2019 of 19.6× (30% premium), 2020 NTM estimate of 25.3× (67% premium), 2021 est. of 19.6× (30% premium), and 2022 est. of 17.9× (20% premium).

Cyclical Adjusted Price to Earnings (CAPE)

We can see by the graph above that the simple use of just the TTM PE has its challenges, especially since there are spikes like in 2009 when the TTM PE was 71×! As is common with most market-related issues, we turn to Ben Graham for the answer. He believed to smooth out the lumpiness of a company's annual PE ratios, it made the most sense to take a longer look at them over a 10- or 20-year period, essentially smoothing them out. Robert Shiller, an economist at Yale, adopted the methodology taking a moving average of ten years of earnings, adjusted for inflation. According to Shiller's Cyclical Adjusted Price to Earnings (CAPE), which is defined as price divided by the average of ten years of earnings adjusted for inflation, the S&P500 is trading at 36× as of June 2025 well above the average CAPE of 15.2× for the 20th century implying the market is overvalued. High CAPE have preceded market crashes in 1929, 1999, and 2007. There have been several criticisms of the CAPE including the accounting behind market earnings, which is reported differently today (Figure 3.1).

Housing Market

The stock and housing markets are important barometers for consumer confidence as consumers typically have a large portion of their net worth in both. We turn our attention to the housing market. The S&P/Case-Shiller Home Price index is a monthly composite of single-family home price index looking at 10- and 20-city composites. The index has a standard value of 100. There

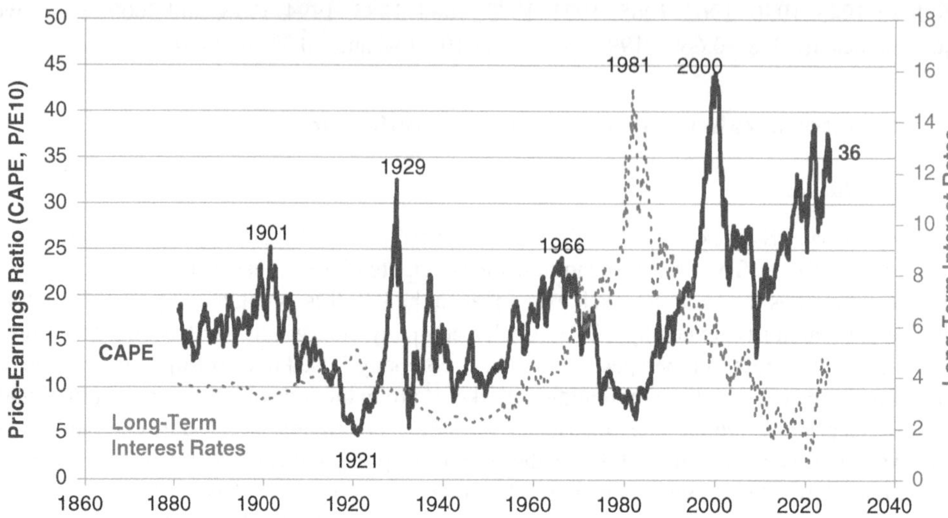

Figure 3.1 Price to Earnings Ratio (CAPE, PE10).

are options and futures traded on the Chicago Mercantile exchange based on the index. The index has been above 200 since 2016 and crossed 300 beginning in 2022.

Confidence

There are two final areas to look at in determining where we are in an economic cycle from a market perspective: **consumer** and **business confidence**. There is a strong link between confidence or psychology and the market. The Consumer Confidence Indicator (CCI) is a monthly metric based on 5,000 households published by the independent economic group, The Confidence Board. It measures the degree of optimism in the outlook for the US economy exemplified by consumer confidence in their spending and savings activities. The CCI declines during recessionary timeframes including recent periods like the early 1990s, 2000s, and 2020–2021 (Pandemic). The first quarter of 2025 experienced a decline as well. The CCI is looked at by the Federal Reserve when considering interest rate changes.

Business confidence can be measured in a couple of ways. The Organization for Economic Co-operation and Development (OECD) publishes a monthly business confidence indicator based on its opinion surveys on development in production, orders and stocks of finished goods in the industry sector. Numbers above 100 indicate confidence and below 100 pessimisms. The business confidence level has been below 100 since 2020.

Our final metric is the National Federation of Independent Businesses (NFIB), who monitors small businesses confidence in the US economy. The NFIB small business optimism index was in the 98 range as of mid-calendar 2025 close to its 51-year historical average of 91.

Putting It All Together

It is impossible and futile to predict the future. The best we can do is look at the data in front of us and try to make sense of where we are in the market cycle to measure the risk associated with investing in it. Markets and stocks are the same in they have two separate parts, price and

Table 3.4 Business Cycle Indicators

BCI Indicators	*Avg*	*1990s*	*2010s*	*2020s*	*2021*	*2022*	*2023*	*2024*	*1Q25*	*2025E**	*2026E**	*Long Term*
Macro Factors												
Real GDP	2.3%	3.2%	2.0%	1.8%	−2.6%	6.1%	2.5%	2.9%	2.0%	1.9%	1.8%	1.8%
Unemployment	5.9%	5.8%	5.9%	5.9%	3.7%	3.3%	3.5%	3.8%	4.4%	4.4%	4.4%	4.4%
Interest rates (10-year T Notes)	4.2%	6.4%	4.1%	2.1%	1.5%	3.8%	3.9%	4.6%	4.2%	3.9%	3.9%	3.8%
Inflation (PCE price index)	2.0%	2.3%	2.1%	1.5%	3.3%	4.9%	3.3%	2.8%	2.6%	2.6%	2.1%	2.0%
Consumer spending (PCE expenditures)	2.7%	2.8%	2.9%	2.4%	5.8%	5.0%	2.6%	2.6%	2.3%	N/A	N/A	–
Consumer credit (US Fed)	5.3%	6.6%	4.3%	5.2%	5.7%	7.6%	2.7%	2.0%	2.0%	N/A	N/A	–
Market Factors												
Stock market valuation (PE TTM)	16.0	21.0	29.6	20.5	33.9	21.5	24.1	28.2	22.8	24.1	21.1	–
Stock market valuation (CAPE)	15.0	26.5	25.7	27.2	38.3	28.3	31.5	37.7	34.8	N/A	N/A	–
Home price index (SP Case-Shiller-10 City)	100	81.6	168.8	202.1	297.5	311.2	333.4	350.6	358.7	N/A	N/A	–
Consumer confidence index (CCI)[a]	100	97.5	89.6	96.3	112.7	104.5	105.4	104.5	93.9	N/A	N/A	–
Business confidence index (BCI-OECD)[a]	100	99.7	99.7	100.0	99.8	97.3	98.3	99.1	–	N/A	N/A	–
Foresi's Current Business Cycle Forecast	Economic Weakness											

Source: SPCapitalIQ, Federal Reserve, CBO, Bureau of Economic Affairs, Bureau of Labor Supply, SP Case-Shiller, CCI, OECD.

[a] Uses annual average for CCI and OECD: Average between the CBO and Fed most recent estimates as of O1 25.

fundamental value. I suggest using a *Mosaic Theory* approach to understanding where we are in the market cycle. A mosaic approach is when a financial analyst uses a variety of sources to draw a conclusion. The good news is we have a lot of real-time data to be able to measure the fundamental strength of the market and its relative price.

I would describe the US economy as of the beginning of 2025 as showing signs of weakness. Although the stock market valuation remains historically well above average, GDP has moderated along with consumer spending and confidence. It does not appear to be a particularly attractive stock market to invest from a historical standpoint as market valuation is high while fundamentals appear to be softening. My commentary regarding the present state of the economy is based on the data as of the beginning of 2025. I would of course update the data quarterly to have a good understanding of where we are in the economic cycle (Table 3.4).

Black Swan

The stock market is susceptible to Black Swan events or highly improbable or unexpected events with significant impacts. A "Black Swan" event impacted society in 2020 when COVID-19 forced businesses to shut down and people to quarantine globally beginning in March 2020, which is when I developed my Mastercard case study. The net result pushed the economy into a recession, which was signaled by the NBER providing the investor with a good understanding of where we are from a fundamental perspective. The Macro factors are behaved as you would expect in the 1H20 with GDP declining −5%, unemployment spiking to double digits, and consumers moving to cut spending and deleveraging quickly. However, remarkably except for a brief period in March, the value of the stock market did not decline and remained above its historical average, thus **not** providing investors, particularly fundamental investors, with an opportunity to capitalize on a market pullback except for the small window when it declined. The historically low-interest rate environment forced investors to look for a return into the stock market, which was being helped by a government stimulus package. A key indicator of recession is the inversion of the yield curve, which, although it is flattening, has not inverted yet.

Booms, Busts, and Bubbles

As we have seen by examining the business cycles, the economy is plagued by economic fluctuations, which provide times of prosperity or "Booms" and hardship or "Busts." These cycles create "Bubbles" at the top of the "Boom" cycles, which are particularly dangerous. A look at Booms, Busts, and Bubbles is equal parts history and pattern recognition.

A Neat History Lesson-Drew's Trick

The name Wall Street itself is derived from the Dutch "de WaalStraat," which was an actual wooden wall on the northern boundary of the New Amsterdam settlement built to protect against outsiders who included Native Americans, pirates, and the British. In the 1600s, Wall Street developed into a marketplace where auctioneers and dealers would meet to conduct trade. By the 18th century, traders and speculators were meeting at the buttonwood tree at the foot of Wall Street to trade securities. In 1792, the traders formalized the association through the Buttonwood agreement, which was designed to add structure to the market. The Buttonwood agreement was the origin of the modern New York Stock Exchange.

Financial historian Charles R. Geisst in his book *Wall Street: A History* provides a comprehensive look at the history of modern Wall Street. Geisst suggests there has always been a "tug-of-war" between business interests on Wall Street and the authority of Washington D.C. Geisst breaks down

Table 3.5 Major Historical Wall Street Trends

Title	*Timeframe*	*Description*
Early Years	1790–1840	Market transforms from outdoor market to major marketplace
Railroad and Civil War	1840–1870	Stock Exchange becomes source of financing from railroads to Civil War
Robber Barons	1870–1890	Robber Baron's take over Gould, Rockefeller, Morgan, and Schiff
Age of the Trust	1880–1910	Development of Trust Co. among banks. Panic-1894, 1903, and 1907
Money Trust	1890–1920	Money Trusts and development of the federal reserve. W-St. gains power
Booming Twenties	1920–1929	Boom and bust of the 1920s. The higher it goes the further it falls
The New Deal	1930–1935	Washington exerts influence on the market through 1933 and 1934 Acts
Struggle Continues	1936–1954	WW-II puts the market on hold, but 1950s sees a return from investors
Bull Market	1954–1969	Antitrust suit against Wall Street dismissed setting off Bull market
Bear Market	1970–1981	1970 Wall Street Crisis marked by high interest rates and inflation
Mergermania	1982–1996	Merger trends take off along with corporate raiding. Crash in '87

Source: Wall Street: A History by Charles R. Geisst.

the history of Wall Street into different time segments. A quick glance at the history appears to show a pattern of boom, bust, big business, and big personalities. One of my favorite stories is one known as Daniel Drew's trick or simply "Drew's Trick." Daniel Drew was a speculator in the mid-1800s. The story is that Drew, who was a notorious short seller, wanted to get the price of a stock (Erie Railroad) up as high as he could before he sold it short. One hot day Drew visited a New York City club where the stock traders congregated. He pulled out a handkerchief to pat his brow. As he patted his brow, a piece of paper fell out of his pocket, which no one told him about. The piece of paper that was left behind had positive news on the stock. The traders frantically bought shares the next day, driving the stock price to new highs, which was Drew's opportunity to sell them short and wipe them out. There are many great takeaways from this story including a view of the manipulative behavior of Wall Street characters, the ability to capitalize on market inefficiencies, and a glimpse of early Wall Street behavior, which continues today! Below is a look at the major historical trends throughout the history of Wall Street, which complement our theory that historically Wall Street has experienced different investment paradigms (Table 3.5).

Financial Crisis-Wash, Rinse, and Repeat; But Never the Same

There is an old saying, "History never repeats itself, but it does rhythm." Drew's Trick and the other Wall Street Manias, even the paradigm shifts, appear to repeat themselves.

Charles Kindleberger in his 1978 classic *Manias, Panics, and Crashes: A History of Financial Crisis* outlines for his readers the patterns associated with financial crisis. Kindleberger and Hyman Minsky describe the seven phases of the cycle. (1) Displacement, (2) Expansion, (3) Euphoria, (4) Distress, (5) Revulsion, (6) Crisis, and (7) Contagion. A displacement (Step 1) occurs in the economy shifting expectations concerning profits one way. A displacement is a shock to the system, it can come in many shapes or forms ranging from technological innovations to war. The displacement creates an area of speculation leading to a "boom." Expansion (Step 2) is necessary to fuel the displacement and create the bubble. Expansion comes in the form of liquidity (bank credit, increased leverage, margin buying power, etc.). Expansion becomes Euphoria (Step 3) when trading becomes based on price alone and not on fundamentals. Distress (Step 4) is a classic crisis when there is concern about the strength of the market or an end to liquidity. Distress can persist, and the crisis can be avoided, or it can turn into revulsion. Revulsion (Step 5) is a sharp shift in actions and expectations caused by new information or an event. The "insiders" sell during revulsion while the "outsiders" are still buying, meanwhile liquidity is drying up causing "discredit." Crisis (Step 6) is caused by the rush to liquidity. Finally, Contagion (Step 7) sets in. Kindleberger believed there were three ways to stop the crisis: (1) A fire sale where buyers are brought back into the market at some point because the prices decline to low levels, (2) Trading is halted by an authority, and/or (3) A lender of last resort provides liquidity.

Seven Steps of a Financial Crisis

Kindleberger's seven steps of a financial crisis are enlightening. First, Kindleberger believes financial crises are part of a process. He thinks we need to understand the process to avoid repeating it. Kindleberger submits that financial crises are linked to human nature and thus inevitable. We agree with Kindleberger. Remember the market is unpredictable, just like people. We believe behavioral science is helping investors understand the behavioral challenges humans face when investing. Second, financial crises arise out of excessive optimism about innovation, economic prospects, and policy control. Humans must contend with the contradiction that the same optimism is an important driver of growth and innovation. Third, a central policy question is how to control all avenues of money expansion, personal wealth, and credit demand. An important indicator of excess leverage is when cash requirements are too low relative to the prevailing and prospective price. Fourth, Jawboning does not help. Central banks' cautioning is often rejected. Fifth, the process of displacement can take years even decades, while the period of excess is typically very short. As a result, the efforts to reduce the crisis must be ongoing and cannot be introduced during the peak when it is too late. Sixth, revulsion, takes years as well. The lender of last resort helps the healing process, but the temptation to force the process often

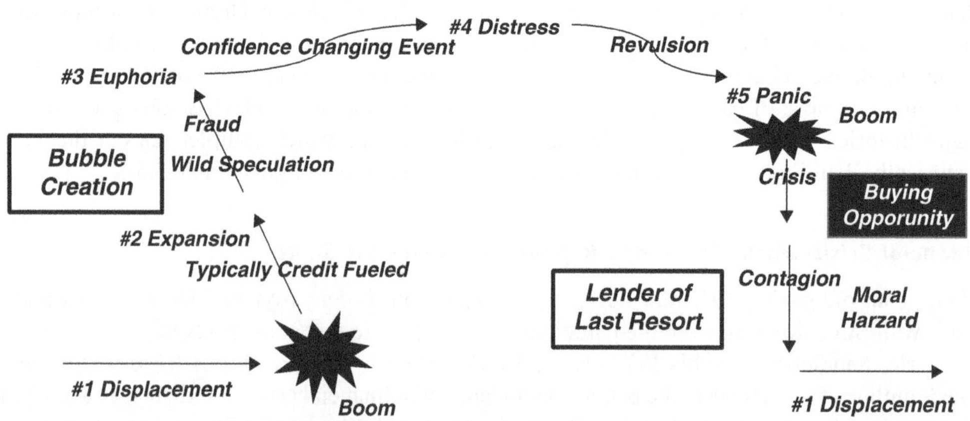

Figure 3.2 Kindleberger/Minsky Anatomy of "Bubble" (Interpretation).

quickly creates a new problem, and seventh, most modern financial crises are international in scope (Figure 3.2).

Golden Rule: Although the steps for a financial crisis are similar, the crises are never the same.

Bubbles

We encourage investors to keep an eye out for a "bubble." A bubble is an economic cycle characterized by rapid escalation of asset prices followed by contraction. It is created by a surge in asset prices unwarranted by fundamentals and driven by exuberant behavior. One of the most famous bubbles was the tulip crazy of 1637 in Holland. The crazy saw rare tulips, which were a sign of prosperity sell for as much as 15× or 20× the salary of a skilled craftsman. Other notable bubbles include South Sea, Roaring Twenties, Soaring Sixties, Nifty Fifty, Roaring Eighties, The Japan Bubble, and the Internet Bubble. I believe it is much harder to pick or call the "Tops" of markets than the "Bottoms." "Tops" are usually marked by asset bubbles. "Bottoms" are in the news making them much easier to define and identify. The problem investors encounter during market bottoms is having the guts to act.

The 2000s Bubbles

Dot-Com

We can look at examples of bubbles from the 2000s including Dot-com and Great Recession. The 1st bubble of the 2000s was a technology bubble created by speculation in internet companies. The 1990s saw an explosion in the use of the internet by households as computer ownership increased to 35% from 15% from 1990 to 1997, according to the Department of Labor *Issues in Labor Statistics*-1999, which in turn led to an increase in internet usage. The next stage is credit-fueled expansion. There were a couple of factors helping with the expansion including lower interest rates, taxes (Taxpayer Relief Act of 1997), and favorable legislation including the Telecommunications Act of 1996. The increase in internet usage led to euphoria as venture capital companies and investment banks satisfied the demand for dot.com companies regardless of viable revenue streams, profitability, or valuation. The peak may have been marked by dot-com companies purchasing 20% of the advertisement spots costing roughly $2 million for 30 seconds for the 1999 Super Bowl. The Federal Reserve under Alan Greenspan announced they would raise interest rates in February 2000. The dot-com companies began to run out of cash marked by a Barron's headline in March "Burning up; Warning; Internet Companies Are Running Out of Cash Fast" in March 2000. The panic set in as the S&P 500 lost roughly −76% from 2000 to 2003; while the NASDAQ composite fell roughly −200%. Economic crises typically help reveal fraudulent activity as swindlers find it increasingly difficult to hide their activity in these difficult environments. The dot-com bubble bursting revealed scandals at companies like Enron, WorldCom, and Adelphia. There are many books written about crashes and scandals, which are topics that fascinate the public. The book *The Smartest Guys in the Room* published in 2003 authored by Bethany McLean is a fascinating account of the Enron scandal and well worth the read in my opinion. The book was eventually made into a movie. The market buying opportunity was from late 2001 to 2002.

Irrational Exuberance

I would caution that any investor should always keep an eye out for "Irrational Exuberance," which typically signals the top of a market. The term "Irrational Exuberance" was first uttered by Federal

Reserve Chairman Alan Greenspan on December 5, 1996. The comments were taken as an indication that the market was overvalued during the dot-com bubble of the 1990s. The phrase was used by Robert Shiller (Yale Professor) for the title of his 2000 book. Shiller was reportedly Greenspan's source for the phrase. Professor Shiller's book focused on several arguments regarding how the stock market was overvalued at the time. The market collapsed the month the book came out.

Great Recession

No sooner has one bubble popped than another is forming. The Great Recession from 2007 to 2009 was caused by a boom in the real estate market, whose seeds were planted during the dot-com bubble. The Federal Reserve (Alan Greenspan) lowered interest rates to 1% in 2001 to help with the previous dot-com challenges. The lowering of interest rates combined with a favorable George W. Bush "aggressive housing agenda" in the form of moderation drove home prices higher. The lower interest rates allowed millions to refinance their homes using the refinancing as a source of cash, often using adjustable-rate mortgages. Housing prices started to rise in 2001. The rise was fueled once again by a credit expansion. Investment institutions began to lower their lending standards repackaging the mortgages into Subprime Mortgage Backed (SMB) securities, which were incorrectly rated "blessed" by the ratings agencies, and bought by investors for their high yields. The housing market peaked in 2006 and declined to a low in 2012. The bubble began to pop when homeowners started to default on their mortgages, which caused the banks to pull back on lending. Panic set in and a credit crunch ensued. As liquidity dried up, there was a bank run on the shadow banking system, whose estimated size rivaled the depository system (Paul Krugman; *Does He Pass The Test*). Banks like Bear Sterns and Lehman Brothers began to fail. The government stepped in bailing out the banking system serving as the lender of last resort and providing liquidity. The result was a global economic recession. As is typical of financial crisis, there was a fair share of scandals including Bernie Madoff's Ponzi scheme and the ratings agency failure to downgrade the debt. The S&P 500 lost roughly −70% from the end of 2007 to the beginning of 2009; while the NASDAQ composite fell roughly −90%. The market buying opportunity was from late 2008 to early 2009.

As we discussed previously, there are many books written about crashes. Michael Lewis, a well-known financial writer, wrote *The Big Short: Inside the Doomsday Machine* published in March 2010, focused on the crisis. It discusses the causes and players associated with the "Great Recession." The book provides its readers with an inside view of the inner workings of a recent financial crisis. The book was a success and later made into a movie. As a side note, we have already seen three ways to be successful writing finance books: (1) Write a personal finance best seller, (2) Write or co-author a book by a successful investor, highlighting their methodology, and (3) Write a book about famous Wall Street excesses, collapses, and/or scandals, which may even be made into a movie (Table 3.6).

Golden Rule: The only thing that can happen with bubbles is they will pop!

Black Swans

An investor's road to success is filled with hidden landmines, which can destroy any thoughtful approach or portfolio in an instant. As if it isn't difficult enough to try to: learn the business cycle-Booms, Busts, and Bubbles, develop a general understanding of where we are in the cycle, and use it to invest wisely, we also must contend with Black Swans. The term Black Swan was popularized in the 2007 book, *The Black Swan* by Nassim Nicholas Taleb. Taleb believes a Black

Table 3.6 2000's Bubbles

	Dot-Com	*Great Recession*
Timeframe	1995–2000	2007–2009
Areas of speculation	Internet	Real estate
Expansion facilitators	Lower rates; taxes; legislation	Lower rates; subprime lending
Euphoria	Demand for Dot.Co's	Demand for real estate
Pin prick	Greenspan rate hike	Defaults on subprime mortgages
Distress/panic	Internet Co.'s run out of cash	Liquidity or credit crunch
Scandal's	Enron, WorldCom, Adelphia	Madoff; rating agencies
S&P500	Roughly-76% from '00 to '03	Roughly-76% from '07 to '09
NASDAQ	Roughly-200% from '00 to '02	Roughly-200% from '07 to '09
Buying opportunity	Late '01 to late '02	Late '08 to early '09
New displacement	Housing market	TBD

Swan has three characteristics: It is an outlier compared to anything in the past, has a massive impact, and we make excuses as to how it was "explainable and predictable" after the fact. The term "Black Swan" refers to how Europeans believed that all swans where white until 1697 Dutch explorers first saw one in Western Australia. A Black Swan is an improbable event. It changes the reality of those who aren't aware they are coming. Black Swans can be positive like the landing on the moon or negative like the 9/11 attacks. What Black Swans tell us is not to use the past to predict the future, which exposes the flaws associated with any specific approach to investing particularly Speculation and Academic, but also to some degree fundamental analysis. Black Swans and the ever-changing market are why we recommend focusing on a revisable process rather than a specific methodology. It reminds us not to rely on business cycles delivering easily identifiable repeatable patterns. We seek these patterns as humans. It is natural to us. The existence of Black Swans makes it difficult, if not impossible, to try to assess real-world risk like it is a game. It can often lead to bad choices. We are particularly reminded of the Black Swan given the recent COVID-19 pandemic, which seems to have surprised just about everyone, except maybe Bill Gates.

Golden Rule: Be Aggressive When Others Are Fearful.

Selling at the Top or Investing at the Bottom

Investors ideally want to sell (or short) at the top and buy at the bottom. Warren Buffett says, "Be fearful when others are greedy and greedy when others are fearful." The problem is "The Trend is your friend" on the way up and trying to call the bottom is as difficult as "catching a falling knife." We will explore some psychological reasons why it is so difficult to do this in our psychological factors section. I do not recommend market timing, but rather believe it is important to be able to understand the characteristics of market cycles and attempt as best you can to capitalize on them. We would recommend the same approach for stocks. It is more about getting the odds in your favor and putting yourself in the best position to succeed, a common theme of this book. As a side note, the existence of business cycles could be considered proof how capitalism is flawed.

The methods for trying to call the top or bottom of markets are similar to individual equities in that both use fundamentals and include sentiment and/or technical analysis. Stock markets like individual stocks should have an inherent (intrinsic) value. Investors should be able to benefit from recognizing the movements away from the intrinsic value. Stock market fundamentals include economic prospects (GDP, inflation, unemployment, etc.), earnings projections and revisions

(S&P500), and market valuation (S&P500). Market sentiment can be measured through methods like 52-week (High/Lows), the Vix or "Fear" index, and Bullish percentages. Market technical indicators include signs of exhaustion, Moving Averages Convergence Divergence (MACD), and Relative Strength Index (RSI).

Warren Buffett closed a fund in 1969, essentially calling the top of the market. Buffett's fund returned roughly 25% over a decade vs. a 7% return for the Dow. Buffett complained, leading up to his decision to close the fund, he did not understand the market or its new investment style. He was having trouble finding good ideas and did not want to risk investor capital. Buffett eventually returned to investing over time, and the rest is history.

Macro and Market Pendulums

Howard Mark's in his 2018 book *Mastering the Market Cycles* describes business cycles as pendulums swinging back and forth from optimism to pessimism. I like the analogy and want to take it to another level. The "Swinging" back and forth or business cycle movements from expansion to recession to trough to recovery provide what I believe are typically opportunities. Graham and Buffett call this the erratic behavior of Mr. Market. Soros refers to it as reflexivity. I recommend buying when others are fearful and selling when they are overly optimistic, which is no surprise. The economy itself provides investors with the opportunity to make these purchases if they can remain calm.

Golden Rule: Use a Pendulum-Know Where You Are in the Market.

A description of a standard pendulum can provide a nice analogy for the market's volatility. A pendulum works by converting energy back and forth. The bob has its maximum stored energy or potential energy when it is at its highest point. The potential energy is converted to kinetic energy or energy of movement as it moves downward. The energy is then converted back to potential energy as it climbs up again. The pendulum switches back and forth between potential and kinetic energy. It is a harmonic oscillator. The distance and time between the oscillations are slowed through friction. The analogy of the economy or market being a pendulum rather than the typical equilibrium is very interesting. I think academics should explore the topic in greater detail. It may be a better way of explaining economics than the current equilibrium format.

Let's think about economic fundamentals and stock markets as two separate pendulums, the macro and the market. We can first look at them separately and then combine them to get a sense of where we currently are in the market and if we should be aggressive in our investment. Let's use a three-step process of: (1) The macro, (2) The market, and (3) A combination. You can think of this as a way of zooming in on the business cycles. The volatility of the 2020 pandemic serves as a good example.

Macro Pendulum

The macro pendulum moves through different stages of the business cycle. I first need to establish the different stages on the pendulum. Let's look at each stage. On one side of the pendulum, we have a recession leading to a trough. A recession is typically signaled by two consecutive quarters of negative GDP contraction, which coincides with high unemployment. The NBER signaled a recession in June 2020 due to a −5% decline in GDP and 11% unemployment resulting from the pandemic. On the other side of the pendulum, there is economic expansion leading to a Peak. The economy was performing very well before the pandemic with historically low unemployment and solid GDP growth perhaps putting it in Peak territory.

Market Pendulum

The market pendulum relates to the valuation of assets, specifically the stock market. The market pendulum should move in sync with the macro pendulum, but as we saw in June 2020 that is not always the case. The market pendulum follows the same path as the macro pendulum through the business cycle. The market pendulum is marked by Boom, Bust, and Bubbles. We mentioned earlier that the Boom cycle can and often does become a Bubble. The COVID-19 pandemic is closer to a Black Swan event than a Bubble scenario, which is not to say the economy was not close to a Bubble scenario prior to the pandemic. The macro pendulum had been pointing to the right side just four short months ago.

The reason the market pendulum carries greater importance for investors is the risk associated with investing. The cheaper the market or a stock on an absolute basis, the potentially lower the risk after purchasing it and vice versa. I typically recommend increasing investments when the risk is low or on opportunistic market pullbacks and increasing the availability of cash or capital to make purchases as we move up the pendulum. The aggregate and average market multiple appears to be increasing over time as well as. Let's take a quick look at market levels pre- and post-COVID-19. The SP500 began 2020 at 3200 level with a PE TTM of 22×. The market pulled back to roughly 2600, a –20% pull back, on March 31st, with a PE TTM of 15×, which provided a brief buying opportunity. It recovered to the 3,000 level in June, a 21× valuation, eliminating the opportunity in our opinion.

Where We Are in the Business Cycle

The amazing thing about the market and stocks is that you can be strategic waiting until the right opportunity to deploy capital, especially during low inflation environments. The 2025 stock market has a historically rich valuation but declining fundamentals making it less attractive from an investment standpoint. This is different from March of 2020 when the market valuation declined for a brief period providing an opportunity to buy the market or purchase stocks on your preferred purchases list (more on this later). The two pendulums will eventually come close to lining up again, although no one knows the timing, which is the difficult part. It would only make sense that the market pendulum should move toward the macro pendulum, as economies contract quickly, but take time to recover.

What to Buy during Cycle Downturns

I have presented a methodology of thinking about the general position of the market and how to think about allocating capital. It is important to remember this is not exactly science. It is one practitioner's opinion just like any others. It is valuable because it presents a workable framework, which can be utilized when the opportunity presents itself.

How do we know the opportunity is presenting itself? As stated earlier, it is much easier to tell when things are not going well. The signals are obvious from the headlines and market movements. The headlines during the Great Recession involved, "The possibility of breaking $1 on the money markets" or "Lehman Brothers going out of business." The Black Swan COVID-19 Pandemic involved headlines like, "The possibility of 240,000 Americans potentially dying," although it now appears the total amount will be much higher. Markets react to these headlines providing an opportunity to buy fear. The hard part is putting aside your emotions to make the purchase. We would submit a 20% downward market movement as a buying signal, especially if it coincides with multiple trading halts. These may be rare, but market pullbacks seem to be happening more and more frequently: 2001, 2007, and 2020. It appears the length of business cycles is contracting.

There are many ways to benefit from the cyclical downturn. The average investor should think about just simply buying the market through SP500 indexing opportunities, especially during economic downturns. One method would be to pre-set up a call option to buy the SP500 20% below the current market value and update the level monthly or quarterly, which would take some of the emotion out of the purchase. The other option is to try to buy certain stocks during different parts of the business cycle. There have historically been different sectors that have performed better than others in different phases of the cycle. The best late-cycle sectors for Recessionary periods (and Troughs) have tended to be energy, utilities, healthcare, and consumer staples. Consumer cyclicals, financials, and bonds are favorable early stage, expansionary sectors. Investors may find opportunities in areas like industrials, information technology, and basic materials during the late stages or Peaks of the cycle. These recommendations help provide a framework, but the challenge is identifying the correct stage of the business cycle. History does not repeat itself. Just because these sectors worked in these stages before there is no guarantee they will again!

I would instead suggest identifying the best, long-term stock opportunities in the market and keeping a Shopping List of those names with regularly updated entry and exit points to choose from in the event of a pullback. There may be some companies on the list, whose prospects may have changed because of the economic pullback, but if you have constructed your shopping list properly and filled it with stocks you would hold "forever" or the next ten years, there will be plenty of opportunities. We will make our transition to finding the right stocks for our shopping list beginning in the next chapter of the book.

The Way It Should Work

The Age of Macroeconomic Modeling

I have thus far presented our rudimentary and admittedly archaic way of describing fluctuations in the macroeconomic environment and market. There have been advancements in macroeconomic modeling as societies have turned to modeling to better understand changes in the macroeconomic environment. The development of these models is an evolution with each updated version of the model adding details and complexity. Similar to the financial modeling we will perform in relation to individual stocks, economists are trying to predict the future, which is rendered virtually impossible by the dynamic natures of market, irrational behavior, and potential Black Swan events. Macroeconomic models typically look at factors like GDP, unemployment, consumption, and inflation, as we touched on earlier. We run through the debate over the different types of models, their individual positives and negatives below. These models can be *static* or representing a given point and time or *dynamic* representing over a given period.

The Different Approaches

Original Models

The original, basic models can be found in the Keynesian or Neoclassical schools referred to earlier. The Keynesian school promotes approaches like the IS-LM and Mundell-Fleming model. The neoclassical growth theory aligns with the Solow model. These models were simple in nature looking at basic aggregate economic factors and describing their interaction. Macroeconomic modeling has evolved from these early origins to better account for forecasting, anticipating, and guiding change.

Empirical Forecasting Models

The empirical forecasting macroeconomic models of the mid 1900s were the next, logical evolution. These models were increasingly detailed across inputs, subsectors, including multiple equations primarily using time series analysis. An early pioneer in the development of the empirical forecasting model was Jan Tinbergen, a Dutch economist, whose 1930–1940s work advanced the foundation set by the basic economic models. Momentum continued to build until the first global macroeconomic model, "Wharton Econometric Forecasting Associates LINK project," was developed by Lawrence Klein in the 1980s. The progress in macroeconomic models resulted in the awarding of the Nobel Prize for Jan Tinbergen and Lawrence Klein.

Dynamic Stochastic General Equilibrium Model (DSGE)

The late 1900s saw the emergence of DSGE, which further took into account rational choice at a micro level. The advancement in modeling was a response to the inability of the earlier models to accurately predict economic movement like the Phillips curve. The DSGE model breaks down the economy into Micro foundations or the individuals or agent level where the entity is expected to make rational, optimal choices (rational expectations). Agents are entities such as businesses or individuals. DSGE models have been used to look at our business cycle challenges presented earlier on a quarterly basis. Computable General Equilibrium (CGE) modeling is an alternative, long-term-oriented, micro-founded model.

Agent-based Computational Economics (ACE)

The ACE model has similarities to the DSGE and CGE model. The ACE model is an agent-based, micro foundational model. The primary difference between the ACE and DSGE is that the ACE model focuses on the agents' specific strategies instead of their defined preferences like the DSGE model. The ACE strategies can then be adjusted and computed. Both the DSGE and ACE models have flaws. The DSGE runs into challenges related to its inflexibility around rational expectations. The ACE model finds it faces challenges regarding strategies.

Macro Models in Action

Although macro modeling is beyond the scope of our book, we encourage the reader to search around for these macro models, particularly DSGE or ACE models, and test them out yourselves. There are great online resources looking at the various models. As an example, the World Bank offers an excel-based Long-term Growth Model (LTGM). Its neo-classical growth model is based on the Solow-Swan. The World Bank model considers factors like productivity, human capital, and demographics. If you are reading this book in the future and can't find this model or it seems dated, we would not be surprised. We only expect the next generation of macro-models to become increasingly more complicated and accessible over time. Unfortunately, they will continue to face the insurmountable challenge of not being able to account for the irrationality of the market and unexpected events.

Golden Rule: No model is good enough to consider irrational behavior and outlier events.

The Realities of a Flawed System

A good investment process is the key to great investment success. The question then is, "How do you arrive at a good investment process?" My answer is to focus on the process not necessarily the results and continually review and revise.

The first step in almost any endeavor is the hardest. The good news is we took our first step in the *Foresi Investment Process*, which is to understand where you are in the market cycle, but it is not any easy one. The truth is despite all the many well intentioned and extremely intelligent Wall Street economists, **no one** knows what the future will bring, **no one**. It is impossible to predict. I wouldn't even begin to try. The good news is we do have some useful pieces of information to help us navigate this very unpredictable and dark road.

I believe markets follow a pattern or cycle. The causes and the timing of these cycles are debatable, but we know they exist. Capitalism is flawed, which means there have always been and will always be booms, busts, and crashes. They are inevitable. At a very high level, these cyclical patterns serve as a type of map we can use to help us navigate our market roads. It helps us understand how much capital should be allocated to stocks and different asset classes and just as importantly when to do it.

In addition to our business cycle map, we are given markers to help us on the way in the form of macro and market factors, which help us understand the fundamentals or strength of the economy vs. the market price. We can use the data points to get a rough idea of where we are in the business cycle.

Our market analysis serves as our first exposure to the difference between price and value. I believe there are two different pendulums. We can thoughtfully measure these pendulums and graph them out. The rough intersection between price and value is where you would buy the market. If you can manage to do this during a bust cycle, you will become very wealthy. As we will see shortly, stocks work in much the same way as markets, having a separate price vs. value, but on a much more micro level.

Our hope for the long-term success of capitalism is that we continue as a society to be able to better navigate all the different market cycles, especially the busts, which can have a catastrophic effect on individuals and society. We are hopeful advancements in modeling techniques and government policy help us on our way shedding more light on our dark, dark road. Ultimately, the success of these models will be in trying to capture the unexpected.

Bibliography

Burning Up; Warning; Internet Companies Are Running Out of Cash Fast. (2000, March). *Barrons*.
Burns, A. F., & Mitchell, W. C. (1946). *Measuring Business Cycles*. National Bureau of Economic Research.
Clear, J. (2018). *Atomic Habit*. Penguin Random House.
Geisst, C. R. (2004). *Wall Street: A History*. Oxford University Press.
Keynes, J. M. (1936). *The General Theory of Employment, Interest, & Money*. Palgrave MacMillan.
Kindleberger, C. P. (1978). *Manias, Panics, and Crashes*. John Wiley & Sons.
Krugman, P. (2014, July 10). Does he pass the test? *The New York Review*.
Lewis, M. (2010). *The Big Short: Inside the Doomsday Machine*. W. W. Norton & Company.
Marks, H. (2018). *Mastering the Market Cycles*. Houghton Mifflin Harcourt.
McLean, B., & Elkind, P. (2003). *The Smartest Guys in the Room*. Penguin.

Nikolai, K. (1925). *The Major Economic Cycles.* Moscow Institute of Conjuncture.
Schumpeter, J. A. (1939). *Business Cycles.* McGraw Hill.
Shiller, R. J. (2000). *Irrational Exuberance.* Princeton University Press.
Sismondi, J. d. (1819). *Nouveaux Principes d'economie politique.* ou, De la richesse dans ses rapports avec la population. Delaunay.
Taleb, N. N. (2007). *The Black Swan.* Random House.
Vernon, R. (1966). International investment and international trade in the product cycle. *The Quarterly Journal of Economics*, 80(2), 190–207.

Chapter 4

Find Your Calling

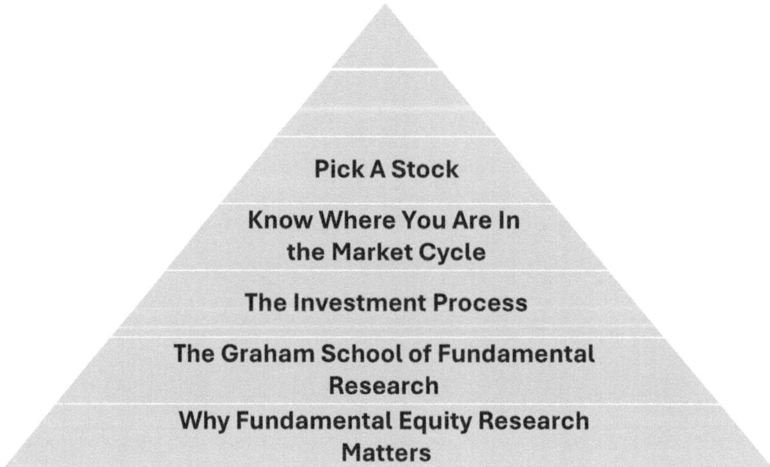

Circle of Competence

I touched upon earlier in the book a piece of wisdom worth revisiting. Warren Buffett talked about investing in what you know or your circle of competence. A circle of competence is the subject area matching your skills or expertise. Buffett recommends sticking to investing within your area of expertise. I call it avoiding "buying blind" or making an investment in something you really don't understand.

Over the years, I have developed the skills necessary to build multiple circles of competence. You can develop these skills as well, even if you don't currently have them. It has taken me well over a decade to understand how to do this. I began my career by developing a circle of competence around the outsourcing trend, then added professional services, and more recently FinTech. I am never done building circles of competence. I just continue to expand them in investing and in life. I recently learned how to ski, completed my doctorate, and published academic papers. You will learn in this chapter how to build a circle of competence in a much shorter time than it took me. You will have a lot of work ahead of you as Charlie Munger has 100s of these circles of competences, which he calls mental models.

A Word on Expertise

I mentioned in the introduction the recent cultural emphasis on specialization and expertise. The paradigm has been encapsulated by the notion of the 10,000-hour rule, which essentially states to

DOI: 10.4324/9781003686644-7

be good at something or an expert you must devote 10,000 hours to it. I believe the 10,000-hour rule can and does work in select instances, but like any other paradigm, the shift toward specialization has swung too far out. You don't need to devote 10,000 hours to creating a circle of competence. You just need to understand the process of creating the circle and then re-apply it. In fact, you may have an advantage by developing a range of expertise overtime as suggested by some recent authors including David Epstein's 2019 book *Range*, which we would recommend for those interested in the subject.

In fact, the whole point of this book was to help the reader expand their knowledge base as they develop a circle of competence in fundamental equity research. We continue to expand our knowledge base as we build toward our stock-specific work. We have thus far taken an in-depth look at: the fundamentals of finance (Foresi Wealth Creation Equation), different approaches to investing (Speculating vs. Fundamental) deciding on a process focused, fundamentally based approach, and the business cycle. We are currently in a recession as of the time of the writing of this book (Mid-2020), but it is not necessarily a buying opportunity as the market valuation has not been corrected.

I can now move on to our second step, pick an industry or subsector. Once we have picked a sector, we can build a circle of competence in this industry or subsector. The process of developing a circle of competence involves a couple of steps, which mirror to an extent doing due diligence on a specific company. Let's get started.

Step 2 of Investment Process: Pick an Industry or Subsector

Golden Rule: Don't buy blind. Invest in what you know.

Invest in What You Know

Knowledge is potentially the key to everything in life. The same holds true for equity research. Peter Lynch suggests, "Invest in what you know." I completely agree. I will present a couple of different approaches for picking an industry and stock, but with an anecdote. I am often asked by friends or family for my opinion on stocks. For example: "What do you think of GE? I bought some a couple months ago." I always answer, "I don't know the company well, so I have no opinion," or "I don't give friends advice on stocks until I have done the work."

I call going out and buying a stock you know nothing about just because you got a tip or have a hunch, "Buying Blind." It is pure speculation. When you do this, you are throwing your money away. Yes, you might get lucky and be right for a short period of time, but it won't last. Investors who buy individual stocks this way (academics call them uninformed investors) by participating in the market provide an advantage for the sophisticated (Informed) investor, like you will be at the end of this book. An educated investor knows if they should get involved with a company like GE based on the homework they have done in getting to know GE's business model, i.e., its strengths and weaknesses, outlook, valuation, etc. Let's be clear here. I'm not suggesting you have insider information or anything of the sort. Ethics is all you have in life. I am suggesting you gain a considerable advantage in understanding the opportunity a stock presents compared to the investors who don't do the work or put in the effort. The rest of the book shows you how to do your homework.

Different Approaches to Picking a Sector

The equities investment universe is enormous. As a result, it might make sense to begin with what you know. For example, perhaps you work in the utilities industry and understand the utilities business model. It would make sense for you to think about beginning your equity portfolio by investing in Utility stocks. It's simple, but it is often overlooked and makes a lot of sense.

I would suggest an aspiring investor follows one of three possible methods to pick a sector and stock to study. An investor can: (1) Take advantage of their background as mentioned above, (2) Pick an industry or stock through our method, and/or (3) Use screens. The decision on whether to invest and when only comes after you have done the work. The unfortunate thing about equity research is you may do the work but not invest or choose not to invest. Although this may seem like a waste of time, it may be a good thing for several reasons.

The benefits of doing the work include the knowledge you gain, the mistakes you avoid (losing money), and the serendipity of uncovering a stock that you would not know about otherwise. In that case, you can decide on a price you're willing to pay for the company and be ready to buy when the market allows. If you buy enough of these great companies at great prices, you will achieve the goal, a great stock portfolio.

Sector and Stock Selection Method

In addition to taking advantage of what you know, investors can follow either an industry (top down) or stock-specific (bottom's up) approach to selecting investment opportunity. Our method for sector or stock identification involves the early identification of an emerging trend, doing your homework, developing a thesis, and if you take the sector approach having, a top (favorite) picks among the group. The process takes time, but practice will allow a person to develop an expertise (circle of competence) in a specific area, assuming one doesn't already exist, creating a competitive advantage when it comes to investing. As we mentioned earlier, we have covered three different sectors in our equity analyst career thus far: IT Services, Professional Services, and FinTech. We were able to build expertise in these areas over time without having worked in the industry, which probably would have enhanced our knowledge. If this seems like too much work, have no fear, you can simply skip forward to our section on stock-specific analysis. However, the ability to develop the skill set necessary to develop industry knowledge, which is replicable, and to have the knowledge itself is incredibly valuable. Especially if the industry you pick has strong, underlining, long-term fundamentals, which can drive performance (Table 4.1).

Identify Emerging Trends

Golden Rule: Develop a "spot the trend" skill set.

The ability to identify a trend is a **key** skill set to investing. A good place to start is by gaining an understanding of the makeup of the S&P500. It will give us a good overview of the different sectors and how they are being represented. The largest sector in the S&P500 in mid-2020 is Information Technology (27% of the S&P) followed by Health Care (14%) with Communication

Table 4.1 Sector/Stock Selection Process

Identify emerging trend
Do your homework
Create your circle of competence
Develop a sector thesis
Come up with top picks

Services, Consumer Discretionary, and Financials (11% Each). These sectors and their weightings are impacted by shifts in economic priorities or what Schumpeter called "Creative Destruction." The percentage of weighing of each sector has changed over time as different sectors have different levels of importance and opportunity. For example, financials used to have a much larger representation as a percentage of S&P500. Sectors like companies and the economy itself rise and fall as capitalism follows its various cycles. It is no surprise that Information Technology is currently the largest sector, especially given the important role technology plays in the business cycle, particularly at the peak of the cycle, which is where we believe the economy roughly was before the Pandemic.

I have benefitted from developing a spot the trend or trend identification skill set multiple times during my career. These trends shift in their level of importance as we move from one innovation to another over time. For example, my career began by covering outsourcing in the early 2000s. The globalization of the modern workforce, particularly the movement of IT work from the US to India, was an astonishing transformation. The outsourcing movement began with Y2K, progressed to wide-scale adoption, and eventually commoditized over a ten-year period. The secular trend reached the height of its popularity around the time of Thomas Friedman's 2005 book *The World Is Flat*, which was published during the growth phase of the industry life cycle. We watched the globalization trend, particularly offshoring, move through its different phases including embryonic, growth, shakeout, maturity, and declining. My approach to investing in the sector was based on my evaluation of the different stages. Once I mastered the skill set around developing industry knowledge, a thesis, and top picks, it was transferable to new sectors. As outsourcing began to mature, I moved into new areas like Professional Services and FinTech. I was able to condense the time it took to develop "expertise" in a new industry by capitalizing on the lessons learned from my original work with outsourcing. The three areas that I am currently focused on for the next wave of technological disruption are FinTech, Disruptive Software, and Artificial Intelligence (AI).

The process of identifying a trend is not easy. It involves extensive research, trial and error, and even when the trends are identified, it is hard to profit from them, especially in the public market. It is particularly difficult with new technology, which is probably an excellent topic for another book. I have found the best types of technologies have similar characteristics such as they add efficiency to life and/or are cost-effective, generate revenues, and have a competitive advantage, which is particularly difficult to maintain. I have often wondered while writing this book: If Warren Buffett had taken up technology investing: How would he do it? Would he be any good at it? Is his smartest move not to do it at all? I have seen his reluctance to take on the challenge, which needs to be weighed against the importance of technology to not only the market, but as we saw in the prior section, the overall business cycle. The importance of technology to the economy and stock market has risen, while other areas like energy, utilities, and financial services have seen a decline.

Do Your Homework

There are many ways to select a trend to focus on, but they all involve doing your homework. The trend could be something you know a lot about or find interesting. These trends typically need to have two key characteristics. They need to be innovative and investable. Once you have identified a couple of potential trends, then the world is your library. There are several different sources you can use in building your industry knowledge including media, books, company filings, and conversations with industry participants to name a few. We found the industry exploration part of our research to be the most exciting. Each time we took on a new industry, we found it more and more interesting. We were always looking to identify a unique, investable, long-term trend, which can lead to multiple successful investments leading us to say, "The Trend is Your Friend."

We now come to a crossroad. You can either build the industry knowledge by putting together an industry report (Top Down) or you can do the work on a specific company (Bottom's Up), which allows you to back into the industry knowledge. Let's assume you decided you were going to look at the opportunities in FinTech, an industry I know very well. You would first need to decide if FinTech is innovative. After looking at numerous periodicals, books, media, and consulting industry veterans, you may decide the answer is yes. FinTech stands for Financial Technology, which has several subsectors like payments, Neobanks, and InsurTech. FinTech is the use of technology to efficiently, effectively help with everyday financial functions. The size of the industry, growth, and penetration rates are very attractive. The second question is can you invest in FinTech? The answer I found was once again yes. There are many public and private companies involved in several subsectors within FinTech.

Industry Analysis

We will take the approach of conducting an industry or *top-down* analysis first as opposed to a company-specific or *bottoms up* analysis, which we will also demonstrate later in the book, to provide added value to the reader. **Although either approach is an option, we prefer and endorse the bottoms up analysis**. As you will see, industry reports are **very** similar to company-specific analysis. Industry reports are useful in understanding a company's or sector's business model, opportunities, and potential portfolio performance attributions.

Creating Your Circle of Competence

The circle of competence analogy is one of our favorite analogies for a couple of reasons. We believe it is a crucial part of being a successful investor, you can build multiple circles in different areas, and it serves as a great metaphor. The circle and knowledge in general start small and grow.

The building of a circle of competence takes time and effort. The investor's opinion or thesis of the industry changes over time as we move through the industry's life cycle. This book primarily focuses on a bottoms up approach, but I include the key topics of an industry report, a description of those topics, and an **abbreviated** look at the key sections as applied to our industry analysis of FinTech below with a hyperlink to the section in our abridged industry report in Appendix II (Figure 4.1).

Develop a Basic Industry Knowledge

A top-down approach begins broadly and then narrows its focus. Industry analysis begins by defining the industry and understanding its growth prospects. We start by getting a basic understanding of the FinTech industry, which includes defining the industry, its sub-segments, and mapping out its growth rates, then continuing to narrow our understanding until we come up with investable ideas. It's important to note that all industry sizing and growth rates should be taken with a measured approach as there is no exact science for determining these numbers. They are often more "guesstimates" than "estimates."

What Is FinTech?

FinTech stands for Financial Technology. FinTech is a very large industry encompassing several subsectors. Three of the larger areas are Technology (bank/investment), Processing (payment/

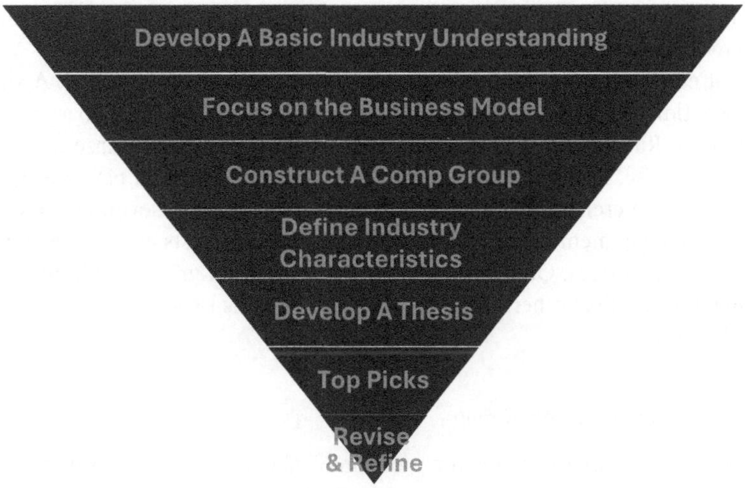

Figure 4.1 Top-Down Industry Analysis.

ATM), and Lending (card networks/prepaid). Other areas include blockchain, wealth management, and insurance. The total industry is estimated to be $310 billion in size by 2022 growing, 25% CAGR according to a report by Edge Malaysia.

Focus on the Business Model

Our funnel of industry understanding begins to narrow as we focus on a specific sub-segment of FinTech. The aspiring investor can pick the sub-segment based on several different characteristics. We recommend choosing a sub-segment based on its potential attractiveness from an investment standpoint. We chose the payment industry. Some of the potential basic questions you are looking to answer here are things like:

How do these companies make money?
What kind of economic environment do they need to make money?
What are the basic economics of the business?
What is the industry's size and growth rate?
What are its drivers?

There are several additional questions, but the answer to these questions is a good start. I looked at all the different sub-segments of FinTech and chose the payments industry because we felt the business model, which charges merchants a fee on **every** customer purchase is attractive from an investment standpoint.

What Is the Most Attractive FinTech Industry from an Investment Perspective? Why? How Do Payments Work?

The answer to what is the most attractive FinTech industry sub-segment from an investment perspective is subjective. We choose the payments industry because of the high recurring revenue, low capital expenditure nature of the business model. The payment processing business is an eco-system, involving several different players, each playing a specific role including the card networks, merchant acquirers, and gateways.

The payment eco-system has a high recurring revenue nature to its model. A simple explanation is that every time a consumer makes a card payment, the merchant is charged a fee called the Merchant Discount Rate (MDR), which is about 2%–3% on every purchase taken from the total amount of the purchase. For example, a customer buying a $100 item pays the $100 total price, with $98 going to the merchant and $2 being taken as a fee going to several payment processors.

There are multiple payment industry catalysts. The basic catalysts are general consumption and cash-to-card conversion rates. Omni-channel retail is a driver of growth with different purchasing channels growing faster than others. The industry in general is expected to grow at a 10% CAGR over the next five years.

Construct a Comparison or "Comp" Group

The development of a comparison or comp group may take time. There are several sources serving as great starting points for developing the comp group. There are typically industry analysts and/or reports, which group or display the companies as we have in our example industry report. If you cannot find these charts, there are software systems like FactSet, S&P Capital IQ, and online sources that may be helpful in locating the information. The easiest approach is to find a public company in the comparison group and check the company's 10K business section, which often lists competitors. Once you have located this group, you can then begin to compare market share and financial metrics like growth rates, margins, etc. to get a better understanding of overall market positioning. A good rule of thumb to remember is typically a company that has a higher than industry growth rate is taking market share and vice versa. Ideally, an aspiring investor would want to find a group of companies with similar revenue drivers and cost structures.

Who Is the Comparison (Comp) Group? How Does It Match Up?

The comp group for payments should be sub-divided in a couple of different ways. The first logical division is to divide the companies up by their roles in the eco-system. If we perform this function, we find the group divides into five segments. Here are the five segments with a sample set of relevant public companies: merchant acquirers (Adyen, EVO Payments, First Data (FISV), WorldPay (FIS), Global Payments, MercadoLibre, PagSeguro, Repay, Square, and Stone), card network (Mastercard, Visa), banks, gateways (Adyen, MercadoLibre, PayPal, and Square), and ISOs. You may notice some companies show up in different segments because they perform multiple functions. Developing a comp group is discretionary, but we have narrowed our focus to a couple of areas like merchant acquiring, gateways, and card networks, which have public company opportunities.

The financial profile of a US payment processor is dependent on their geographic and eco-system positioning. The US Gateways (SQ, PYPL) tend to be the fastest growers producing mid to high teens annual growth followed by the card networks (MA, V) in the high single, low double digit range followed by the merchant acquirers (GPN, EVOP) in the mid-single digits over the long term. The card networks have by far the best margin profile at an impressive 60%–70% EBITDA margin. The earnings profile for the group implies +20% earnings growth.

Define Industry Characteristics

We can then look at industry specific characteristics including topics such as life, business, and product life cycle stages, short and long-term growth prospects, economic sensitivities (GDP,

Interest Rates, Inflation, etc.), competitive dynamics (market share, competitive moats, pricing power) and forces (Porter Five Forces), influences (governments, technology, and social), and risks. These industry characteristics can then be compared to other industries to identify superior/inferior returns.

Is FinTech a Competitive Industry? What Are the Industry Characteristics?

I chose to focus on three primary characteristics for our industry analysis: market share, return on equity, and valuation. Visa has the largest US market share at 50% followed by 20% by Mastercard. PayPal has roughly 20% of the US eCommerce payment market. Global payments have roughly 10% market share of the merchant acquiring market.

The payments industry has several unique competitive dynamics. Historically, the industry had high barriers to entry which have come down over time as retail has moved to omni present, multi-channel environment from in store. The group has a healthy ROE well above market averages. Payment's other attractive qualities including growth rates and margins stack up well vs. other sectors within the S&P.

The payment group has competitive financial metrics compared to the market. The group ROE is above industry average. Gateways sell at an extremely large premium to the 5 Yr. Avg. PE, while the card networks trade at roughly a 50% premium and merchant acquirers at a 30% premium.

Value Added Sections

After you have developed a solid foundational understanding of the industry, you can then focus on the two or three areas where you can add value. These data points can then be aggregated and used to help someone select a few companies to focus on. Typically, you want these companies to be the best positioned to take market share. We can then derive an overall sector thesis and refine the thesis based on our Mosaic. There are several similarities between industry and company analysis, just like there are similarities between stock and overall market values vs. intrinsic values.

Potential Value-Added Sections?

There is a wide variety of potential value-added sections, which change throughout an industry life cycle. We should think of these value-added sections in three categories: Opportunity, risk, and challenges to our thesis. Below are potential areas where current investors can add value. We do not include a value-added section in our appendix as they tend to fluctuate. The most effective value-added sections are those measuring risks to a sector or company's business model and/or potential opportunities.

- Threat of Regulatory Changes
- Alternative Payment and Settlement Methods
- Changing landscape of technology in the payment eco-system
- Impact of cryptocurrency on the eco-system
- Opportunity for global expansion including China

Develop a Thesis

The most important aspect of building an industry knowledge is being able to start to form a FinTech industry investment thesis, which as we will see is very similar to a stock-specific investment thesis. It should generally be a memorable one liner or sentence. It is a summary of your belief on how to identify the best investment opportunities in the sector through certain characteristics. Below is a sample of our industry investment thesis for the three areas we covered as of 2020. Thesis change, evolve, and should be tested over time.

- **FinTech**-"We like the stock best positioned at the point of sale, friction fighters, and the international players where cash conversion rates were accelerating. Our top picks are Mastercard, PayPal, and Adyen."
- **Tech Services**-"We like those best positioned to capitalize on the fast-growing Digital movement and the BPO players. Our top picks are WNS, EPAM, and Accenture."
- **Professional Services**-"We believe the *Trend Is Your Friend* preferring companies with dominant positions in spaces with accelerating economic trends. Our top picks are S&P Global, MSCI, and Exponent."

Step 3 of Investment Process: Screen for the Best Stock Opportunities

Find Your Investable Ideas

Our top-down method of selecting an industry and developing an understanding and preliminary thesis should lead you to be able to identify the companies in a sector you should be doing additional work on as potential investment opportunities. These would be your potential selections for your portfolio on the Buy Side and/or coverage if you were on the Sell Side. Industries can be homogenous, which allows you to easily apply the knowledge of one company to others, helping to expand your pool of potential investment opportunities by easily comparing the group. Remember as Buffett says, "Knowledge compounds like interest." The challenge is less homogenous sectors where the nuance to each company makes them less of a group.

Top Picks

We can now rank the names we have researched in each sector from our favorite picks to our least favorite. The approach to ranking the companies can be customized in the characteristics you choose to use, the weighting you put on those characteristics, and the timing you choose when updating the list. I would recommend using the ranking system or *Foresi Five Factors* I propose later in the book as a starting point. However, there are different methodologies including ranking your top picks based on valuation or risk/reward or any of the five factors individually.

I would routinely rank each of our picks by month prioritizing our top two or three picks, which would not be necessary on the buy side where it is important to simply find your best investment opportunities. We included a ranking in our investment summary statement examples provided above. My top picks by subsector as of mid-2020 before the Pandemic were: FinTech-Mastercard, Adyen, PayPal; Tech Services-WNS, EPAM, Accenture; and Professional Services-S&P Global, MSCI, and Exponent. These top picks were selected for a variety of reasons, but the overall reason was that they were the best companies providing the greatest opportunities. Ideally, you would want your top picks to represent the best risk/reward, but valuation metrics don't always allow for that.

Stock Screening Methods

Screening for Individual Stock

There are over 4,000 companies listed on the exchanges, so how do we know which one/s are the right ones? Our method would be to identify a powerful, early stage stock-specific or industry trend. However, there are other potentially quicker, useful, practical methods. These screens only help identify potential investment opportunities. We **do not** endorse making investments based solely on the screens, which would be a speculative approach. Instead, the screens are useful for identifying potential opportunities and then performing fundamental analysis. They are helpful identifiers not strategies.

The first question you may have would be, "What stock screens do the greatest investors use?" (see Chapter 2). The answer is we simply don't know the specific screens. Successful investors like Warren Buffett provide clues as to what they look for in stock, but do not map out a standard criterion. We have clues as to what Warren Buffett looks for from looking at his mentor Ben Graham, who does spell out investment criteria to an extent, and Buffett's letters to shareholders, public comments, and holdings list. We know Buffett looks for the best companies with competitive moats in industries he knows very well (more on this in upcoming chapters). These companies' characteristics include strong free cash flow, solid earnings track record, and above industry margins and Return on Equity (ROE). An investor could turn these criteria into screens, but unfortunately, Buffett and the great investors only leave clues, not specific directions.

Popular investment professional William J. O'Neil in his 1988 book, "How to Make Money in Stocks." lays out popular characteristics under the acronym CANSLIM. O'Neil was a famous entrepreneur, stockbroker, and founder of IBD, Investor Business Daily, and the brokerage firm William O'Neil & Co. in 1963. CANSLIM was one of the original, popular screeners.

CANSLIM screens:

Current Earnings: quarterly earnings per share are up 25% or more
Annual Earnings: five-year average compound earnings growth rate greater than 24%
New Highs: stock is within 15% of a new 52-week high and is breaking out of a period of consolidation
Shares Outstanding: number of shares outstanding is less than 50 million with a recent increase in trading volume
Leading Stocks: market leader reflected by a Relative Strength Value (RSV) of 80 or higher
Institutional Ownership: Institutional sponsorship should be minimal but at least one major holder
Market Conditions: market edge should be bullish

The author/reporter Jack Hough turns into a stock selecting detective in his 2008 book, *Your Next Great Stock: How to Screen the Market for Tomorrow's Top Performers*. Hough points to five signs of a winning strategy for stock screening: (1) They have worked well in the past (*correlation*), (2) There is a good explanation for why they work (*cause*), (3) There are no other, hidden explanations (*no lurking variables*) (4), They are practical, and (5) They can be translated into stock screening tools. It is important to remember Hough is suggesting you use these screens to **identify** potential stock opportunities. He would then recommend you do **further research** into the stock. I would highly recommend doing further research after identifying a potential investment. Hough breaks his screens into two categories: growth and value stocks. We highlight for the

Table 4.2 Your Next Great Stock Screen

Name	*Method*
Buy high, sell higher	Momentum opportunities companies doing well continue to do so
Impatient value	Value investing with a momentum bend
Surprise, surprise	Post Earnings Momentum Drift (PEAD)
Tomorrow's breakthroughs	Low P/R&D Ratio combined with increasing R&D
New dogs	Dow Stocks with high net payout ratios
Bold is beautiful	"Out of consensus" earnings estimates and revisions
Rising expectations	Look for Industries of stocks with a positive change in sentiment
Follow the leaders	Track "insider buying" by executives
Accrual to be kind	Compare earnings to free cash flow to find how aggressive accruals are used
Sales on sale	Finding low P/S valuation metrics
Combo platter	Finding low P/B valuation metrics

Source: Your Next Great Stock (Hough).

reader a couple of the screens Hough presents, which I find potentially useful below, providing a short synopsis with relevant supporting research when applicable (Table 4.2).

Buy High, Sell Higher

The *Buy High, Sell Higher* is a momentum screen. It looks for stocks at 52-week highs. There is academic research supporting the idea of strong continuous stock performance. Narasimhan Jegadeesh and Sheridan Titman in their 1993 paper, "Returns to Buying Winners and Selling Losers: Implications for Stock Market Efficiency," published in the *Journal of Finance* looked at stock returns from 1965 to 1989 found that stocks that outperformed the market maintained the momentum for a short period of time 3–12 months, but unfortunately then it reversed. The study was followed up by a more meaningful study by Thomas George (University of Houston) and Chuan-Yang Hwang (Hong Kong University of Science and Technology) in 2004, "The 52-Week High and Momentum Investing" in the *Journal of Finance* looked at the stocks within 5% of their 52-week highs. The study found the 52-week high/low portfolio comprised of long stocks within 5% or their 52-week and short stocks within 5% of their 52-week low beat the market by roughly 8% with the returns staying strong for more than five years from 1963 to 2001.

Buy High, Sell Higher screens:

- Share Price Within 5% of 52-week High
- Sales are greater than $100 million
- Average daily trading greater than 100,000 shares

Potential Additional Screens:

- One-year sales growth is greater than 20%
- Insider ownership greater than 5%

Contrarian Screens

Hough's *Buy High, Sell Higher* methodology using a 52-week screen reminds us of some legendary contrarian investors. John Neff, who was a notable contrarian and value investor, used a contrarian version of the 52-week method to identify possible value opportunities. Neff outlined his methodology for screening for potential opportunities in his book *John Neff On Investing*. Neff would scan the market for 52-week lows for stock opportunities. He was looking for stocks that were 40–60% of the market average. He further down selected stocks by looking for steady, sustainable earnings growth (7–20% growth) driven by sales growth and Free Cash Flow. He used a "Total Return/PE" ratio-

$$\text{Total return/PE} = \left(\text{earnings growth rate} + \text{dividend}\right)/\text{PE}$$

Neff headed the Vanguard Windsor fund, which became the highest returning and largest mutual fund in existence during his management. Neff ran the fund for 31 years (1964–1995) returning 13.7% annual average vs. 10.6% for the S&P500.

Whereas John Neff is considered a tactical contrarian investor who placed emphasis on the fundamentals, David Dreman is more of a statistical contrarian. Dreman outlined his investment philosophy in his book, *Contrarian Investment Strategies*. Dreman believes an investment approach should account for behavioral (crowd psychology) and interpretational obstacles (predicting future estimates) in investing. These challenges often lead stocks to be over bought or sold and move further away from their intrinsic value, which can reverse within one year. Dreman's approach is to screen for the lowest price-to-earnings stocks (bottom 40%). He chose price-to-earnings as he sees it as a valuable metric with other methods like the dividend discount model containing flaws due to forecasting difficulties. He then looks for medium to large market capitalization names believing it is more unlikely these names will go out of business than smaller companies. The third screen is for financial strength looking at ratios like debt-to-equity ratios (compared to their group). The fourth screen is for the highest, safest dividend yield (1.5%). The fifth screen is for earnings growth above the S&P500. Once these screens have been run, Dreman recommends a diversified portfolio of 15 to 20 stocks in 10 to 12 industries.

Once the sector is chosen you can screen for opportunities. The lower valuation stocks or cheaper stocks provide a positive risk/reward. The higher the valuation, the less opportunity the market risk goes up. Hough himself suggested a version of value investing using momentum-oriented screens. He called it the *Impatient Value Screen*. The screen is his version of a successful screen used by the American Association of Individual Investors, which uses a *Value on the Move* screen, which had reported solid returns in the early 2000s.

The Impatient Value Screen:

- Price/Earnings/Growth (PEG) ratio below 1.5
- PEG ratio above 0.2
- Share price within 5% of 52-week high
- Trailing 12-month sales greater than $100 million
- Average daily trading volume greater than 100,000 shares

Potential Additional Screens:

- Lower the PEG ratio to 1.0
- Look for a rise in out year earnings estimate

A Couple of Additional Hough Screen Suggestions

Surprise, Surprise

The *Surprise, Surprise* screen is a momentum screen based on earnings results, which coincides with the idea of stocks needing a catalyst, which is one of our five factors. Catalyst can take on many forms. One catalyst is the potential for upside to results. The screen is based on what is known as *Post Earnings Announcement Drift*, or PEAD. PEAD was first reported by Raymond Ball and Philip Brown in their 1968 paper, "An Empirical Evaluation of Accounting Income Numbers." There have been numerous studies since validating the PEAD approach according to Hough. Narasimhan Jegadeesh (Emory University) and Joshua Livnat (NYU) in 2006 published a paper entitled "Revenue Surprises and Stock Returns." in the *Journal of Accounting and Economics* that found a cross-sample of the top 20% of companies that surpassed Street revenue and earnings estimates beat the market by more than 10% on an annualized basis. Hough accurately points out top line beats are much harder to manipulate than bottom-line results.

The Surprise, Surprise Screen:

- Past-quarter upside to earnings surprise greater than 5%
- Past-quarter upside earnings surprise above industry average
- Past-quarter sales surprise greater than 5%
- Past-quarter sales surprise above industry average
- Standard deviation of estimates below industry average
- Trailing Twelve Month (TTM) sales greater than $100 million
- Average daily trading volume greater than 100,000 shares

Potential Additional Screens:

- Lower the PEG ratio to 1.0
- Look for a rise in out year earnings estimate

New Dogs

The *New Dogs of the Dow* screen is a spinoff of the original strategy only the new screen looks at the *net payout yield*. The original *Dogs of the Dow* screen was popularized in 1991 by Michael O'Higgins in his 1991 book *Beating the Dow*. The original *Dogs of the Dow* screen suggested choosing ten companies in the Dow Jones Industrial Average with the highest dividend yields and buying them every year. The strategy showed strong historical results with the Dogs beating the Dow by three percentage points a year over the 50 years ending in 1995 but lagged the Dow over the next 11 years. You might recall Burton Malkiel's list of ineffective strategies, which included the *Dogs of the Dow*. The *New Dogs of the Dow* screen focuses on finding the Dow stocks with the highest *net payout yield*. A 2004 paper by Jacob Boudokh (Cornell), Roni Michealy (NYU), Matthew Richardson (UPenn), and Michael Roberts (Arison-Israel) titled, "On the Importance of Measuring Payout Yield: Implications for Empirical Asset Pricing." looking at performance of the Dogs of the Dow from 1983 to 2005 based on Net Payout Ratio showing a return of 19% per year. The screen would be on Dogs of the Dow stocks for net payout ratios.

The Net Payout Ratio Screen:

$$\text{Net payout ratio} = \frac{\text{dividend} + \text{repurchases} - \text{issuance}}{\text{Market cap}}$$

Sale on Sale

The *Sale-on-Sale* screen looks at the Price-to-Sales (P/S) ratio for opportunities. The standard valuation metric is the Price-To-Earnings (P/E) ratio. We know it is easier for managements to manipulate earnings by making other valuations like P/S more useful. James O'Shaughnessy referred to the P/S metric as "the king of the value factors" in his 1996 classic *What Works on Wall Street.* O'Shaughnessy found that low P/S stocks produced annual returns of about 16% annually.

The Sale-on-Sale Screen:

- Trailing Twelve Months (TTM) sales greater than $200 million
- Avg. daily volume greater than 100K shares
- P/S ratio below 1.5
- Positive one-year earnings growth
- Three months better than average share price appreciation
- Six months better than average share price appreciation

High Quality Stock Screen

Our screening method attempts to identify high-quality stocks. The point of investing is to minimize your risk, while maximizing your return. Investors can minimize their risk in a couple of different ways including buying the best companies at the most attractive valuation, below the intrinsic value building in a margin of safety. How should investors identify opportunities worth continuing to research? Our own *High Quality Stock Screens* is presented below. Once these opportunities are identified, investors can then do more work on the individual companies to see if they are indeed strong opportunities

***High Quality Stock* Screens:**

- Strong Return On Invested Capital (ROIC), Return on Equity (ROE), and Return on Assets (ROA) using a thoughtful analysis
- Healthy commanding, preferably growing Market Share
- Solid Free Cash Flow (FCF) generation (thoughtful capital allocation as a plus)
- Manageable Regulatory Concerns

Additional Stock Screens:

- Positive Sector Trends
- Expanding Total Addressable Market (TAM)
- Attractive Valuation

The return ratios (ROIC, ROE, and ROA) are among the most important in all of finance. The ratios essentially measure management's performance. They answer the very important question of how efficiently businesses are being managed and a company's ability to deliver returns to shareholders. All three ratios benefit from an increase in net income. The ROIC is the amount of money a company makes above what it pays for its invested capital (debt and equity). The simplest form of this equation is the company's net income minus dividends divided by its total capital or debt plus equity. The ROE and Asset ratios are the net income divided by shareholder equity and assets.

Investors should be careful when evaluating these formulas. For example, let's look at ROE. There are basic challenges with calculating and understanding ROE. There are inherent issues regarding the accounting of ROE, which can be manipulated and often excludes off-balance sheet accounting. There can be challenges with the consistency of a company's net income, which is often not comparable. ROE does not account for leverage focused on shareholder equity and potentially penalizes companies for holding too much cash, even though it may be the right decision. Managements are potentially incentivized to manipulate ROE. These formulas can accelerate, decelerate, and be volatile over a short period of time, so a longer-term record may provide a more accurate view of a company's potential. If we look at the Top 25 Companies in the SP500 in 2019, we see Mastercard ranks in the Top 25 in ROIC-#8, ROE-#14, and ROA-#3.

We can then select the best companies from the list. We already know a couple of the names on the list including Mastercard, S&P Global, and Moody's as we had previously evaluated the names from an investment perspective. We can add additional metrics around strong FCF generation or FCF Margin. We can then cut the list down to a couple of names performing tertiary work. We know we are on the right path! An additional data point validating for us that these companies have commanding market share is the threat of regulatory action, which is a positive sign assuming the risk is manageable. The regulatory risk exists in most of these names. We eventually decide on Mastercard, as it is not only a monopoly in our opinion but is expanding its TAM in FinTech a very powerful, positive trend.

We now need to perform a further fundamental analysis on Mastercard, which we will walk the reader through in Chapter 5. The analysis will help us determine short and long-term growth rates, whether they are accelerating, and confirm our belief that the TAM is expanding. The best time to own companies with commanding market share or any company for that matter is when the company is accelerating growth rates, expanding their addressable market, and taking market share. We will be able to determine if the stock is worth buying by calculating an intrinsic value, identifying a margin of safety, and establishing a reasonable entry and exit point.

There were ultimately several reasons I chose to use Mastercard for our exemplary stock. Mastercard fits well with our positive thematic commentary from an industry (FinTech) and company-specific perspective. I know the name well from my analyst days. I believe it serves as a good teaching name given its unique characteristics, which I won't spoil by revealing ahead of time. Lastly, Warren Buffett owned the name as the initial writing of the book. A note to the reader: Although I chose Mastercard, there is a vast array of companies out there, several of which are on the list, which are worth researching. I have been able to develop a talent around identifying names like these, which means although the companies may differ, the methodology and steps taken to understand them remain the same. I would encourage you to learn the framework, provide feedback, and eventually develop your own approach.

Trend Identification

I have presented a few starting points to identifying companies that can outperform the market. The logical starting point for aspiring investors is to invest in what you know or your "circle of competence." For example, if you are an airline pilot, you should think about investing in the airline industry. These "circles of competence" can be built.

There are two stock identification methods. My recommended method is identifying a long-term secular trend, establishing a foundational understanding of those trends, and then locating the best stock opportunities. A second method is to use stock screens to locate "high-quality" companies. There are unfortunately no short-cuts. Only two things will help you get better at "spotting the trends" experience and hard work. Once these names are spotted, you can then research them and see if they make sense for your portfolio. Most of these names will not make sense for your portfolio, but you will be smarter and a better analyst for having gotten to know them.

Bibliography

Ball, R., & Brown, P. (1968). An empirical evaluation of accounting income numbers. *Journal of Accounting Research, 6*(2), 159–178.

Boudoukh, J., Michaely, R., Richardson, M., & Roberts, M. R. (2007). On the importance of measuring payout yield: Implications for empirical asset pricing. *The Journal of Finance, 62*(2), 877–915.

Dreman, D. (1998). *Contrarian Investment Strategies: The Psychological Edge.* Simon & Shuster.

Epstein, D. (2019). *Range: Why Generalists Triumph in a Specialized World.* Riverhead Books.

Friedman, T. (2005). *The World Is Flat.* Farrar, Straus, Giroux.

George, T. J., & Hwang, C. (2004). The 52-week high and momentum investing. *The Journal of Finance, 59*(5), 2145–2176.

Hough, J. (2008). *Your Next Great Stock.* John Wiley & Sons.

Jegadeesh, N., & Livnat, J. (2006). Revenue surprises and stock returns. *Journal of Accounting and Economics, 41*(1–2), 147–178.

Jegadeesh, N., & Titman, S. (1993). Returns to buying winners and selling losers: Implications for stock market efficiency. *Journal of Finance, 48*(1), 65–69.

Neff, J. (2001). *John Neff on Investing.* Wiley.

O'Neil, W. J. (1988). *How to Make Money in Stocks.* McGraw Hill.

O'Shaugnessy, J. P. (1996). *What Works on Wall Street.* McGraw Hill.

Chapter 5

The Anatomy of a Stock

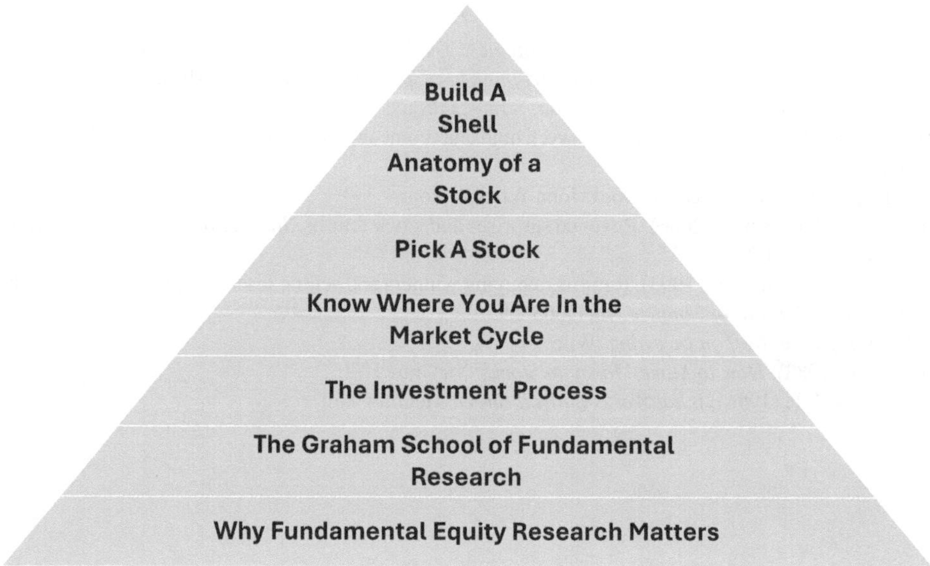

The Midas Touch

Investing has been compared to Alchemy, a medieval type of science and philosophy aimed at changing base metals into one of the most coveted metals on the planet, gold! The comparisons make a lot of sense. Investors, like alchemists, try to create wealth without increasing their individual labor. The difference is that investors are focused on growing their wealth by thoughtfully allocating their capital to obtain a return. Investing benefits from the power of compound interest providing at least part of the formula for magically turning one dollar into many over time. The comparison between Alchemy and finance makes a lot of sense, so much so you may remember George Soros used it for the title of his book!

Investors like Alchemists are constantly looking for ways to help assure quicker and larger returns. Every couple of years, Wall Street discovers a "new" method or formula for producing what it believes will be consistent, market outperforming investment results. I covered a number of these different approaches throughout the book. Examples include methods like technical and quantitative analysis. These different approaches often get labelled with memorable names. One memorable formula was the "Nifty Fifty," which was the term used to describe the 50 "best" stocks

DOI: 10.4324/9781003686644-8

on the New York Stock exchange in the 1960s and 1970s. These stocks eventually underperformed the stock market in the 1980s.

I expect the discovery of "new," successful investment approaches to continue in perpetuity. Thomas Kuhn in his 1962 book *The Structure of Scientific Revolutions* introduces the reader to the idea of a paradigm shift, which may help to explain the "boom and bust" phenomenon of the different Wall Street investment approaches. A paradigm shift in its simplest form is a fundamental change in the basic concepts and experimental practices. Kuhn was applying the paradigm shift to changes in the scientific landscape. I believe these shifts are constantly taking place in regards to the various Wall Street approaches to investing. However, the dynamic and unpredictable nature of the stock market itself renders each new formula obsolete. Over time, these new approaches appear to be more fads than winning formulas. Our solution to this problem is that we suggest the reader focus on studying the anatomy of a stock and the process of using this knowledge to identify the best investment opportunities, instead of following the latest Wall Street paradigm shift.

Anatomy of a Stock

We are now ready to truly understand stocks and how they work. We begin by developing a foundational understanding of *The Anatomy of a Stock* through the identification of its most important factors or characteristics.

We have covered a lot of ground thus far. We began by establishing the opportunities and challenges associated with active management and what important characteristics are helpful for outperformance. We then looked at the different methods of investing, deciding fundamental analysis was the best approach. We figured out where we were in the business cycle and picked a sector and a stock.

The remaining part of this section focuses on a deep understanding of how stocks work. We want the reader to focus on the process, especially the characteristics of successful equity investments, rather than any specific methodology. The process and its constant improvement should be the center of attention ahead of the positive outcomes. If investors get the process right, the results will follow. We remind the reader of the unpredictability of markets, which leaves almost all investment methodologies obsolete, especially over the long term. We will interweave an in-depth examination of the important characteristics or anatomy of a stock with a bottom's up, practical, step-by-step evaluation of our focus company, Mastercard. I have created an exemplary appendix, which puts together an abbreviated version of our outlook for the company.

Introduction to Foresi Five Factors

We turn our attention to the general framework or anatomy (characteristics) from which you can evaluate all equities, which we like to call, "Foresi Five Factors." These five factors can be looked at for every company you examine. The factors are: competitive advantage, catalyst, valuation, quality of management, and psychology (Table 5.1).

Table 5.1 Five Factors

Competitive advantage
Catalyst
Valuation
Quality of management
Psychology

You Need to Be Flexible

Investors need to adopt a flexible approach when looking at these factors. They are not ranked in any order. The reader may want to personally rank order them after reading the book, which we will explain in further detail a little later, but for now we want to briefly introduce you to the different factors. The challenge is that only experience will allow an individual to develop a deep understanding of each factor. Practice makes perfect. It would make sense to periodically review the most important factors and update their ranking. There may be additions, subtractions, and/or changes to the list of factors over time.

The current list of factors is competitive advantages catalyst, valuation, quality of management, and psychology. I have personally found through my experience that the hardest characteristic to find is a discernable, sustainable competitive advantage. Catalysts come and go based on the industry, product life cycle. However, if you can invest in a stock opportunity at the early stages of a catalyst, it can pay off for a long time. The upside and downside to the estimates are often a derivative of the strength of the catalyst or unfortunately sometimes financial engineering on the part of management. Valuation is more of an art than a science. It can be performed based on an intrinsic and relative basis. An investor's flexibility around valuation can be determined by the stage of the business cycle. I believe there is a difference in the quality of management, but ultimately it is the strength of the business model that **truly** determines the performance of the business and thus the "quality" of the management. Finally, psychology is a factor we must all deal with as investing is a difficult task for the structure of the human mind as we each must work to control our emotional selves.

Our Anatomy Analogy

The book is entitled *The Anatomy of a Stock* because we think of a stock as a living breathing organism. It adds a second dimension and helpful way to remember the different characteristics, which ultimately leads to optimal stock selection and market outperformance. There are two parts to the market and stocks: the fundamentals (physical) and the psychological (mental), just like human beings. If the reader indulges us, the five factors can **loosely** be related to different aspects of human anatomy and their functions. The *Competitive Advantage* is the arms and legs, which provide a company with the ability to defend itself. *Valuation* is literally and figuratively at the heart of the matter. It fuels everything. The *Catalyst* is similar to physical capabilities like running, which is what you would want the stock price to do after you purchase it. In fact, investors often use the phrase, "The Run Up in the Stock" to describe stock price appreciation. *Catalysts* drive the *Upside or Downside* to Street expectations and the performance of the stock often following the underlining businesses life cycle. *Quality of management* is the management running the company like your brain runs your body. Finally, the markets and humans have both a psychological and logical aspect to them. It is imperative that investors understand how both the psychological and logical parts of their mind interact in making decisions in order to better protect themselves ironically from themselves and try to make our psychological flaws work for us, not against us.

To complete our analogy, an investor can think of financial ratios as a way of tracking the performance of management similar to how we track our human statistics like height, weight, pulse, etc. Think of earnings results as your regular doctor's visit. The following is a brief look at each factor before we dive into building an understanding of a specific company followed by the company's analysis.

Competitive Advantage (Offense and Self-Defense)

A discernable, defensible competitive moat is the most important characteristic and toughest to find in any company. Generally, it is beneficial to find companies that are oligopolies or monopolies, but not always. Monopolies can face erosion and decline like any business. There may be challenges to the monopolies that provide better investment opportunities. We note that the ability to develop a competitive moat is sometimes dependent on an industry's natural characteristics. Competitive moats tend to run a life cycles. We would suggest investors start by focusing on the competitive advantage themselves creating these moats. Competitive advantages can have several different features such as commanding market share, high switching costs, pricing power, and cost advantages.

If you can find a monopoly with a distinct, discernable, defensive competitive position (moat) that is not only defending their market share but also expanding their Total Addressable Market (TAM), well congratulations, you have found a very, very special company. You have found a leprechaun and need to catch it! If you haven't found it, well you should be looking for it. Why is this so important? Remember investing is about risk, which can be reduced by investing in great companies.

The standard methods for understanding competitive dynamics are strategy-based methods like Porter's Five Forces or an S.W.O.T analysis. Developed by Harvard Business School's Professor Michael Porter, Porter's Five Forces analysis focuses on a company's buyer power, supplier power, threat of new entry, threat of substitute, and competitive rivalry. A SWOT analysis looks at a company's Strengths, Weaknesses, Opportunities, and Threats. We will touch on each of these analytical methods and explore others in further detail when we take an in depth look at our First Factor. We would encourage readers to go beyond the basic analyses like Porter or SWOT, if possible, and take a closer look at the company's strategy. A solid short and long-term strategy is crucial to expanding or protecting the current competitive advantages and moats. Perhaps the most important reason for needing a good strategy is that it potentially creates the next set of competitive advantages, which is extremely difficult to do.

Catalyst (Physical Capabilities)

A catalyst is a catalytic agent driving stock movement. We note catalysts can come in many different shapes or forms having different levels of importance and impact. Catalyst-type events range from earnings announcements to analyst days to management changes, etc. It is important to separate these events from the company's long-term drivers. We believe consistently reporting results above Street expectations is a good thing. However, we discourage investors from "playing" or trading stocks based on their expectations regarding the company's performance vs. expectations when reporting quarterly results. Instead, we encourage investors to take a long-term approach looking for sustainable long-term catalysts, which take the form of significant changes in demand or outlook, profitability, and/or capital allocation much in the same way we described approaching competitive advantages.

Valuation (The Heart of the Matter)

Valuation is an art, not a science. Valuation can be performed in two ways from an intrinsic and relative value perspective. A company is worth the sum of its future discounted cash flows, which is known as its intrinsic value. A crucial aspect of investing, which is often forgotten, is the process of establishing an intrinsic value for a company, but then **most importantly** building in a margin of safety to account for the inherent risk associated with the investment, essentially establishing a price you would actually want to buy the company at. Investors may want to build in an automatic adjustment for upward or downward market movements into their valuation framework. We are exploring this and other ways of potentially improving what we consider to be a dated valuation methodology. Valuation methodologies change throughout the life cycle of a company. Valuation can be used as a way of establishing the true value of a company and at what price levels it would make sense to buy and sell the stock.

Quality of Management (Intelligence)

There are a couple of different ways to measure management. One of the most telling is the examination of their monetary incentives, which can be found in the company filings. Investors want to make sure compensation incentives match up with ways to drive shareholder value. We can look at the company's past performance over the last 8–12 quarters vs. guidance (their targets) and consensus (Street expectations). Investors can meet management and use a Socratic-like method asking the management questions about their business and measuring their response. Psychologists would contend there is marginal value in meeting with management and applying the Socratic Method given our inherent biases. The argument could also be made that the quality of management is the least important of the five factors. The quality of management is primarily dependent on the strength of the business model!

Psychology (Inside an Investors Mind)

Did you know there are two different parts to the human mind with different agendas, making it difficult to invest? The two-part system is made up of System 1 (X System), which is the emotional part. System 2 (C system) is the logical system. The problem is System 1 often gets in the way of System 2 when we make decisions. System 2 requires effort and energy, as a result it tends to be "lazy." We often need to engage or wake up-System 2. We can counteract the challenges by (1) being aware of them and (2) building into our process best practices to counteract them. These best practices range from keeping an investment diary to seeking out the opinions of those who disagree with us.

Performance Metrics (Regular Checkups)

Companies routinely report their progress on a quarterly or semiannual basis in the form of earnings results. Investors should think of these earnings results and other such events as a type of checkup, like going to the doctor, consistent with our anatomy analogy. It allows the investor an opportunity to check how the company is doing vs. their expectations, primarily the five factors we have laid out. Investors should be specifically looking for any "significant" changes in the company's narrative or direction, which would cause them to rethink their investment thesis. Typically, the quality of the earnings results is just as if not more important than the earnings themselves. The quality of earnings is not typically reflected in sell-side reports, which is a huge mistake in our opinion, but provides an opportunity for the investors willing to spend the time deciphering the authenticity of the results. We caution one quarter does not make a trend, but several quarters over the long-term certainly do. Perhaps even more important than the quarterly results are company analyst day events. Here investors get the opportunity to exam a company's strategy, which is crucial to developing and maintaining a strong competitive advantage.

Scorecard (Annual Physical)

One option for investors is to create a five-factor scorecard, which we do in the next chapter. A scorecard would have several advantages. It would force the investor to think through the different factors and rank them, allow them to compare vastly different investment opportunities on a similar scale, and keep track of specific investments on a regular basis. We suggest using a simple Likert scale for each of the five factors, from 1 to 10 with ten being the best and one being the poorest, then weighing each score based on the relative importance investors place on each factor as it relates to overall stock performance. The weightings and potentially even the factors themselves can change over time. For example, I would currently argue competitive advantages carry more weight in determining a stock's ability to outperform the market than its quality of management. However, I did not make the same argument earlier in my career. At one point in time, I believed the quality of management was the most important factor. My experiences over time have changed my mind and will likely change the reader as well. However, I still believe if you truly do not like or trust a management team, then you should never own the company's stock.

Process Focused Results

One of the truths regarding the ability to consistently generate above-average Wall Street returns is that there are no short-cuts or special formulas to generate the returns. The challenge is that Wall Street "experts" are all too comfortable coming up with the next investment formula for success. These formulas are unfortunately doomed to fail.

My suggestion is instead of focusing on the results and/or a specific investment approach to those results, investors should focus on the process itself. I introduce the reader in this section to five characteristics, which I believe currently lead to a company being able to outperform the market over the long run: competitive advantage, catalyst, valuation, quality of management, and psychology. I refer to these characteristics as the anatomy of a stock. I currently believe aspiring investors should apply this process to individual companies using a scorecard method to identify the best opportunities. The factors themselves and their weightings have evolved since I began covering stocks. I expect the evolution to continue. I will examine each factor for my example company, perform a company-specific analysis, and then put together a five-factor scorecard or ranking in the upcoming chapter.

Bibliography

Kuhn, T. S. (1962). *The Structure of Scientific Revolutions.* University of Chicago Press.
Porter, M. E. (1980). *Competitive Strategy.* Free Press.

Chapter 6

Building a Basic Understanding of a Stock

Variety of Research Methods

We return to the subject of science for help in understanding research methods. Research methods come in different varieties and forms. Perhaps the most famous research method is the scientific method. The origins of the scientific method go all the way back to Aristotle in Greece in the 300s BCE. The basic steps of the method involve: (1) Asking a question, (2) Doing background research, (3) Constructing a hypothesis, (4) Testing the hypothesis, (5) Analyzing the data, and (6) Drawing a conclusion.

Equity research is more art than science, yet there are similarities between the scientific method and fundamental equity research. Like a scientist, the aspiring investor begins by asking a basic question. The initial questions for an equity investor are typically the same question. The investor wants to know, "Is this stock a good investment?" The investor begins their background research or due diligence by gathering qualitative and quantitative data. Our process suggests organizing the qualitative information into the different logical sections of an investment report. The quantitative data comes in the form of financial statements that can be captured and converted into a spreadsheet incorporating the proper operating and liquidity ratios. The common Wall Street term for converting financial statements into excel spread sheets and forecasting out potential future results is known as, "modeling." Once the information is in spreadsheet form, we can then analyze the key financial ratios and assess the "quality" of a company's earnings results providing us a good foundational understanding of the company. As a preview of what's to come, the *Foresi Five Factors* described in the earlier section will serve as a valuable analytical tool on our road to developing an investment thesis (hypothesis) and more importantly a conclusion!

Let's Get Started

We can begin our due diligence by putting together a shell or skeleton report for our example company, Mastercard. A shell report contains the essentials needed to understand a company's investment prospects. There are a couple of natural questions you may have at this point like:

- How much information or data will I need to collect?
- Where is the information located?
- What information am I looking for?
- How should I organize the information?

There are a couple of ways to think about the amount of information needed to evaluate a company. One option is to collect as much information as possible. A second method is to use an 80/20 rule

DOI: 10.4324/9781003686644-9

or Pareto Principle with 20% of the information driving 80% of the outcome. A third option and the one we recommend is to use our process, which is designed to focus the aspiring investor on the most important information and organize the information in a logical manner providing the investor with the best opportunity to produce a successful outcome. Our stock-specific approach involves developing a basic understanding of the business, examining the most important issues, focusing on the five factors, coming up with an investment thesis, making a decision, and then looking for evidence to prove or disprove the thesis.

We will see in the section on psychology, humans are wired to want to have as much information as possible before making an investment decision. Although having more information adds to a false sense of confidence, it does not necessarily lead to better decisions. The best investment decisions are produced by focusing on the development and use of a successful investment process and continually working to refine the process. It is about having the "right" information for the process organized in logical manner. We would usually not decide on whether to buy, hold, or sell stock until the end of the due diligence process, not because we needed more information, but rather because it takes time to complete the first step, which is building a strong foundational knowledge of a company. It is only after completing the first step that you can focus on the few crucial pieces of information and your opinion on them, necessary to make the correct investment decision, at the end of the process. These pieces of information are the difference between success and failure.

We begin the process of getting to know a company by performing basic due diligence using a three-step process: (1) Gather the information, (2) Aggregate and understand the information, and (3) Build a financial model. We will begin by locating the different sources of information. We then sort through the material looking for the essential pieces of qualitative information needed to understand the potential investment opportunity. We use an outline of a standard equity research report to help us identify the basic pieces of information we should focus on. We finish the section by using quantitative data to build a historical financial model. As the reader will see, the process of putting together a shell equity research report and basic financial model is designed to help the aspiring investor develop a strong preliminary understanding of the company. We will then analyze the company using our *Foresi Five Factors* beginning with a thorough understanding of each factor and applying those individual factors one by one to the company.

Step 4 of Investment Process: Begin Due Diligence

Where to Find the Information

There are key sources you will need to consult to find company-specific information. The most productive source of information is typically the company's Security and Exchange Commission (SEC) filings, specifically the business section of 10-Ks, which is a great place to start. Company filings and press releases including 10 & 8-Ks, earnings results and presentations, and conference call transcripts are all very helpful. You can go back in time researching a company as far as you feel is necessary, although in most cases three to four quarters is sufficient. Analyst days and investor presentations are very useful, particularly for understanding the strategy behind the company and how management feels about the business.

All the company-specific information you will need can typically be sourced online through the investor relations website. The world's biggest library (the internet) presents an opportunity to find information well beyond the company's specific filings, etc. There are helpful software systems like FactSet, Bloomberg, and S&P Capital IQ, which serve as great, comprehensive sources of data and information. These software systems have become crucial to the equity research process.

I would recommend speaking to industry experts, management, and especially contrarians or those with an opposing view, as part of your final step.

What to Focus On

Once the information is located and aggregated, we can then begin sorting it, searching for the basic pieces of information. We recommend using the standard outline for writing an equity research report to help us identify the important pieces of qualitative information necessary to understand the company from an investment lens. You do not need to write an actual report on the company or even collect all the suggested information necessary to put together a report to make an investment decision, but just knowing the basics of what is in an equity research report is extremely helpful and recommended.

The *CFA Institute* provides a rough outline of the essential sections of an equity research report including basic information, investment summary, business description, management and governance, industry overview and competitive positioning, valuation, financial analysis, and investment risk. We provide a brief description of what is typically contained in each section along with our commentary below.

Basic Information

An equity research report should contain basic information on the company like its description, stock ticker, sector, stock market recommendation, and price target. Other key attributes like market capitalization (caps), float, volume, and largest shareholders are important. The reader will become familiar with these basic pieces of information over time. A knowledge of these basic pieces of information has practical uses, for example, small market capitalization (cap) names with low volumes tend to have comparatively volatile stock prices because the trading activity of just one investor can have a large impact on the stock price. The volatility of these small cap stocks may make them unattractive investment opportunities.

Investment Summary

The investment summary is the most important section of the report. It tells the action being recommended and investment thesis behind the action including the catalysts. I would recommend keeping the investment summary to just a couple of very concise sentences, which include why your opinion is different than consensus, which is the average opinion of all the Wall Street analyst, or the market in general, assuming it is different. It is a good opportunity to highlight the crucial investor questions regarding the story and your opinion on those questions as well. Investment thesis like hypothesis is meant to be routinely tested, can be wrong, and can change.

Business Description

The business description section is typically thought of as the least interesting part of the report. I disagree with this general characterization. One of the most important questions you can ask a company is, "How do you make money?" You would be surprised how difficult it is for companies let alone potential investors to answer this question. Analyzing the validity and sustainability of a company's response to the question, especially over the long run, could help in separating the good vs. the bad investment opportunities. It is crucial that investors understand the business model of any company and believe in its long-term merits before they invest in the business. At the very least, the business description section should provide an understanding of the business model and its economics.

Management

The management section is also a typically underutilized opportunity. Most Wall Street reports just fill in the section with management biographies. The real focus of this section should be on the quality of management. A good place to start is by looking at management's track record of execution. However, there are other crucial pieces of information including compensation, incentive structure, succession plans, stock ownership, and board diversity and independence. The management and governance section has historically been an area where the analyst just doesn't spend enough time and they should.

Industry Overview and Competitive Positioning

The industry overview and competitive positioning segment is one of our favorite sections, especially if you come across monopolies or oligopolies. These sections typically look at market share and competitive dynamics through exercises like "Porter's Five Forces." A detailed examination of competitive positioning can help identify a company's competitive advantages, moats, and just as important their sustainability over the long term, which is the most important of our five factors, in our opinion.

Valuation

The valuation section is a thorough examination of what the potential relative (P/E, P/S, etc.) or absolute valuation (intrinsic value) of the company may be based on conventional valuation metrics and formulas. The CFA Institute recommends using multiple valuation metrics. I agree and include a look at the intrinsic and relative valuations. All too often the valuation sections exclude the important "Margin of Safety" aspect, whose inclusion provides suggestions for potential entry or buying point price levels. I believe these sections need to include intrinsic values and entry and exit price points. I warn aspiring investors that way too many Wall Street reports incorrectly base valuation solely off the current price of the stock and don't take into account the underlining value!

Financial Analysis

The financial analysis section has several key components including ratio analysis, industry comparison, and forecasting. An examination and comparison of the company's financial ratios helps you understand what kind of company you are researching. For example, software companies tend to have high gross margins and large SG&A. A ratio analysis can help identify discrepancies between companies that need to be investigated. The aspiring investor can analyze a business' earnings results to get a sense of the quality of the results and where the company stands from an execution and life cycle perspective. Most importantly, the financial analysis section provides the foundation for forecasting future results, which serve as the basis for determining the true value (intrinsic value) of a company.

Risk

The investment risk section is extremely important. I would encourage aspiring investors to go beyond just taking the risks from the company's filings. There is a risk section located in the 10-K SEC filings. An analyst can add significant value by deriving their own potential set of risks. It is extremely important because you should be building in the amount of risk you would be taking on into your valuation considerations. Remember investing is about risk management.

Environmental, Social, and Governance (ESG)

The ESG section is the newest addition to equity research reports. The inclusion of ESG into what are considered essential sections of an investment report is a sign of the trends increasing relevance and importance. ESG brings up key questions which need answering, for example: How does the company interact with the natural world? How does the company account for people and relationships? What are the rules for running the company? The answers to these questions touch on a variety of important issues including topics like climate change, diversity, and corporate governance. I expect ESG compliance to become increasingly more important over the short and long term, potentially having an impact on a company's investment prospects and valuation.

Value Add

The *CFA Institute* does a good job of outlining the basic sections of a report. However, they missed a crucial section in my opinion. The most important part of any equity analysis or research report is the ability to **add value** or the value-add section by discovering information the market may have missed, may not have dedicated enough importance to, or might not be doing their homework on!

Let's be clear I am not suggesting finding an unethical edge, but I am suggesting finding an ethical one. There will be one to three questions that a potential investor in a company is going to need to thoroughly understand and answer by doing additional research, which will not only determine the performance of the stock but also provide you with confidence for your investment thesis and recommended action Buy, Hold, and/or Sell. The answers to these crucial questions confirm you are on the right path. I believe the value added to the crucial questions section is the most important section of the report (Table 6.1).

Table 6.1 Sections of a Company Report

Basic information
Investment summary
Business description
Management and governance
Industry overview and competitive position
Valuation
Financial analysis
Investment risk
Value added to crucial questions

Step 5 of Investment Process: Build a Shell

Financial Modeling

We begin by building a historical financial model. The process is a very common one on Wall Street known as financial modeling or just "modeling." There are three basic financial statements a company reports: income statement, balance sheet, and cash flow. I would start by building each of these statements in their own excel tab on a quarterly and annual basis going back a couple of years. The length of historical modeling would depend on what I felt comfortable with and the value the modeling provided to our future estimates. There are key financial ratios, which I would build into each individual financial statement in excel.

Each financial statement focuses on a specific aspect of a company's business. The income statement focuses on profitability. The balance sheet on liquidity. The cash flow statement on cash. I include a brief description of the potential key metrics per statement below. The formulas themselves are listing in Appendix IV. These ratios may be applicable to a specific company depending on the type of business or industry they are in.

Modeling like any other skill takes experience to become proficient. It is one of the foundational skills every financial analyst must have. However, we would caution you that modeling is only part of the formula for making a good investment decision. It rarely is the determining factor in the investment process in our opinion.

Financial Ratios

Ratios and metrics are a crucial way of measuring the performance of a company and comparing it to others. You can think of financial ratios and metrics as the financial analyst's tools. The analogy makes a lot of sense. A carpenter needs tools and practice to eventually become proficient at carpentry and building. Similarly, the aspiring investor needs tools in the form of financial ratios and practice by looking at different companies to help them become better analysts and at identifying investment opportunities. The aspiring investor is building an investment portfolio.

These tools come in the form of basic operating performance ratios found on the income statement, which relate to how well management is running the business. A change in these ratios can be either positive or negative. Liquidity ratios found on the balance sheet and cash flow statements measure a firm's financial health and its ability to pay its liabilities. These ratios are very important, especially for those who take on debt. Think of quarterly or annual reported earnings results as an opportunity to perform a routine checkup on these ratios. I provide a summary of the different ratios below and a table, which you can click on, and it will bring you to Appendix IV where you will find the actual formulas.

There are a few measurements which are particularly important and worth pointing out. These measurements are: net income, Free Cash Flow (FCF), Return on Equity (ROE), and dividends. Net income is the amount of income available to shareholders. FCF is the cash available to shareholders, essentially the life blood of an organization. ROE compares the net income to each unit of shareholder equity (net worth). Remember our *Foresi Get Rich Formula.* The same formula (ROE) applies to companies. Finally, the opportunity to pay dividends, the amount paid, and their continuous payments are important.

Golden Rule: Cash is the only REAL thing; The MORE Cash the better.

Income Statement Ratio

GROWTH RATES

Investors tend to focus on the income statement, which is the most popular of the three statements, but not necessarily the most important in our opinion. As we stated earlier, the income statement is a measurement of how well the management is running the company. The most exciting metric on the income statement has always been growth, particularly revenue growth rates. It is arguably the most popular of all financial metrics. Revenues are often referred to as "top line" because they are reported at the top of the income statement. Investors show a high degree of irrational exuberance over companies producing strong revenue or top-line growth. The faster the revenue has historically grown, the better from an investor standpoint. The infatuation with growth is understandable, but beware. The real focus should be not on the strength of the growth rate, but rather on its sustainability. The reality all too often is the faster the growth rate, the quicker the slowdown, the faster the decline in the stock price. Earnings or "bottom line" growth rates are important as well and usually are the result of strong top-line growth.

Revenue growth can be calculated in two ways. The standard way to calculate the growth rate is by comparing it to the prior quarter or year and converting it to a percentage. The comparisons are written as quarter over quarter (q/q) or year over year (y/y). This is the most common. The other growth rate calculation is performed by taking the retention rate or the percentage of earnings not paid out as a dividend and multiplying it by the return on equity. The challenge of using this method is that the input ratios used can be skewed or outsized, often making it difficult to perform the calculation.

PROFITABILITY

The income statement measures profitability. There are three primary measures of profitability: gross, operating, and net profit margins. Margins are usually stated as a percentage of revenue. The gross margin is typically the total of the revenue minus what is known as Cost of Goods Sold (COGS) as a percentage of revenue. Operating margins are revenue minus COGS minus Sales, General, & Amortization (SG&A) as a percentage of revenue. There can be different accounting issues including one-time items, which routinely impact operating margins, making it tough to make comparisons. As a result, investor use Earnings before Income Tax (EBIT) instead of the standard operating margin formula to help "smooth" out the numbers and to be able to make a comparison. Net margin is simply the net income as a percentage of revenue. The percentage changes in margins are calculated in basis points, which can be tricky for new analysts.

These calculations seem simple but are messy. Things happen in the regular course of business, which do not fit into the standard accounting format, yet need to be accounted for. Managements make it more difficult by reporting Non-GAAP results (vs. GAAP or IFRS), which allows them to decide what is accounted for and what isn't. You may need to re-read that statement. That's right! Within certain limitations, managements have discretion on what numbers they report, which can of course impact their stock price. As we will see in an upcoming section, the "quality" of earnings or results being reported matter.

Balance Sheet Ratios

Return

Although the income statement gets all the attention, it's the balance sheet that shows off the amount of progress the company is making. One of our favorite formulas is Return on Equity or

ROE. You might remember the formula from our prior discussion. ROE measures how much profit a company earns in comparison to the amount of shareholder equity. Simply put, it is your return on your equity investment. Higher ROE implies the business can generate more profits internally. The basic formula for ROE is net profit over average shareholder equity, but there are alternative ways to calculate ROE. Return on Assets or ROA follows the same methodology as ROE; the only difference is that ROA uses assets instead of equity.

Cash and Debt

Other important ratios on the balance sheet involve cash, cash management, and debt. I highlight a few of the frequently used formulas. A larger list is contained in the Financial Analyst's Tool Set table below. The current ratio divides current assets by current liabilities measuring a company's short-term liquidity. Days Sale Outstanding or DSO's divides the days by the receivables turnover, essentially measuring a company's ability to collect its receivables. There are ratios measuring the servicing of the debt through an interest coverage ratio which is EBIT divided by the interest and the size of the debt through a debt-to-equity ratio.

Cash Flow Statement Ratios

Cash Generation

The cash flow statement is the most important of the three statements because it measures the generation of cash. Here, the most important metric perhaps for the whole company is the calculation of FCF. The simplest calculation of FCF is operating cash flow minus net capital expenditures. There are other methods of calculating FCF including direct and indirect. We can measure the FCF yield as well. FCF is important because it is the life blood of the organization without it the organization will die. As we will see coming up, it also impacts valuation. **We provide a summary of the different ratios in the table below; you can also look at the appendix where you will find the actual formulas** (Table 6.2).

Table 6.2 Financial Analyst Metric Tool Set[a]

Income Statement	*Balance Sheet*	*Cash Flow*
Growth	*Return ratios*	*Cash flow ratios*
Growth rate	*Return on equity*	*Free cash flow*
Retention rate	*Return on assets*	*Direct, indirect method*
Basic, diluted EPS	*Liquidity ratios*	*FCF yield*
Profitability	*Current, quick ratio*	*Dividend*
Gross margin	*Defensive interval*	
Operating margin	*Cash management*	
Net margin	*Receivables, inventory, payables turnover*	
	Days sales outstanding	
	Cash conversion cycle	
	Asset turnover	
	Total, fixed, working capital turnover	
	Debt ratios	
	Debt-to-equity, total debt	
	Interest, fixed charge coverage	

[a] See Appendix for detailed formulas.

Quality of Earnings

There are plenty of reasons for a management to want to "display" or even manipulate their financial metrics like the ones presented above in a positive manner. The difference between reporting positive or negative financial results to Wall Street also known as "The Street" has wide-ranging implications and the margin for error is often very narrow. Positive financial results are often measured in a company reporting better than the Street or consensus expectations and their own guidance. Positive results often translate into stock price appreciation, which in turn creates shareholders' value, and results in a happy management team and board. However, the opposite can happen as well, where negative or disappointing earnings results lead to a contraction in the stock price, which in turn could lead to a decline in shareholder value and eventually result in management losing their jobs!

I am reminded of Thornton O'Glove's 1987 book *The Quality of Earnings*, a must-read for all aspiring investors. Thornton was an equity analyst who examined the **quality** of each earnings report. He noticed companies were consistently manipulating their ratios to deliver above Wall Street expectations. I am very skeptical of the current accounting practices, which continue to stretch the limit of accounting rules every year. One of our golden rules is *Cash is the only thing that is real.* The actual cash a company holds physically in its bank accounts is ultimately the only thing that can be counted. Many fraudulent companies "cook the books" or falsify their reported results and are caught because the auditors check the cash balances at the bank and they cannot verify them. I have seen this several times throughout our career. I have covered fraudulent companies or "frauds" like Satyam, an Indian based IT Services Company, and Longtop, a Chinese-based IT Services Company. As we have seen throughout the history of Wall Street, fraud can take place almost anytime, anywhere, and in many forms. No matter how smart you think you are, no one is smart enough to detect fraud! As an investor, you need to trust the auditors, who are often also fooled by fraud. We would steer clear of any company where there are rumors regarding fraudulent activity. If you need to check with the auditors regarding the validity of the cash balances, then the stock is not a good buying opportunity. Period! Rather, you should consider it on the short side. Short sellers borrow the stock, sell the stock, and then buy it back returning it to the lender. Short sellers "short" the stock, essentially betting on a decline in the stock price. I have found that if there is even a sniff of impropriety on the part of management, it makes the most sense to just stay away. If you are wrong, the results can be disastrous, including the rapid and massive destruction of wealth. It could even cost you your job if you are an investment professional! However, even if you are right, it could cost you a tremendous amount of time and effort, two very valuable resources. It is probably best to just make a case for it on the short side or most likely just move on!

Revenue Build

Two challenging aspects of investing are: the past means nothing and the future is uncertain, as the saying goes. How then do you build credible forward-looking forecasts? The answer is it isn't easy. One option is to create what is known as a revenue build to help with forecasting overall revenue or top-line estimates. The revenue build is a separate excel tab, which splits the total revenues into different subcategories allowing the analyst to further break down the revenue outlook into parts or components. The revenue build allows the analyst to forecast out different factors, which can be used to test out different scenarios and functions on your financial model. Revenue builds are often built based on the specific company's geographic or service line revenue breakdowns. We note that a revenue build must be based on regularly published quarterly or annual metrics. I built my Mastercard's revenue build off the company's revenue drivers and segment break down, which are both reported by the company and flow off each other. I would suggest beginning by first inputting the historical metrics into the revenue build and drivers excel tabs. You should now have five historical tabs in your Mastercard model: revenue drivers, revenue build, income statement, balance sheet, and cash flow statement. A snapshot of the statements can be found in Appendix III: Revenue Drivers, Revenue Build, Income Statement, Balance Sheet, and Cash Flow. Our next section will demonstrate the building of a basic, qualitative understanding of the company.

Understanding the Business Model

We can now build a qualitative foundational understanding of Mastercard's business model. There are a couple of key questions, "What is Mastercard? How does it work? How do they make money? How do they break down their business?" A good source of basic information on a public company is its 10-Ks, which can be found on a company's website. These filings tend to be verbose, so it helps to simplify what the company does in one sentence after organizing the information. For example, one sentence to describe Mastercard would be: Mastercard is an international payment network that charges participants a fee every time a payment is used on its network. We include highlights of our abbreviated answer to the key questions below. We encourage the readers to look at our Business Description section for further details.

What Is Mastercard?

Mastercard is a payment network. The company's primary business is the authorization, clearance, and settlement of digital payment transactions through their international, multi-rail network. Mastercard offers services in the areas of security, analytics, consulting, and rewards programs. The company has Automated Clearinghouse (ACH) and real-time payment processing capabilities as well.

How Does It Work?

Mastercard is part of the payment ecosystem. There are four participants in the ecosystem: account holder (customer), card issuer (bank), merchant, and merchant acquirer. Mastercard is a network meaning they do not issue cards, extend credit, collect traditional fees, or establish the Merchant Discount Rate (MDR).

How Do They Make Money?

Mastercard generates revenues (fees) based on volumes (Gross Dollar Volume (GDV)), transaction switching fees, and other payment-related products and services.

How do They Break Down Their Business?

There are five segments to Mastercard's business: Transaction Processing Fees, Domestic Assessments, Cross Border Volume Fees, Other, and Rebates and Incentives, which is a contra account. Transaction Processing Fees are the fees accumulated for the authorization, clearance, and settlement of domestic and cross-border transactions. Domestic Assessments are the fees Mastercard charges issuers and acquirers for transactions in which the merchant and issuer country are the same. Mastercard's 3rd largest source of revenue is cross-border volumes fees, which are fees charged to issuers and acquirers for transactions where the merchant and the issuer country are different. These segments each have a different fee schedule. The company's Other revenue segment consists of fees for consulting, data analytics, research, safety and security services, loyalty and reward solutions, and program management services. The Other category is Mastercard's fastest-growing category. Rebates and Incentives is a contra-revenue account, which is deducted from total gross revenues, consisting of long-term contracts with financial institution clients, merchants, and strategic partners for various programs.

What Products Do They Offer?

Mastercard offers a wide variety of products. The company divides its business into three core products: consumer debit and prepaid, consumer credit, and commercial credit and debit. Mastercard provides value-added offerings in different areas including security, data analytics and consulting, and digital payments.

Due Diligence

Equity research has similarities to the scientific method. A crucial step in both processes is the gathering and organizing of information. It is important to start by developing a strong foundational understanding of a company to help ensure a successful evaluation of the company as a possible investment opportunity.

I recommend a multi-step process for developing a basic understanding of a company. Company specific information can come in qualitative and quantitative forms. In the previous chapter, I made recommendations on where to find the information and how to organize it. The qualitative information can be sorted and organized into different sections of a "shell" report. Quantitative data can be used to build a financial model, which is known as modeling. Once we have performed the basic due diligence on a company, we are now ready to analyze it through our five-factor analysis as we make progress toward developing an investment opinion.

Bibliography

CFA Institute. (2020, September). Equity research report essentials. https://www.cfainstitute.org/sites/default/files/-/media/documents/support/research-challenge/challenge/rc-equity-research-report-essentials.pdf

O'Glove, T. L. (1987). *Quality of Earnings.* The Free Press.

Chapter 7

Five Factor Analysis

The Science

It is only appropriate we return to science one last time to set the stage for the presentation of our five factor analysis. Alina Bradford's article "What is a Law in Science?" helps to clear up a common confusion among the public. Many people mistakenly believe that in science evidence turns a hypothesis into a theory, and if the theory turns out to be true, it becomes a law. Facts, hypotheses, laws, and theories are all different things. As Bradford points out, the statement, "there are three apples," is a fact, while "Apples fall from a tree" is a law. These laws serve as the foundation for science, can change, and are often converted into mathematical formulas.

Over a long equity research career, my market observations have led me to hypothesize companies who excel at the following five characteristics or factors are best positioned to deliver long-term returns. I believe my five factor analysis compliments the practice of fundamental equity analysis. I concede the hypothesis and the factors themselves could change, but even if they serve as just a starting point for a much bigger conversation concerning what factors result in outperformance than they have more than served their purpose. I believe Ben Graham had it right, when like Isaac Newton and the law of gravity, he pointed out what he believed where the "laws" of the market like, for example, the fact that there is a difference between the price on an asset and its underlining value. Like science, analysts come across mathematical formulas, like those used to describe intrinsic value in our analysis, to help us on our journey.

I am not suggesting Ben Graham is Isaac Newton. In fact, ironically, Newton faced challenges when trying to invest. *Wall Street Journal* reporter Jason Zweig in the *Intelligent Investors* tells the story of how Newton lost millions in the market. Newton owned share of the South Sea Company in 1720, one of the most popular stocks in the market. Newton sensing the stock was overvalued famously said, "He could calculate the motions of the heavenly bodies, but not the madness of the people." He sold his South Sea Share for 100% profit, but succumbing to irrational exuberance, he bought it back shares at a higher price and eventually lost £20,000 or more than $3 million in 2002–2003 terms. Newton forbade people to talk about "South Sea" in his presence for the rest of his life.

The Analysis

The purpose of the *Foresi Five Factor* analysis is to accurately identify and evaluate the crucial elements of a company leading to its long-term outperformance. I begin by analyzing an industry and company using various potential methods to understand its competitive dynamics. I am looking to identify the company's competitive advantages, sustainable moats, and addressable market.

DOI: 10.4324/9781003686644-10

Once we have established the company's positioning, we can then look for the crucial catalysts driving growth and determine their strength and sustainability.

My analysis builds upon the basic foundational understanding we developed in the prior section. We will proceed by forecasting or modeling out the company's future earnings by incorporating different pieces of information and ratios, building off our historical model. Our newly completed model will allow us to evaluate the quality and implications of future earnings and synthesize them into our forecasts on a go forward basis. Our forecasts will serve as the basis for deriving intrinsic value.

Finally, we will learn about the art of valuation and how the different valuation methods change throughout the business life cycle. We will determine another of the Five Factor's quality of management based on performance, incentives, and business model. We conclude by examining the final factor, psychology, by looking at the different cognitive biases and heuristics and how to avoid them in the investment process. Our analysis will be crucial in making the "right" investment decision and just as importantly avoiding the "wrong" ones. My five factor analysis is based on fundamental equity research and should not be confused with the academically grounded Fama-French Five Factor analysis.

Factor 1: Competitive Advantage-Keep Opponents at Arm's Length

Businesses compete against each other every day for revenues. Some will succeed, while others will fail. Why does this happen? What characteristics do the winners have vs. the losers? These questions are very important to investors as the ability to find companies that are well positioned to succeed often results in superior, above average investment returns. As we will see in this section, companies that have discernable competitive advantages tend to be successful over the short and long term. It has been our experience throughout our career that finding a company with a large, sustainable competitive advantage or moat is the hardest, but the most rewarding characteristics for being able to drive long-term, above-average returns.

Competition is generally thought of as a positive, important component of any market helping to solve the problem of scarcity or lack of resources. I am reminded of our discussion of business cycles and creative destruction in Chapter 3. The economic definition of competition is a condition where different economic firms seek to obtain a share of a limited good by varying the elements of the marketing mix, price, product, promotion, and place (*Wikipedia*). Classic economics describes competition as a process where profits attract new entrants to an industry looking to capture those profits. Competition encourages firms to innovate and improve productivity. Product improvement and price declines due to competition are long-term positive for consumers but potentially negatives for companies.

Different Market Structures

Markets have varying degrees of competition. Economists have developed four market structures to help better understand competition: *perfect competition*, *monopolistic competition*, *oligopoly*, and *monopoly*. These varying types of market structures are defined by their different characteristics including number of firms, pricing power, barriers to entry, and advertising expense. *Perfect competition* is an industry with a number of firms with no pricing power, low barriers to entry, and homogenous products. *Monopolistic competition* is an industry with a number of firms, limited pricing power, low barriers to entry, differentiated products, and large advertising expenses. *Oligopoly* has a few firms with significant pricing power, high barriers to entry, and products may be homogenous or differentiated. A *monopoly* is a single firm with significant pricing power, high barriers to entry, and advertising used to compete with substitute products. Profits are maximized in all markets where marginal revenue equals marginal cost.

Competitive Advantages

So what separates the competition? Why do some companies survive while others fail? The answer is their competitive advantages. A competitive advantage is an advantage allowing a company or organization to outperform its competitors. Competitive advantages come in all forms, ranging from a differentiation in the cost to produce or service a customer to more niche strategies. The most compelling aspect of competitive advantages is a company's value proposition, which is essentially the reason why customers should use the company's innovation, service, or product instead of their competitions. An effective value proposition can translate into a competitive advantage.

An authority on competitive advantages is the Harvard professor, Michael Porter, who lays the foundation for understanding competitive dynamics in his 1980 book, *Competitive Strategy*. Porter believes companies can institute a competitive advantage in two ways: cost and differentiation advantages. He lays out his framework for evaluating competition through Porter's five forces. It draws from industrial organization economics, which is used to determine the competitive intensity of an industry in terms of its profitability. The most unattractive industry would be industries whose competition is pushing them toward normal profitability. These forces in the microenvironment affect its ability to service its customers and make a profit. There are three forces of "horizontal" competition: the threat of substitute products or services, the threat of established rivals, and threat of new entrants. There are two "vertical" forces: the bargaining power of suppliers and bargaining of customers. Porter's views were considered unique at the time because he unified different strategies like what we are trying to do with our current five factor analysis, only ours is focused on fundamental equity research. Porter was writing at the beginning of what would be a positive explosion in management consulting.

Porter's Five Forces was developed in reaction to the then popular SWOT. analysis. A SWOT analysis helps the individual identify Strengths, Weaknesses, Opportunities, and Threats as they relate to a business or project. Strengths and Weaknesses are often internally related, while Opportunities and Threats are externally related.

Since Porter's writing, Alan Bradenburger and Barry Nalebuff from Yale added a 6th force, the concept of complementors. They used "game theory" to try to explain the reasoning behind strategic alliances. Bradenburger and Nalebuff coined the term co-opetition, which is the concept of cooperation between competitors. They lay out the concept in their 1996 book entitled *Co-opetition*. Porter has disputed the existence of other forces.

Beyond Michael Porter

Porter's Five Forces or a SWOT analysis are the most popular methods used when performing competitive analysis, but there are other potentially useful ways to analyze the competitive dynamics of an industry. Craig Fleisher and Babette Bensoussan in their 2007 book, *Business and Competitive Analysis,* evaluate 24 valuable competitive analysis models. They re-enforce the idea of using business strategy to create, improve, and/or defend competitive advantages. Fleischer and Bensoussan lay out the challenges associated with Business and Competitive Analysis (BCA) including addressing the proper questions, known as Key Intelligence Question (KIQ), collecting and aggregating the information, and routinely presenting it to management. We list the 24 different analyses and highlight a few of the more relevant ones based on their work below for the reader who is looking to go "beyond" Porter. Although Porter and SWOT tend to be flexible enough to be applicable across a broad range of industries, the aspiring investor should focus on trying to use the competitive analysis, which fits best with the industry or company they are looking at and will deliver the most value to their company-specific analysis (Table 7.1).

Table 7.1 Strategic Tools and Analysis

Tools/Analysis	*Description*
Nine forces	STEEP/PEST Analysis Combined w/ Porter's Five Forces
Competitive positioning	Examines Co. place in industry relative to competitors
Business model	Measures Strength of a Business Model to generate economic rents for a product
SERVO	Strategy, Environment, Resources, Values, Organization (Leans toward Org. Behavior)
Supply-chain management	Evaluates a company's supply chain vs. competitors and in general to drive improvement
Benchmarking	Examining other firms looking to incorporate their best ideas into your business
McKinsey 7S	(Structure, Strategy, Systems, Style, Staff, Skills, Shared Value) Connects Environment to Organization
Shadowing	Closely monitoring specific markets or competitors looking for useful competitive comparable data
Product line	Involves examining different product lines from a capital allocation, competitive, and viability standpoint
Win/Loss	Collection of data around sales wins (strengths) and losses (weaknesses) performed in a politically viable manner
Strategic relationship	Looks are strategic inter-firm relationships and their competitive impacts
Corporate reputation	Soliciting corporate reputation feedback through focus groups, stakeholders, or reputation quotient
Critical success factors	Understanding what the critical factors of a business are and the information and action necessary to execute them
Country risk	Look at the different positives and negatives of global expansion into new countries
Driving forces	Identify the drivers of the industry and how it will change the structure and competitive dynamics
Event and timeline	Creation of an event and timeline isolating the activity of competitors and others to form a trend
Technology Forecasting	Uses multiple elements (time horizon, specific tech, perfect level, prob. of outcomes) to forecast Tech trends
War gaming	Creating a role-playing simulation game where the participants play the role of competitors to test strategy
Indications and *warning*	System put in place to warn companies of potentially risky situations
Historiographical	Tracks strategic issues from historical inception to today
Interpretation of statistics	Application of statistical analysis to data to help predict outcomes
Competitor cash flow	Analysis of historical and future competitors' cash flow
Competing hypotheses	Encourages users to list competing hypotheses simultaneously to compare and contract and protect against bias
Linchpin	Search for the most important issues or Linchpin issues

Source: Fleisher and Bensoussan-Business and Competitive Analysis.

Competitive Positioning Analysis

The competitive positioning analysis examines a company's current competitive position. The areas of focus are market share, client perception, marketing, pricing, and costs. The idea is to use these data points to develop, maintain, defend, and/or improve a competitive advantage or exit a market. The tools/analysis presented above can be used in the competitive positioning process. The analysis is very useful for understanding a firm's positioning, but collecting competitive intelligence can be difficult. The development of matrices or perceptual maps may be useful in understanding a firm's competitive positioning.

Business Model Analysis (BMA)

A BMA examines the strength of a company's business model and its ability to generate revenue from a product or service. BMA focuses on the company's business model accounting for different aspects including value, target market, value chain analysis, revenue/profit, and overall strategy. The strength of the approach is its comprehensive, detailed, and focuses on value in exchange for revenues, but the weakness is it may not cover innovation.

Benchmarking

Most analysts are familiar with benchmarking, which uses data from a similar outside organization as a comparison. According to Fleisher and Bensoussan, benchmarking involves taking the best ideas from other world-class organizations and incorporating them into your own to drive competitive advantages. There are four kinds of benchmarking: internal, external/competitive, other industry, and best practices. Porter himself does not believe benchmarking is a strategy as it only promotes operational effectiveness. He sees benchmarking more along the lines of mimicking others, which does not necessarily create a new competitive advantage.

There are simple quantitative methods for understanding a company's competitive positioning vs. its competition. One method we have used in the past involves comparing its growth rate to the industry and competitors, which is similar to benchmarking. If a company is growing faster than the industry and/or its competitors, it is most likely to take share, especially if the company's specific growth rate is faster than the industry growth rate. The opposite is true for slower than industry growth rates. It is important to keep in mind that growth rates can be skewed by size. The same comparative analysis can be done based on margins and other financial metrics or ratios like the ones presented in an earlier section.

Product Line Analysis

A product line analysis evaluates each company's product line. Each product line should provide a return on its capital and fit into a broader strategic plan. Companies can get into trouble by wasting valuable time and money on new and old products. The use of tools like the product life cycle (PLC) analysis and others can help save precious resources. The analysis is done by looking at a product line through various characteristics. They often include graphs like perpetual maps. However, PLC analyses can sometimes be short cited, focusing too much on the product and not the consumer or overall strategy.

Competitive Moats

A competitive advantage can be very large. In fact, it can be so large it can be considered a moat or competitive moat. Warren Buffett (remember him) is a proponent of finding these types of companies, no surprise, so am I. Remember the point of investing is trying to minimize the risk, while reaping the benefit of the return. Investors can lower the risk profile by finding the highest quality companies, which have the best opportunity to succeed in continuing to increase shareholder value over the long term.

Golden Rule: Moats are hard to find, but worth the effort, especially if they are expanding.

Here is where things get a little tricky. We know by now the best companies to own are consistently increasing returns, typically measured through return on investment (Return on Invested Capital (ROIC), Return on Assets (ROA), or Return on Equity (ROE)), which is essentially the *Get Rich Formula* only for companies. We also know companies with robust competitive advantages or moats are best positioned to do this. The challenge is finding the companies with the competitive moats, which are sustainable or expanding, and deciphering when the "enemy" or competition has successfully crossed the moat and presents a challenge.

Pat Dorsey in the 2008 book *The Little Book that Builds Wealth: The Knockout Formula for Finding Great Investments* attempts to help investors find great companies with large competitive moats. Dorsey's approach to some extent mirrors those of Buffett's and the one I suggest. He is looking for companies with high ROIC believing large economic moats help the companies that have them sustain their ability to drive returns over a longer period, thus increasing their long-term value. He provides a checklist of the characteristics to look for when evaluating companies with competitive moats including:

- *Intangible Assets* like brands or patents creating a barrier to entry for competitors
- *Customer switching costs* may be high leading to pricing power
- *Network Economics* can create a large competitive moat
- *Cost Advantages* through process, location, or access to unique assets

Dorsey evaluates each of these four characteristics and provides further details. He makes the important distinction regarding *intangible assets* between simply popular brands and popular brands with actual moats noting the challenges associated with patents and regulations. *Switching costs* can come in many shapes and forms including the amount of effort it takes to switch, integration and retraining costs, and the monetary aspects associated with switching. A company's ability to display pricing power is a positive sign when evaluating its potential competitive moat. The *network* effect is enhanced as the number of users increases. *Cost Advantages* can be achieved through process, location, or access to unique assets. However, these advantages can decline easily, especially process cost advantages.

Moat Opportunities

Competitive moats come in different sizes. These sizes range from small to expanding to huge to shrinking. All companies start out with small competitive advantages or small moats. These moats tend to expand, which is ideally the best time to own a company. Unfortunately, moats can also easily erode or shrink, which is when you don't want to own the company. Moat erosion can come from different forms including changes in technology, regulation, commoditization, and/or misallocation of capital. A company's ability to create a competitive moat and sustain it is often the result of the natural characteristics of its industry. Some industries provide a company with a better opportunity to create or even sustain a competitive advantage than other industries. These takeaways lead Dorsey to conclude the quality of management is overrated. In our opinion, a company's success is more heavily dependent on the characteristics of the business, industry, and ability to create and sustain a natural competitive advantage through those characteristics than any management team, a theme echoed by Dorsey.

Our View of Competitive Moats

I believe there is a life cycle to competitive moats. I will try to explain the hypothetical life cycle below. My competitive moat life cycle theory is a company's born with an original, organic competitive advantage. If the competitive advantage is strong enough, it becomes a moat. There are a lot of factors going into whether the original competitive advantage can become a moat. Some of these factors are dependent on things like the industries' natural characteristics and outside of the individual company's control. The company then capitalizes on its competitive moat driving returns, which can then be allocated through a thoughtful business strategy to create additional competitive advantages, which then in turn adds to the number of moats. I call this expanding the Total Addressable Market or TAM. You want to own companies that not only have a competitive moat but are also expanding their TAM at the same time. The problem is the continuation of expansion into further competitive advantages and moats works in theory, but in practice, it is often very difficult to do, so what ends up happening instead is the original competitive advantage deteriorates over time, and eventually the company falls prey to Shumpert's creative destruction (Figure 7.1).

Mastercard Industry Evaluation

We can now expand our basic understanding of the company (Step #5) to include an industry analysis. I used the Nine Forces method, but the reader should feel free to use different or multiple methods as stated earlier. My evaluation goes well beyond simply defining the market share.

I look at the competition, competitive advantages, competitive moat, and addressable market. Mastercard has multiple competitors, but its main competitor in the western world is Visa. It competes with other payment methods like cash. The company's competitive advantage is its infrastructure for processing payments. Mastercard's competitive moat is its payment infrastructure, and it has a healthy market share. The company has an expanding addressable market with multiple catalysts.

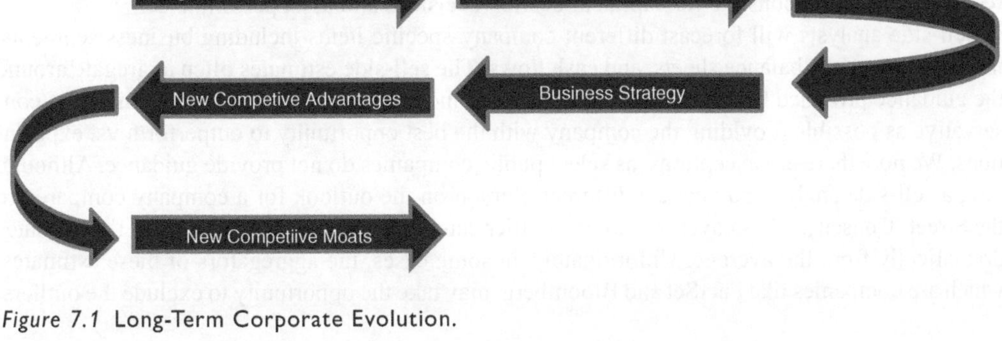

Figure 7.1 Long-Term Corporate Evolution.

Factor 2: Catalyst-Growing and Building Strength

We are making progress toward building out our understanding of the investment process and example company. We have built a historical model, examined its industry and business model, and developed an understanding of its competitive dynamics (advantages/moats). The next step is to look at the potential catalysts. A stock without a catalyst is like a car with no gas or no electricity, completely useless.

We can start by defining a catalyst. A stock catalyst is an event causing the price of a stock to move significantly. Examples of catalysts include earnings announcements, analyst days, changes in analyst estimates, product launches, management changes, and significant dividend or stock buyback announcements. (Wikipedia) One of the conclusions we can draw from the definition is that a catalyst is an unexpected positive or negative event or announcement, which changes the way Wall Street views a company's prospects, and most likely changes its stock price.

Catalysts can come in many different forms at the market and individual stock level. In Chapter 3, we touched on the different pieces of economic data like the unemployment rate or GDP, which could have a positive or negative impact on the overall direction of the stock market. The same logic applies to individual stocks. There are different pieces of stock-specific information, which impact the trajectory of stock prices. The most common of these are earnings announcements, which give the Street an opportunity to evaluate their investment thesis, forward-looking forecasts, and intrinsic valuation for a company.

Measuring a Company's Performance

Golden Rule: Gravity Rules. Numbers go up, stocks go up. Numbers go down; stocks go down.

A company's performance vs. Wall Street or Street expectations is a **crucial** factor in investing. Public companies report earnings results to the street on a regular basis, which can be quarterly (in the US) or half a year (in Europe). The company's reported earnings results are compared to what is known as consensus or street estimates, which is the average of all the sell side (brokerage houses) analyst's forward looking estimates, broken down by quarter or half years, over multiple years. It is important here to make a distinction between the sell and buy side analysts. The sell side is analysts employed by brokerage houses to provide written coverage of companies, which the brokerage houses often have corporate relationships. Sell-side research has been controversial because of the potential conflict of interest between the authenticities, independence of the research vs. its promotional nature toward existing corporate relationships. Sell-side research is sold to the buy side and often published in the public domain. The average of all the sell side analyst's estimates is known as consensus. The buy side analysts are the analysts who work at asset managers, consume sell-side research, and are responsible for capital allocation decisions and asset performance.

Sell-side analysts will forecast different company-specific items including business segments, income statements, balance sheets, and cash flows. The sell-side estimates often aggregate around the guidance provided by the management, who are incentivized to keep Street estimates as conservative as possible providing the company with the best opportunity to outperform vs. expectations. We note there are exceptions, as select public companies do not provide guidance. Although rare, a sell-side analyst may have a different opinion on the outlook for a company compared to the Street. Consensus is an average, so one outlier can make a difference, especially if it deviates dramatically from the average. Unfortunately, in some cases, the aggregators of these estimates, which are companies like FactSet and Bloomberg, may take the opportunity to exclude the outliers.

A company's performance is periodically measured by comparing their reported earnings results to the Street. Reported earnings results either meet, beat, or fall short of Street expectations. A company's ability to report earnings results that differ from Street estimates to either the upside (better than expected) or downside (lower than expected) is an important component of investing, so important that we contemplated making it a standalone factor.

Taking a Position Ahead of the Quarter

I want to be clear, before going any further. I do not promote the idea of "playing" the quarter, which is essentially betting or taking a position on the long (buy) or short (sell) side on how a stock price will do or react to upcoming reported earnings results, especially results that vary dramatically from consensus. I view this type of activity as a "fools" game and more about speculation than investing. Even though I don't promote playing the quarter, it is important to understand the relationship between reporting earnings results and the market's reaction, because the ability to deliver long-term upside results translates into positive, long-term stock appreciation.

Let's walk through a basic example to get a better understanding of what we are talking about. Company A reports quarterly earnings of $3.50 vs. the Street, which is looking for earnings of $3.00. The upside results vs. consensus are referred to as a "beat" in reference to beating expectations by analysts because reported earnings exceeded expectations. A "beat" is a positive quarterly catalyst. Even better than a "beat" is a "beat and raise," which is when a company's reported earnings exceed Wall Street expectations and then raises guidance! The stock trades up 5% on the news of the earnings "beat."

There is theoretically a mathematical reason for the stock price appreciation. When Company A reports quarterly earnings above expectations, the analyst community, all else being equal, will then raise their full-year forecasts and longer-term price targets or intrinsic values accounting for the new encouraging news regarding the outlook. The size of the stock price movement should in theory reflect the upward revision to estimates. I believe providing upside to numbers is a positive occurrence, pushing stock prices higher. I am reminded of the stock screens mentioned earlier particularly the Post Earnings Announcement Drift (PEAD). The opposite tends to take place when earnings come in below expectation. If the reported results are below expectations, then stocks tend to react negatively or decline, which may or may not provide an opportunity depending on whether you are short the stock or like the company as an investment opportunity and are waiting for an opportunity to purchase it. As we know, Mr. Market is volatile providing opportunities and challenges.

There are plenty of reasons why stocks don't react the way they should to either positive or negative earnings announcements vs. expectations. Let's take the same example where Company A reports better than expected quarterly earnings of $3.50 vs. Street expectations of $3.00, but the stock price is down −5%. There are a lot of reasons this could happen. It is very difficult to pinpoint the exact reason for the problem. Here are some examples of what might have happened.

- Company A's stock may have appreciated 20% since its last reported earnings as the investment community expected the company to report better than expected results, and the +$0.50 better than expected result was already built into the stock price or below the "whisper" or unpublished expectations.
- Company A may have "beaten" the quarter by $0.50 but not changed full-year guidance or worse brought it down because although the quarter was positive, the longer-term outlook has changed.

- Company A's management may have said something on the earnings call, which changed the analyst's mindset. Analysts now believe despite the better-than-expected performance the outlook for the company will be worse than originally expected.
- Mr. Market may just be having a bad day. The stock may be trading off in line with much broader negative market or other company news.

I believe it is important for a company to report better than consensus or Street estimates. I would argue that if, for example, a company guided to $3.00 in earnings for the year and delivered $3.00, which most likely would have been reflected in consensus, then assuming the Street believed they would achieve $3.00 then the company should be worth the same from the very beginning of the year to the end. However, if they guided to $3.00 and delivered $4.00, then the stock would be worth more because of the embedded +$1.00 increase in earnings. The positive momentum from the earnings upside carries over into future forecasts, driving the forecasts and intrinsic values higher, which is typically a good thing. It is helpful if a positive upside surprise comes in an area affecting valuation metrics like cash flow or earnings. The higher the earnings the more likely the higher the valuation assuming a constant Price-to-Earnings or PE ratio. The same logic applies to the income statement, balance sheet, and cash flow statements reported items affecting valuation. The higher the reported results vs. the expectations on these financial statements, typically the higher the forward-looking projections, thus the higher the valuation, and the better it is for the stock, which we will discuss in the next section.

Let's take an abbreviated look at Mastercard's 2019 quarterly performance vs. Street estimates as an example. Below is a table looking at Mastercard's reported earnings results including the date the company reported, Mastercard's reported revenue or "top line" and earnings or "bottom line" results vs. consensus. We see from the table below that Mastercard tends to slightly outperform expectations in each quarter, but there was little reaction from the stock price to the results on the day they reported, which in my opinion implies the news was expected. The good news is that the reported numbers were increasing. Remember our golden rule for the most part, numbers go up, stocks go up. Mastercard stock appreciated nearly +60% in 2019, despite the marginal quarterly stock price movements. There is unfortunately a tremendous amount of gamesmanship in the reporting of quarterly earnings as the reader can tell (Table 7.2).

Table 7.2 2018–2019 Performance vs. Street Expectations (Mastercard)

Date	*1Q18*[a]	*2Q18*	*3Q18*	*4Q18*	*1Q19*	*2Q19*	*3Q19*	*4Q19*
Revenue								
Reported	$3,580	$3,665	$3,898	$3,807	$3,889	$4,113	$4,467	$4,414
Consensus	$3,252	$3,651	$3,859	$3,798	$3,854	$4,081	$4,426	$4,398
Upside/downside	10%	0%	1%	0%	1%	1%	1%	0%
Earnings								
Reported	$1.50	$1.66	$1.78	$1.55	$1.78	$1.89	$2.15	$1.96
Consensus	$1.25	$1.53	$1.68	$1.52	$1.66	$1.83	$2.01	$1.87
Upside/downside	20%	8%	6%	2%	7%	3%	7%	5%
Stock performance	+3.1%	−3.2%	−1.7%	+3.5%	+2.9%	−1.2%	−0.60%	0.00%

Source: FactSet.

[a] 1Q18 represents first fiscal quarter 2018.

Modeling a Realistic View of the Future

Investors are sometimes able to figure out the potential for upside or downside to Street estimates through extensive modeling work. We would recommend keeping up to date excel models and intrinsic values on all our investments. There will be instances where the forward-looking guidance or estimates appear either too low or too high. The key is to recognize the discrepancy between where guidance is and what you believe will happen. We believe there is an opportunity to spot the discrepancy, but the amount of times you can capitalize from an investment performance perspective from extensive modeling efforts is extremely low, in our opinion.

So, if we believe reporting continuously better than expected or improving results drives long-term shareholder value, what is one good way to make sure we are investing in stocks that can do this? The answer is finding stocks with a discernable catalyst or multiple discernable catalysts, which can drive their reported results over the long term.

Different Types of Catalysts

I presented earlier the notion that catalysts can take on many forms as they are essentially new pieces of information driving the price of stocks or markets up or down. Here, I want to separate the short-term, one-time drivers of stock performance from the long-term drivers. Short term, drivers of stock performance tend to be one-time items like news items or earnings results, which can be manipulated. Although these short-term catalysts can be positive, we want to make a distinction between these short-term catalysts and what we are looking for, which is a long-term, discernable catalyst. Long-term, discernable catalysts are meaningful changes in demand or outlook, profitability, and/or capital allocation. Our financial tool set presented in the earlier section will come in handy here in being able to identify and measure these changes.

Changes in Demand

The purest and most popular catalyst is the strength of demand, which is typically measured by revenue growth (percentage changes). Demand can vary in relative strength. It can be either strong, steady, or even weak. The demand for a company's product or service is strongest either when a company or industry is new or when it has a new service, product, or innovation to offer. The strength of demand peaks during the early stages of a new product or offering because the company is taking market share or creating a whole new market. As the company or industry matures, growth rates moderate. Demand and/or growth rates are not solely a function of the age of the company. Other factors may include the strength of the demand in a particular vertical or industry, the relative strength of the overall economy, price of the product, level of competition, and/or product mix.

Changes in Profitability

A company's change in profitability can be a driver of stock performance. The change is typically measured by the changes in the company's margin structure. Profitability improvements can come from areas like economies of scale and/or cost efficiencies. A rise or fall in profitability can happen for different reasons. A company may push through positive productivity gains on an annual basis causing margins to rise on a consistent annual basis. Some companies may push through large takeout programs. The opposite may happen when margins decline because the business is being commoditized at a rapid pace. The order of magnitude and sustainability of a change in profitability will determine its impact on stock price performance. Changes in profitability have been less of a driver of stock performance over the long term than changes in demand in our opinion. There are rare cases when a company reports a positive improvement in revenue growth and margin expansion at the same time, which we affectionately call a "double whammy," which is a healthy combination of catalysts to say the least.

Changes in Capital Generation/Allocation

Capital generation and allocation may be a catalyst in addition to growth and profitability. Capital allocation can come in different forms, including strategic acquisitions and/or the return of capital to shareholders through dividends or share buyback. A company's ability to generate incremental cash flows is positive as it can drive up valuation through the Discounted Cash Flow (DCF) method, which we will see later, or it can be allocated to building the business organically through capital expenditures, inorganically through acquisitions, or returned to shareholders. The three factors demand, profitability, and capital allocation often work in tandem. There may be cases where better than expected demand and/or an improvement in profitability will in turn accelerate cash flow generation and vice versa.

Putting It All Together

In their 2001 book, *Expectation Investing* authors Alfred Rappaport and Michael J. Mauboussin tackle the topic of expectations. The authors look at the misplaced Wall Street emphasis on valuation metrics such as PE. Instead of chasing growth, the authors suggest looking at the quality of the growth. Growth is often driven by an increase in expenditure, when in fact they should be focused on the company's ability to generate cash flow that keeps pace with the growth, so the companies are in fact creating not destroying shareholder value. The authors suggest using a "reverse" engineering of the stock price using the price itself to determine what is built into the model from a cash flow generation perspective. The investor can then decide if the stock can surpass the Price Implied Expectation (PIE). I believe there is some value to the author's unique perspective. My favorite section of the book is the authors' framing of the value "triggers" (or catalysts): sales (volume, price and mix, operating leverage, and economies of scale), costs (cost efficiencies), and investments (investment efficiencies).

Our case study Mastercard has several catalysts. I break these catalysts into three categories: industry, technology, and company-specific initiatives. I would recommend a deeper dive than we present here into each of the catalysts and five factors when looking at a potential investment opportunity as it could provide an edge. The strength of Mastercard's catalysts is impressive as essentially the company is working to "put cash (itself) out of business" or serve as a payment alternative to cash. My back-of-the-envelope calculations indicate the potential for a high single-low -double-digit annual growth rate in a normalized environment for Mastercard.

Forecasting

We have made progress in understanding Mastercard from several different angles. We built a historical model and an understanding of the company's industry, business model, competitive advantages, and catalysts. It is now time to financially model future projections.

Forecasting is controversial in the sense that no one knows the future, which is impossible to predict. The best an analyst can try to do is take in all publicly available information within reason and use it to make educated forecasts of what the future could look like. These forecasts are often skewed for various psychological and practical reasons. So why do they even make them? I believe they serve a specific purpose and fill a knowledge gap, but I would not put too much emphasis on them. The available information to make your forecasts comes from different sources. Two of the more common sources are the industry and company reports cited earlier, particularly the SEC filings and quarterly earnings reports.

Gather Available Public Information

We have already completed the 1st step in modeling, which is building a historical model. It is now time to move on to the 2nd more exciting step in creating your forecasts for a company. I begin the second step by looking at the most recent quarter for all available public company information regarding their future expectations or outlook. You can do this by looking through press releases, quarterly earnings reports, transcripts, and analyst days.

Mastercard reported its most recent quarter on July 30th, 2020, as of the time of the writing of this book. By the time the book is published, and you are reading it, Mastercard will have reported additional quarters or even years providing further data points. The company may even be an uninteresting investment opportunity! However, as I have mentioned, the Mastercard example is simply for learning purposes. I am reminded of the many investment books I have read in the past citing many outdated opportunities ranging from railroads to high-flying tech stocks of bygone eras. I am aware that times change quickly, especially on Wall Street.

I would not over emphasize the importance of a company's quarterly results. Mastercard's 2Q20 quarterly results are particularly insightful, especially because the company reported the results during the COVID pandemic. Mastercard reported quarterly results above expectations or consensus (average of analyst's estimates) on the top (revenue) and bottom lines (earnings). We take a closer look at Mastercard earnings results in Appendix III. Revenues declined −19% (−17% in constant currency), while earnings declined −26%! The results were negatively impacted by lower consumer spending because of the COVID-19 pandemic, which had a negative impact on overall results, particularly cross-border fees, as travel has been restricted due to the pandemic.

There are multiple ways for analysts to benefit from a detailed examination of quarterly earnings results. Quarterly results allow analysts an opportunity to test their overall investment thesis on a stock for validity similar to how a scientist tests their hypothesis during the scientific method. There are different sources available for quarterly information including press release, company presentations, earnings transcripts, and sell-side analyst reports. An analyst can compare the quarterly results and commentary to the estimates in their model to determine the accuracy of their current and future predictions. They can examine the results to determine the quality of earnings. Thornton O'Glove wrote a great book in 1998 focused on the *Quality of Earnings* as the title suggests through financial statement analysis, which I would highly recommend. I believe earnings can easily be manipulated by managements with the Street typically accepting the final reported number without questioning its quality. I am sure Thornton agrees with me.

I attempt to measure our case study Mastercard's "Quality of Earnings" analysis in Appendix III. Any measurement of a company's quality of earnings should be extensive and performed over a longer timeframe. I performed an abbreviated analysis of quarterly results to give the reader a sample of how the process of measuring the quality of earnings could work. I use a three-category rating system. The quality of earnings can be good, fair, or poor. The choice of ranking is subjective with companies, who drive earnings through revenue upside or operational excellence as opposed to non-operational items such as other income and lower taxes receiving a lower rating. I rated Mastercard's 2Q20 quality of earnings as fair. The company offset the impact on earnings resulting from a large revenue decline due to COVID-19 by lowering costs, particularly in marketing. However, the company did get additional help from lower non-operational expenses. I looked at the current quarter's reported earnings compared to a year ago to get a sense of what caused the change in earnings. I remind investors one quarter does not make a year. All analysts should be looking for positive or negative **multi-year trends**.

Golden Rule: One quarter does not make a year. Look for multiyear trends.

Time to Make Some Forecasts

We are now ready to bring all the information together to forecast or model future results over the next one, three, five, and ten years. Let's begin by looking at all the relevant public information regarding management's commentary on the most recent quarter and sell-side estimates to get a sense of the short-term outlook. Try to be careful not to fall into an anchoring trap when looking at either consensus or management's guidance. Anchoring is a psychological term referring to the cognitive bias where the individual depends too much on an initial piece of information during the decision-making process. I will talk more about cognitive biases when we look at our fifth factor, psychology. Remember these forecasts tend to be conservative.

Wall Street has unfortunately become very short-term oriented. The sell side is transaction oriented (trading) and thus more focused on the short term and potential volatility, which leads to higher trading volumes and larger commissions. I discussed earlier some of the general challenges associated with making estimates. Sell-side analyst estimates can be flawed. Sell-side analysts' models tend to be too short term in my opinion as they only model out a couple of years of estimates. I believe they should model out five to ten years of future estimates. Hedge funds tend to focus on the short term as well. Unfortunately, even longer term, buy and hold-oriented investors known as "long only's" are becoming increasingly more short-term oriented to comply with the institutional investors demand for outperformance and the investors' ability to quickly, easily move their assets, if they are dissatisfied with performance. I understand the need for the short-term focus but taking a longer-term view as an investor is becoming increasingly more unique and may even be your own unique, competitive advantage as an investor should you choose to do it.

Analyst forecasts have a sense of mysticism to them. The job of the analyst is to take all reasonably available qualitative and quantitative data, especially guidance, and translate it into a numerical picture or prediction of the future. The forecasts are carefully constructed from the bottom up. Analysts begin by forecasting out the individual revenue drivers and business segments. Those forecasts are then rolled up into a short- and long-term revenue outlook and flow through the income statement. Investors can often gain insight and guidance regarding their income statement estimates from sources like guidance and managements' comments on earnings calls. The income statement then drives balance sheet and the very important cash flow statement estimates. I would recommend estimating out ten years to be able to take a long-term view. Finally, the cash flow estimates are used to calculate an intrinsic value. The goal of forecasting is to ultimately be able to develop a reasonable and reliable prediction of the future stock price allowing the investor to calculate the true (intrinsic) value of a company.

The challenge is that managements typically have poor visibility into the prospects of their business and are reluctant to provide guidance, which adds to the daunting task associated with an analyst's ability to make accurate forecasts, especially when unforeseen events like wars, pandemics, economic crises, and tariffs take place. The process I suggest accounts for all reasonably available public information and incorporates it into our forecasts. We look at our case study Mastercard's short-term outlook, long-term outlook, and balance sheet and cash flow estimates.

Factor 3: Valuation-Getting to the Heart of the Matter

We've made tremendous progress with our company. We built a solid foundation around a basic understanding of the industry and business model. We then identified the company's specific competitive advantages and catalysts. We have finally arrived at the crucial intersection between our Ten Step Process and Five Factors. We are at the heart of the matter, valuation.

Equity valuation is a complex subject. There are volumes of literature on it; in fact, I did my dissertation on it. I have attempted to provide a simplified framework to help us understand the topic of valuation and its inputs. I encourage the reader to try to not to get overwhelmed by the formulas and math. The equations may look difficult, but they represent simple calculations. Both the equations and examples are in the appendices. Readers can easily access them by clicking on the links. The real challenge will be finding the correct inputs. I walk the reader through my Mastercard valuation example in detail in Appendix VI. The use of a framework rather than a specific definition is a practical approach to understanding valuation in my opinion. At the heart of all investing, the most important question an investor can ask themselves is, "What is this asset worth (value)?"

The Art of Valuation

Golden Rule: Valuation is an art, not a science. It requires flexibility.

A good place to start is establishing parameters. Valuation is neither an art nor a science, but rather a mixture of the two. As we will see, valuation is more art than science. In its simplest form, valuation is the search for intrinsic value or the actual value of an asset or company based on the underlying perception of its true value including all aspects of its business both tangible and intangible. The intrinsic value of an asset often differs from its market value, which presents an opportunity. If the intrinsic value is above the market value, investors would look to buy the asset, if the difference between the intrinsic and market value or price provides a comfortable margin of safety. If the intrinsic value is below the market value, investors could do nothing or possibly short the stock.

I have already discussed earlier in the book the method of establishing an intrinsic value then building in a margin of safety from which you would establish a price at which you would buy the stock or entry point. I believe the art of finding a valuation itself is inherently flawed. Investors can protect against the inherent flaw by building a margin of safety, which essentially helps mitigate or reduce the risk of the investment. I would recommend considering adjusting valuation metrics to support overall market movements to keep them relevant. My dissertation further explores the role of valuation in the investment process. I've included a link for those who are looking for an academic point of view.

Company valuations should be derived through an arbitrary process not backed into to support a preconceived investment thesis. Please reread the prior sentence. It is crucial to the success of all investment decisions that valuation calculations remain as autonomous as possible. There are cognitive biases at play in deriving a valuation for a company. Two of the more prominent are confirmation and anchoring biases, which cause the average investor to want to have a valuation matching their positive or negative investment thesis on the stock. I will address these issues in more detail in my section on psychology. We now come to another golden rule.

Golden Rule: Attractive valuation means positive risk/reward, REMEMBER to use a margin of safety.

Three Risk Mitigating Steps

It is important to remind readers that equity investing is a risky business. I try to mitigate the risk by doing three things. First, I look for very good companies with large competitive moats, expanding addressable markets, and catalysts to spare. Second, I want companies with strong balance sheets and great Free Cash Flow (FCF) generation, which allow the company not only the opportunity to sustain itself but also to grow. Finally, I am looking to buy these companies for my portfolio at prices below their intrinsic value building in a "margin of safety."

I believe the value of a financial asset is equal to the cash flows you expect to receive from the assets discounted into present value form. An aggregate stock price then can be separated into two pieces: (1) The intrinsic value or value of future cash flows and (2) The market speculation/expectations or noise, which is anything above the intrinsic value. This view of a stock is consistent with the academic Noise trader model presented earlier.

The price of a stock or the level a stock is trading at is a combination of the intrinsic value plus market speculation. An investor would ideally want to buy an asset at a discount (margin of safety) to its intrinsic value. The concept is simple, but as we will see, the practical application is much more difficult. I will review the different types of formulas used to perform these calculations and their necessary inputs in the next section.

Let's take a simple example. XYZ Company is trading at $500. Our intrinsic valuation calculation implies a value of $350 over a five-year period. I assume based on my intrinsic valuation calculations the market is assigning a $150 market premium on the stock. I would note intrinsic and relative valuations computations rarely match. I then look at relative valuation, which accounts for the price the stock is trading at in the market. I found out XYZ company's current multiple is trading at a premium to the average multiple of its peer group despite its in-line growth and margin profile.

Situations like these, especially when the market premium is large, often have investors wondering, "What does the market know that I don't know that would allow the stock to trade at such a large premium?" The true answer is only time will tell if the market knows something you don't and what the information is. In fact, stock price movements are time-stamped daily, meaning at any point and time you could be right or wrong depending on the mood of Mr. Market on the day. Although easier said than done, I would suggest maintaining a high level of conviction in your work and taking a long-term approach, as these short-term discrepancies are solely attributable to Mr. Market's volatile nature or noise, as it is referred to in academia, which can be used to the investors' advantage.

Valuation Methods

There are a variety of different valuation methods that fit into different asset pricing scenarios. We turn to NYU professor Aswath Damodaran, who is the authority on valuation, to help us sort through the different methods and scenarios. Damodaran's views can be found in his 1994 book *Damodaran on Valuation* and 2011 book *The Little Book of Valuation.* He breaks valuation into two methods: intrinsic and relative. The *intrinsic valuation method* of a stock is the present value of all future cash flows. The typical method used to derive the intrinsic values is the DCF method, which is utilized by value investors like Warren Buffet. The positive aspect of DCF is it forces the analyst to look at cash flows, fundamentals, and risks. The drawbacks to the DCF approach are it can produce estimates having nothing to do with intrinsic value, requires a lot of information, and can lead to overvaluation, especially during bull markets.

The *relative valuation method* is derived by the market compared to its outlook and its peers. Relative valuation metrics are based off the stock market price. Relative valuation is helpful as it can be used in all types of markets (Bull or Bear). The negative aspect of relative valuation is that it builds in the inherent market biases or market premium mentioned earlier, and comparables may be difficult to find or may not be comparable at all. As noted above, the intrinsic and relative valuation methods can lead to two different conclusions about the same asset.

The natural question is, "Isn't the value of something always the same? Shouldn't all valuation methods lead to the same result?" The unfortunate answer is "No." Valuation like investing is more art than science.

We see examples of relative vs. intrinsic valuation discrepancies quite often in everyday life in markets like real estate. A home is often the largest purchase a person can make. A home's value is primarily determined by its relative value or comparison (comps) to other similar homes in the same location. There are however other less popular intrinsic valuation methods for valuing real estate like the income approach, which converts the properties' potential income into an intrinsic value. I encourage you to try these different real estate valuation methods in evaluating your current home, a prospective home purchase, or even just looking at different homes in your neighborhood. I believe you will come up with very different values for the market or comparisons vs. the income approach. Most homes sell for a price based on their relative value, which is why everyone is happy, when the house down the street sells for a high price!

Valuations can be very challenging regardless of the method chosen. Damodaran believes the simplest, easiest form of valuation is typically the best. He notes certain groups of assets like financial services, commodities, and technology/biotech lend themselves better to certain types of valuation methods. As we will see, these valuation methods change over the life cycle of a company as well.

Intrinsic Valuation Method

The intrinsic value of a company is an objective calculation (intrinsic) of an asset value based on the financial modeling of its future cash flows, dividends, or earnings, which are discounted back to present value terms. The primary intrinsic value method is known as the *DCF method.* The calculation of the present value of the future cash flow is performed by using a discount rate, which accounts for the various risks future cash flow may not materialize. There are various methods for deriving intrinsic value including *Dividend Discount*, *FCF*, and *Residual Income Model.* I review these valuation methods in the Financial Analyst Tools below. We will familiarize ourselves with the different types of inputs used in deriving intrinsic value including cash flows, cost of equity and debt, and growth, in Chapter 8.

Relative Valuation Method

The relative value of a company is found by comparing the price or the asset to other similar (relative) assets in the market. It is important to note that the relative valuation method uses the market as a tool to measure the value of an asset. Relative valuation is performed by finding a comparable group of companies and determining the market multiple of a specific company or asset compared to the group multiple based on its characteristics vs. the group. For example, a company having a higher growth profile than the group tends to be assigned a relatively higher multiple or premium and vice versa. The dislocation of stock prices measured through multiple premiums or discounts to the comparable or comp group is used to identify opportunities. There

Table 7.3 Financial Analyst Valuation Tool Set[a]

Intrinsic Value		*Relative Value*	
Dividend Discount Model		*Price Multiples*	
Single period	FCFE	Price/earnings (P/E)	Price/sales (P/S)
Gordon Growth Model (GGM)	FCFF	*Leading P/E*	Price/CF (P/CF)
Multi period		Trailing P/E	EV/EBITDA
Residual Income Model	RIM	Price/book (P/B value)	

[a] See Appendix for formulas. We walk through a step-by-step example of the Valuation method in Appendix VI.

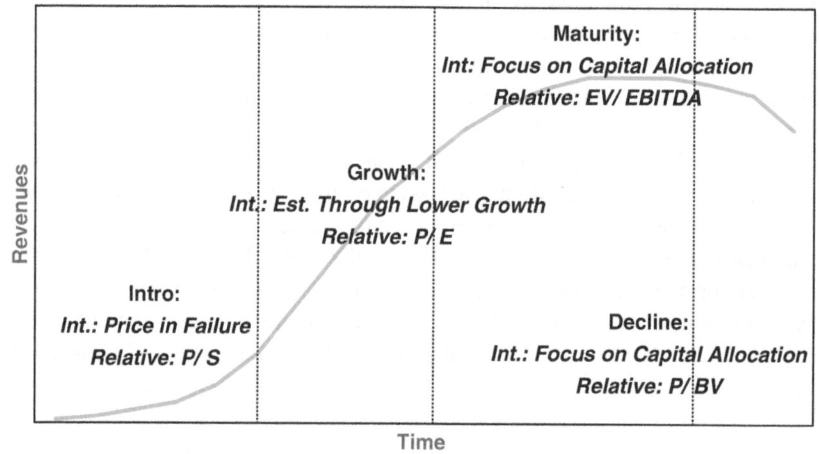

Figure 7.2 Intrinsic and Relative Valuation through Life Cycle (Damodaran).

are many different relative valuation formulas including price to earnings, cash flow, sales, and book value. We see many inherent dangers in relying on relative valuation, especially given the difference between price and value and the natural volatility associated with markets. I take a look at the various relative valuation methods in Chapter 8 including a summary table below linked to the actual formulas in Appendix IV. I present a multi-point valuation analysis (three, five, and ten years) for Mastercard (Table 7.3).

Changing Valuation Methods

The appropriate intrinsic and relative valuation method will change throughout the life cycle of a business. A businesses life cycle can be divided into four categories: introductory, growth, maturity, and decline. Companies in each stage of the life cycle have different characteristics, which lend themselves better to certain valuation methods vs. others. For example, companies in the introductory life cycle phase should price in the chance of the failure of the business from an intrinsic value standpoint. Investors should use a price-to-sales relative valuation methodology given the lack of cash flow typical during this stage. We provide further details in Chapter 8 regarding and the graph below as a preview (Figure 7.2).

Factor 4: Quality of Management—Using Your Head

We've made significant progress in making our way through the five factors and applying them to our case study, Mastercard. We now move to a crucial piece of the puzzle, which is evaluating the quality of management. As with most of the factors, there is an element of subjectivity. I currently use a couple of different elements to evaluate management including past performance, management meetings and incentives, and the quality of the company's business model and strategy.

Past Performance

I begin by looking at a rudimentary form of evaluating management's ability to execute by looking at their quantitative past performance or execution. I encourage investors to take a measured approach to historical metrics. Management can manipulate earnings results. It is very important to remember past performance has little or nothing to do with the future. History doesn't repeat, it rhythms.

The evaluation of a company's past performance is a straightforward exercise. It can be performed by looking at recent execution. I chose a period of eight quarters, but the reader should feel comfortable using different timeframes. The key question is, "Has the company been able to meet or consistently exceed Street expectations over the last two years?" My measurement as mentioned in the last section is reported earnings results vs. consensus or the average of the analyst expectations. There are various reasons leading to over and under performance vs. consensus including gamesmanship in both the way management reports results and how the sell side creates their estimates. As we saw earlier, Mastercard has performed very well over the last two years 2018–2019 vs. consensus. Although the company's performance should be taken with a measure of caution, I believe it is a net positive.

Earnings Are Your Periodic Check Up

Companies report earnings results on a periodic basis. The results are typically reported quarterly in the US and semi-annually in Europe. You should think of earnings as an investor's opportunity to check in on how their investment is doing. Earnings results provide new pieces of information allowing investors to test their thesis and assumptions, update their long-term forecasts, and gather new data points. We provide a condensed look at earnings in our Mastercard report. For the most part, despite potential stock reactions, earnings tend to be a non-event if you have chosen your investments wisely. An unwarranted stock price movement around earnings may provide an opportunity or short-term headache from an investment perspective. Remember we are playing the long-term game; one quarter does not make a trend. We are looking for the "forever" stocks.

Many companies hold analyst days for their investors on an annual basis. The analyst days are partially self-serving on the part of management. However, they do provide an update on the company's strategy, remember strategy is crucial as it is the creator of competitive advantage, and long-term financial targets. The information disseminated at a company's analyst day is particularly helpful if you are working on developing a foundational understanding of a company. The long-term fundamental investor enjoys analyst days because they focus on two very important topics: strategy and long-term financial targets, which can be compared to an analyst's long-term forecasts.

Management Meetings

To meet or not to meet; that is the question.

In addition to examining management's record of execution, the investor may have the opportunity to speak with the members of the team.

The decision to talk to management is not as easy as it sounds. You could make the argument talking to management is negative because rather than helping your judgment, it clouds it. There are several reasons why a meeting with management may cloud your judgment based on the cognitive biases we will present in our next section on psychology. Malcolm Gladwell touches on the challenges in "reading" other humans in his entertaining 2019 book *Talking to Strangers*. He speculates humans tend to "default to truth," which means we as humans tend to believe what others tell us, even if we should know better. Gladwell provides different examples in his book where the default to "truth" mindset is an issue, including the famous case of Bernie Madoff. Gladwell's hero in the Madoff scandal is an equity analyst named Harry Markopolos, who uncovered the Madoff fraud. Markopolos is a skeptical person by nature, so skeptical that he doesn't meet with management, because he doesn't want it to skew his judgment!

There are multiple cognitive biases at work when you meet with management. Investor's want to inherently believe what managements are telling them due to what Gladwell calls the "truth" mindset. Managements tend to be likeable individuals by nature, which is how they got to be management! This creates a "Halo" effect, which is the tendency for a positive impression in one area to influence another. Analysts tend to think they know more than most, which may lead to a second psychological challenge known as, the overconfident effect. Analysts are looking for data points to confirm their thesis, particularly on the positive side, which leads to a third challenge, confirmation bias. I followed a few of the companies the great investor Warren Buffett owned as an equity analyst. I would always ask the management of these companies if they had talked to Warren Buffett. I was surprised he did not talk to them all that much and quiz them about their business. In retrospect, perhaps Buffett potentially through the influence of his partner Charlie Munger may just be smart enough to recognize the limited or possibly negative value in having those conversations based on these and other cognitive biases.

Use the Socratic Method

The decision to meet with management is a personal one. I would recommend meeting them and asking pointed questions using a Socratic method about their business to help you form an opinion on the company. The more sources you can locate to help you form an opinion, particularly sources that disagree with you, and "scuttlebutt," typically the better you will feel about the investment. You may even be able to potentially pick up on their non-verbal cues, but be careful, unless you have years of interrogation experience in the CIA, you will never be able to determine if someone is lying to you. Managements or individuals who want to deceive you will not show the signs you are looking for. I understand this may not be possible for the average investor but would recommend at least a phone call with a company's Investor Relations or member of executive management, especially if you are trying to understand the details of a company or industry specific topic you are researching.

The initial questions you ask of management should be basic questions about the business. I list our typical ten questions below. The most important question you can ask management is, "How do you make money?" It sounds like a very simple question, but you would be surprised how many very smart investors forget to ask the question. The answer to this one question and your evaluation of the answer is the single biggest determinate of whether you should invest in the company and how good management truly is. By evaluating the quality of

Table 7.4 Ten Management Questions

1	How do you make money?
2	Can you give some background on yourself?
3	Who are your competitors? What do you do differently from them?
4	What do you consider to be your competitive advantage?
5	What are the catalysts in your business?
6	What are two or three investor's topics you get asked the most about?
7	How do you think about the long-term growth of the company?
8	How do you think about the long-term margin profile?
9	What are your thoughts on capital allocation?
10	How do you value your company? Acquisitions

the business model based on a company's ability to make money, you have already begun to develop the important skill of being able to separate good businesses and management from bad. It all starts with you applying common sense to determine the strength of the business model (Table 7.4).

The list above is a generic list of questions, but it should put any investor on the right track to understanding a business model. The first question on the list is of course the most important. There are questions specifically aligned with the five factors including questions about competitive advantages, catalysts, and how management handle Street expectations. One of the more interesting questions is, "What are two or three investor topics you get asked about?" The question has several implications. I believe the push and pull between bulls and bears is really an investor debate over the two to three most relevant topics. The winner of the debate, either the bull or the bear, ultimately decides stock appreciation or depreciation. I often tried to isolate these crucial topics and produce deep dives on them, which we called Value Added Pieces.

The notion that an investor can gain an advantage through asking the right questions of the right (company) people was introduced by Philip Fisher in his 1958 book, *Common Stocks & Uncommon Profits*. Fisher (known as the father of growth investing) believed you could get a better picture of the investment prospects of a company through industry scuttlebutt. He developed a 15-point checklist to help you understand which companies present the best investment opportunity. A company does not need to satisfy all 15 points below, but it is helpful to satisfy as many as possible. Fisher was a proponent of a buy-and-hold investment approach, only recommending selling when the earnings peak has already been achieved (Table 7.5).

There are additional qualitative cues to think about if you have a face-to-face meeting with management. Joseph Navarro, a former FBI agent, sets a solid foundation for understanding body language in his 2008 book, *What is EVERY Body Saying*. Humans have a limbic system in their brain producing body language consistent with our internal emotions. Navarro presents the underlining meaning behind different body movements by body part. Protection of the head and neck is a sign of nervousness. The legs and torso tend to be the most truthful part of the body. The legs show relaxation (crossed) or nervousness (kicking) or favoritism (leaning or mimicking someone). Protecting the torso is a sign of being uncomfortable, showing the torso is a sign of comfort. Arms can show excitement (overhead), protection (crossed), or fear (less movement). Hands can show confidence (praying) or nervousness (wringing). The head and face can be and often are the most deceiving part of the body. The reaction should always match the emotion.

Table 7.5 Philip Fisher's 15 Points

1	Does the company have the products or services with sufficient market potential to make possible a sizeable increase in sales for at least several years?
2	Does management have a determination to continue to develop products and processes that will increase total sales potential when the growth potential of currently attractive products lines have been exploited?
3	How effective are R&D efforts in relation to the company's size?
4	Does the company have an above average sales organization?
5	Does the company have a worthwhile profit margin?
6	What is the company doing to maintain or improve profit margins?
7	Does the company have outstanding labor and personal relations?
8	Does the company have outstanding executive relations?
9	Does the company have depth to its management?
10	How good are a company's cost analysis and accounting controls?
11	Are there other aspects of the business, somewhat peculiar to the industry involved, which give the investor clues as to how outstanding the company may be in relation to its competition?
12	Does the company have a short and long-range outlook for profits?
13	In the foreseeable future, will the growth of the company require sufficient equity financing so that the large number of shares then outstanding will largely cancel the existing stockholder's benefit from the anticipated growth?
14	Does the management speak freely to investors when things are going well but "clam up" when times are difficult?
15	Does the company have a management of unquestionable integrity?

What Happens When You Fail to Read Management?

A major reason why you shouldn't rely on or trust management too much is because reliance on management could be catastrophic. I cannot stress enough that investing is risky business. We have already learned that humans are psychologically programmed to be terrible lie detectors. If we rely on management too much, we will not be able to tell when we should no longer be relying on them. It could cloud our judgment on when to buy, hold, or sell a stock.

Let's look at a hypothetical example. You have developed a relationship with XYZ management team over the years and own the company's stock, which has outperformed the market in the time you owned it. You read one day there are potential accounting irregularities at XYZ Company. Naturally, you call management and ask them for their opinion about the rumors. The management responds with what appears to be a legitimate explanation of the accounting in question. You think, "Hey I have known this team for a long time." I will hold on to the stock. Here you are running into several of the previously mentioned psychological traps. You think to yourself the management has always been "honest." The short interest or number of investors taking a short position on the stock starts to increase and more data points come out about there being problems with the accounting. You talk to the management again. They assure you there are no problems. You think to yourself, "Well they can't be lying" with your cognitive biases remaining firmly in place. There is no other way to get the information you need to decide on the accounting issue, except from the management, so you continue to maintain a position in the stock. The next thing you know, you wake up one day to the headline of the stock depreciating −40% on the news the auditor resigned due to the accounting irregularities they just discovered. You would not be surprised to know. Investors continue to hold on to names even after multiple rounds of damaging news. Now investors are dealing with two additional cognitive biases: confirmation and sunk cost. Finally, it comes out that the management was misleading investors all along. The stock is down −250%. Now you hit the sell button. It is already too late to salvage the investment, but it may be too late to salvage your career as well.

The example above unfortunately happens all too many times. I have unfortunately seen many similar situations like it throughout my career including well-known frauds like Satyam and Longtop. When it comes to fraud, if management tries to deceive you, they will be successful! It often makes the most sense to sell or "punt" to use the football analogy "troubled" investments at the first sign of concern. The only way to obtain a high level of conviction on potentially "troubled" names is to verify the company's cash balances at their respective banks because at the end of the day cash is the only thing that is "truly" real from an accounting perspective. The company's auditors are responsible for verifying the cash balances, and even auditors can be deceived. It often will cost investors way too much of their valuable time in trying to deal with "problem" stocks, which is an added incentive to just sell or punt the stock.

Golden Rule: Punt (Sell) your troubled companies IMMEDIATELY!

I want to be clear here. When I say sell your troubled companies, I am referring to the companies facing possible fraud or other (ethical) questionable practices, which should not be confused with companies that are facing business challenges. Troubled companies not only present challenges, but they may also present opportunities. If you own a troubled company, you should sell it. You also have the option of shorting the stock if you have conviction that the magnitude of the problem will continue to put downward pressure on its share price. Shorting a stock is when an investor borrows shares and immediately sells them in the market hoping the investor can buy them at a lower price and return them to the lender while pocketing the difference. Short selling is generally considered to be risky and speculative, as a stock technically has no limitation on its potential appreciation.

The 1996 Kathryn F. Staley book *The Art of Short Selling* is the best book I have read on short selling. The author presents several examples of companies that have set out to deceive investors. My favorite example was Snapple, the juice beverage company. Snapple had rapid sales when it first hit the market. However, when sales slowed, the company would ship the product ahead of time and perhaps without demand, so it could book the product as revenue. Snapple was essentially "stuffing the channel." Short selling takes guts and requires high conviction, but it can result in a lucrative payoff.

Management Incentives

The incentive theory is the concept that people are pulled toward actions leading to rewards and pushed away from actions leading to negative consequences. In short, the theory leads us to believe people tend to do what they are incentivized to do. The same goes for management teams. In fact, you could argue, the individuals who make it to the C suite have figured out how to maximize their incentives. Investors can look at the information in the company's proxy filings and annual shareholder meetings for details regarding management's incentives (compensation). These documents provide a rough understanding of what the company and management value or focus on from a business performance perspective and what actions we can expect them to take to.

Our case study, Mastercard, has a detailed compensation plan that lines up to an extent with shareholder interests. The plan is short and long-term in nature based on adjusted net revenue and net income targets. We include a look at the management team and incentives in our sample company report.

Bottom Line on Managements

I believe there is a real difference in the quality of management, but ultimately, the success of any business is primarily dependent on the strength of its business model. Below-average management teams can appear successful if they are backed by a strong business model. The best management team can appear weak if it is supported by a poor business model. Regardless of the business model, the incentive structure helps guide these managements to make the right decisions assuming the incentives are aligned with shareholder values. I would encourage investors to meet with management. However, they should not put too much emphasis on their responses and keep in mind the cognitive biases I discussed earlier. Management will be most useful in furthering your understanding of a specific topic or issue.

Our analysis of this point brings us to the next Golden Rule below. As a reminder, the golden rules are all located in the Appendix.

Golden Rule: Go with Strength of Business When Deciding Between "The Good, Bad, & Ugly."

Factor 5: Psychology – "You Win Some, You Lose Some"

My first four factors are designed to provide a general framework for evaluating investment opportunities. We will eventually assign a point system to all our factors and apply them to our case study in the next section. With our general framework securely in place, we can add the final piece of the puzzle, which is psychology. The psychological category is to some degree separate from the others but is an invaluable addition to any investment process. In this section, I will look at the psychological aspect of investing and then build this knowledge into the investment process. I am reminded of Charlie Munger's two-step decision process: (1) Understand the forces at play, and (2) Understand how your subconscious might be leading you astray.

Behavioral Finance

Behavioral finance is a relatively new area of study that looks at how psychological influences can affect market decisions and outcomes. The origins of behavioral finance trace their roots back to the early 1900s with the 1912 publishing of *Psychology of the Stock Market* by G.C. (George Charles) Selden. Selden outlines in his book the "human" aspect of markets up and downs and explores the notion of how the mental state impacts the trader. There were numerous other complementary works from various authors to follow, but the subject remained unexplored for the next 50 years.

It wasn't until 1979 when Daniel Kahneman and Amos Tversky, two pioneers in the field, published their work, *Prospect Theory: A Study of Decision Making under Risk* that behavioral finance began to take off. Kahneman and Tversky's work looks at the flaws in human (investor) decision-making. They look at how investors are more likely to focus on the purchase price of a stock than calculating the universe of potential outcomes and choosing the most rational. Investors are inherently loss averse and willing to take on risk to protect their gains. Richard Thaler would soon join Kahneman and Tversky as a pioneer in the field of behavioral finance.

Is There Any Such Thing as a Stock Market Expert?

The reader should have a solid understanding around fundamental equity research at this point in our journey. The idea would be that like other vocations, by practicing the principles and processes you learn in this book, you would become an expert over time. Yet the statistics would tell you otherwise as fewer than 10% of active managers outperform the market. So, if practice makes perfect, then, "How come there aren't more expert stock pickers?"

The lack of stock picking expertise raises the question of whether anyone can become an expert stock picker. Maybe not. Daniel Kahneman in his 2011 book *Thinking, Fast & Slow* makes an interesting observation about experts. The most often cited example is the devotion of 10,000 hours to learning a skill should make a person an expert. There have been studies proving the development of expertise in chess using the 10,000-hour rule to be true. Kahneman would agree with the idea that a person can indeed become an expert. However, he believes expertise is limited to learning activities with **structured rules**. Financial analysts cannot be experts because the game they play (the stock market) may have defined rules everyone follows, but there is always the element of unknown risk making all predictions of the future outcomes riskier than they already appear. Financial expertise is a lot different than learning how to play a defined, rule-based game like chess or basketball or baseball.

Kahneman was awarded a noble prize in economics in 2002 for his work in behavioral finance. He essentially proved where he felt Bernoulli went wrong. Humans began measuring risk by using a weighted average of probabilities. Bernoulli did not believe the weighted average was the correct way to measure risk because, for example, a rich person would not miss $1 million as much as a poorer person. Bernoulli thus assigned weightings to risk. Kahneman took it one step further and said behaviorally humans are more concerned with loss on the margin, so they will act irrationally. Losses hurt two times as much as wins!

A Two-System Problem

Kahneman provides other observations that are helpful to incorporate into an investment process. He believes your thought process is separated into two systems. System 1 is known as the X-system. It is your reactionary (automatic) system. It can lead you to jump to conclusions. System 2 is known as your C System. System 2 is your logical system (reflective), which needs to be summoned to logically think through risk. He believes humans can avoid making mistakes based on inherent behavioral flaws by summoning System 2. He suggests taking a "You win some, you lose some approach" to investing. Investors can be more productive by using a broader framing approach, developing a risk threshold policy, and checking your finances once a quarter. Kahneman's suggestions begin to directly address Munger's second step. We will explore others way investors can protect themselves ironically from themselves as we make our way through our fifth factor (Table 7.6).

Cognitive Biases and Heuristics

We come to my favorite part of the book defining and recognizing cognitive flaws. These flaws are in the form of heuristics and biases. A heuristic is a mental shortcut that eases the cognitive load of decision-making. A cognitive bias is a systematic pattern of deviation from norm or rationality in judgment caused by heuristics. Although we are not conscious of the biases, we all have them, so they are consistent and widespread. These are fun, fascinating ideas. Some of the more common biases impacting investing include anchoring, confirmation, framing effect, fear of missing out (FOMO), gambler's fallacy, halo effect, herding, and loss aversion. It is a long list!

Table 7.6 Two System Thinking

System 1-Reactionary (Animal)	*System 2-Logical (Evolved)*
X-System	*C-System*
Parts of the Brain	
Amygdala	Anterior cingulate cortex
Basal ganglia	Prefrontal cortex
Lateral temporal cortex	Medial temporal lobe
Holistic	Analytic
Characteristics	
Affective (what feels good)	Logical
Associative	Deductive
Rapid parallel processing	Slow, serial processing
Concrete images	Abstract images
Slower to change	Changes with speed of thought
Broad generalizations	More highly differentiated
Context specific processing	More highly integrated
Experienced passively	Experienced actively and consciously
Automatic and effortless	Controlled and effortful
Self-evidently validity	Requires justification from logic

Source: Montier (Behavioral Investing); Epstein (1991) and DrkW Macro research.

A "Thoughtful" Example

Let's look at some of these biases at work in an example of an investor who is looking to make an investment like our Mastercard example. Let's say you are a typical investor looking for your next investment. You read an article published by a reputable source talking about how attractive a specific company is as a potentially good investment. You are naturally inclined to like the stock after reading the story because of the framing effect. You start to dive deeper into the research associated with the investment and find out the company has a commanding market share in the card market. Now you're even more excited due to the anchoring effect. You are a "rational," thoughtful investor, so you want to do more research. You see many positive attributes to the company including its expandable, addressable market and solid growth rates. You may now be experiencing confirmation bias and only selectively looking at the good pieces of information that comes across. Once the research is complete, you decide to talk to management. You find management to be very likeable. The company may be benefitting from the "Halo" Effect. You have enough information together and decide you like the stock for purely "objective" reason. You start by calling other investors who have already made a lot of money owning Mastercard. There is a FOMO. The stock keeps going up every day as it becomes evident all investors like the name. The group think is leading to a herd mentality. You now think, "Well maybe I should wait. The stock can't go up forever!" as in the gambler's fallacy. You wait to buy the stock on a down day, but while you are waiting it goes up for 20 straight days and moves 20% higher. You finally give in and buy the stock and sure enough right after the purchase it finally goes down 10% and you are suffering from loss aversion as it hurts twice as much. Are you exhausted yet from this example? You should be! Let's explore these biases and make suggestions on how to improve our own investment process.

What's the Solution to Our Biases?

James Montier's 2007 book *Behavioural Investing: A Practitioner's Guide to Applying Behavioural Finance* and his 2010 book *The Little Book of Behavioral Investing,* which we would recommend, provide the reader with a helpful road map to understanding our inherent biases. Montier picks up to some degree where Kahneman left off discussing the conflicts between investing and human's two system brains.

Inability to Override System 1 (System X)

Montier believes humans are wired for the short term. Our natural tendency is unfortunately toward System 1, as our self-control is a muscle, which gets worn out, making it difficult to "override our emotional reactions." In his Practitioner's Guide, he cites the work of social psychologist Roy Baumeister (2003). Baumeister conducted an experiment designed to test self-control by asking participants to skip lunch. These participants were then divided up, and some were tempted to eat sweets, while others were not. The different groups were then given problems to solve. The net result was those participants who used up their self-control to resist the sweets gave up on the problems quicker than those who had reserves. Montier found Baumeister's (2003) key finding very applicable to investors:

1 **Emotional distress** causes people to shift toward favoring high-risk, high-payoff options, even if these are objectively poor choices.
2 **Threats to self-esteem** cause people to become upset and lose their ability to self-regulate. Individuals with high opinions of themselves are especially susceptible. They will rush to prove something great about themselves.
3 **Self-regulation** is a limited resource, which can be used up. Self-regulation is important to make good long-term decisions. A lack of self-regulation leads to instant gratification decisions.
4 **Decision-making** is a limited resource. Having to make too many **important decisions** can lead to fatigue, which in turn leads to bad decisions, like self-regulation.
5 **Belonging** is a key to human existence. Humans react poorly to rejection with irrational and self-defeating acts.

Montier goes on to compare contrarian strategies to the investment strategy of seeking out social pain. He combines this with research on the part of Eisenberg and Lieberman comparing the following of the contrarian strategy with the equivalent of having your arm broken!

Suggestions

Montier helps us narrow the list of bias and heuristics to the ones that most readily apply to investors. He then provides suggestions to help us navigate this dangerous world.

There are a couple of examples he gives, which I experienced first-hand as fundamental equity analysts. My experience and "success" over my many years as an analyst left me exposed to overconfidence, self-attribution, and hindsight bias and the regency effect. One suggestion to overcome this bias may be to keep an investment notebook or journal where you can write down why you bought the stock to confirm if your original thesis was correct or if it was lucky. It will help in clearing up the challenges associated with hindsight, self-attribution bias.

A key piece of information you may want to keep in the investment journal would be your exact potential entry and exit points on a stock. Like our section on the speculators, Montier suggests presetting specific entry and exit points on a stock when you initiate a position. If the investor does this before investing, they may be better positioned to overcome any emotional or X system biases that may crop up. It allows us to keep in mind the power of loss aversion. It is important to sell the losers, which may be easier to do with entry and exit points. I believe it may be helpful to track other things in the investment notebook like cost basis, changes in valuation, and stock performance. It may even make sense to chart out the changes in investment thesis and intrinsic values on a quarterly or annual basis.

There are other interesting takeaways from Montier's works. Montier makes the point that more information is not necessarily better, but investors seek more information because it gives the illusion of control. He suggests focusing on a couple of key factors when investing. We have provided our version of those key components to focus on with our five factors. As a side note, there were many times during our research where we felt we were trying to learn EVERYTHING about a company when really the 80/20 rule was probably good enough.

We all suffer from confirmation bias, which is we are looking for information to confirm our theory, rather than contrarian views. The sell side has what is known as "consensus buys," which are stocks all analysts tend to believe are good companies to own. Instead of listening to analysts, who share the consensus views to feed our confirmation bias we should have been searching for out of consensus or opposite views, so we can check these alternative views vs. our potential investment thesis.

Anchoring is a constant challenge, especially around setting forecasts and price targets or intrinsic values. An analyst typically comes up with forward forecasts and price targets influenced by guidance and consensus and where the stocks were trading after seeing the company's stock price movements over a longer period. Montier would suggest not using forward forecasts at all from an estimate perspective. He would suggest reverse engineering the current stock price to find the implicit growth rate expectations to see if they match the company's ability to deliver results (Tables 7.7 and 7.8).

Table 7.7 Common Flaws in Investor Thinking

Heuristic or Bias	*Montier's Thoughts*
Overconfidence bias	*Be less certain in your views, especially if they are forecasts* *You know less than you think you do*
Illusion of control	*More information isn't better information* *Try to focus on the facts, not stories*
Confirmation bias	*Listen to those who disagree with you*
Self-attribution bias	*Examine your successes and mistakes, failures aren't just bad luck*
Hindsight bias	*You didn't know it all along, you just think you did*
Anchoring	*Reverse Engineer Market Prices for growth and see if they make sense*
Representativeness heuristic	*Judge things by how statistically likely they are, not how they appear*
Regency effect	*Don't overweight personal experience*
Framing	*Don't take information at face value; think carefully about how it is presented*
Loss aversion	*Sell your loser and ride your winners*
Endowment effect	*Don't value something more because you own it*

Source: Montier, Behavioral Finance.

Table 7.8 Overcoming Investment Bias and Heuristics

Montier Suggestions
– Decide your entry and exit points on a stock before buying them to avoid emotional X system responses
– Keep an investment notebook so you can check your thinking to address self-affirmation and hindsight bias
– Use trailing estimates and reverse engineered current price growth rates to address anchoring issues
– Focus on just a few key factors (Foresi Factors) as you don't need all the information-Illusion of Information
– Seek out those who disagree with you, rather than those who agree to avoid confirmation bias
– Skip talking to management, it may only skew your judgment. You may fall victim to the Halo Effect, among others
– Only invest when you find something compelling, avoiding the bias to action

Source: Montier, Behavioral Finance.

Everyone Can Use a Little "Nudge"

Richard Thaler and Cass Sunstein in their 2008 book "Nudge" attempt to provide a solution to the problem of everyday cognitive bias. Their solution is *libertarian paternalism*. Thaler and Sunstein believe people can be "nudged" through the arrangement of choice architectures in a way allowing them to maintain their freedom of choice, while still guiding or "nudging" them toward the optimal choices. The authors use the need for individuals to save more for retirement, as an area where a "nudge" could be used. The "nudge" would be to create better default retirement plans or a "Save More Tomorrow" plan, which would have default features like automatically saving more when you get a pay raise. The "nudge" idea is not without controversy, but the good news is it starts a conversation about finding a solution for overcoming inherent cognitive flaws. I hope by following the methodologies of this book, the author is "nudging" you toward the correct investment process. Thaler himself is trying to put his ideas to work in the investment process through his firm, Fuller and Thaler Asset Management.

Addressing Our Psychological Flaws

I believe the psychological battle to protect ourselves from ourselves when investing is a perpetual one. I would address the challenges associated with these flaws in a couple of ways. First, I believe investors must have the proper mindset, which is developed over years of training. The proper investor mindset is skeptical and contrarian in nature. Just be careful to separate this mindset from your personal life. Second, I would create a checklist of biases to go through before making an investment.

Finally, I would create an investment notebook designed to protect us against our inherent biases. An investment notebook has a thesis, establishes an entry and exit point, and provides a contrarian opinion. It essentially keeps the investor "honest" and protects against some of the psychological biases. We would use company earnings results and news to test, revise, and/or change our thesis.

The Five Factors

Wall Street is littered with the remnants of failed investment approaches due to the dynamic nature of the market, a trend I expect to continue. I have introduced the reader here to our five-factor approach, which addresses the problem by changing the focus from the latest Wall Street fad to the study of how stocks work. My method shifts attention to developing a deep understanding of the anatomy of a stock and using it to identify the stocks best positioned to succeed.

The hardest thing about doing equity research is getting started. I typically begin with trying to get a foundational understanding of a company by gathering the basic qualitative and quantitative information. I suggest organizing the qualitative research into the basic sections of a standard equity research report such as basic information, business description, etc. The quantitative historical information can be divided into the income statement, balance sheet, cash flow statement, and converted into an excel model along with the relevant financial ratios. The process is known as modeling and will take practice to get better at. I note modeling is important, but not crucial as you are predicting the future.

The key question throughout this process is, "How does this company make money?" The answer to this question and its sustainability over the long term is at the crux of every investment thesis. You will come across two or three very important questions for a given company while researching its business. Your ability to add value to these questions will make a difference in making a good or bad investment decision. Most of your efforts should be spent on these value-added sections.

Once we have a foundational understanding of a business, we can then perform our Foresi Five Factor analysis. We believe there are currently five factors making up the anatomy of a stock: competitive advantages, catalysts, valuation, quality of management, and psychology, which can be used to measure the attractiveness of any opportunity.

- A well-positioned company must have a discernable, sustainable competitive advantage and moat, which in our opinion is the hardest thing to find.
- Investors should focus on identifying companies that have a long-term, sustainable catalyst, which can come in the form of changes in the demand outlook, profitability, and/or capital allocation.
- Valuation is an art, not a science. We use a mosaic approach to valuation utilizing intrinsic and relative methods. Investors should try to purchase stock at a favorable price or entry point. The probability of successfully achieving this objective can be enhanced by building a margin of safety regardless of the valuation approach.
- It is important to have a high-quality, trustworthy management team, but often the ultimate success of a business comes down to the strength of its business model and strategy.
- Psychology plays a major role in the investment decision-making process. It is important to be aware of the psychological challenges. I recommend developing the best practices like an investment notebook to use the psychological challenges to your advantage and protect against them.

Remember it is about identifying the factors, developing a process, and testing and revising the process on our quest for the next "Forever Stock."

Bibliography

Bradenburger, A. M., & Nalebuff, B. J. (1996). *Co-opetition.* Crown Business.
Damodaran, A. (1996). *Damodaran on Valuation.* John Wiley & Sons.
Damodaran, A. (2011). *The Little Book of Valuation.* John Wiley & Sons.
Dorsey, P. (2008). *The Little Book That Builds Wealth.* John Wiley & Son.
Fisher, P. A. (1958). *Common Stocks and Uncommon Profits.* John Wiley & Sons.
Fleisher, C. S., & Bensoussan, B. E. (2007). *Business and Competitive Analysis.* Pearson Education.
Gladwell, M. (2019). *Talking to Strangers.* Little, Brown and Company.

Graham, B. (Revised 2006). *The Intelligent Investor*. Harper Business.
Kahneman, D. (2011). *Thinking, Fast and Slow.* Farrar, Straus and Giroux.
Kahneman, D., & Tversky, A. (1979, March). Prospect theory: An analysis of decision under risk. *Econometrica, 47*(2), 263–292.
Montier, J. (2007). *Behavioural Investing.* John Wiley & Sons.
Montier, J. (2010). *The Little Book of Behavioural Investing.* John Wiley & Sons.
Navarro, J. (2008). *What Every BODY Is Saying.* Harper-Collins.
O'Glove, T. L. (1987). *Quality of Earnings.* The Free Press.
Porter, M. E. (1980). *Competitive Strategy.* Free Press.
Rappaport, A., & Mauboussin, M. J. (2001). *Expectations Investing.* Harvard Business School Publishing.
Selden, G. C. (1912). *Psychology of the Stock Market.* Ticker Publishing Company.
Staley, K. F. (1997). *The Art of Short Selling.* John Wiley & Sons.
Thaler, R. H., & Sunstein, C. R. (2008). *Nudge.* Yale University Press.

Chapter 8

Art of Valuation

Close Is Close Enough

We are incorrectly taught from an early age that there is winning and there is losing and really no in between. The value of winning is reinforced physically, psychologically, and socially. Physically, winning produces testosterone, which converts into the pleasure chemical dopamine making us feel better. Psychologically, the "winner effect" is a biological term describing how an animal that has won a few bouts against weak opponents is likely to then win against stronger opponents. Socially, we praise and hold winners in high esteem. They rank higher in our social hierarchy. The need to win has driven us to precisely measure and judge outcomes.

The same need for precision ironically is not the case in determining intrinsic valuation. Valuation is more art than science. It is at best an approximation of a current but moving target. The art of valuation has more similarities with games like horseshoes, golf, archery, and darts, where although the objective is to hit the center of the target, there are points for being close, then winner takes all games like basketball and baseball. It may have been the famous hall of fame baseball player Frank Robinson who said, "Close only counts in horseshoes and hand grenades." However, in the investing world, we follow the advice of Warren Buffett who said, "It is better to be approximately right than precisely wrong." Finding intrinsic valuation is about being close enough.

I view valuation as one of my five factors crucial to determining the success of an investment opportunity. There are two different methods for determining valuation: intrinsic and relative. Most investors prefer the Discounted Cash Flow (DCF) method when applicable. The following chapter is a detailed review of the different types of valuation methods and their application to our example companies. I finish this chapter by reviewing what valuation method to use depending on the stage of the company life cycle.

Intrinsic Valuation Methods

Discounted Cash Flows

The foundation of the DCF model is the theory behind the present value of money. The present value of money is a method for figuring out what the value of future cash flow generation is in today's terms. There are various risks to future cash flow including giving up the present purchasing capabilities, inflation, and the possibility that the future cash flow may not materialize. The method of figuring out present value is known as discounting with the discount rate accounting for the uncertainty associated with the future. Theoretically, the longer the period, the more uncertain the cash flow, the lower the present value. We will need to familiarize ourselves with the different types of inputs used in deriving intrinsic value including cash flows, cost of equity and debt, and growth.

DOI: 10.4324/9781003686644-11

Different Types of Cash Flows

There are different types of cash flows. These cash flows include annuities and perpetuities. An annuity is a consistent cash flow over a specified period. Cash flows can come at the end of a period, known as an ordinary annuity, or at the beginning of a period, known as an annuity due.

A perpetuity is a cash flow happening at regular intervals forever. There is a type of perpetuity known as a growing perpetuity, which is essentially a cash flow that grows forever. The growth rate of a growing perpetuity must be less than the discount rate, the rate of return used to discount the cash flows back to present value. The growth rate must be slower than the economy, since no growth rate can grow faster than the rate of the economy forever. You may recall that the goal of our earlier company-specific forecasting efforts was to estimate out Mastercard's cash flow, which can then be used in combination with other inputs mentioned below to derive its valuation.

The Cost of Capital

I discussed earlier how important capital is to an organization. Capital is the life blood of organizations or an economy, which cannot survive without it. If capital is the life blood, then cash flow is the air. Capital can come in the form of equity or debt. We can measure the cost of capital, equity (Capital Asset Pricing Model or CAPM) or debt (Weighted Average Cost of Capital or WACC), the required rate of return for the capital, and the returns on equity and capital (Return on Equity or ROE, Return on Capital or ROC).

Cost of Capital (Equity)

Let's review the risk models. The primary model for measuring risk is the CAPM, one of the most important concepts in finance. The "CAPM," as the model is often referred to, relates the Expected Return of an Asset or Cost of Equity to a Risk-Free Rate plus the Beta of the Asset multiplied by its risk premium or the market risk above the risk-free rate. The risk-free rate is the rate of a long-term bond. Beta can be either historical, fundamental, or accounting and essentially measures the volatility of the asset vs. the market. The risk premium would be either a historical premium or an implied premium. The historical premium is the geometric average of 4.84%, earned by stocks over treasury bonds between 1928 and 2004, according to Damodaran. The CAPM's flaws are that it fails to fully capture the impact to small firms and privately held businesses.

The CAPM is the most popular way of measuring the cost of equity. Other ways of measuring the cost of equity include looking at the return differences across stocks over long periods of time and backing out the implied cost of equity from stock prices. The equation would be the dividend divided by the stock price plus the growth rate. The assumption in finding the cost of equity is from the perspective of the marginal investor, who is assumed to be well diversified, and cannot diversify away the equity risk.

Cost of Capital (Debt)

The cost of debt is the rate at which firms can borrow money today depending on the default risk embedded in the business. Default risk can be measured either through bond rating or by looking at financial ratios. Tax advantages from tax-deductible interest expense will reduce the after-tax cost of borrowing. The cost of capital is known as the WACC.

The Weighted Average Cost of Capital is the weighted average sum of its total value of the required rate of return on its: debt tax adjusted for interest expense plus preferred stock plus the cost of equity.

Table 8.1 Financial Analysts-Valuation Component's Tool Set[a]

Present Value	*Capital Measurement*	*Capital Efficiency*	*Growth*
Present value	Cost of equity	Return on equity	Growth
Annuities	Capital asset pricing model	Equity reinvestment	Retention rate
Perpetuity	Cost of debt	Reinvestment rate	
Growth perpetuity	Weighted average cost of capital	Return on capital	

[a] See Appendix for formulas and on individual topics for examples.

Stewards of Capital

It is possible to measure a firm's ROE and capital to get a sense of how efficient they are at managing capital as we discussed earlier. ROE is the amount of net income returned as a percentage of shareholder equity. It essentially measures how efficient the company is making use of the investments in the business. There are different methods for measuring ROE including the DuPont Analysis. All companies are investing capital at a specific rate or equity reinvestment rate. The return on capital or ROC or ROIC is the amount of net income returned as a percentage of total capital. It is a very important formula as it measures how efficiently a company is allocating capital under its control to generate returns. It can be compared to the WACC to get a sense of whether the company is using capital efficiently.

We Can Use These Concepts to Find Growth (g)

The formula presented above can be used to derive a growth rate for the business. Growth rates can be derived either through multiplying the retention rate by the ROE or the reinvestment rate by the ROC. These growth rates can be used in different valuation models. Investors can back into a growth rate known as the implied growth rate used by the market given by reverse engineering the formula using the current stock price (Table 8.1).

DCF Valuation Methods

There are different methods of valuing equity through DCF). These methods include the Dividend Discount Model (DDM), Free Cash Flow to Equity (FCFE), and Free Cash Flow to Firm (FCFF). The DDM is the oldest method based on dividends, which are the only thing investors can "really" lay claim to. FCFE works in much the same manner as DDM but uses FCF assumptions. DDM methods tend to yield a lower valuation compared to the FCFE. The challenge of using FCFE is that it's often difficult to compute.

How Do You Decide What DCF Model Works for You?

I would reiterate Damodaran's belief that investors should use the easiest valuation method. The information a company provides often dictates what valuation method can be used. I would recommend looking at a company from an intrinsic and relative valuation perspective. The DDM model should be used when the company has a dividend history and policy as it relates to earnings. Investors typically use an FCF model when the company being valued lacks the dividend characteristics.

FCF valuation methods are helpful in companies where FCF has an impact on profitability. Our experience has been that FCF valuations are used more often than the actual dividends when deriving valuations. There are different ways to find relative valuation, which we will look at shortly.

Dividend Discount Method (DDM)

The DDM uses dividends and their growth rates to determine valuation. The value of the stock is the expected dividends divided by the cost of equity minus the growth rate. The different DDM models include constant growth, Gordon Growth Model (GGM), and/or multistage growth models. Investors should use the stability of the expected growth rate to determine which model to use. The constant growth model is used for companies that pay constant dividends. The growth rate in the constant growth model should be interchangeable with earnings. The GGM assumes a perpetual dividend growth rate, which is typical of mature companies. The multi-stage growth model can be used for unstable growth rates. Multistage growth models can be either one stage, two stage, or three stage, a combination of the two stage and H stage model.

DDMs have positives and negatives. The positives of the DDM method are that it uses dividends, which investors can lay claim to. Dividends are sustainable and easier to forecast than FCF. The negatives are that dividends ignore claims to cash balances and FCF and overvalues the use of debt to pay dividends. The DDM is most useful when it forms a baseline valuation for firms whose FCFE exceeds dividends. The DDM is useful for mature companies that pay dividends and when it is difficult to make FCF estimates. The cost of equity and growth components are sensitive. It is important to remember as the gap between the two (cost of equity and growth) widens; the value of stocks falls and vice versa. A critical assumption of the DDM is that the growth rate can never exceed the cost of equity, or the math will not work. We note investors may choose to modify the DDM by adding stock buy backs. There are different formulas for handling different dividend situations based on changes in growth rate or valuation period.

Free Cash Flow to Equity (FCFE)

FCFE is a general version of the DDM. An important distinction of the FCFE is it substitutes potential dividends for actual dividends. There are advantages to the FCFE valuation. Investors are no longer bound to dividend policy itself. It is especially effective for firms that are under paying their dividends, as a result FCFE will typically have a higher valuation vs. DDM. FCFE can be negative due to the complications in determining the FCFE because of a changing capital structure. FCFE valuations work much in the same way the DDM works in they can be single and multi-stage. Warren Buffett's "owner's earnings" calculation ignores the net cash flow from debt making it a more conservative version of cash flow to equity.

Free Cash Flow to Firm (FCFF)

FCFF is the amount available after expenses and reinvestments. Both FCFE and FCFF represent the cash flow after taxes and reinvestment and can be negative. However, the main difference between FCFF and FCFE is that FCFF is before debt cash flows, whereas FCFE is after accounting for debt. FCFF calculates the amount available to equity and debt holders, as opposed to FCFE, whose calculation is for just equity holders. You typically start with operating earnings instead of net income when calculating FCFF subtracting out taxes and reinvestment. Like other calculations,

Table 8.2 Financial Analysts Valuation Method Tool Set[a]

Intrinsic Value		*Relative Value*	
Dividend Discount Model		*Price Multiples*	
Single period	FCFE	Price/earnings (P/E)	Price/sales (P/S)
Gordon growth model (GGM)	FCFF	Leading P/E	Price/CF (P/CF)
Multi period		Trailing P/E	EV/EBITDA
Residual income model	RIM	Price/book (P/B value)	

[a] See Appendix for formulas. We walk through a step-by-step example of the Valuation method in Appendix VI.

a common challenge FCFF faces is the debate over what does and does not belong in the calculation and if companies are representing the inputs accurately. Tables 8.2 and 8.3 contain the different types of DDM methods.

Example of Intrinsic Valuation

After looking at the different inputs and calculation formulas, we are now ready to find the intrinsic value of a company. We will look at the company from both an intrinsic and relative value standpoint. It's worth noting that using the intrinsic method to derive valuation can be complicated leading to potential errors, which brings us to another golden rule.

Golden Rule-keep valuation methods as simple as possible.

The process of finding intrinsic value is a three-step process. Step 1 is to estimate out the FCF for the next ten years, which I performed in my forecasting section. Step 2 is to figure out the inputs like cost of equity, debt, and growth. Step 3 is to perform the calculation by discounting back the cash flows for each year and coming up with a terminal value, which will be discounted back to present value. I provide my step-by-step method for calculating FCFE and FCFF in Appendix VI. I encourage readers to go to Appendix VI, which contains a complete step-by-step calculation of intrinsic value for our example company. We have now established our three-, five-, and ten-year intrinsic value based on DCF. Our five-year DCF calculation results in an intrinsic value of $377 with the stock trading at roughly $350 at the time of the calculation, a sub 10% premium. Not too much to get excited about.

The result of our efforts leads us to believe Mastercard is fairly valued from an intrinsic value perspective, at least in the short term. However, if you take a longer-term view and use the ten-year intrinsic value of $485. It implies there is still +35% upside to the stock over the long term. I would build in a margin of safety on the $485 intrinsic value, putting the real buying opportunity somewhere in the roughly $350 range. I encourage investors to make their own assumptions regarding future forecasts once the historical and future estimates are inputted into an excel model. These calculations led me to the conclusion that there is a considerable amount of upside to the stock, especially if the long-term growth assumption is higher than expected!

Residual Income Valuation Method

The residual income model (RIM) is another method used to derive an intrinsic value for a company. Although I did not use this valuation method in the case study in the book, it deserves mention and possible future consideration as a viable intrinsic valuation method. The RIM substitutes the incremental income a company generates for FCF and discounts it back to present value. RIM is better known in the academic community than Wall Street, who use DCF. I believe there is merit to using RIM. My doctoral thesis, "Valuations Role in the Investment Process" (https://digitalcommons.uri.edu/oa_diss/1667/) studied the forecasting abilities of different intrinsic and relative valuations to forecast stock performance for S&P500 companies over a ten-year period. The study found that the Residual Income Method had the highest predictive power among the intrinsic valuation methods and refining the inputs to the model has a positive impact on its outcome.

Relative Valuation Methods

We turn our attention to our second valuation method known as relative valuation. Relative valuation is a market-based method of comparing similar companies to see if there are any opportunities. Relative valuation is a quicker, easier calculation than intrinsic value, thus it tends to be used more often. We turn our attention once again to Damodaran who highlights for the reader in *The Little Book of Valuation* three steps in relative valuation: (1) Find comparable assets priced by the market, (2) Scale the market prices to common variable to generate standardized prices comparisons, and (3) Adjust for differences across assets when comparing their standard values.

Different Relative Valuation Comparison Options

There are several different ways to compare companies from a relative valuation perspective. I will touch on a few of these valuation comparisons using Mastercard. Relative valuations can be impacted by variables like overall market fluctuations and/or aggressive financial accounting. A stock price may experience a large spike or short-term price appreciation or depreciation at any moment. These movements are based on increased investor expectations around potential short-term catalysts like the announcement of a new offering. Short-term stock movements (appreciation or depreciation) rarely have to do with a fundamental change in the business.

Investors' irrational enthusiasm or disappointment is captured by stock price trading levels and relative valuation. Managements are unfortunately incentivized to "stretch" or manipulate accounting practices to inflate or deflate metrics to position the company well from a valuation perspective. I would argue that the shift to the use of "Non-GAAP" reported numbers opened the door to further accounting manipulations negatively impacting the average investors. The problem is compounded by the fact that psychologically speaking humans tend to take mental short cuts and often just accept the reported "Non-GAAP" number as being valid because it would take too much mental energy to sort through the financial statements looking for potential accounting irregularities. The challenges don't stop there. If a sell-side analyst's estimate does not conform to consensus, their estimate can be excluded and/or worse, they could lose their job! The system needs reform, but the good news is there is an inherent advantage to the long-term, value-oriented, patient investor who is willing to do their homework.

Price Multiples

There are a variety of different price multiples. One of the most common metrics is the P/E or Price/Earnings ratio. P/E's can be either leading, which looks at the next 12 months forecasted EPS, or trailing, which looks at the previous 12 months. Leading P/E's tend to be the valuation metric of choice. As previously mentioned, the P/E ratio can be skewed by Price appreciation, which captures irrational behavior, and aggressive accounting practices on the part of management impacting Earnings. Below is a list of Price Multiples.

Build a "P/E" Context

The method for calculating P/E ratios appears simple, but multiples should be put into context and effort made to ensure the investor is using accurate comparisons. Investors should build a comparison or "comp" group. A comp group includes a group of similar companies, so the investor can put into perspective how expensive or inexpensive a stock is vs. its competition. Investors should look at the historical multiple ranges to get a sense as to how expensive the stock is vs. the past. Finally, investors should look carefully at the comparison of the multiples to make sure the companies being compared are reporting their earnings results in a similar manner, so it is a fair comparison.

Let's take a closer look at our Mastercard example through its comparison or comp table. Click here for a complete relative valuation comparison table. I began the table by including the key variables, price and forward earnings per share for 2020, 2021, and 2022. I included my forecasts instead of consensus for Mastercard, which I have already built into the financial model. The next step is to find the comparisons for Mastercard. There are both direct and indirect comparisons. Mastercard's direct competitor is Visa, which I include in the comp. The broader comparative or comp is our roughly defined FinTech industry.

We can get a better context for Mastercard's P/E multiple by looking at the comparison. Mastercard is trading at a P/E in the mid to high 30× multiple (39× 2021). The 39× P/E multiple is an 8% premium to Visa, which trades at 36× 2021. The premium in relation to the FinTech group and overall market is even larger. Mastercard trades at almost a 100% premium to the market with the S&P500 trading at a P/E of 20× 2021. Historically, Mastercard has traded in a P/E range of 16× to 38× over the last ten years with a five year average P/E of 34×. The bottom line is no matter how you look at it. Mastercard is trading at a rich premium, which is another way of saying it is expensive.

What Multiples Should We Use?

There is no definitive answer to this question. Any answer is primarily opinion based, which is what makes investing so difficult. There has been an attempt to ground price multiples in fundamentals such as cost of equity, growth, etc. rather than let them be solely market determined. A justified multiple is the estimated fair value or intrinsic value for the multiple based on forecasted fundamentals. The challenge with justified multiples is they are only as good as their inputs, which can vary. Justified multiples can diverge tremendously from their solely market-based counterpart.

Here, we run into another one of our problems. A justified P/E for Mastercard can be found by dividing its payout ratio (20.6%) by its cost of equity (5.83%) minus its growth (3%). If we follow the math, the multiple for Mastercard should be 7×! However, we know the market is putting a 39× P/E multiple on it, which doesn't make sense. These types of inconsistencies are the norm when we try to mathematically derive a target P/E. If we hold the payout ratio (20.6%) and cost of equity (5.83%) constant with our assumptions, we can back into a growth rate of 5.3% to get 39×, which is higher than the 4.7% financial growth rate we found and the 3% growth rate we are using.

We have learned a couple of important data points regarding Mastercard. We know the terminal growth rate is probably in the range of +3%–5%, but we get dramatically different valuation some astronomically high if we use the upper end of this range, so our growth rate assumptions are crucial. We know Mastercard is trading at a premium to its direct peer (Visa) and at the upper end of its historical trading range. Let's keep filling in the picture with other relative valuation metrics to get a better sense of how Mastercard matches up.

Enterprise Value (EV)/Earnings before Interest Taxes Depreciation and Amortization (EBITDA)

We take a look at a second valuation metric known as EV/EBITDA. Investors sometimes prefer the EV/EBITDA valuation metric to the P/E because they believe it is less likely to be manipulated. It can be applied across a larger group of companies as earnings can sometimes be erratic or even negative, which is something I will discuss shortly. If we perform the calculation for our sample company Mastercard, the net result is a ratio of 40× EV/EBITDA 2020. If we use our 2021 and 2022 EBITDA estimates, we get 31× and 28× (Click Here for Example).

The relative valuation comparison table includes EV/EBITDA. I included my forecasts instead of a consensus for Mastercard. I am hoping to get a better perspective on relative valuation by using a second metric. Mastercard is trading at a low 30× EV/EBITDA multiple (31× 2021). The 31× multiple is a 10% premium to Visa, which trades at 29× 2021. Historically, Mastercard has traded in an EV/EBITDA range of 16× to 38× over the last five year with an average EV/EBITDA of 23×. Our second relative metric appears to be consistent with the conclusions of the first metric, which is that Mastercard is richly priced.

Price to Cash Flow (P/CF)

We take a look at our third and final relative valuation metric I will use for Mastercard the Price divided by P/CF per share. The Price to Cash flow valuation metric adds another dimension to the P/E, EV/EBITDA metrics previously mentioned. Cash flow is potentially more difficult to manipulate than earnings and EBITDA. If we divide the price per share from the cash flow per share, the Price to Cash Flow per share is: $357/$8.03 or 44× for 2021. The P/CF for Mastercard for 2020 is 56× and 2022 is 39×.

Our Mastercard three-point relative valuation comparison is now complete. The table below contains comparisons on a forward P/E, EV/EBITDA, and P/CF basis. We have included our estimates for Mastercard. The company is trading in the mid-40× P/CF (44× 2021). The 44× multiple is an 18% premium to Visa, which trades at 36.7×. Historically, Mastercard has traded in a P/CF range of 23× to 55× over the last five year average P/CF of 34×. All three of our relative valuation metric appear to be consistent, Mastercard is richly priced.

Valuation Methods Change throughout a Business Life Cycles

Mastercard has attractive company-specific characteristics like positive earnings and healthy FCF generation allowing investors to use standard valuation methods. However, "What does an investor do when run into issues like negative earnings? Or no cash flow? When trying to value a company?" The answer is there are different intrinsic and relative valuation methods, which can be used during the different stages of a business's life cycle: introductory, growth, maturity, and decline. We turn again to Damodaran whose provides guidance for valuations in the different stages of a business's life cycle in *The Little Book of Valuation.*

Golden Rule-Companies characteristics dictate what valuation can be used.

Introductory Stage

The introductory stage of a business' life cycle is the most difficult from a valuation perspective in my opinion. I believe it contains the most unknowns. A company in the 1st stage of its business life cycle has little or no historical record, small revenues, and high operating losses. The company probably does not have any cash flow. An investor focused on finding the value of a company in this stage would need to estimate revenue, operating profit, and cash flow. General assumptions regarding market penetration, industry reinvestment rates, and taxes can be used to come up with these estimates. To find an intrinsic value, a discount rate can be found using industry rate assumptions with perhaps a premium given the age and risk of the company. Damodaran suggests putting a discount on the terminal value of the firm based on the business's potential failure rate. He suggests estimating out the business over a period and then applying a discount based on the slower growth rates and the business' chance of failure to find the relative valuation.

I utilize a Price to Sale or P/S valuations for startup or early-stage firms. The positives to using a P/S ratio is sales are hard to manipulate and perhaps not as volatile as other metrics. The drawbacks to the P/S ratio are that sales recognition can vary, it doesn't account for different cost structures, and sales do not always translate into profits or cash flows. Like other price multiples, there is a fundamental approach to finding a justified Price to Sales Multiples.

Growth Stage

The challenges associated with valuing an asset tend to change as we move to the company's growth stage from its introductory stage. There is a debate on what constitutes a growth company, but we believe the definition of a growth company relates to the acceleration or above-average revenue growth a company displays for a sustainable period, as new companies rapidly take market share. Growth and growth rates are then expected to moderate. One of the challenges of valuing a growth company is handling the margin profile after growth moderates. Theoretically, the margins profile should expand as growth moderates due to a declining rate of investment. Damodaran would suggest forecasting estimates and variables through the moderation of the growth phase to determine intrinsic value.

I typically use Price to Earnings (P/E) multiples and P/E over Growth (PEG) for growth stage companies when looking at relative valuation. Companies must have positive earnings to establish a PE ratio. The challenge with the ratio is earnings can be manipulated, which makes it difficult to make fair or an "apples to apples" company comparison. PE ratios are sometimes used in conjunction with PEG, which is PE divided by earnings growth. A PEG below 1.0 is often considered desirable, while over 1.0 implies a rich valuation. There are justified formulas for figuring out leading and trailing PE as well.

Maturity Stage

The maturity stage of a business provides different valuation options. Mature businesses deliver stable growth (GDP plus Growth) and margins. Companies generate healthy FCF, so capital allocation is part of their valuation either through acquisitions or returning it to shareholders through dividend and stock buyback. There are multiple challenges associated with valuation including a deterioration of core organic growth rates and measuring the impact and performance of acquisitions. Damodaran suggests looking at changing capital allocation programs and potential changes in management when thinking about valuing mature businesses. He believes and I agree it is about the management being able to maximize the firm's potential through the various options presented to them. There are multiple relative valuation options available to investors given the large amount of information available for mature companies.

I have used formulas like EV/EBITDA and P/CF for my relative valuation comparison of mature companies. Both formulas depend on inputs like Cash Flow and EBITDA, which are theoretically harder to manipulate than Earnings Per Share (EPS). The challenge with using EBITDA is that several companies report an "Adjusted" EBITDA, which skews the number usually in the management's favor from multiple perspectives. Depreciation expenses can be manipulated. The problem with cash flow calculations is they can be lumpy. We looked at these specific metrics when performing a relative valuation on my example company. I would encourage readers to check out our EV/EBITDA and P/CF formulas and examples.

Declining Stage

A company in the declining stage of its business life cycle most likely has plenty of the metrics Necessary to perform different valuations. We have now seen the life cycle of a business: Introductory, growth, maturity, and decline. Mature companies are marked by declining growth rates (potentially below GDP and inflation) compared to rapid growth in the growth stage and moderate growth in the mature stage. The slowing growth rates can have a negative impact on margins. As opposed to growth companies who are looking to add to their business through acquisitions, mature companies are looking to divest their assets (remember "Creative Destruction") and pay high dividends or buy back stock. Declining businesses may even be looking at bankruptcy. Damodaran notes the long-term growth rates, whether the company will improve or

Table 8.3 Different Approaches to Valuation through the Business Life Cycle

Stage	*Business Life Cycle*	*Characteristics*	*Damodaran Intrinsic Valuation*	*Relative Valuation*
1	Introduction	Small revs; operating losses	Est. revs, EPS, cash flow; discount business for possible failure	Price/sales (P/S); forward forecasts and discount for slower growth and failure
2	Growth	Accelerated arbitrarily high growth rates with profits; then moderation	Est. out forecasts and valuation factors through the end of the growth phase and discount back	Price/earnings (P/E) or PE/growth (PEG) from forward forecasts
3	Maturity	Moderating growth rates; stable margins; capital allocation	Focus on capital allocation and debt structure; change in management	Ent. value/EBITDA (EV/EBITDA) and Price/cash flow (P/CF); multiple options
4	Decline	Growth rates slow margins decline assets could be sold	Value co. focused on a return to steady state; discount based on possibility of distress	Price/book value (P/BV); value vs. other distressed co.'s

Source: Damodaran.

continue to decline, and possibility or distressed debt should be taken into consideration when looking at intrinsic value.

We look to ratios like Price to Book Value (P/BV)_for relative valuation for declining companies. A company's book value per share essentially measures its asset value. Challenges to book value include the accounting being used, and book value never equals market value. Damodaran suggests finding other similar company valuations and building a discount for distress or finding similar distressed companies. We can use fundamentals to derive a price-to-book-value multiple as well.

Toughest Part of Valuation

Valuation is an art not a science. The challenge to valuation is surprisingly not the arithmetic but rather finding the "right" valuation approach for the company you are researching. There have traditionally been two methods for defining valuation: Intrinsic and relative valuation. The most often used method by institutional investors is the DCF valuation approach for a variety of reasons. Companies with established, reliable cash flows tend to deliver the best risk/reward. If you cannot perform a DCF valuation, there are other valuation methodologies. Relative valuation is an option, but remember relative valuation relies on market prices, which are sentiment driven, making it inherently flawed. The inherent flaw with relative valuation tends to make it more of a data point than a primary methodology. Unfortunately, it is often difficult to widely and successfully apply the DCF valuation method. As a result, investors may need to utilize a variety of different methodologies throughout the company's business life cycle we have presented in this chapter. The good news is we are now ready for our final and most important step, which is making a decision.

Bibliography

Damodaran, A. (2011). *The Little Book of Valuation.* John Wiley & Sons.

Foresi, J. D. (2024). *The role of valuation in the investment process.* Open Access Dissertations. Paper 1667.

Chapter 9

Putting It All Together to Make a Decision

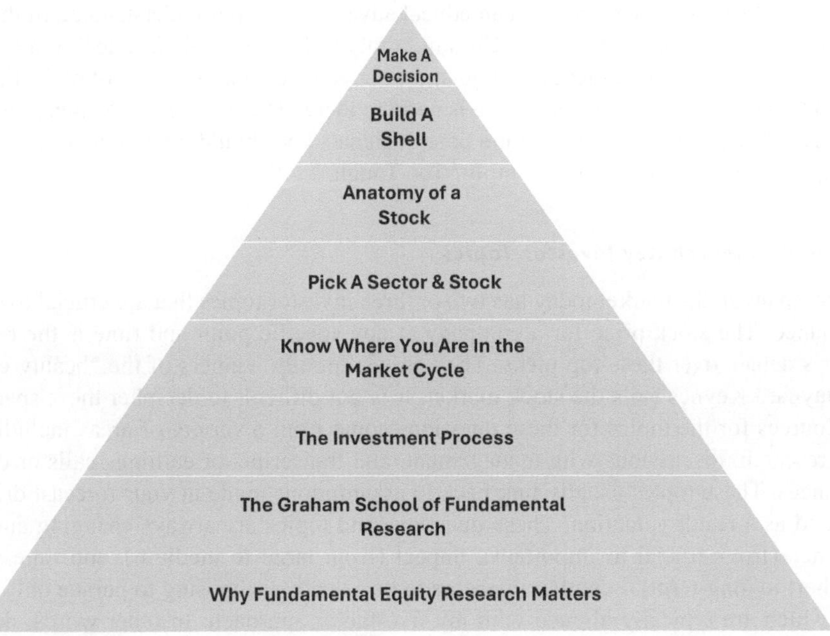

The "Hillary" Step

We encounter the final steps to processes all the time. Some are ordinary and routine like locking the door before leaving the house or brushing your teeth before bed. Others are breath taking to hear about. One inspiring final step is the "Hillary" Step, which is the name of a vertical rock face about 39 feet high located near the top of Mount Everest. The step was named after Sir Edmund Hillary, who was the first person to ever scale the summit in 1953. The Hillary step was the final tough climbing challenge before reaching the top of the summit. As a side note, there are rumors that the Hillary Step has disappeared due to changes in the climate. For those who are interested, a great book on mountain climbing is 1997 *Into Thin Air* by Jon Krakauer.

Throughout this book, we have climbed our fundamental equity research "mountain" of sorts, but we have one more final step, our version of the "Hillary" Step. I concede there is a very large difference between our journey and those of the great climbers of Mount Everest, but the final steps, small or large, are typically the hardest.

DOI: 10.4324/9781003686644-12

The Final Step

The final steps of the investment process are where we put all the pieces together. The reader should be proud of what has been accomplished. We have completed a basic understanding of the company and looked at it through the lens of the five most important factors. The final steps in the process presented below will lead us to decide on whether to buy stock and at what level to do so. To use the words of Mr. Munger, we are deciding if we are, "In, Out, or Too Tough."

Step 6 of the Investment Process: Gain an Ethical Advantage

Investors may be able to gain valuable insight into the key factors leading to stock outperformance. There are two pieces to the last step (1) define the two or three most relevant issues (factors) investors are focused on that will determine the success or failure of the investment, and (2) "deep dive" into these topics to see if you can gain an ethical advantage in your understanding of them. I have often called this step of the process, "Chasing a rabbit down the rabbit hole." Sometimes these research efforts lead to great success as you find what you are looking for. Most of the time you get to the bottom of the rabbit hole, and there is nothing there! The inability to "capture" the rabbit is completely okay and typical. Most of the time, it signals you should do nothing because things or the company you are researching is simply "Too Tough."

Define and Research Key Investor Topics

Every company in the market today has two or three investor topics that are crucial to the stock's performance. The stock price for a company at any specific point and time is the result of an investor's debate over these top picks. They are essentially winners of the "beauty contest" as John Maynard Keynes calls the stock market. It is not difficult to decipher these specific questions. Sources for the topics for these questions come from a variety of areas including fundamental research, discussions with management, and transcripts of earnings calls or conference appearances. These topics usually link back to assumptions made in your forecast driving your model and as a result valuation. These questions and topics are always changing and range in importance (from crucial to important), impact (from large to medium), and time sensitivity (from short to long-term). I caution investors to be selective, choosing to pursue only important topics, which are typically aligned with my five-factor approach. In other words, don't chase every rabbit, just the most important ones.

Golden Rule: Figure out what the (stock market) judges are looking for and if your company has what it takes.

What Are the Key Topics Affecting Mastercard?

The key topics are always changing and matter of opinion. As of the time of the writing of this book, I believe the top three topics are:

1 What will be the impact of COVID on short and long-term results?
2 How will Mastercard adjust its model to account for this impact?
3 Can Mastercard continue to expand its addressable market? Deliver double-digit growth rates?

Table 9.1 Deep Dive Suggestions

Step 1: Start with question
Step 2: Pull all relevant info
Step 3: Find second- or third-party sources
Step 4: Link conclusions to math or your model
Step 5: Run conclusions by management if possible

I think it is crucial to stick with just two or three top questions. It forces the potential investor to focus. These questions are up for debate and **always** changing. The list of crucial questions prior to COVID was most likely completely different. Mastercard could suddenly face an antitrust suit or make a significant acquisition making those topics extremely relevant. We performed "deep dives" in the areas of margin profile, B2B payment opportunity, and China expansion as it relates to Mastercard in the past to give the reader an idea of the range of potential important company-specific topics. "Deep Dive" refers to doing extensive, thorough research on a topic. In general, it is best to try to pursue a topic consistent with the five factors, if possible. For example, a topic consistent with the catalyst factor would be a topic like Mastercard's potential B2B payment opportunity, which would impact our thesis and estimates. B2B payments would be an important, high quality topic worth investigating.

Performing a Successful "Deep Dive"

There is no set formula for performing a successful "deep dive" on a topic. I purposely did not include a deep dive in this book as the reader may develop their own effective method. I can however point the reader in the right direction when performing a deep dive. I would suggest starting with three simple, but meaningful questions like the ones outlined above. The next step would be to research and aggregate all relevant, publicly available information on the topic using sources like earnings releases, transcripts, conference appearances, and analyst days. Analyst days typically are the most useful sources of information for the deep dives, but it varies. The next step is to use outside resources like the world's biggest library a.k.a. the internet and properly vetted experts. I would remind investors and researchers to be ethical in conducting their research, especially with the emergence of expert network systems. Ethics is all you have. Pushing too hard to get an edge on a stock could compromise your ethics. After you have a good understanding of the topic, see if you can link it back to the forecasts or wrap numbers around your conclusion. The last step would be to potentially run these conclusions by management. Why run them by management? Management may provide color or say nothing at all, but it may be helpful to get a reaction. Once the process is complete, you may or may not have gained enough information to help you in developing your investment conclusion. One thing is for certain deep dives may be frustrating, but they provide a competitive advantage in developing an understanding of a stock ahead of the other investors, who don't have the time to do the work (Table 9.1).

Step 7 of the Investment Process: Develop an Investment Thesis

The basic components of an investment thesis are formulaic, but the value of the thesis is derived from the quality of work put into each company report. An investment thesis tends to be a five- to seven-sentence paragraph. We can deconstruct the thesis line by line to get a good understanding of what goes into using our Mastercard thesis.

Construct an Investment Thesis

Line #1 is used to describe the action/s you are recommending. The tendency after performing research on a stock is to want to describe an immediate, specific action. The three typical action categories used by Wall Street are buy, hold, or sell (the stock). I encourage the reader to try to resist the tendency to feel obligated to recommend an action! Most of the company-specific investment research you conduct will result in taking no action or acting at a later date, which can be very disappointing over the short term, but incredibly rewarding in the long run. I believe investors would be lucky to come up with only a couple of actionable investment ideas per year. Despite the lack of actionable items, there is still quite a bit of value in the research itself. There are several positives even if you are not going to buy or sell (short) the company. Positives include discovering stocks you would purchase at the right price, not purchase at all, and/or finding out something new about companies you already own.

We will look at the different approaches to an investment conclusion from both the buy and the sell side equity analyst perspective. As a reminder, buy-side analysts are analysts who typically work at large fund companies making investment decisions, while the sell-side analysts are employed working at large brokerage to write sometimes promotional research on companies. The buy side is incentivized by capturing Asset under Management (AuM) through strong portfolio performance, while brokerage houses derive their revenues from transactions.

Sell-side analysts have a propensity to write generic investment conclusions. The sell side tends to promote companies on behalf of the investment bank/bankers. They (not all) are stewards of the corporate relationships, not necessarily stock pickers, which is widely understood. Consequently, they are not incentivized to be negative. The majority of sell-side analyst ratings are positive, either buys or holds. A sell rating would be considered a negative view potentially damaging the corporate relationship. If you come across a sell rating on a stock you like, it is extremely valuable to try to speak with the analyst to find out more regarding his contrarian view. Below are examples of Line #1 of sample investment conclusion from the sell side and a more "realistic" version.

Line #1-Sell Side-Action Recommendation-"We initiate coverage of Mastercard with a BUY rating and a twelve-month price target of $333."

Line #1-Realistic Buy Side-Action Recommendation-"We would initiate a position in Mastercard in our portfolio. Our 5-yr discounted cash flow valuation of $360 and 10-yr valuation of $485. We think a reasonable margin of safety would imply buying the stock as close to $300 as possible."

The other lines of an investment conclusion are essentially summaries of other areas where the analyst has performed extensive research in the report itself. These lines would most likely be similar regardless of whether you are on the buy or sell side. They are essentially summaries of the other categories you have done research on.

Line #2-Value Add or Competitive Edge Conclusion-"We believe Mastercard is well positioned to benefit from an acceleration in the cash to card conversion rates as we come out of the pandemic."

Line #3-Summarizes Catalysts-"The company has a number of catalysts in place to drive long-term high single, low double digit growth rates including: consumption, global cash to card conversion rates, new opportunities, and services."

Line #4-Competitive Advantages-"Mastercard has multiple competitive advantages including healthy market share in the card network market, which has high barriers to entry, and a multi-purpose global network."

Line #5-Risks-"The largest risk to Mastercard's business model is regulatory challenges."

What Is Mastercard's Investment Thesis?

I would recommend investors with a long-term (five to seven years) time horizon add Mastercard at $300 and below. The $300 or below level implies a reasonable discount to our $485 ten-year discount cash flow target, but you would need to purchase the stock well below the $300 level if you were using a shorter time horizon. I believe Mastercard is well positioned to benefit from an acceleration in the cash-to-card conversion rates especially as we exit the pandemic. The company has catalysts in place to drive long-term high single, low double-digit steady state revenue growth rates including consumption, global cash to card conversion rates, new opportunities, and services. Mastercard has multiple competitive advantages including healthy market share in the card network market, which has high barriers to entry, and a multi-purpose global network. The largest risk to Mastercard's business model is regulatory challenges.

The Importance of an Investment Thesis

An investor's sector or stock-specific investment thesis is very important for several reasons. I discussed in Chapter 5 the loose similarities between the scientific method and equity research. An investor's investment thesis is like a scientist's hypothesis. It is a theory based on limited information. The analyst or investor can then test the information against the different data points we get from earnings results and the market. Our thesis can then be changed or altered causing a change in our approach to the stock or sector. For example, I may own a stock for a specific reason and because our thesis changed over time, I may sell it, which brings us to the investment decisions.

Step 8 of the Investment Process: Buy, Hold, and Sell

Take Action

The decision to buy, hold, or sell a stock is not an easy one. It requires conviction. The reader can tell by the rigorous, methodical steps and factors presented in this book. It takes time to build up conviction. Most of the time high levels of conviction are unattainable. The practice of looking at a variety of different companies in different sectors helps you to get better at this part. The best thing to do is to collect all your facts first. Once they have been collected and organized, you can work on adding value. Typically, you gather the information regarding the five factors and then find answers to the two or three crucial questions, which provide an investor with a level of conviction high enough to set buy and potentially sell price points or targets. Once you have completed your due diligence, you can then form an opinion on the name and make your "call" on the stock. I would recommend waiting until the very end before making the decision. Most of the time the final moments of your research will be the most rewarding as they tend to uncover the most valuable information in determining the outcome of your research.

Golden Rule: Make your conviction based, actionable decision after having "enough" facts.

Tying Up the Loose Ends

Congratulations! You have successfully learned how to analyze a stock. The key lessons you learned in the prior seven chapters can be applied to any company you research. Practice on different companies will allow you to get better over time. I conclude this chapter by looking at how to build a portfolio, when to start selling positions, and the future of investing. Our next chapter looks at modern portfolio theory.

Step 9: Build a Portfolio

Building a Portfolio

One approach an investor can take to building an investment portfolio is what I would call, "The No Shortcuts Approach." The approach would be based on trying to find the 10–15 best companies in the market, doing extensive work on each company, setting potential buy price targets by building in a margin of safety near the intrinsic value, and then adding these high-quality stocks to your portfolio when the market provides a buying opportunity, while selling them when they get too expensive. A company like my case study Mastercard could be put on a list containing other high-quality names to be monitored and purchased when and if the opportunity presented itself. The investor could theoretically set up a five-factor analysis for Mastercard and other names. Potentially setting parameters like a competitive advantage and catalyst rating of +7 on a Likert scale of 1–10 to warrant additional research. A total score of +7 or greater would get a company added to the portfolio.

It should be noted that this is a new, untested method. However, it makes intuitive sense. I would suggest you look at all different factors, then go back and check your thought process by reviewing the potential psychological flaws and then score each factor. Below is how I would have scored Mastercard on a scale of 1–10 in our different categories with 10 being the best and 1 being the poorest. I weighed the different categories based on their overall impact on long-term shareholder value. The advantage I have is my decade plus of market experience probably leads me to a better scorecard. **It is important to note that the market is a dynamic ever-changing environment. My original five-factor scorecard has changed over time. I expect the scorecard to continue to evolve. Readers should consider developing their own scorecard.**

Five Factor Scorecard

See Table 9.2.

Table 9.2 Five Factor Scorecard[a]

Factors	*Rating*	*Weighting (%)*	*Total*
Competitive advantage	8.5	40	3.4
Catalyst	7.5	20	1.5
Valuation	3.0	20	0.6
Quality of management	7.0	10	0.7
Psychology	8.0	10	0.8
Total		100	7.0

[a] Margin of safety implies buying below $300.

Portfolio Construction

The Search for the Northwest Quadrant

Richard Ferri attempted to tackle the challenges of portfolio construction in his 2010 book *All about Asset Allocation*. Ferri promotes a multi-asset-class approach. He focuses on the different asset classes, their historical correlation, and how the combination impacts risk/return. Ferri constructs portfolios based on his forecast for each asset classes expected return using multiple ETFs to diversify and lower volatility, which ultimately delivers higher returns. We are reminded of the work of Markowitz and other academics who diversified away risk when constructing a portfolio. We will talk about this more in our next chapter on modern portfolio theory.

Ferri makes several helpful observations even though he is not specifically focused on individual stock picking. We believe his observations would translate well into the construction of any long-term investment portfolio. Ferri agrees with the academic view of the risk presented earlier. He believes risk to the individual investor is much simpler. The individual investor is concerned about not losing money, especially because losses can cause irrational behavior.

Ferri believes no asset is truly "risk-free" (so do we), especially given investment fees, inflation, and taxes. He would recommend keeping costs and taxes low, which is why he promotes indexing. From a portfolio perspective, Ferri supports a strategy of keeping volatility in check through diversification, while trying to maintain a steady average annual return. Diversification is managed by holding assets with low correlation, which is hard to do as correlations between asset classes are constantly fluctuating. New asset classes can be discovered and incorporated as necessary. Ferri believes his diversification method works up to about 12 asset classes and then the costs outweigh the benefits. A long-term diversified asset allocation approach is an effort to increase annual returns by a couple of basis points per year. Ferri supports a multi-decade strategy requiring long-term commitment. The objective is to optimize the portfolios positioning in the Northwest quadrant, which is the mathematical section of the efficient market frontier where risk reward is the most balanced. We will learn more about the *Northwest Quadrant* in the next section. The portfolio should be systematically, annually rebalanced. The rebalancing takes place as the winners (outperforming assets) are sold, and the losers (underperforming assets) are purchased to improve diversification while maintaining returns. A scheduled annual rebalancing appears to be positive given what we learned about in our section on psychology, as it essentially takes the emotion out of investing. Rebalancing can take place due to a variety of other factors including a change in life circumstances, etc.

Ferri promotes a four-step process: (1) Determine your portfolio risk level based on long-term financial needs and risk tolerance translated into asset allocation (equity vs. fixed income), (2) Evaluate assets based on risk, expected return, correlation, and tax implications, (3) Pick the ETFs, and (4) Rebalance. My book focuses specifically on equities, but a well-balanced portfolio would include a multi-asset class approach as Ferri suggests.

The criteria Ferri uses for his approach include using assets that are different from each other, expected to have a higher return than inflation, and convertible into low-cost funds or products. Ferri highlights a couple of different potential asset classes to choose from: US Equities (Large Cap, Small Cap, Growth, and Value), International Equities (Developed, Emerging), Fixed Income (Investment and Non-Investment Grade, International), Real Estate (REITs), and Alternative Investments (Collectibles, Commodities, and Others). Naturally, he suggests different asset allocations based on risk tolerance and stage of life. For example, he would suggest a 70% Equities/30% Fixed Income for young, just starting out investors with moderate risk tolerance. The percentage allocated to fixed income would increase over time as the investor progresses through the different stages of life. The book cites the "Your age in bonds" rule of thumb, which suggests the percentage of your portfolio in bonds should be dependent on your age. For example, a 40-year-old would have 40% of his portfolio in bonds. The rule of thumb is not a hard and fast rule. Ferri is of the opinion that REITs should not represent more than 10% of a portfolio. He does not promote getting involved with commodities as they are asset price plays and rely too much on timing in his opinion.

I believe the goal of all investors would be to create the next great portfolio. I talked about it in my introduction comparing investing to being a painter. Your equity portfolio should be your Picasso. Your portfolio of equities is your masterpiece painting including the best colors, the stocks themselves. However, over time, you would want to expand your portfolio to include other asset classes like bonds, real estate, commodities, etc. Think of it as expanding your skill set beyond paintings to sculpting (Bonds) or woodworking (real estate). I am stretching the analogy to its outer limits, but you get the point.

Step 10: Rinse and Repeat

Research Determines the List; Market Determines Timing

I have come to the end of our ten-step process. I will cover a lot of the major conclusions from the research we have presented in the next chapter. However, I want to provide one final thought on the process. Let the research you perform on the stocks lead you to your list of names you would like in your portfolio, while the stock movements themselves can determine when those names are added.

Forever Stocks

I can now tell you about my true obsession. I am consumed with the search for the optimal portfolio, particularly a basket of the best possible group of stocks you can own. There should of course be an element of diversity in the basket of stocks.

A *Forever Stock* is my invention. There is no standard definition, but in general, you can think of a forever stock as a select group of the "very best" stocks you can own each with a ten-year time horizon. A company must have a combination of characteristics to be considered one of the "very best" stocks. I have outlined these characteristics for you throughout the book. These characteristics include dominant end market positions, expandable addressable markets, and potential for great free cash flow generation, and thoughtful capital allocation. I know forever stocks exist because I have seen them throughout my career. They are extremely rare, but they exist.

My ideal or optimal portfolio would be constructed with a diverse group of these forever stocks. I would suggest thinking of it as a portfolio of just 10–15 stocks, which would provide the proper amount of diversity, while at the same time by holding to a limited number requires you to have strong conviction in every name that you add to the portfolio. You would then develop a circle of competence in the most relevant potential sectors, picking a potential forever stock from each of these sectors. Once you have identified these forever stocks, you would then keep a running list with specific entry and exit points adding and trimming positions based on the opportunity presented by the markets.

Potential Future of Investing: Social Responsibility

Socially Responsible Investing (SRI)

I may be adding a SRI score to our list of crucial investment factors in the future. SRI investing is the practice of investing in areas where there are positive social impacts in addition to looking for a financial return. SRI encompasses a broader set of objectives from a social perspective including subjects like human rights, environmental protection, and positive consumer impacts. These focuses change with the times. Investors typically look at SRI through what is known as an ESG or Environmental, Social, and Governance lens.

Impact investing is a subset of SRI. Impact investing is the idea that capital can be used for positive change. The difference is that impact investing is specifically geared toward investments focused on social change. It currently appears that momentum in SRI, ESG, and Impact investing could continue in the future.

Jeremy Balkin addresses the topic of impact investing in his 2015 book *Investing with Impact: Why Finance Is a Force for Good.* Balkin believes the 2007 financial crisis exemplifies the failure of the current economic system and its participants, including the financial services participants and governments, who fell into the trap of their own greed. We learned in our section on business cycles; capitalism is inherently flawed. The challenges of the financial crisis were perhaps most acutely felt by the Millennials, who now can determine their destiny.

Balkin believes Millennials and future generations can use capitalism as a force for good. Impact investing can be the mechanism for the change. Impact investing directly links financial results and positive social impact. He believes impact investing is a more powerful tool than SRI. SRI focuses on filtering out the companies that lack socially acceptable criteria, thus excluding potential financial gains. On the other hand, impact investing empowers select companies to drive social change while reaping financial rewards. Balkin submits his 6E framework for evaluating impact investments. The 6E's are economics (valuation), employment (job creation), empowerment (diverse stakeholders), education (compliance and workforce), ethics (moral code), and environment (planet earth).

Bibliography

Balkin, J. K. (2015). *Investing with Impact.* Bibliomotion.
Ferri, R. A. (2010). *All about Asset Allocation.* McGraw Hill.
Krakauer, J. (1997). *Into Thin Air: A Personal Account of the Mount Everest Disaster.* Villard Books.

Chapter 10

Modern Portfolio Theory

Truly a Story of Chance

Modern Portfolio Theory (MPT) uses a mathematical framework to assemble a portfolio maximizing the expected return for the level of risk. Although the theory itself is a way of effectively measuring and managing risk, the interesting part of the story is the development of MPT itself is also a story of chance.

The story of the development of MPT involves random, chance-driven events. For example, Harry Markowitz, one of the founders of MPT, whom we will meet in a moment, met a random person in the lobby while waiting for his thesis advisor, Professor Marschak. The person suggested he do his dissertation on the stock market. Markowitz of course took the advice. Chance shows up again when Markowitz goes to the library one afternoon and while he was browsing different, random books, he gets the idea for his thesis. All in one afternoon! Chance shows up a third time when Professor Paul Samuelson and his colleagues stumble across the works of an early 1900s French Mathematician Bachelier, whose work itself is about randomness and chance, which is then applied to describe stock movements!

My prior work throughout the book focused on stock or market-specific analysis. The upcoming section looks at investing at the portfolio level from a mathematical standpoint. I will touch on very important theoretical notions including the efficient frontier, measurements of portfolio risk/reward, and the capital asset pricing model (CAPM). Although not always easily applicable, the theories behind this notion changed investing and continued to sculpt its future. It is the academic contribution to the eternal search for the optimal portfolio.

The Academy

Time for a History Lesson

A look at the academic approach to Wall Street is really a history lesson. Academia is a practice where advancements are made with one academic often building off the work of another. Academics were focused on several different stock market phenomena. They attempted to solve these challenges not by looking at the fundamentals of the stocks, but rather by applying statistical analysis to stock price movements themselves. The academics are focused on how to handle risk, searching for the optimal portfolio. A group of academics believe stock price movements are essentially random. A validation of the academic approach would imply an element of market efficiency and in turn be a dismissal of active management's ability to outperform the market. If markets are random and/or efficient, indexing is really the only possible successful approach for investors, which is the topic we discussed at the beginning of the work.

DOI: 10.4324/9781003686644-13

History of Finance

Luckily, we have the great author Peter L. Bernstein to guide us through our journey. Peter wrote valuable books on the history of finance including *Capital Ideas*, *Against the Gods*, *The Power of Gold*, and *Capital Ideas Evolving*. These books are captured in Peter L. Bernstein's *Classic Collection*. The academics, like speculators, were more focused on the stock price movements themselves than on the fundamentals driving the movements. Academics were concerned with the relationship between risk and reward. They wanted to be able to diversify the risk away and create the optimal or efficient portfolio. It is interesting that both academics and fundamental analysts are focused on the "Search for the Perfect Portfolio." Academics believe stock prices movements are random with as much opportunity to go up as down and volatility increasing over the long-term. They feel to some extent that the market is efficient, making it very difficult to beat. They would recommend you buy the market or index rather than trying to personally beat the market (Table 10.1).

Capital Ideas by Peter L. Bernstein lays out the history of finance providing us with a very good roadmap to understanding the intersection between academia and Wall Street. The roots of the movement start in 1900 with Louis Bachelier, a French mathematician, who was completing his dissertation for a Doctor of Mathematics at the Sorbonne. Bachelier's 70 pages dissertation entitled, "The Theory of Speculation," was the first effort to apply mathematics to understanding the market. He saw the movement of stock prices as random. His work used the concept of stochastic processing, which analyzes the random movement among statistical variables. Bachelier's thesis builds on the theory of Brownian motion. The theory is based on the work of Robert Brown was a Scottish botanist studying a species of pollen known as pink fairies in the late 1820s. The pollen grains Brown observed under a microscope seemed to bounce around randomly without stopping. The grains were moving in a "Brownian motion." Bachelier believed stock prices are an equilibrium between buyers and sellers, so the probabilities of a rise and fall are 50/50 on each day. However, the size of the stock fluctuations grows larger as the time horizon expands. It gets larger as you move from a day to month to a year to years. Stock prices move in accordance with the square root of time in a random fashion. For example, over a 12-month period stock prices will range $\sqrt{2}$ or 3.5× more than in one month.

Table 10.1 Academic Approach

Academics	*Approach*	*Nobel Prize*
Louis Bachelier	Applied statistical analysis to the market's using the theory prices were random	N/A
Harry Markowitz	Balanced risk and reward achieved through diversification (covariance) and placement on efficient Frontier	1990
James Tobin	Separation Theorem-separate the risk from the less risky assets to find the optimal portfolio (the market)	1981
William Sharpe	Found easier way to calculate efficient portfolio and CAPM model	1990
Paul Samuelson	Believed the present stock prices reflect the intrinsic value	1970
Eugene Fama	Father of the efficient-market hypothesis	2013
Modigliani & Miller	M&M or Irrelevant Capital Structure Theory	1985, 1990
Black & Scholes	Black-Scholes Option Pricing Model	1997

Modern Portfolio Theory

Harry Markowitz-The Efficient Frontier

> A good portfolio is more than a long list of good stocks and bonds. It is a balanced whole, providing the investor with protections and opportunities with respect to a wide range of contingencies.

The road to MPT picks up again half a century later in the 1950s with Harry Markowitz. Markowitz, a 25-year-old graduate student at the University of Chicago, published a paper entitled, "Portfolio Selection" in March 1952 edition of the *Journal of Finance*. The paper was the foundation for Markowitz's dissertation and his 1959 full-length book, *Portfolio Selection: Efficient Diversification of Investment*. He updated his thoughts in his 1987 book, *Mean-Variance Analysis in Portfolio Choice and Capital Markets*. His decision to choose the topic is based on chance as he ran into a stockbroker on the way to a thesis meeting who encouraged him to use the stock market as a topic.

Markowitz was not interested in identifying specific stocks to buy, but rather he was interested in how to handle the relationship between risk and reward within a portfolio. He started by going to the library to research how to value assets by reading John Burr Williams 1938 classic, *The Theory of Investment Value.* Williams's theory of asset valuation is based on the ability to forecast out dividends and then find the intrinsic value of the dividend stream (Dividend Discount Model). Williams was suggesting you essentially own the shares of a company you like the best. Markowitz immediately noticed the challenge here. Investors take greater risk by investing in just one asset, not to mention most people own more than one asset: real estate, bonds, stocks, etc., thus you need to balance risk/reward.

Here, we run into a difference of objectives and opinion. The investment community wants to maximize its return, especially fund managers who will gain more assets if they have strong returns. The quickest way to do this is by investing in a small group of well-known stocks, which can provide you with the highest return. A fundamental investor, like Buffett or Munger, would suggest you invest in what you know in a concentrated couple of names. Whereas Markowitz recommends that you balance the risk/reward through diversification. There is an inherent collision here! Fundamental investors build a circle of competence, in a sector or stocks, which takes time. They want to invest in the "best" opportunities. Both Markowitz and speculators to some extent suggest you diversify. They seem to take a "portfolio" first approach based on stock price movements without fundamentally looking at the assets you are investing in. The compromise would be to find a large number of stocks where you have done a large amount of extensive research, which solves both desires, but the challenge is that it would take a tremendous amount of time, perhaps more than one lifetime!

Markowitz did NOT stop with just suggesting diversification. He wants to add a second dimension to ensure diversity and low covariance. A single stock portfolio with one high-quality technology stock is **not** diverse. A 10–15 stock portfolio with 15 technology stocks increases diversity compared to one stock, but only a marginal amount of diversity as the stocks have a high covariance, meaning they move up and down with one another. True diversity would be a portfolio with several stocks that have low covariance, meaning their movements are separate from each other. Variance itself means distance from the average. Ultimately, Markowitz is driving toward what is known as an efficient portfolio, which is a portfolio offering the highest amount of return for a given level of risk. There are two separate calculations to figuring out where a portfolio sits on the efficient portfolio frontier. Step One: is to estimate the return of the portfolio or expected return. Step Two: is to calculate the covariance of those securities. These portfolios would be put on an efficient frontier. The lower the covariance, the lower the risk. An investor could choose the portfolio he was looking for based on their pension for risk. We present the important formulas necessary for calculating the efficient frontier like expected returns in our formula section. We walk the reader through Steps 1 and 2 and an example of the efficient frontier in our analyst workshop where the Northwest quadrant is the most advantageous part of the frontier.

The academics rely heavily on statistics. I would strongly recommend anyone who wants to fully understand the academics approach start with a basic understanding of statistics, which can be accomplished by taking college-level courses or through the CFA program. I provide examples and formulas with explanations of where and when necessary, but they are limited and abbreviated.

A.D. Roy-Safety-First Ratio

A.D. Roy was also working to understand the relationship between risk/reward. He was teaching at Sidney Sussex College at Cambridge when he published an article, "Safety First and the Holding of Assets." The article was published in 1952 around the same time as Markowitz's work, although Roy's work was limited in approach. A.D. Roy developed Roy's *safety-first ratio.* Roy's *safety first* criterion says the optimal portfolio is one minimizing the probability that the portfolio returns fall below the minimum required rate of return, or shortfall risk. If the portfolio has normal returns, the optimal portfolio will be the one with the highest safety ratio. The *safety-first* ratio measures the excess return per unit of risk. The goal of the ratio is to minimize the left tail, which is the probability the portfolio returns less than the threshold. The value represents the number of standard deviations below the mean. For example, a ratio of one would be one standard deviation below the mean, so the higher the ratio, the smaller the tail. We include the Roy's Safety formula and an example.

James Tobin-Separation Theorem

As we mentioned in the introduction, MPT is evolutionary as with most academic endeavors with one academic adding to what another has already put in place. Markowitz and to an extent Roy had a breakthrough in their approach, but there were practical problems to their suggestions. There were multiple problems with the Efficient Portfolio frontier including forecasting, choosing the right portfolio, and the impracticality associated with being able to do the large numbers of calculations. Enter Professor James Tobin, a 40-year-old Sterling Professor of Economics at Yale. Professor Tobin published an article entitled "Liquidity Preference as Behavior Toward Risk" in *The Review of Economic Studies* in 1958. Tobin wanted to expand on Markowitz's work by applying it to economic theory and including other less risky asset classes compared to equities like bonds or cash. Tobin developed the idea known as Separation Theorem, which argues that Markowitz's process of selecting securities for an efficient portfolio is **separate** from the decision of how to divide up the total portfolio between risky and risky free assets. Tobin believes we can arrive at a one super-efficient portfolio combination which could apply to all investors. He felt you could start by first finding the optimal combination of risky assets and then deciding to lend or borrow depending on the investor's aptitude for risk. It then showed if there is only one portfolio plus borrowing and lending, it's got to be the market.

William Sharpe-The Sharpe Ratio

> What if your advisor talks only about returns, not risk?...It's his job to take risk into account by telling you the range of possible outcomes you face. If he won't (tell you) go to a new planner, someone who will get real.

William Sharpe made a significant contribution to finance primarily building off Markowitz's work. Sharpe began working on the project with Markowitz in 1960. He came across the relationship with Markowitz in an unconventional manner. Sharpe was working on his doctoral thesis at UCLA on transfer pricing. It was not going very well, so his professor suggested he talk to Markowitz. The relationship was made even more unconventional by the fact that Markowitz was not a professor at UCLA where Sharpe was doing his work. Sharpe published his findings in a 1961 paper entitled "A Simplified Model for Portfolio Analysis." It appeared in the January 1963 issue of *Management Science*. Sharpe presented what was known as the single-index model. Sharpe's calculation eliminates the need to calculate covariance. Instead, the investor calculates the relationship of each individual security to the dominant factor, which is typically the index. If the price of the security is more volatile than the dominant factor, the security will make the portfolio more variable or risky, and vice versa. The average of these relationships can then be used as a measure of volatility.

The Sharpe ratio measures an investments risk adjusted return over a specified timeframe. The Sharpe ratio formula is the portfolios' risk premium (return minus the risk-free rate) divided by the standard deviation of the portfolios' return based on a normal distribution. The ratio measures the return or compensation for risk. The Sharpe ratio carries similarities to *Roy's safety-first ratio*. Generally, the higher the Sharpe ratio; the better. Below 1 are considered poor, 1 to 1.99 are acceptable, 2 to 2.99 are good, and 3 and higher are excellent. We provide an example of the Sharpe Ratio.

The Capital Asset Pricing Model

Sharpe's truly revolutionary breakthrough happened in 1964 when he along with others (Jack Treynor, John Lintner, Jan Mossin) developed the CAPM. Sharpe published his ideas in the 1961 paper, "Capital Asset Prices: A Theory of Market Equilibrium under Conditions of Risk." The CAPM is a model used to determine the theoretically appropriate required rate of return of an asset to make the best decision about adding assets to a well-diversified portfolio. The CAPM can be used to derive the cost of equity. As we saw in our section on valuation, the cost of equity is a crucial factor in determining valuation.

Here, we need to explain some important pieces of terminology. **Systematic risk** is the risk associated with the market. **Unsystematic risk** is the risk associated with individual assets. Unsystematic risk can be diversified by adding more companies to the portfolio. A portfolio of 30–40 names would be appropriate in a developed market. **Beta** is a measurement of the risk arising from exposure to general market movements. The market portfolio has a beta of 1.0, above 1.0 means the assets are more volatile than the market. A beta below 1.0 means it is less volatile. The **risk-free rate** is the rate of return of a hypothetical investment with scheduled, reliable payments over a fixed period. Investors typically use a risk-free bond issued by the government for the risk-free rate. The **risk premium** is what the investor is willing to pay for an asset above the risk-free rate. A risk premium is necessary to induce an investor to hold the asset. The **Security Market Line (SML)** graphs the results from the CAPM with the x-axis representing the risk (beta) and the y-axis representing the expected return. The invention of the CAPM points to the market itself as being the most efficient portfolio that Markowitz, Tobin, and Sharpe were all looking for with no one able to beat it without taking on risk. We include the CAPM formula and an example of the CAPM and an example of the SML.

Challenges to the CAPM

There have been academic challenges to the validity of the CAPM pricing model. Two challenges have identified possible areas of opportunity from a value and size effect. Sanjoy Basu, a finance professor at McMaster University at the time, published a 1977 paper entitled "Investment Performance of Common Stocks in Relation to Their Price-Earnings Ratios: A Test of the Efficient Market Hypothesis." in *The Journal of Finance* describing what is known as the **value effect**. He looked at share prices of 1,400 stocks from 1956 to 1971. Professor Basu found that the returns for low Price-to-Earnings (P/E) stocks exceeded the returns for high P/E stocks by seven points per year and the low P/E stocks were less volatile. His work was followed by Rolf Banz, a Swiss economist, who published a study entitled "The Relationship between Return and Market Value of Common Stocks." in 1981 in the *Financial Journal of Economics* showing the shares of the 50 smallest companies outperformed the 50 largest by 1% per month from 1931 to 1975, which is now known as the **size effect.**

On the Shoulders of Giants

Academia is a collaborative effort. Markowitz and Sharpe's work served as a spark for the financial revolution. They believed investors were rational and could trade off risk for a reward in an optimal manner. Bachelier theorized that the prices of stocks were as likely to go up as down, and the passage of time would expand the range according to the square root of time remained dormant until the 1950s when Jimmie Savage, an American mathematician and statistician brought it to the attention of none other than Paul Samuelson from earlier in our book in 1965.

MIT Professor Paul Samuelson is perhaps best known for his 1948 textbook *Economics*. Samuelson was a prolific writer publishing more articles by the age of 25 than the years he was old. Samuelson contribution to the efficient market approach to the stock market appeared in his 1965 article in MIT's *Industrial Management Review* entitled "Proof That Properly Anticipated Prices Fluctuate Randomly." Samuelson argues that there is an intrinsic value associated with each stock hiding in the shadows of the market. He puts forth the idea that the actual trading price of the security on that day represents the intrinsic value or shadow price. The trading price is in effect the equilibrium.

The progress being made on the random movement of stock prices is perhaps best exemplified in the 1964 classic book *The Random Character of Stock Prices* written by MIT Professor Paul Cootner, who aggregated the advancements in theory of random stock price movements. Cootner included his analysis along with the works associated with Bachelier, Kendall, Osborne, Working, Cowles, Alexander, Fama, and others. This book is dense but serves as a good reference tool.

The "Noise" Trader Model

Fischer Black later added his own twist to the thesis delivering his entire presidential address to the American Finance Association in 1986 on "Noise," which challenges Samuelson's conclusion in the "real" markets. "Noise" arises when investors trade off rumor or bad information. If this can affect stocks, then their stock prices cannot reflect their true intrinsic values. The existence of Noise presents a challenge to stock prices to ever get to a true intrinsic value, but presents an opportunity for those with better information. If you are a fundamentally oriented investor, then the existence of noise presents an opportunity, especially if the asset price contracts to a level below your intrinsic value building in a margin of safety.

The emergence of the Noise Trader Hypothesis attributable to the contribution of academics like Fisher Black, Joseph Stiglitz, Sanford Grossman, and Robert Shiller among others was a convergence of academic market theory and fundamental equity analysis. It put forward the notion that markets were indeed irrational or inefficient and that investors or active managers could in fact beat the market. Professor Grossman and Stiglitz 1980 paper in *The American Economic*, "On the impossibility of Informationally Efficient Markets" described a stock market as one in which stock prices represent the amount of information in the market as represented by the total amount of professional investors (arbitrageurs). The lower the number of informed investors, the lower the amount of information, the higher the stock price, and the larger the "noise" and vice versa. They theorized that price movements reflect the transfer of information from the professional to the amateur investor. The existence of "noise" attracts an increasing number of investors and efficiency increases as information becomes more widespread. The market continues to reach greater efficiency theoretically leading to a "noiseless" market, where there is no need to trade. Since we know markets do indeed trade, then markets must by default contain some "noise." The Noise Trader Model sounds a lot more like the stock market described by Ben Graham and Warren Buffett than the Random Walk Theory or the Efficient Market Hypothesis.

Fama and French-Multi Factor Model

You may remember Eugene Fama from Chapter 1 as the father of the Efficient Market Hypothesis (EMH), which eventually set the tone for passive investing. Fama continued to have a large impact on financial academic thought, well beyond EMH. Professor Fama teamed up with Ken French in 1992 publishing in the *Journal of Financial Economics* a paper entitled "The Cross-Section of Expected Stock Returns." The paper put forth the theory the performance of a diversified US equities portfolio relied on three primary factors, as opposed to the one variable in the CAPM, to determine its returns. The three factors were: (1) Beta, (2) The percentage of small-cap stocks vs. large cap, and (3) Percentage of value orientation, Book-to-Market (BtM) or P/B. The contribution of the small cap stocks and value orientation was measured by market weight. Fama and French believed they could determine with 95% accuracy how a portfolio would perform based on these three factors in relation to the stock market without knowing actual returns. I include the three-factor formula in our appendix.

Five Factors Model

The French Fama model was extended to a five-factor model in 2015. The Professors added profitability and investment. The profitability factor is the difference between firms with high and low operating profits. The investment factor is the difference between the returns of firms that invest conservatively vs. aggressively. There is controversy in the academic community regarding the accuracy of the three and five-factor models. Eugene Fama was awarded the 2013 Nobel Memorial Prize in Economic Science. I include the five-factor formula in our appendix. Although the two are NOT comparable, I have included a comparison of my five factors vs. the academic model (Table 10.2).

Table 10.2 Fundamental vs. Academic Five Factors

Fundamental	*Academic*
Catalyst	Market risk
Competitive advantage	Size
Quality of management	Value
Valuation	Profitability
Psychology	Investment

Modigliani and Miller-M&M Theory

> You only need to make one big score in finance to be a hero forever.

Franco Modigliani and Merton Miller combined to make a significant contribution to modern economic thought. Miller and Modigliani developed and published their theorem when they were professors at the Graduate School of Industrial Administration (GSIA) at Carnegie Mellon. The two were assigned to teach a corporate finance course and found the material to be lackluster. The Modigliani-Miller (M&A) theorem known as the capital structure irrelevance principle is quite simple, it states the value of the firm is unaffected by how the firm is financed, in the absence of taxes, bankruptcy, agency costs, and in an inefficient market. The value of the firm is not related to whether capital is raised through equity or debt or its dividend policy. A world where taxes are relevant would mean the use of debt vs. equity would be a better way to raise capital as interest is tax deductible. They published their results in June 1958 in the *American Economic Review*. M&M theory would imply savvy investors who have market experience would be able to estimate out earnings and can develop market-leading performance.

Black and Scholes-Option Pricing Model

> In the end, a theory is accepted not because it is confirmed by conventional empirical tests, but because researchers persuade one another that the theory is correct and relevant.

Fischer Black and Myron Scholes created an options pricing model named after them. They published the formula supporting their pricing options model in 1973 article entitled "The Pricing of Options and Corporate Liabilities" in the *Journal of Political Economy*. Robert C. Merton was the first to expand on the mathematical model and coin the term. The Black-Scholes formula gives a theoretical estimate of the price of European-style options showing the option has a unique price regardless of the risk of the security and its expected return. The formula replaces the expected return with the risk-neutral rate. Edward O. Thorp mentioned earlier claimed he was the originator of the option pricing model. He lays out in his 2017 autobiography *A Man for All Markets from Las Vegas to Wall Street, how I beat the dealer and the market* not only how he came up with the formula, but how he profited from it, until the Black Scholes model was widely disseminated.

The Quants

The academic impact on investing had positive and negative implications. I discussed earlier how the efficient market hypothesis eventually led to passive investing. Another natural extension of the academic work being performed is quantitative investing, which presents an interesting opportunity, especially given the computing power of computers and the ability to take the emotion out of investing. However, remember markets are dynamic and quants face the same risks as any other market participant in a potentially unusual, black swan-like event. In the future, we surmise you will need a combination of quantitative and fundamental analysis.

Quantitative (Quant) investing presents an interesting opportunity. We know from our section on psychology about how emotions (bias, heuristics) get in the way of humans being able to make consistently good investment decisions. Humans have a limited brain capacity as well. Quant investing seems to solve these problems as computers have no emotion but do have comparatively more computational power than humans. A quantitative approach to investing can examine large data sets, using empirical evidence, and a systematic, consistent approach. However, the flaw with quant investing is the same thing, which makes it great, markets are just as much, perhaps even more human than they are fundamental or mathematical. History has taught us that when irrational events take place, neither humans nor computers are ready.

The beginning of the quant movement has its origins in academia. Quants base their trading patterns on mathematical formulas and algorithms, which are built into computerized trading programs. The Quants take the academic research and convert it into mathematical models. The math doesn't care about the company, management, business fundamentals, etc. in the way fundamental human analysts do. Quant models can include elements like a scoring system for individual stocks (assets) based on the specific characteristics, which can range from valuation parameters to growth rates, and then ranked, known as factor investing. The portfolio will then hold these stocks and be rebalanced periodically.

There are different types of quantitative investing outside of the factor investing mentioned above.

Quantitative analysis can be used in a variety of ways including to help mitigate risk (risk parity), take advantage of events (event-driven arbitrage), and find attractive bargains (quantitative value). There are even hybrid models, which use fundamental and quantitative analysis, which we believe is probably the best of both worlds. Quants have begun to look at Big Data and AI, which could provide future opportunities.

Scott Patterson 2010 book *The Quants* maps the development of the quantitative or "quant" movement on Wall Street. Patterson's story picks up where our section on the academics leaves off. He considers Edward O. Thorp, who was mentioned earlier in our book, to be the "godfather" of the quants. As we have seen throughout the book, each Wall Street "movement" has a person, who is credited with its origination. Thorp was the mathematics professor, who designed a successful card-playing approach. He was one of the first academics to actively cross into the Wall Street world setting up hedge funds designed to mathematically enable traders and computers to benefit from arbitrage opportunities.

The general idea behind quantitative analysis is that there are profit opportunities in the market that can be identified through mathematical formula. These opportunities can then be programmed into a computer to execute them. It seems inevitable that the academics, Harry Markowitz and others, will attempt to put their academic theories to work in the market by utilizing computers. One of the early examples of these identifiable patterns was statistical arbitration (stat arb.), which is essentially finding mispriced assets based on factors like the Law of One Price (LOP) or the relationship of one asset to another.

Patterson looks at the careers of well-known "quants" such as Jim Simons (Renaissance Technologies), Ken Griffin (Citadel), Cliff Asness (AQR), Peter Muller (BARRA/Morgan Stanley), and Boaz Weinstein (Deutsche Bank). These "quants" have connections to the academics. For example, Griffin looked to Thorp as a mentor starting with a convertible bond trading strategy. Asness studied under Fama at the University of Chicago.

Quants have benefited from the latest trends in the stock market. Their success is real. However, they face the challenge of abnormal market movements just like any other historically successful

Wall Street trends. I have seen a few of these anomalies. The 1987 crash was further fueled by the quantitative strategy associated with portfolio insurance. Patterson points out just how statistically unusual the 1987 crash was. The crash was a statistical anomaly akin to, "A 27 standard-deviation event tantamount to flipping a coin a hundred times and getting ninety-nine straight heads" (p. 118). The quants failed again in 1998 as the aforementioned Long-term Capital Management (LTCM) collapsed, as Russia defaulted on it bonds. Outliers are bound to continue to happen, presenting challenges to all market participants, including quants!

What's the Best Approach-Speculating, Fundamentalist, Academic?

We have looked at three approaches to the stock market: speculating, investing, and academic. Each approach has its positives and negatives. The speculative or trading approach teaches an investor to bet in small amounts and cut their losses quickly, but the efficiencies in the market, randomness of stock movements, and availability of information make it very difficult to spot or benefit from singular or stock-specific trends. Technical analysis has been proven to be ineffective over time, especially since it rests on historical price data. The fundamental approach appears to be a sound approach. I believe it is most successful when combined with a value-based investing style. It is the one I prescribe to and support. It promotes finding the best names, their intrinsic value, and building in a margin of safety before buying. However, it requires a lot of effort, time, and patience, so even if you find a name you are interested in, you need to wait until it gets to an attractive level building in a margin of safety. Fundamental analysis fails to account for technology investing and to an extent shorting stocks. It may be very difficult to be a fundamental investor in different types of markets, particularly "Bullish" environments. Finally, the academics' approach promotes using statistics to understand the market; it views stock price movements as random and believes risk should be diversified away. The challenge with the academic approach is that it has historically been impractical or impossible to translate it into a useful everyday approach to the market. Academic approaches fail to account for outlier events (Table 10.3).

Table 10.3 The Different Approaches

Characteristic	*Trading*	*Investing*	*Academics*
Type of investing	Active	Active	Passive
Belief	Follow the trend	Market volatility provide opportunity	Random stock movements
Objective	Protect principal and grow	Protect principal and grow	Diversify away risk for efficiency
Working to identify	Trends	Under valued stocks	Asset prices relationship
Tools	Technical analysis	Fundamental analysis	Statistics
Key metric	Moving avg., relative strength	Intrinsic value, margin of safety	Efficient portfolio, Sharpe ratio
Size of position	All small bets (1%–5%)	Concentrated positions (10–15 names)	Indexing
Upside	Let winner's ride	Own until intrinsic value is reached	Long-term market participation
Downside	Cut loses quick/limit order	Build in margin of safety	Buy the market on dips
Card game	Poker	Bridge	Poker
Founder	Jesse Livermore	Ben Graham	Bachelier, Markowitz, Fama

In Support of Fundamental Analysis

I did not start writing this book with the agenda of defending fundamental analysis or supporting the use of value-based investing. The original goal in writing the book was to take a holistic view of the different approaches to drive better than market returns and create the optimal portfolio.

There are useful elements or takeaways from each of the three different approaches to investing. Speculators teach us to cut our losses quickly and bet moderately. Fundamental analysis suggests an investor searches for the best companies, calculates an intrinsic value, and builds in a margin of safety before you buy. The academics focus on diversity by holding multiple, different names in their portfolio.

There are reasons why fundamental analysis should outperform the other investment approaches over time. Speculating and the academic approach are to a degree based on stock price movements, which is inherently dangerous and flawed. We know short- and long-term stock price movements are erratic and unpredictable, which instantly renders speculating and technical analysis insufficient, especially since it is based on historical price movements. Although academia attempts to account for the randomness of these stock price movements, we have seen time and time again that the size and timing of the movements cannot be captured by any one formula over the long term. This may change over the long run, but the recent historical examples of the academic approach have ended poorly.

If you believe in the future and therefore the market is unpredictable, then you have no choice but to support fundamental analysis. I would reiterate, "The only thing predictable about the market is it is unpredictable." This is one of the few "laws" of the market which include other cornerstones of fundamental analysis like the difference between price and value. Fundamental analysis solves these inherent market problems by suggesting we use human judgment to evaluate opportunities. We know human judgment is flawed, so we must correct it by following a value-based investing approach and reviewing our psychological flaws before investing.

Fundamental analysis using a value-based investing approach is by no means perfect and certainly not the end of the quest for the optimal portfolio. We have constantly seen revisions to the paradigm particularly around the areas of what type of characteristics you look for in the companies you invest in and valuation metrics. The great investors like Buffett, Munger, Lynch, and others have stretched the original Dodd parameters to adjust to an ever-changing market. Although they have been stretched, the original thesis remains intact. Our investment process and especially our five factors are our humble attempt to contribute to the body of knowledge.

We see our approach as a beginning, not an ending. The five factors as well as the market continue to evolve. In fact, the ranking of the factors and the factors themselves have changed over the years. We fully expect them to possibly change along with the markets, but they are a good starting point to continue to the search for the best stocks and the optimal portfolio, which can be done by focusing more on improving the process, than just the results.

What We Learned

The writing of this book brought about as many questions as it answered.

Investing is hard work. It begins by taking a personal inventor of our finances and how we psychologically feel about them. The formula for creating wealth remains the same protect principal, while thoughtfully investing to increase cash flow and build wealth.

We moved forward with an examination of the different approaches to investing. We learned each approach: trading, academics, and fundamentals have positives and negatives. The average individual investor would benefit from an indexing strategy. However, for the investors interested in actively investing in equities, currently the best approach is a fundamental-based one focusing on identifying great companies with potentially strong cash flow, which can be bought at a discount building in a margin of safety. The different approaches provide lessons which can be incorporated into a fundamental-based strategy. Traders are quick to cut losses. The academics help with risk mitigation. Investing is at its core about managing risk.

Markets are dynamic. A general knowledge of how markets operate is crucial to all investing processes. Capitalism is flawed causing market cycles, which provide challenges and opportunities. There are two very different elements in terms of the current trading prices of both stocks and the market: fundamentals (intrinsic value) and psychology (noise). These elements reflect their participants, humans. They are very different elements. However, if you know the two are going to eventually converge, it provides you with an advantage. As an investor, you will not only be prepared against the possibility of outlier events, but you will be ready to buy when the pendulum swings in your favor.

We finish our examination of equity investing by providing our own approach. We looked at the anatomy of a stock. We believe there are five crucial characteristics separating successful equity investments from unsuccessful ones. The elements are: competitive advantage, catalyst, valuation, quality of management, and psychology. These elements should not all be weighed equally. They may even change overtime. They do provide a framework to evaluate opportunities and make comparisons. We encourage readers to research several companies in different industries, and the experience will sharpen their ability to rate each factor and even come up with their own factors. We conclude the book by walking the reader step by step through a practical example of a company and how to evaluate it.

The market is constantly providing lessons. The problem is that you must pay to get those lessons. The markets are dynamic, so should be your approach as an investor. We remain flexible in our thinking about the markets absorbing daily lessons and willing to change our approach to incorporate these lessons at any time, including in future editions. Some areas where we believe there is the opportunity for further exploration: the use of pendulum economics as opposed to the standard idea of economic equilibrium, attempting to measure the psychological element of stock prices, adjusting valuation metrics to incorporate shifts in the market or sentiment, and the further development of quantitative and SRI investing including how it interacts with the markets and stocks.

It has truly been a pleasure. Thank you for taking the time to read this book. I know how valuable time can be. Happy Investing!

Bibliography

Bachelier, L. (1900). *The theory of speculation.* Annales scientifiques de l'École Normale Supérieure, 17, 21–86. https://doi.org/10.24033/asens.476

Banz, R. W. (1981). The relationship between return and market value of common stocks. *Journal of Financial Economics*, *9*, 3–18.

Basu, S. (1977). Investment performance of common stocks in relation to their price-earnings ratios: A test of the efficient market hypothesis. *The Journal of Finance*, *32*, 663–682.

Bernstein, P. L. (1996). *Against the Gods.* John Wiley & Sons.

Bernstein, P. L. (2000). *The Power of Gold.* John Wiley & Sons.

Bernstein, P. L. (2005). *Capital Ideas.* John Wiley & Sons.

Bernstein, P. L. (2007). *Capital Ideas Evolving.* John Wiley & Sons.

Black, F. (1986a). *Lecture/Presentation at CMU (2002, October).* As cited in Derman, E. 2004). My life as a quant: Reflections on physics and finance. Wiley

Black, F. (1986b, July). Noise. *The Journal of Finance, 41*(3), 528–543.
Cootner, P. H. (1964). *The Random Character of Stock Prices.* MIT Press.
Fama, E. F., & French, K. R. (1992). The cross-section of expected stock returns. *The Journal of Finance, 47*, 427–465.
Grossman, S. J., & Stiglitz, J. E. (1980). On the impossibility of informationally efficient markets. *The American Economic Review, 70*(3), 393–408.
Markowitz, H. M. (1959). *Portfolio Selection: Efficient Diversification of Investments.* John Wiley & Sons.
Markowitz, H. M. (1987). *Mean-Variance Analysis in Portfolio Choice and Capital Markets.* Wiley.
Miller, M. H. (1999). The history of finance: An eyewitness account. *Financial Analysts Journal, 55*(6), 11–15.
Patterson, S. (2010). *The Quants.* Random House.
Roy, A. (1952). Safety first and the holding of assets. *Econometrica, 20*, 431–449.
Samuelson, P. A. (1965). Proof that properly anticipated prices fluctuate randomly. *Industrial Management Review, 6*, 41–49.
Sameulson, P. A., & Nordhaus, W. D. (1948). *Economics.* McGraw Hill.
Sharpe, W. F. (1963). A simplified model for portfolio analysis. *Management Science, 9*, 277–293.
Sharpe, W. F. (1964). Capital asset prices: A theory of market equilibrium under conditions of risk. *The Journal of Finance, 19*, 425–442.
Sharpe, W. F. (2007, July 6). What if your advisor talks only about returns, not risk? (J. Zweig, Interviewer).
Tobin, J. (1958). Liquidity preference as behavior towards risk. *The Review of Economic Studies, 25*(2), 65–86.
Williams, J. B. (1938, 1997). *The Theory of Investment Value.* Fraser Publishing Company.

Appendix I

30 Golden Rules of Investing

Foresi's 30 Golden Rules of Investing

1 Investing is risky, buy great companies with strong cash flow at great prices.
2 Market movements combine psychology and fundamentals, two separate things.
3 Ca$h Is King.
4 Thoughtful Capital (Cash) Allocation Creates Wealth.
5 Follow the Power of Compound Interest.
6 Protect Principle while Seeking the Best Returns for a level of risk.
7 Investing is hard work.
8 Stocks represent ownership, but they don't know you own them.
9 Best approach: a flexible, fundamental approach, incorporating the best of the different methodologies and focused on risk mitigation.
10 Fundamental analysis is about finding great companies, establishing an intrinsic value (typically off of cash flow), and building in a margin of safety to come up with an entry point, then being patient for market volatility to provide an opportunity.
12 If capitalism exists, business cycles will take place, regardless of when or why.
13 Know where you are in the business cycle.
14 Although the steps for a financial crisis are the same, the crises are never the same.
15 The only thing that can happen with bubbles is they pop!
16 Be aggressive when others are fearful.
17 No model is good enough to account for irrational behavior and outlier events.
18 Don't buy blind. Invest in what you know (Circle of Competence).
19 Develop a "Spot the Trend" Skill Set.
20 Cash is the only REAL thing; the MORE the better.
21 Moats are hard to find, but worth the effort, especially if they are expanding.
22 Gravity Rule-Numbers go up, stocks go up. Numbers go down; stocks go down.
23 One quarter does not make a year. Look for multiyear trends.
24 Attractive Valuation Means Positive Risk/Reward; REMEMBER to discount using a margin of safety.
25 Keep Valuation Methods as Simple as Possible.
26 Companies characteristics dictate what valuation can be used.
27 Punt (Sell) your troubled companies IMMEDIATELY.
28 Go with Strength of Business-When Deciding Between. "The Good, Bad, & Ugly."
29 Figure out what judges are looking for and if your team has what it takes.
30 Make your conviction-based, actionable decisions after having "enough" facts.

Appendix II

Mastercard Case Study

The Mastercard Case Study-*Master the Possibilities**

Investment Summary. We would recommend investors with a long-term (five to seven years) time horizon consider adding Mastercard at a price level of roughly $350 or more ideally below as of mid-2020. The $350 or below level implies a reasonable discount to our $485 ten-year discount cash flow target. Investors would need to buy it at an even lower price level, if they have a shorter investment time horizon. Mastercard is one of the few companies that would qualify on our list of high-quality stocks, which we would recommend owning, market price permitting.

Company Description. Mastercard is a card network facilitating transactions across the payment eco-system including card users (credit, debit, prepaid, or commercial), issuers, merchants, and acquirers. Card networks utilize their network capabilities and infrastructure to facilitate the authorization, clearance, and settlement of payment transactions. Mastercard facilitates payments within a four-party model, where the issuer and acquirer are different entities.

Mastercard has a distinct, defendable competitive advantage. The company has a healthy market share (26%) in the card network market. There are high barriers to entry into the market, including the infrastructure associated with establishing a network. Mastercard's network has an advantage over other players in the payment industry in they can move funds with limited friction on a global level.

Catalysts are in place to drive long-term results. We believe Mastercard is a GDP plus business meaning it will grow at the pace of GDP due to consumption with additional growth drivers. We believe Mastercard is well positioned to benefit from an acceleration in the cash-to-card conversion rates, especially as we come out of the pandemic. Additional growth drivers/catalysts are the global cash to card conversion rate, new opportunities (additional "rails," Int'l, etc.), and services. Near-term acquisitions could provide key, long-term technological advantages. **Mastercard can deliver an annual high single, low double-digit growth with margin expansion over the long-term.**

Risk. Government regulation of fees and the payment industry is a significant risk. Mastercard can be impacted by economic changes affecting consumer spending patterns and revenues. The company faces competitive threats from incumbent and new players, particularly on the technology front.

Numbers. Mastercard is an expensive company compared to its peer group and competitors making it crucial to build an adequate margin of safety. We build in 18% growth rate and $8.88, 31% growth for 2021. We build in ~10% revenue and ~12% earnings growth over the next three to five years. **We believe Mastercard can deliver an annual high single, low double-digit growth rate with margin expansion in a normalized environment over the long-term.**

**-Please note the example provided is abbreviated and meant to exemplify what an initiation report should look like. If we were publishing, we would spend more time in different areas trying to find conviction and add value. The report is a snapshot taken at a specific point and time.*

Appendix III

FinTech Industry Report (April 2021)

The FinTech Industry

FinTech

The Financial Technology (FinTech) industry presents a large opportunity. FinTech is a line of business using technology to deliver financial services. FinTech companies are disruptive to incumbent, service-oriented vendors. FinTech is currently having its biggest impact in the areas of funds transfer and payments and commercial banking putting pressure on the banking industry.

The Global FinTech market is expected to reach $310 billion, a 25% CAGR, through 2022. Investment in the industry remains healthy with Venture Capital investment in FinTech totaling $128 billion, nearly half of all VC investments in 2018. (*The Business Research Company*) The industry is beginning to show signs of early maturity after its explosive growth following its 2008 birth post, the Great Recession. FinTech funds are reaching their end of life, and new technologies are evolving resulting in later-stage investing.

FinTech covers a broad landscape. Several Financial Services sectors are facing increasing competition from technology-fueled competition. Three of the larger areas are Technology (bank/investment), Processing (payment/ATM), and Lending (card networks/prepaid). Other FinTech areas include blockchain, wealth management, and insurance.

Industry Thesis: We like the companies best positioned at the point of sale, friction fighters, and the international players where cash conversion rates are accelerating. Our top picks are Mastercard, PayPal, and Adyen.

Industry: Financial Technology (FinTech) is a large industry encompassing several subsectors. Three of the larger subsectors are Technology (bank/investment), Processing (payment/ATM), and Lending (card networks/prepaid). Other areas include blockchain, wealth management, and insurance. The industry is estimated to be $310 billion in size through 2022 growing, 25% CAGR.

Payments: Payments are an attractive investment opportunity given the recurring nature of the revenues and low capital expenditures. There are several catalysts driving industry growth including consumption, cash-to-card conversion rates, omni-channel retail, and frictionless experiences. These catalysts have different growth rates making individual and company market positioning very important from a growth rate and market share perspective. The industry is expected to grow at 10% CAGR.

Comparison Group: The financial profile of a payment processor is dependent on their geographic location and position in the ecosystem. The baseline annual growth rate for the industry is low to mid-single digits with aggregate annual growth rates trending toward mid-single digits for Merchant Acquirers, high single to low double digit growth rates for the card networks, and mid-teens to low twenties for the gateways. The card networks have compelling EBITDA margins in the 60% range followed by the merchant acquirers in the 35%–45% range and finally the emerging gateways, whose business models particularly SQ remain in their early stages. The earnings profile for the group implies +20% earnings growth.

Competitive Analysis: Visa has the largest US market share of any player in the group at roughly 50% of the card network market followed by 20% for Mastercard. PayPal has a 20% market share in eCommerce, while Global Payments has roughly 10% market share among the Top 10 merchant acquirers. The barriers to entry vary based on where the players are in the payment ecosystem. The card networks have a high barrier to entry given their position as the "network" the payments are processed on. Gateways have a first mover and competitive technology advantage, while the merchant acquirers have a low barrier to entry.

Financials: The payment group have competitive financial metrics compared to the market. The group ROE is above industry average. Gateways sell at an extremely large premium to the 5-Year Average PE, while the card networks trade at roughly a 50% premium and merchant acquirers at a 30% premium.

Welcome to the Payment Ecosystem

Payment processing is an ecosystem. Each time a consumer makes a digital or card payment, the transaction moves through the system. There is a chain of different providers participating in the system, each charging a fee for their services. There are many ways a transaction can be processed, and different participants take part in its processing. We look at the three Ps below what participants are involved in a "typical" transaction, how it is processed, and what price or fees are potentially charged below.

The Participants

There are several different players involved in the payment ecosystem. We provide a brief, simplified definition of each and examples of the participants below. We list the names of the companies we are very familiar with in each category (former coverage) bolded below. We note payment participants can reside in more than one area.

- **Merchant Acquirer/Processor**: signs merchants to contracts to process online and in-store payments.
  Names: Adyen, EVO Payments, First Data (FISV), WorldPay (FIS), Global Payments, MercadoLibre, PagSeguro, Repay, Square, Stone
- **Card Network**: network the payment's travel on.
  Names: Mastercard, Visa, American Express, Discover (Domestic)
- **Issuers**: banks
- **Gateways**: refers to online (e-commerce) payment processors
  Names: Adyen, MercadoLibre, PayPal, Square
- **ISOs (Independent Sales Organization)**: provide merchant services to banks, but not part of card system

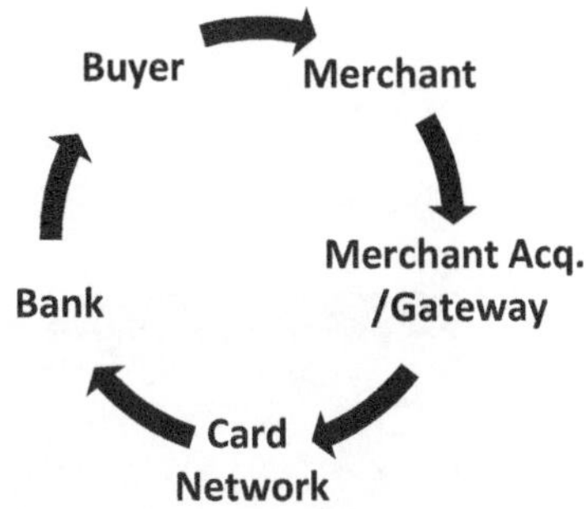

Figure AIII.1 Payment Processing Ecosystem.

The Processing

Payment processing is a multi-step process taking just a few seconds. The process begins with a customer using their card for payment of a product with a merchant. A customer can purchase a product in an increasing number of ways through physical contact, contactless, etc. in several different venues like in stores, online, etc. The place where a product is purchased is considered the Point-Of-Sale (POS). The merchant sends the transaction information to the acquirer either through manual feed, swipe, contactless, or other. The gateway then authorizes the payment for processing. The acquirer or processor sends the transaction info to the card networks, which is referred to as "riding the rails." The issuing bank validates the transaction by paying the card association after deducting its charge. The card network (e.g., Mastercard, Visa) deducts its charge and pays the acquirer or processor. The processor deducts its charge and credits the merchant's account for the transaction. The issuer bills the buyer, and the buyer settles the bill. The transaction is considered complete at the end of the process. All in a matter of seconds (Figure AIII.1).

The Price

Every company gets a slice of action. Participants of the payment-processing ecosystem, who are part of the transaction, each get a fee whenever a payment is processed. The fees known as the Merchant Discount Rate or MDR are charged to the merchant. The MDR is the total fees covering interchange (issuers), networks (card networks), and merchant acquirers. The typical fee amount is in the range of 2p–3% of every transaction. These fees can be "all in" or "cost plus." The fees and percentages each participant collects vary based on how the transaction is being processed and what players are involved. The card network fees are standard (15–18 bps), banks/issuers get the largest fees, and the remainder goes to the processor. Issuer fees are typically referred to as interchange fees. These fees add up to trillions of dollars globally per year (Figure AIII.2).

An example of a "typical" payment may help. Let's assume a merchant is selling a product for $100 with a MDR of 2%. If a consumer pays for the item through card or digital payments, the merchant receives roughly $98. The MDR of $2 would be split between the bank would get $1.50, the card network would receive $0.15, and Acquirer/Processor/ISO/MSP would collect the remaining $0.35. **Please note these are very rough assumptions, and the MDR changes based on participants and geographies.**

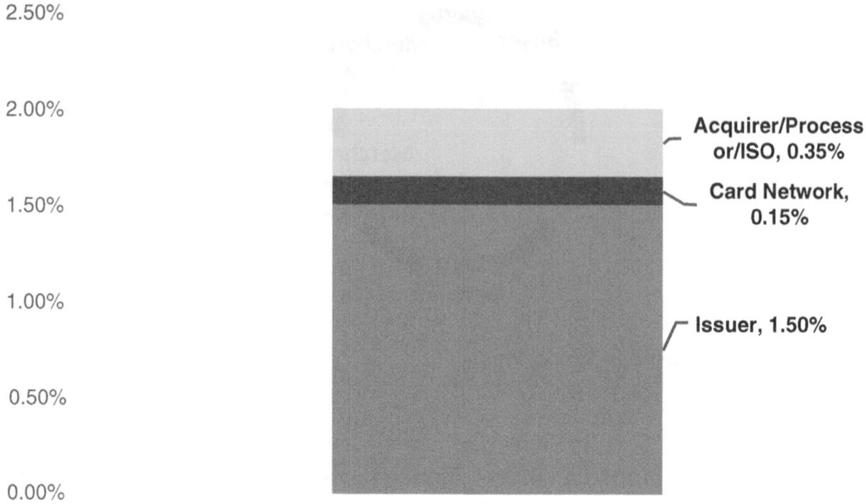

Figure AIII.2 Merchant Discount Rate (MDR) 2%–3%.

Payment Growth Drivers

Global payments processing industry expected to grow at 10% CAGR over the next five years. According to reportlinker.com, the global payments industry is expected to grow to $121 billion in 2025 from $74 billion in 2020.

We believe there are several catalysts for industry growth including global consumption, cash-to-card conversion rates, and omni-channel retail. These drivers each present an opportunity to drive payment volumes. The natural driver is Gross Domestic Product (GDP). Consumption can vary, but GDP tends to be in the low single-digit range. Non-cash payments should take place globally wherever they are available and there is consumption.

A second powerful catalyst is the global cash-to-card conversion rate, meaning the increased use of card vs. cash at the point of sale (POS). Payment companies will continue to benefit as card usage naturally continues to increase vs. cash over time. Card usage is relatively high in the US vs. the rest of the world with cash being used roughly one fourth of the time. Cash usage tends to be higher in emerging markets and surprisingly in countries like Germany and Japan. We expect card usage to continually rise over time.

A third catalyst is omni-channel retail. Historically, retail ran primarily through one channel, in store. The ability to purchase items has changed over time in how and where they are purchased. Consumption can be performed through several vehicles including cash, card, contactless, and wearables. It can happen online and in store. The growth rates associated with these different vehicles vary, making the positioning of potential in these areas important. For example, in store annual consumption growth rates tend to be in the low single digits, while eCommerce is in the mid-teens making positioning in eCommerce important to growth rates and market share.

There is the powerful notion of "friction" within payments. The easier it is to perform a payment, the more likely it is for consumers to purchase things. General consumption has increased as we have moved to card from cash because we have taken friction out of the system. The same is true as we continue to move away from card purchases to the internet. The natural conclusion is the better the payment processor is at taking friction out of the system, the more effective they will be.

Payment Industry Individual Company Comparison Group

The financial profile of a payment processor is dependent on their geographic location and positioning in the ecosystem. We note our initial focus here is on the US payment's ecosystem as an initial view into the world of global payments. We can see below that the US Gateways (SQ, PYPL) are the fastest growing with well over 20% annual growth followed by the card networks (MA, V) and the merchant acquirers (GPN, EVOP) at low double digits.

There is a discrepancy among the payment players in their margin profile. The card networks have compelling EBITDA margins in the 60% range followed by the merchant acquirers in the 35%–45% range and finally the emerging gateways, whose business models particularly SQ remain in their early stages. The earnings profile for the group implies +20% earnings growth.

Competitive Analysis

Market Share

A thorough understanding of an industry or company's overall market, market share, and whether the participant is gaining or losing share is crucial to a top-down industry analysis. We take an abbreviated look at the payment industry including the card networks, gateways, and merchant acquirers.

According to Nilson that publishes annual reports on the payments industry, the total card purchases volume reached over $7 trillion in 2018 and was expected to reach $10 trillion by 2023. The card networks accounted for roughly 70% market share with Visa making up roughly half the market and Mastercard accounting for 20% market share. The US eCommerce industry was estimated to be about 15% of the US card purchase volume putting it at $1 trillion in 2019 growing double digits. Gateway PayPal accounted for 22% of transactions in 2018, according to Statista. We anticipate the market share for PayPal, and the adoption of eCommerce has rapidly accelerated due to the current pandemic, which has forced consumers to make purchases online. Transaction volume grows to single digits, steady state. Purchase transaction volumes grew roughly 7% to roughly 104 billion in 2019. The top US merchant acquirers ranked by volume in 2019 according to Nelson were: FIS, Chase, First Data, BofA, Global Payments, Wells, and Evalon. Global payments had roughly 10 billion in transaction volume or 9% market share across the top providers (Table AIII.1).

Table AIII.1 Payment Ecosystem Market Share

Company	*Market Share*
Card Networks	
Mastercard[a]	*21% market share in US credit card purchase volume 2018* *22% market share in US debit card purchase volume 2018*
Visa[a]	*50% market share in US credit card purchase volume 2018* *52% market share in US debit card purchase volume 2018*
eCommerce	
PayPal[b]	*22% market share in eCommerce in 2018*
Merchant Acquirer	
Global Payments	*9% market share in merchant acquirers in 2019*

[a] 2019 Nilson Report.

[b] Researchandmarkets.com and Statista.

Competition

The payments industry has several unique competitive traits. Historically, the industry had high barriers to entry, which have come down over time as retail has moved to omni present retail from in store purchases. The card networks have maintained high barriers to entry. The top ten merchant acquirers continue to maintain the largest amount of market share. However, a new group of players have entered the market as commerce has taken to the internet where initially the barriers to entry were low. Gateway providers have a first-mover advantage on the internet and have put pressure on the merchant acquirers who are commoditized and consolidating.

The core driver of payments is consumer demand. The payment business is a low capital expenditure, high recurring revenue business. Growth rates for the payments industry currently have additional drivers like an accelerating cash-to-card conversion rate and technological changes. We compare the payment industry financial characteristics to other SP500 composite sectors.

ROE

The quality of a business model and management can be measured through its return metrics, including the return on equity, investment, and assets. These return metrics measure the strength of the business and its ability to generate excess returns. We can see from Table AIII.2 that the payment players are able to deliver impressive excess returns. For perspective, the long-term average long term average ROE is around 14%, which implies PYPL, SQ, Visa, and especially MA are well above the average (Figure AIII.3).

Financial Comparison

We look at the different sectors of the S&P to get a sense of how payments compare. Payment is a cyclical business delivering a baseline growth rate of mid-single digits with most players delivering a high single-low double digits. The industry average margin is in the 20% range with select vendors delivering higher margins. The ROE for select vendors is above 25%. Payment's compares favorably to other sectors in the S&P.

Table AIII.2 SP500 Sector Comparison

5 Year Avg.	*Technology (%)*	*Health Care (%)*	*Consumer Disc. (%)*	*Financials (%)*	*Industrials (%)*	*Consumer Staples (%)*	*Energy (%)*	*Utilities (%)*	*Materials (%)*	*Real Estate (%)*
% of SP500	27	14	11	11	8	7	3	3	3	3
Growth	4	9	4	4	1	3	−4	−2	1	7
Gross margin	43	32	28	–	25	28	12	28	23	38
Ops margin	20	11	8	–	11	9	4	20	11	19
ROE	25	19	24	9	19	25	4	10	14	8
ROIC	15	10	10	5	9	13	3	4	8	4
FCF margin	19	9	6	–	6	6	3	−4	7	22

Source: FactSet April 2021.

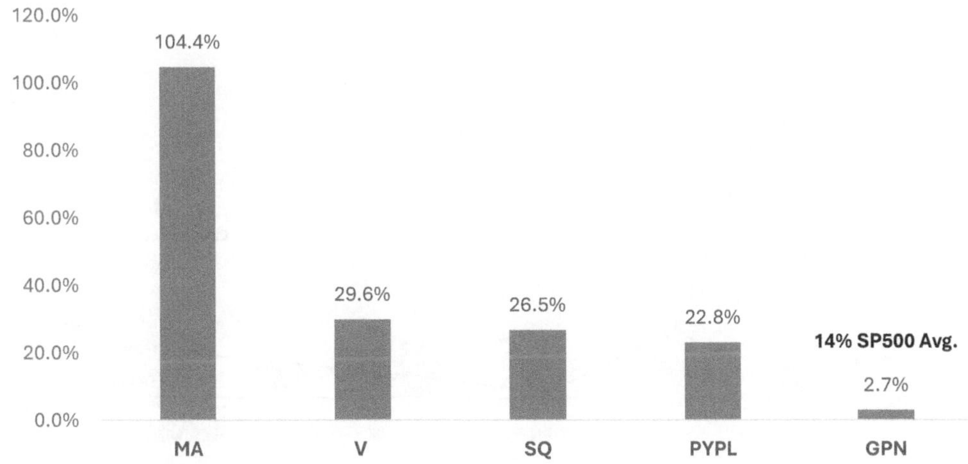

Figure AIII.3 2020 Payment Processing ROE.

Source: FactSet, FY Yr. End, Numbers as of April 2021.

Valuation

We look at the relative valuation for the payments group. The payments group sells at a premium to SP500 whose 5-year average is 23×. The card networks trade at nearly a 50% premium with Gateways trading at a much higher 500% average premium than the card networks, while the Merchant Acquirers are at a more reasonable 30% average premium (Figure AIII.4).

Mastering Mastercard

Mastercard is a card/payment network. The company's primary business is the authorization, clearance, and settlement of digital payment transactions through their international (150 currencies; 210 countries), multi-rail network. Mastercard's revenues are based on collecting fees from the number and dollar value of the transactions it facilitates. It doesn't earn revenues by issuing cards, setting cardholder fees or interest rates, or making loans to cardholders, a common misconception. The company offers services in the areas of security, analytics, consulting, and rewards programs. Mastercard has ACH and real-time capabilities as well.

The company's core network follows the traditional "four-party" system. The four parties include the account holder, card issuer or bank, merchant, and merchant acquirer. The system is like the ecosystem described above. Mastercard serves as the "middleman" in the four-party system facilitating authorization, clearance, and settlement. The company has global capabilities. It switches transactions throughout the world when the merchant country and issuer country differ, known as "cross-border transaction," and when they are the same, "domestic transaction." Mastercard switches nearly half of their transactions and all their cross border transactions.

Mastercard believes its core network adds value. The company has built and maintains a secure, global, 24-hour a day network, enabling its users to confidently expand into new geographies. Value-added services include offerings like fraud scoring and tokenization. Mastercard continues to focus on adapting its system to newer payment initiatives like digital and real-time

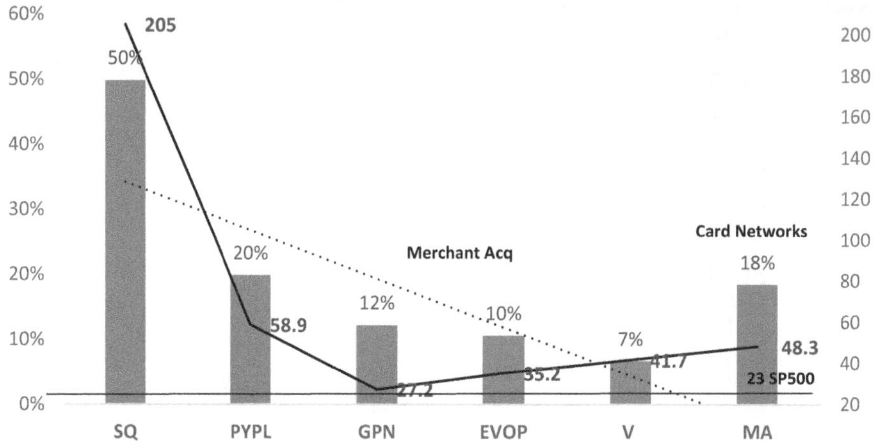

Figure AIII.4 Annual US Revenue Growth and Price to Earnings.

Source: FactSet; FY Yr End; Numbers as of April 2021.

payments. Mastercard only guarantees settlement of transactions from issuers to acquirers known as settlement exposure. The company routinely participates in collaborative global safe and secure payment initiatives.

Mastering the Five Business Segments

Mastercard business is divided into five segments: Transaction Processing Fees (34% of Gross Revenues), Domestic Assessments (27%), Cross Border Volume Fees (22%), Other (17%), and Rebates and Incentives. The company has grown revenues at 10.6% CAGR from 2013 to 2019. We note the Rebates and Incentives segment is a contra account meaning its total is subtracted from the aggregate (Figure AIII.5).

Transaction Processing Fees are earned from authorization, clearance, and settlement of domestic and cross-border transactions. Purchase transactions are core drivers of Transaction Processing Fees, which are roughly $0.08 per transaction. Transaction processing represents about one third of gross revenues growing at a 13% CAGR from 2014 to 2019 (Figure AIII.6).

Domestic Assessments are the fees Mastercard charges issuers and acquirers for transactions in which the merchant country and issuer country are the same. Worldwide GDV (Gross Dollar Volume) drives growth in the Domestic Assessments segment, which is roughly $1 per transaction. Domestic Assessments represent about roughly one fourth of gross revenues growing at an 8% CAGR from 2013 to 2019. Mastercard's worldwide GDV grew to $6.46 trillion in 2019 from $4.50 trillion in 2014, representing a 6% CAGR (Figure AIII.7).

Mastercard's third largest source of revenue is cross border volumes fees, which are fees charged to issuers and acquirers for transactions in which the merchant country and the issuer country are different. Mastercard reports cross-border volume fees, which are roughly $0.90 per transaction. Mastercard's cross-border volumes grew to 5.61 trillion in 2019 from 3.05 trillion in 2014, representing a 9% CAGR (22% of gross revenues). **We provide a comparison of the fees for the three primary segments per Gross Domestic Volume (GDV) below as well** (Figure AIII.8).

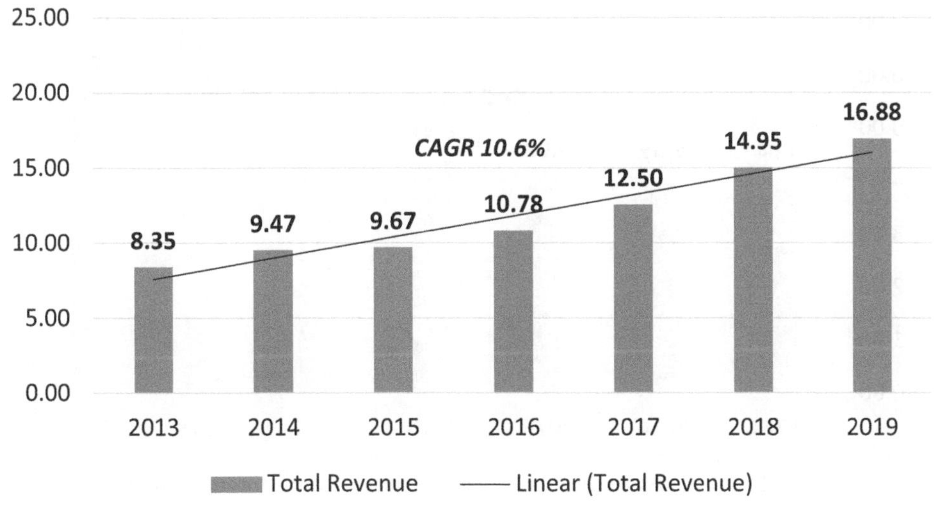

Figure AIII.5 Total Revenue.

Source: Company Reports.

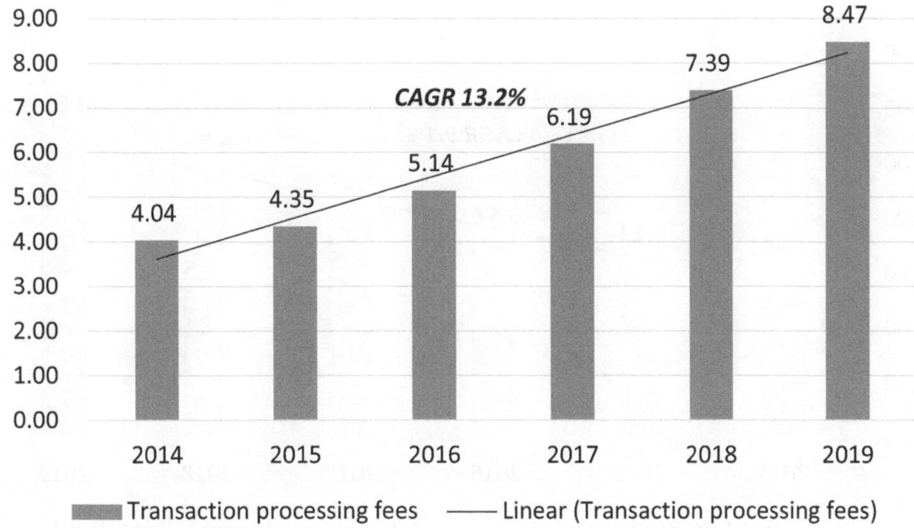

Figure AIII.6 Transaction Processing Fees.

Source: Company Reports.

The company's Other revenue segment consists of fees for consulting, data analytics, research, safety and security services, loyalty and reward solutions, and program management services. Other revenues have accounted for roughly 17% of gross revenues. Mastercard's Other revenue segment is the fastest-growing segment growing at a 16% CAGR from 2014 to 2019 (Figure AIII.9).

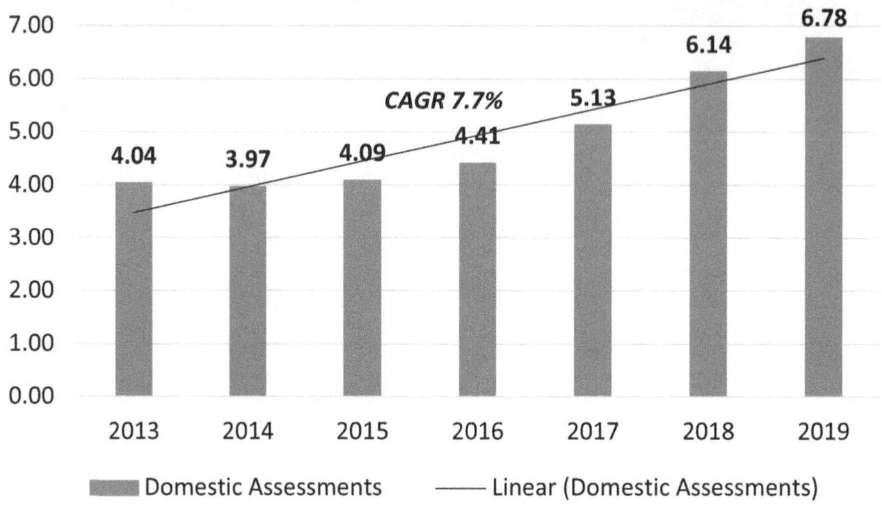

Figure AIII.7 Domestic Assessment.

Source: Company Reports.

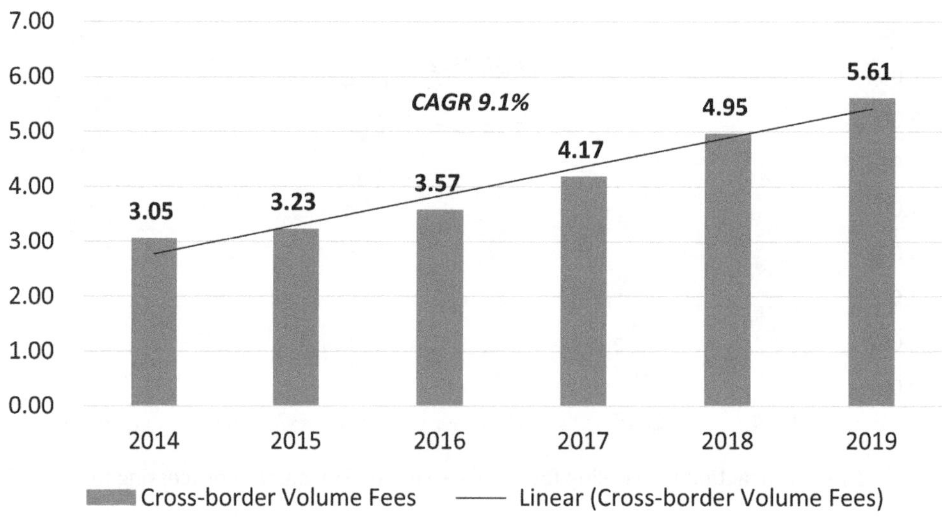

Figure AIII.8 Cross Border.

Source: Company Reports.

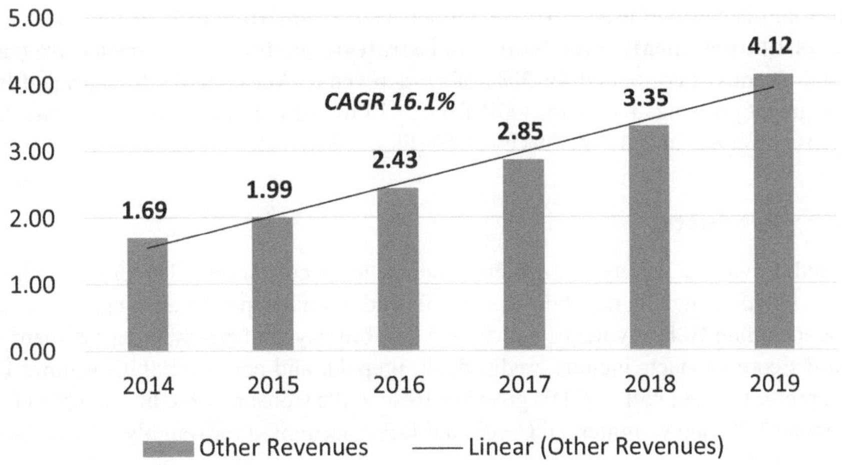

Figure AIII.9 Other Revenue.

Source: Company Reports.

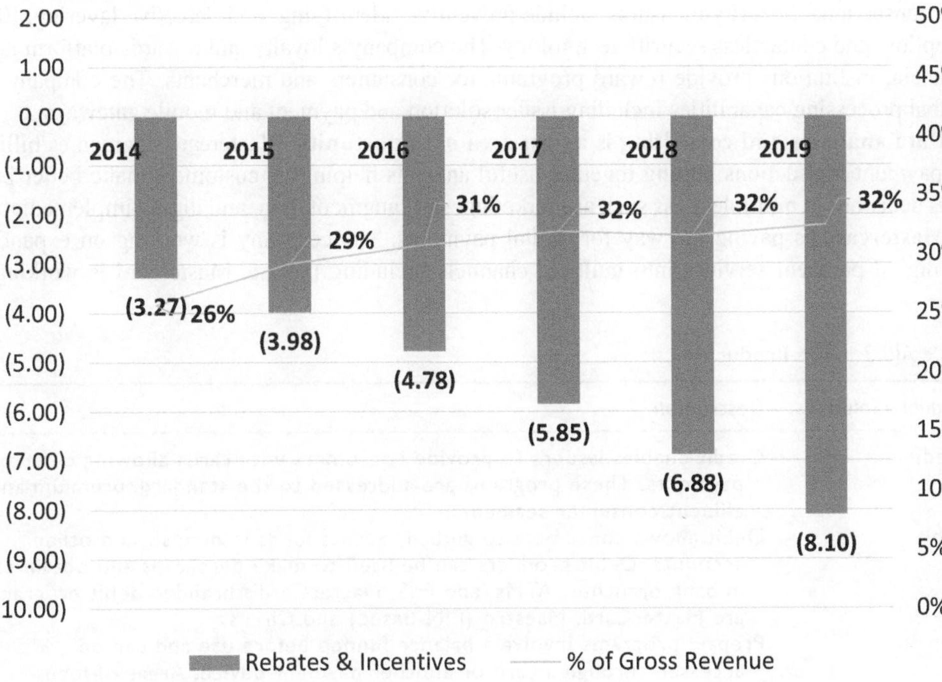

Figure AIII.10 Rebates and Incentives.

Source: Company Reports.

Rebates and Incentives is a contra-revenue account consisting of long-term contracts with financial institution clients, merchants, and strategic partners for various programs. The rebates and incentives accounted for 30% of gross revenue. Mastercard's Rebates and Incentives revenue segment growing at a 16% CAGR from 2014 to 2019. The segment has grown from 26% of total gross revenues in 2014 to 32% by 2019 (Figure AIII.10).

Mastering Products

Mastercard provides a variety of payment products to its customers. The company maintains its core network with switching capabilities but offers additional capabilities to capture a larger payment flow including B2B payments, real-time ACH, bill pay, and cross-border payment transfers. Mastercard's core products include credit, debit, prepaid, and commercial. Consumer Debit and Prepaid represents about half of GDV growing 16%; while Consumer credit accounted for 40% of GDV growing 10% and Commercial Credit and Debit accounted for roughly 10% of GDV growing 14% (Table AIII.3).

Value-Added Products and Services

Mastercard provides value-added offerings like security, data analytics and consulting, and digital payments. Mastercard's cyber and intelligence offering ensures the security and privacy of the transactions. Security measures include preventive, identifying, and detective layering, EMV adoption, and contactless security technology. The company's loyalty and rewards platform helps financial institutions provide reward programs for consumers and merchants. The company has global processing capabilities including issuer solution and payment and mobile gateways.

Data analytics and consulting is a vast area of opportunity. Mastercard aggregates billions of payment transactions putting together useful analysis helping its customers make better business decisions in multiple areas such as marketing, staff augmentation, and digital implementation.

Mastercard is paving the way for digital payments. The company is working on expanding its digital payment services into multiple channels including mobile. Mastercard is working to

Table AIII.3 Core Products

Products/Solutions	*Description*
Credit	Credit enables issuers to provide consumers with cards allowing deferred payments. These programs are addressed to the standard, premium and affluent consumer segments.
Debit	Debit allows consumers to globally access funds in deposit and other accounts. Debit products can be used to make purchases and obtain cash in bank branches, ATMs, and PoS. MasterCard's branded debit programs are MasterCard, Maestro (PIN-based) and Cirrus.
Prepaid	Prepaid programs involve a balance funded before use and can be accessed through a card or another payment device. Areas of focus in MasterCard's prepaid solutions are government, commercial and consumer programs.
Commercial	Commercial products and solutions help large corporations, mid-sized companies, small businesses and government entities with payment processes, expenses and administrative costs. The company's primary offerings are cards, programs and a SmartData tool.

enhance the digital shopping experience enabling secure payments to be made in an omni-channel retail environment through multiple payment methods. There is innovation taking place in areas such as mobile payments, biometric identification, and open APIs.

It's GOOD to Be Mastercard

Mastercard owns the infrastructure necessary to process card payments, which is their key competitive advantage. There is very little, short-term threat to the current network in our opinion. It would be extremely difficult and would take a long time for a new competitor to build a network, not to mention the challenges with getting customers to use and trust the system. There is very little to no pricing pressure with very few alternatives, although pricing is sometimes limited by government regulations.

There is the potential for long-term threats. Governments could push through further regulations, try to directly disrupt the ecosystem, or put pressures on fees. Technological progress, like Venmo, could create or accelerate the opportunity to perform payments outside the traditional ecosystem. There is the looming threat of large technology players like Amazon or Apple, who could try to perform payment processing on their own. Other disruption includes advances in ACH payments, etc.

Mastercard currently has a clear competitive moat in our opinion. The company's moat is supported by its network, which would be extremely difficult to replicate. The company's market share makes it a monopoly/duopoly. Mastercard has additional characteristics, which strengthen its competitive moat, including its global reach and ability to transfer cash through its global network.

Mastercard faces multiple layers of competition. Mastercard is a card network. It facilitates card payment processing serving as the crucial backbone or rails of the transactions. The company competes globally against the use of other forms of payment outside of cards including such methods of payments as cash, checks, and prepaid payments. There are emerging methods of payment including P2P payments through methods like PayPal's Venmo. According to a 2018 Nilson Report, the US is predominantly a card-based transaction system +60% (39% Debit, 21% Credit) with cash representing 25% of transactions. The balance between payment methods varies across countries with some countries being nearly cashless and others having lower cash-to-card conversion rates. Overall, it is believed cash to card conversion rates will increase globally toward card purchases.

Mastercard has domestic and global competitors. According to a 2019 Nilson Report, US purchasing volumes were $6.698 trillion in 2019. The US card network world is divided up between Mastercard and Visa, which is considered Mastercard's main competitor in the Western world. The two companies are essentially a duopoly in my opinion. Visa has a larger portion of the US market from a volume perspective with almost 60% of the purchase volumes (29% Debit-9.8% y/y; 31% Credit-6.8% y/y). Mastercard has 26% market share (12% Debit-9.0% y/y; 14% Credit-12.2% y/y). The remainder of the purchasing volume is divided across American Express (12%) and Discover (2%).

There are six major players in the global card network. The major players are Mastercard, Visa, UnionPay, American Express, JCB, and Discover. The six largest players account for about 441 billion in purchase transactions in 2019, according to the Nilson Report. The three largest card networks Visa, Mastercard, and UnionPay (China) have dominant market share. Mastercard accounted for 108 billion transaction or 24% of the market. Mastercard has consistently represented about 25% of the market over the last decade. UnionPay has 30% of the market. The remaining players American Express, JCB, and Discover each have 1% of the market.

Mastercard Nine Force Competitive Analysis

We view Mastercard as being in a positive strategic position. We look at each of the different Nine Forces below ranking the forces between 1 and 10 from weakest-1 to strongest-10.

Threat of New Entrant-Very Low-2

A new competitor would:

- need to set up a global network to process payments
- sign up global players to be on the network and convince them it was usable, secure
- satisfy the regulatory requirements of each geography

These are all very difficult challenges to overcome.

Bargaining Power of Buyer-Semi Weak-4

- Buyers are banks or financial institutions, who have limited choices between card networks
- Little ability to impact a standard pricing model
- Bargaining power may increase in geographies outside the US where other forms of payment are used

Bargaining Power of Suppliers-Very Strong-8

- Card networks are the primary suppliers of the infrastructure, so they have bargaining power
- They maintain a standard, stable pricing model

Threat of Substitutes-Very Low-2

- There are other options available for payment, but cash to card conversion is moving to cashless

Rivalry across Competitors-Low-3

- MA competes against V, but they essentially own the Western Market w/ few rivals

Government Threat-Moderate-7

- Intervention is always a concern with true monopolies
- Gov.'s often can and do set/cap interchange fee

Social-Moderate-3

- COVID accelerating the movement to cashless society
- Omni-present retail, especially eCommerce, continues to grow faster than in store
- There is push back from Merchant's

Technology-Moderate-5

- Threat of Big Tech (AMZN, AAPL) getting bigger over time
- Technology is increasing the payment options like Venmo, which could go around the system
- Fast payment could be a threat, especially if they use ACH

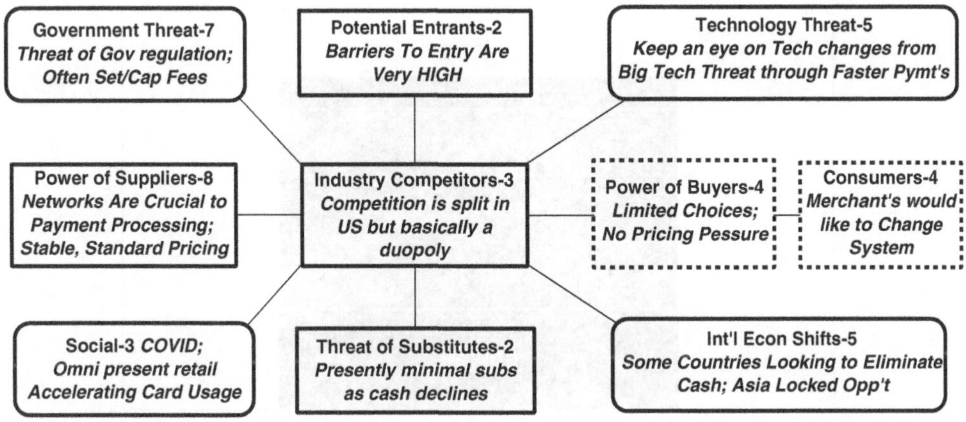

Figure AIII.11 Mastercard Nine Forces (Scale of 1–10; 1-Easiest; 10-Hardest).

***International*-Moderate-5**

- International is an opportunity as areas like emerging markets and Japan are accelerating cash-to-card conversion
- China remains a locked market, but an opportunity (Figure AIII.11).

Company Specific Competitive Advantages

Mastercard has company-specific competitive advantages. Mastercard is often compared to its competitor Visa with other competitors including Discover and American Express. There are subtle differences between the business models. Mastercard appears to be further ahead in developing its technology and other services and its ability to move beyond its core business, essentially expanding its TAM (Total Addressable Market).

Mastercard's acquisition activity and "other" services have helped building out its additional "rails" approach. Significant acquisitions include Vocalink (ACH Capabilities-June 2016) and Nets (Real Time Payments-August 2019). Mastercard's "Other" services account for nearly 20% of the business growing in the mid-teen's pre-pandemic. Other positive initiatives include the advancement into the area of B2B and International expansion (cross-border). I believe Mastercard has an advantage over its competitor Visa given its lower margin profile of a roughly high 50% margin range vs. roughly high 60% margins for Visa in normal environments. The lower margin profile gives Mastercard the opportunity to expand margins over the long-term or protect their margin profile in challenging economic times. **Visa's positive attributes are that the company appears to have a larger domestic market share and signed partnerships compared to Mastercard.**

Plenty of Driver to Go Around

There are several different catalysts driving Mastercard's business. Mastercard has several catalysts to drive results including consumption, accelerating global cash to card conversion rates, global expansion, B2B (Business-To-Business), P2P (Person-To-Person), etc. These catalysts can be broken down into three categories: industry, technology, and company-specific initiatives. The payment industry's annual growth rates are expected to be in the mid to high single-digit range driven by global consumption and cash-to-card conversion rates. The progression of technology

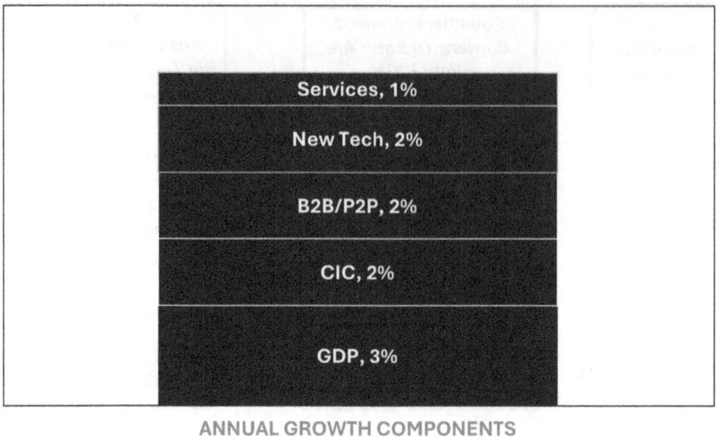

Figure AIII.12 Mastercard Potentially High Single/Low Double-Digit Growth.

is driving the growth in digital payments in the short term through newer retail channels like eCommerce and over the long-term through emerging payment methods like mobile or wearables. Mastercard is working on several initiatives to drive further growth including opportunities like contactless and B2B (Business-to-Business) payments and services offerings. Other opportunities include margin and global expansion, particularly Asia.

The strength of Mastercard's catalysts is impressive as essentially the company is working to "put cash (itself) out of business" or serve as a payment alternative to cash. The foundation of the company's growth rate is supported by global consumption (GDP) and the trend toward card or digital payments away from cash (CIC-Cash-In-Circulation). These secular trends are taking place on a global basis without much effort by Mastercard. The company is focused on expanding its addressable market and can do so in areas like Business-to-Business (B2B) and Services. Mastercard has the capital available to add acquisitions to accelerate its transformation.

Our back of the envelope calculation indicates the potential for a high single-low double-digit annual growth rate in a normalized environment for Mastercard. The company benefits from a core mid-single-digit annual growth rate. It is expanding its Total Addressable Market (TAM) to include a multitude of new opportunities such as B2B/P2P, New Tech (Digital), and Services, which are expected to complement the aggregate high single-digit growth rate over the longer term. Qualitative catalysts often get converted into quantitative catalysts through the process of forecasting as we will see in the next section (Figure AIII.12).

Healthy Industry Backdrop

The core growth rate for Mastercard's business is driven by consumption. Consumption is typically a GDP plus growth rate. There is a global movement away from cash to card usage, especially in the international markets where cash-to-card conversion rates are lower but rapidly accelerating. The net result is a mid-to-high single-digit annual industry growth rate. The forecasted global payment transaction growth rate pre-COVID 19 pandemic can be separated between mature and emerging markets. Emerging markets provide an opportunity as well as omni-channel retail, especially eCommerce, which is growing faster than in store physical payments. *Capgemini World Payment's* report estimates a CAGR of roughly 7% for the mature regions (5% US; 8% Europe) and 24% for developing regions from 2017-22F. Asia could be a long-term opportunity, but the card networks are currently locked out of one of the region's largest markets, China. **Mastercard's business is geographically broken down into 33% in the US, 30% in Europe and Asia and the remainder in Canada and Latam.**

Technology Driving Digital Payments

The trend toward digital payments is a catalyst. Digital payment growth is being driven by the move to omni-channel retail changing the way people pay for and how merchants receive payments, which provides opportunities and potential competition. Currently, the largest opportunity is eCommerce estimated to grow mid to upper teens vs. the single digit growth rates for in store purchases pre-pandemic. For context, eCommerce was roughly $450 billion of retail sales or roughly 9% of the $5 trillion in 2017 according to the US Census Bureau. eCommerce represents roughly 20% of global retail sales, growing at a roughly 20% CAGR from $1.5 trillion in '15 to $4.0 trillion in '20, according to eMarketer. The COVID-19 pandemic was expected to accelerate the use of alternative payment methods away from in store purchases. The ability to process digital payments through multiple devices such as mobile, contactless, and wearables, which are all areas of rapid growth, should accelerate cash-to-card conversion rates benefitting Mastercard. The advent of IoT (Internet of Things) over time is expected to be a continuation of the movement to a cashless society.

Mastercard's Growth Initiatives

Mastercard has several initiatives with the potential to drive future results. The company is working on innovations such as "tap & go" to make the checkout experience faster, more enjoyable. The adoption of contactless payments is efficient and increases card usage while changing customer payment behavior in a favorable manner. The "tap & go" system is being rolled out to New York, Miami, Portland, and Mexico City transit systems. Mastercard is working on penetrating the B2B payment ecosystem through its "MastercardTrack" program aimed at improving the business payment ecosystem. The company estimates the US B2B payment industry is roughly $25 trillion. We estimate only 10% of B2B payments are performed by card (virtual card) with the remaining 90% split between check and ACH providing plenty of opportunity. Mastercard is working on creating opportunities to capture new payment flows in the P2P, B2C, and government disbursement arena through offerings such as real-time payments or FastACH. The company has made acquisitions to enhance its capabilities including VocaLink, Nets, Transactis, and Transfast. Mastercard's service offering is an emerging area of long-term growth potential. The company provides its customers with data analytics, consulting, security, and processing capabilities.

2Q20 Earnings Results

Mastercard Outperforms 2Q20 Expectations. Mastercard reported 2Q20 net revenues of $3.335 billion, a −19% annual decrease (−17% in constant currency), above the FactSet consensus on $3.25 billion. Acquisitions contributed 1% to overall growth. Adjusted EPS was $1.41, above consensus of $1.17. The primary reason for the large decline in revenues was a slowdown in consumer spending due to the COVID 19 pandemic. Domestic assessments (44% of net revenue) were $1.474 billion, −12% y/y, above consensus of $1.423 billion. The biggest decline was in cross-border volume fees of $637 million (19%), −54% y/y, below consensus of $727 million.

Table AIII.4 2Q20 Quarterly Performance Table

FY December	*Jun-20*	*Rate or*	*Jun-19*	*Rate or*	*Mar-20*	*Rate or*	*% Change*	*% Change*
($ in Millions, Except Share Data)	*2Q 20A*	*Margin (%)*	*2Q 19A*	*Margin (%)*	*1Q 20A*	*Margin (%)*	*Y/Y (%)*	*Q/Q (%)*
Domestic assessments	1,474	44.2	1,680	40.8	1,683	42.0	−12.3	−12.4
Cross-border volume fees	637	19.1	1,374	33.4	1,217	30.4	−53.6	−47.7
Transaction processing fees	1,901	57.0	2,053	49.9	2,200	54.9	−7.4	−13.6
Other revenues	1,081	32.4	962	23.4	1,062	26.5	12.4	1.8
Rebates and incentives	(1,758)	−52.7	(1,956)	−47.6	(2,153)	−53.7	− 10.1	−18.3
Net revenue	**3,335**		**4,113**		**4,009**		**−18.9**	**−16.8**
Operating Expenses								
General and administrative	1,368	41.0	1,369	33.3	1,494	37.3	−0.1	−8.4
Advertising and marketing	93	2.8	225	5.5	154	3.8	−58.7	−39.6
Depreciation and amortization	145	4.3	122	3.0	144	3.6	18.9	0.7
Provision for litigation settlement	22	–	0	0.0	6	–	–	–
Operating Income	**1,707**	**51.2**	**2,397**	**58.3**	**2,211**	**55.2**	**−28.8**	**−22.8**
Investment income	8	0.2	24	0.6	16	0.4	−66.7	−50.0
Gain (losses) on equity investment, net	75		0		(174)			
Interest expense	(101)	−3.0	(51)	−1.2	(69)	−1.7	98.0	46.4
Other income (expense), net	1	0.0	149	3.6	3	0.1	−99.3	–
Pretax income	**1,690**	**50.7**	**2,519**	**61.2**	**1,987**	**49.6**	**−32.9**	**−14.9**
Income tax provision	270	16.0	471	18.7	294	14.8	−42.7	−8.2
Other	0		(111)		0			
Adjusted net income	**1,420**	**42.6**	**1,937**	**47.1**	**1,693**	**42.2**	**−26.7**	**−16.1**
EPS	**$1.41**		**$1.89**		**$1.65**		**−25.5**	**−14.7**
Diluted shares	1,008		1,025		1,010		−1.7	−0.2

Source: Company Reports.

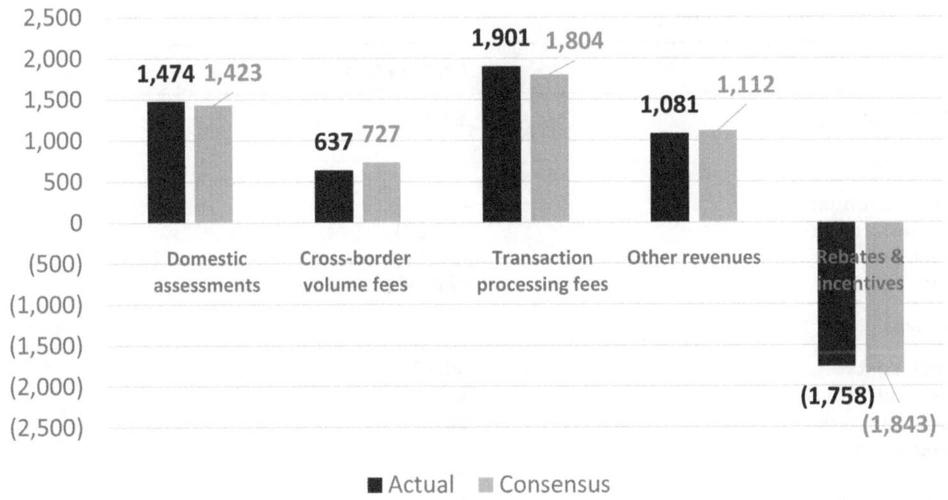

Figure AIII.13 Segment Performance.

Source: Company Reports.

Cross-border fees were negatively impacted by the lack of travel due to the virus. Management noted cross-border declines have stabilized down 45%. Transaction processing fees were $1.901 billion (57%), a −7% y/y decline, above consensus of $1.804 billion. Other revenues were $1.081 billion (32%), a 12% y/y increase (+4% from acquisitions), below consensus of $1.112 billion. Rebates and Incentives were $1.758 billion (53%), below consensus of $1.843 billion (Figure AIII.13 and Table AIII.4).

Revenue drivers show sharp declines across the board. Mastercard's worldwide GDV (Gross Domestic Volume) declined −14% y/y to $1.38 trillion, below consensus of $1.452 trillion. GDV declined on an annual basis by roughly −5% in the US, −15% in Canada, Middle East, Europe, and −33% in Latin America. Worldwide purchase transactions declined by −7% to 24,800 trillion. Purchase transaction volumes declined by −8% in the US and −5% in Europe and the Middle East. It declined by −14% in Latin America and −20% in Canada. Domestic assessments held steady at roughly $1.07, while the cross-border fell to $0.46 as volumes in the business declined dramatically. Overall processing fees remained steady at $0.08.

2Q20 Quality of Earnings

We take an abbreviated look at the "Quality" of Mastercard's earnings. We see through our analysis the impact of the pandemic and what the company is doing to offset the challenges.

We would rate the quality of earnings as fair on a scale of good, fair, and poor. The pandemic had a large impact compared to the prior year with earnings being impacted by about −$0.77 based on our analysis compounded by a higher interest charge. Management is taking steps to offset the impact by lowering costs, particularly through the marketing budget, which helped by about +$0.13. Mastercard noted the decline in expenses, but believes it was due to a delay in sponsorship activity, which will resume in 3Q20. The operational moves plus the contribution from the below the line items helped but could not offset the total impact (Table AIII.5).

Table AIII.5 Quality of Earnings

Category	*Contribution*
2Q19 earnings	**$1.89**
Negatives	
Lower revenues	($0.77)
Provision for litigation	($0.02)
Other income	($0.14)
Sum	**($0.93)**
Positives	
Lower costs	$0.13
Litigation provision	$0.11
Lower tax rate	$0.19
Lower share count	$0.02
Sum	**$0.45**
2Q20 earnings	**$1.41**

Source: Company Reports.

Short Term Outlook (Next Three Years)

Mastercard provides its view of the COVID world. Mastercard expects a slow recovery in spending. The company believes COVID is accelerating the move to digital forms of payment, like eCommerce, click-to-pay, real-time payments, and B2B payments, which is a positive. Mastercard noted seeing an improvement in spending patterns as we headed into the normalize phase of the pandemic with Europe outpacing North America in the recovery process. Management continued not to provide guidance.

Mastercard provided color on a couple of topics from a modeling perspective. Cross-border continues to be weak except for Europe, which is lower yielding. Rebates and incentives are expected to increase as a percentage of gross revenues sequentially due to increased deal activity. Operating expenses are expected to be down low single digits in the 3Q, excluding acquisitions, which are expected to add 1% to growth in 3Q and 4Q, but 6%–7% to expenses in 3Q and 4Q. Interest expense is expected to be about $100 million per quarter. FX is expected to be a 1% headwind in both the 3Q & 4Q. The tax rate is expected to be roughly 17%–18%, closer to the bottom of the range. Mastercard remains committed to its long-term strategy. The company reinstituted its share buyback program.

Short-Term Forecasts

Our September quarter estimates are for $3.795 billion, a −15% decline, compared to FactSet consensus of $3.936 billion, with margins of 56%. We note that all FactSet consensus numbers are as of August 2020. We anticipate margins of 56% or $2,135 million (vs. FactSet consensus of $2,109 million). We forecast an interest expense of −$100 million and a tax rate of 17.5%. Our September quarter earnings forecast is $1.68 (vs. FactSet Current Consensus of $1.65). **We believe there is a possible element of conservatism in our quarterly estimates as consumer spending has seemed to pick up in the US economy in 3Q. There are other areas of conservatism including the cost structure and other below the line items like other income, tax rate, and stock buyback.**

Table AIII.6 Revenue Drivers

FYE Dec	*Mar-20*	*Jun-20*	*Sep-20*	*Dec-20*	*FY*	*Mar-20*	*Jun-20*	*Sep-20*	*Dec-20*	*FY*	*FY*	*FY*
($ in Billions)	*1Q 20*	*2Q 20*	*3Q 20E*	*4Q 20E*	*2020E*	*1Q 20E*	*2Q 20E*	*3Q 20E*	*4Q 20E*	*2021E*	*2022E*	*2023E*
Credit, Charge and Debit Programs GDV												
APMEA	**$472**	**$409**	**$415**	**$450**	**$1,746**	**$465**	**$442**	**$448**	**$486**	**$1,841**	**$1,950**	**$2,096**
q/q growth	−8.9%	−13.3%	1.5%	8.4%	–	3.3%	−5.0%	1.5%	8.4%	–	–	–
y/y growth	2.8%	−14.8%	−15.5%	−13.1%	−10.4%	−1.5%	8.0%	8.0%	8.0%	5.4%	5.9%	7.5%
Canada	**$40**	**$39**	**$42**	**$50**	**$171**	**$45**	**$42**	**$45**	**$54**	**$186**	**$195**	**$205**
q/q growth	−19.1%	−2.5%	7.7%	19.0%	–	−10.0%	−6.4%	7.7%	19.0%	–	–	–
y/y growth	2.6%	−15.2%	−11.3%	1.1%	−6.0%	12.5%	8.0%	8.0%	8.0%	9.1%	4.6%	5.0%
Europe	**$467**	**$398**	**$475**	**$500**	**$1,840**	**$495**	**$475**	**$495**	**$525**	**$1,990**	**$2,150**	**$2,311**
q/q growth	−11.9%	−14.8%	19.3%	5.3%	–	−1.0%	−4.0%	4.2%	6.1%	–	–	–
y/y growth	8.9%	−16.9%	−6.2%	−5.7%	−5.4%	6.0%	19.3%	4.2%	5.0%	8.2%	8.0%	7.5%
Latin America	**$107**	**$74**	**$74**	**$90**	**$345**	**$95**	**$81**	**$87**	**$100**	**$363**	**$385**	**$420**
q/q growth	−13.0%	−30.8%	0.0%	21.6%	–	5.6%	−14.3%	6.9%	14.8%	–	–	–
y/y growth	1.9%	−32.7%	−34.8%	−26.8%	−23.6%	−11.2%	10.0%	17.6%	11.0%	5.3%	6.0%	9.0%
Worldwide less United States	**$1,086**	**$920**	**$1,006**	**$1,090**	**$4,102**	**$1,100**	**$1,040**	**$1,076**	**$1,165**	**$4,381**	**$4,680**	**$5,032**
q/q growth	−11.0%	−15.3%	9.3%	8.3%	–	0.9%	−5.4%	3.4%	8.3%	–	–	–
y/y growth	5.2%	−17.5%	−13.2%	−10.7%	−9.4%	1.3%	13.1%	6.9%	6.9%	6.8%	6.8%	7.5%
United States	**$478**	**$464**	**$500**	**$565**	**$2,007**	**$540**	**$522**	**$543**	**$613**	**$2,218**	**$2,450**	**$2,573**
q/q growth	−5.7%	−2.9%	7.8%	13.0%	–	−4.4%	−3.3%	3.9%	13.0%	–	–	–
y/y growth	6.0%	−4.5%	1.2%	11.4%	3.6%	13.0%	12.5%	8.5%	8.5%	10.5%	10.5%	5.0%
Total worldwide GDV	**$1,564**	**$1,384**	**$1,506**	**$1,655**	**$6,109**	**$1,640**	**$1,562**	**$1,618**	**$1,778**	**$6,598**	**$7,130**	**$7,604**
q/q growth	−9.5%	−11.5%	8.8%	9.9%	–	−0.9%	−4.7%	3.6%	9.9%	–	–	–
y/y growth	5.5%	−13.6%	−8.9%	−4.2%	−5.5%	4.9%	12.9%	7.4%	7.4%	8.0%	8.1%	6.7%
Purchase Transactions (in Millions)												
APMEA	**6,309**	**5,899**	**6,300**	**6,600**	**25,108**	**6,940**	**6,725**	**6,804**	**7,128**	**27,597**	**30,200**	**32,918**
q/q growth	−8.1%	−6.5%	6.8%	4.8%	–	5.2%	−3.1%	1.2%	4.8%	–	–	–
y/y growth	13.8%	−5.1%	−3.7%	−3.9%	−0.2%	10.0%	14.0%	8.0%	8.0%	9.9%	9.4%	9.0%
Canada	**653**	**572**	**620**	**650**	**2,495**	**650**	**625**	**630**	**665**	**2,570**	**2,650**	**2,756**
q/q growth	−13.3%	−12.4%	8.4%	4.8%	–	0.0%	−3.8%	0.8%	5.6%	–	–	–

(Continued)

Table AIII.6 (Continued)

FYE Dec	*Mar-20*	*Jun-20*	*Sep-20*	*Dec-20*	*FY*	*Mar-20*	*Jun-20*	*Sep-20*	*Dec-20*	*FY*	*FY*	*FY*
($ in Billions)	*1Q 20*	*2Q 20*	*3Q 20E*	*4Q 20E*	*2020E*	*1Q 20E*	*2Q 20E*	*3Q 20E*	*4Q 20E*	*2021E*	*2022E*	*2023E*
y/y growth	6.9%	−19.4%	−17.1%	−13.7%	−11.6%	−0.5%	9.3%	1.6%	2.3%	3.0%	3.1%	4.0%
Europe	**10,228**	**9,051**	**9,900**	**10,700**	**39,879**	**11,762**	**10,182**	**10,791**	**11,770**	**44,506**	**48,500**	**52,623**
q/q growth	−5.1%	−11.5%	9.4%	8.1%	–	9.9%	−13.4%	6.0%	9.1%	–	–	–
y/y growth	23.2%	−5.6%	−3.2%	−0.7%	2.5%	15.0%	12.5%	9.0%	10.0%	11.6%	9.0%	8.5%
Latin America	**2,915**	**2,339**	**2,500**	**2,750**	**10,504**	**3,265**	**2,713**	**2,700**	**2,900**	**11,578**	**12,550**	**13,680**
q/q growth	−5.5%	−19.8%	6.9%	10.0%	–	18.7%	−16.9%	−0.5%	7.4%	–	–	–
y/y growth	17.8%	−14.0%	−15.1%	−10.8%	−6.4%	12.0%	16.0%	8.0%	5.5%	10.2%	8.4%	9.0%
Worldwide less United States	**20,105**	**17,861**	**19,320**	**20,700**	**77,986**	**22,617**	**20,245**	**20,925**	**22,463**	**86,250**	**93,900**	**101,976**
q/q growth	−6.4%	−11.2%	8.2%	7.1%	–	9.3%	−10.5%	3.4%	7.4%	–	–	–
y/y growth	18.8%	−7.1%	−5.6%	−3.6%	−0.1%	12.5%	13.4%	8.3%	8.5%	10.6%	8.9%	8.6%
United States	**7,350**	**6,940**	**7,500**	**7,850**	**29,640**	**7,938**	**7,495**	**8,175**	**8,557**	**32,165**	**34,500**	**37,433**
q/q growth	−6.9%	−5.6%	8.1%	4.7%	–	1.1%	−5.6%	9.1%	4.7%	–	–	–
y/y growth	6.6%	−8.2%	−3.3%	−0.6%	−1.5%	8.0%	8.0%	9.0%	9.0%	8.5%	7.3%	8.5%
Worldwide	**27,455**	**24,801**	**26,820**	**28,550**	**107,626**	**30,555**	**27,741**	**29,100**	**31,020**	**118,415**	**128,400**	**139,409**
q/q growth	−6.5%	−9.7%	8.1%	6.5%	–	7.0%	−9.2%	4.9%	6.6%	–	–	–
y/y growth	15.3%	−7.4%	−4.9%	−2.8%	−0.5%	11.3%	11.9%	8.5%	8.6%	10.0%	8.4%	8.6%
Revenue Drivers												
Domestic assessments (millions)	1,683	1,474	1,626	1,754	6,538	1,771	1,687	1,748	1,920	7,126	7,700	8,213
Total GDV (billions)	1,564	1,384	1,506	1,655	6,109	1,640	1,562	1,618	1,778	6,598	7,130	7,604
Domestic assessments per GDV	**$1.08**	**$1.07**	**$1.08**	**$1.06**	**$1.07**	**$1.08**	**$1.08**	**$1.08**	**$1.08**	**$1.08**	**$1.08**	**$1.08**
Cross-border volume fees (millions	1,217	637	800	850	3,504	875	950	1,100	1,250	4,175	4,500	5,000

(Continued)

Table AIII.6 (Continued)

FYE Dec	*Mar-20*	*Jun-20*	*Sep-20*	*Dec-20*	*FY*	*Mar-20*	*Jun-20*	*Sep-20*	*Dec-20*	*FY*	*FY*	*FY*
($ in Billions)	*1Q 20*	*2Q 20*	*3Q 20E*	*4Q 20E*	*2020E*	*1Q 20E*	*2Q 20E*	*3Q 20E*	*4Q 20E*	*2021E*	*2022E*	*2023E*
Total GDV (billions)	1,564	1,384	1,506	1,655	6,109	1,640	1,562	1,618	1,778	6,598	7,130	7,604
Cross-border volume fees per GDV	**$0.78**	**$0.46**	**$0.53**	**$0.51**	**$0.57**	**$0.53**	**$0.61**	**$0.68**	**$0.70**	**$0.63**	**$0.63**	**$0.66**
Transaction processing fees	2,200	1,901	2,186	2,405	8,692	2,567	2,233	2,372	2,613	9,785	10,818	11,745
Total purchase transactions	27,455	24,801	26,820	28,550	107,626	30,555	27,741	29,100	31,020	118,415	128,400	139,409
Processing fees per purchase transaction	**$0.08**	**$0.08**	**$0.08**	**$0.08**	**$0.08**	**$0.08**	**$0.08**	**$0.08**	**$0.08**	**$0.08**	**$0.08**	**$0.08**

Source: Company Reports.

Table AIII.7 Revenue Build

FYE December	Mar-20	Jun-20	Sep-20	Dec-20	FY	Mar-20	Jun-20	Sep-20	Dec-20	FY	FY	FY
($ in Millions)	*1Q 20*	*2Q 20*	*3Q 20E*	*4Q 20E*	*2020E*	*1Q 20*	*2Q 20E*	*3Q 20E*	*4Q 20E*	*2021E*	*2022E*	*2023E*
Revenues by Segment												
Domestic assessments	**1,683**	**1,474**	**1,626**	**1,754**	**6,538**	**1,771**	**1,687**	**1,748**	**1,920**	**7,126**	**7,700**	**8,213**
q/q growth	−5.1%	−12.4%	10.3%	7.9%	–	1.0%	−4.7%	3.6%	9.9%	–	–	–
y/y growth	4.9%	−12.3%	−5.5%	−1.1%	−3.6%	5.2%	14.5%	7.4%	9.5%	9.0%	8.1%	6.7%
Total revenue	42.0%	44.2%	42.9%	42.9%	42.9%	41.2%	38.4%	39.5%	39.3%	39.6%	38.5%	37.5%
Cross-border volume fees	**1,217**	**637**	**800**	**850**	**3,504**	**875**	**950**	**1,100**	**1,250**	**4,175**	**4,500**	**5,000**
q/q growth	−16.2%	−47.7%	25.6%	6.3%	–	2.9%	8.6%	15.8%	13.6%	–	–	–
y/y growth	−3.6%	−53.6%	−47.3%	−41.5%	−37.5%	−28.1%	49.1%	37.5%	47.1%	19.1%	7.8%	11.1%
Total revenue	30.4%	19.1%	21.1%	20.8%	23.0%	20.4%	21.6%	24.9%	25.6%	23.2%	22.5%	22.8%
Transaction processing fees	**2,200**	**1,901**	**2,186**	**2,405**	**8,692**	**2,567**	**2,233**	**2,372**	**2,613**	**9,785**	**10,818**	**11,745**
q/q growth	−2.8%	−13.6%	15.0%	10.0%	–	6.7%	−13.0%	6.2%	10.2%	–	–	–
y/y growth	14.5%	−7.4%	−2.0%	6.3%	2.6%	16.7%	17.5%	8.5%	8.6%	12.6%	10.6%	8.6%
Total revenue	54.9%	57.0%	57.6%	58.8%	57.1%	59.8%	50.9%	53.6%	53.5%	54.4%	54.1%	53.6%
Other revenues	**1,062**	**1,081**	**1,250**	**1,418**	**4,811**	**1,253**	**1,276**	**1,438**	**1,631**	**5,597**	**6,269**	**7,021**
q/q growth	−13.9%	1.8%	15.6%	13.4%	–	−11.6%	1.8%	12.7%	13.4%	–	–	–
y/y growth	26.1%	12.4%	15.0%	15.0%	16.7%	18.0%	18.0%	15.0%	15.0%	16.3%	12.0%	12.0%
Total revenue	26.5%	32.4%	32.9%	34.7%	31.6%	29.2%	29.1%	32.5%	33.4%	31.1%	31.4%	32.0%
Vocalink	**90**	**94**	**85**	**85**	**354**	**90**	**90**	**90**	**90**	**360**	**385**	**400**
q/q growth	–	4.4%	−9.6%	0.0%	–	5.9%	0.0%	0.0%	0.0%	–	–	–
y/y growth	–	–	–	–	–	0.0%	−4.3%	5.9%	5.9%	1.7%	6.9%	3.9%
Total revenue	1.5%	1.8%	1.4%	1.3%	1.5%	1.4%	1.4%	1.3%	1.2%	1.3%	1.3%	1.2%
Gross revenue	**6,162**	**5,093**	**5,947**	**6,513**	**23,899**	**6,556**	**6,236**	**6,747**	**7,504**	**27,043**	**29,672**	**32,379**
q/q growth	−8.3%	−17.3%	16.8%	9.5%	–	0.7%	−4.9%	8.2%	11.2%	–	–	–
y/y growth	9.4%	−16.1%	−9.3%	−3.1%	−4.3%	6.4%	22.4%	13.4%	15.2%	13.2%	352.6%	419.2%
Total revenue	153.7%	152.7%	156.7%	159.3%	156.9%	152.6%	142.0%	152.6%	153.6%	150.3%	148.4%	147.7%
Rebates and incentives (contra revenue)	**(2,153)**	**(1,758)**	**(2,153)**	**(2,423)**	**(8,487)**	**(2,261)**	**(1,846)**	**(2,325)**	**(2,617)**	**(9,049)**	**(9,682)**	**(10,457)**
q/q growth	−6.7%	−18.3%	22.5%	12.6%	–	−6.7%	−18.3%	26.0%	12.6%	–	–	–
y/y growth	23.5%	−10.1%	3.0%	5.0%	4.8%	5.0%	5.0%	8.0%	8.0%	6.6%	7.0%	8.0%
% of gross revenue	34.9%	34.5%	36.2%	37.2%	35.5%	34.5%	29.6%	34.5%	34.9%	33.5%	32.6%	32.3%
Total revenues	**$4,009**	**$3,335**	**$3,795**	**$4,089**	**15,228**	**$4,295**	**$4,390**	**$4,422**	**$4,887**	**$17,994**	**$19,990**	**$21,922**
q/q growth	−9.2%	−16.8%	13.8%	7.8%	–	5.0%	2.2%	0.7%	10.5%	–	–	–
y/y growth	3.1%	−18.9%	−15.1%	−7.4%	−9.8%	7.1%	31.6%	16.5%	19.5%	18.2%	11.1%	9.7%

Source: Company Reports.

Revenue Driver's and Build

Our model is driven by our revenue drivers where we estimate quarterly GDV of $1,506 billion (vs. FactSet consensus of $1,646.8 billion). Our quarterly revenue build breaks down into: domestic assessments estimate of $1,626 million, −5% annual (y/y) decline (vs. consensus of $1,698 million), cross border fees estimate of $800 million, −47% y/y decline (vs. consensus of $903 million), transaction processing fees estimate of $2,186 million, −2% y/y decline (vs. consensus of $2,275 million), Other revenue estimate of $1,250 million, 15% y/y growth (vs. consensus of $1,272 million), and Vocalink estimate of $85 million (vs. consensus of $80 million). We estimate Rebates and Incentives of −$2,153 million vs. consensus of −$2,159 million (Tables AIII.6 and AIII.7).

Short Term Top and Bottom-Line Estimates

We forecast Mastercard to be a high single, low double-digit grower with margin expansion, resulting in a low to mid-teens earnings growth. We estimate revenues of roughly $15 billion in 2020, a −10% decline, resulting in earnings of $6.77, a −10% decline (roughly $7.00). We estimate a rebound in net revenue growth rate to 18% for 2021 and 11% for 2022. We forecast margin expansion of 500 bps to 61% in 2021 and 300 bps to 61% in 2022 off a lower cost structure. Our earnings estimate is for $8.88 in 2021 (roughly $9.00), 31% growth, and $10.06 in 2022 (roughly $10), 13% growth (Table AIII.8).

Long-term Outlook (3-, 5-, and 10-Year Outlook)

We believe over the long-term Mastercard is a high single, low double-digit annual revenue grower with the opportunity to expand margins driving consistently low to mid-teens earnings growth. We build into our long-term model a high single digit, organic annual growth rate declining over time. We expect moderate annual margin expansion of 10–50 bps. Earnings are expected to grow mid double digits on an annual basis. We expect +$10 in earnings over the next three years, $15 in earnings over the next five years, and +$20 in earnings by 2030. We note the long-term estimates do not include acquisitions (Figure AIII.14 and Table AIII.9).

Balance Sheet and Cash Flows

Solid Balance Sheet. Mastercard ended 2Q20 with $11.137 billion in cash and cash equivalents and $12.498 billion of long-term debt on its balance sheet. Its long-term debt has been steadily rising as the company remains active in the acquisition market. Unlevered free cash flow in the quarter was $1.39 billion, 99% of net income (Table AIII.10).

Cash Flow Forecasts

Strong Cash Flow Generator. Mastercard is a strong free cash flow generator. We estimate the company will generate billions in Free Cash Flow per year over the next decade. The company has a Free Cash Flow (FCF) yield in the range of 3%–5% which we expect to continue over the next ten years. We have FCF growing at a roughly mid-teens CAGR over the next three, five, and ten years. FCF has been growing at an 18% rate over the last five years. We believe the healthy and growing free cash flow yield will strengthen the balance sheet and improve cash reserves. Mastercard will have the opportunity to deploy capital in a shareholder friendly manner including thoughtful acquisitions, dividend payments, and share repurchase (Table AIII.11).

Table AIII.8 Estimates

FY December	*Sep-20*	*Dec-20*	*FY*	*Mar-20*	*Jun-20*	*Sep-20*	*Dec-20*	*FY*	*FY*	*FY*
	3Q 20E	*4Q 20E*	*2020E*	*1Q 20E*	*2Q 20E*	*3Q 20E*	*4Q 20E*	*2021E*	*2022E*	*2023E*
Our Estimates										
Domestic assessments	**1,626**	**1,754**	**6,538**	**1,771**	**1,687**	**1,748**	**1,920**	**7,126**	**7,700**	**8,213**
q/q growth	10.3%	7.9%	–	1.0%	−4.7%	3.6%	9.9%	–	–	–
y/y growth	−5.5%	−1.1%	−3.6%	5.2%	14.5%	7.4%	9.5%	9.0%	8.1%	6.7%
Cross-border volume fees	**800**	**850**	**3,504**	**875**	**950**	**1,100**	**1,250**	**4,175**	**4,500**	**5,000**
q/q growth	25.6%	6.3%	–	2.9%	8.6%	15.8%	13.6%	–	–	–
y/y growth	−47.3%	−41.5%	−37.5%	−28.1%	49.1%	37.5%	47.1%	19.1%	7.8%	11.1%
Transaction processing fees	**2,186**	**2,405**	**8,692**	**2,567**	**2,233**	**2,372**	**2,613**	**9,785**	**10,818**	**11,745**
q/q growth	15.0%	10.0%	–	6.7%	−13.0%	6.2%	10.2%	–	–	–
y/y growth	−2.0%	6.3%	2.6%	16.7%	17.5%	8.5%	8.6%	12.6%	10.6%	8.6%
Other revenues	**1,250**	**1,418**	**4,811**	**1,253**	**1,276**	**1,438**	**1,631**	**5,597**	**6,269**	**7,021**
q/q growth	15.6%	13.4%	–	−11.6%	1.8%	12.7%	13.4%	–	–	–
y/y growth	15.0%	15.0%	16.7%	18.0%	18.0%	15.0%	15.0%	16.3%	12.0%	12.0%
Rebates and incentives	**(2,153)**	**(2,423)**	**(8,487)**	**(2,261)**	**(1,846)**	**(2,325)**	**(2,617)**	**(9,049)**	**(9,682)**	**(10,457)**
q/q growth	22.5%	12.6%	–	−6.7%	−18.3%	26.0%	12.6%	–	–	–
y/y growth	3.0%	5.0%	4.8%	5.0%	5.0%	8.0%	8.0%	6.6%	7.0%	8.0%
Vocalink	**85.0**	**85.0**	**354.0**	**90.0**	**90.0**	**90.0**	**90.0**	**360.0**	**385.0**	**400.0**
q/q growth	4.4%	−9.6%	0.0%	–	5.9%	0.0%	0.0%	0.0%	–	–
y/y growth	1.4%	1.3%	1.5%	1.4%	1.4%	1.3%	1.2%	1.3%	1.3%	1.2%
Total operating revenues	**3,795**	**4,089**	**15,412**	**4,295**	**4,390**	**4,422**	**4,887**	**17,994**	**19,990**	**21,922**
q/q growth	13.8%	7.8%	–	5.0%	2.2%	0.7%	10.5%	–	–	–
y/y growth	−15.1%	−7.4%	−9.8%	7.1%	31.6%	16.5%	19.5%	18.2%	11.1%	9.7%
Total operating expenses	**1,660**	**1,705**	**6,791**	**1,810**	**1,760**	**1,760**	**1,760**	**7,090**	**7,787**	**8,434**
% of revenue	43.7%	41.7%	44.6%	42.1%	40.1%	39.8%	36.0%	39.4%	39.0%	38.5%
y/y growth	−8.4%	−15.4%	−5.9%	0.7%	8.1%	6.0%	3.2%	4.4%	9.8%	8.3%
Operating margin	**56.3%**	**58.3%**	**55.4%**	**57.9%**	**59.9%**	**60.2%**	**64.0%**	**60.6%**	**61.0%**	**61.5%**
bps y/y	−318	395	−184	271	872	394	568	519	45	48
Adjusted EBITDA margin	**60%**	**62%**	**59%**	**61%**	**63%**	**64%**	**67%**	**64%**	**64%**	**65%**
bps y/y	−256	407	−119	261	779	365	533	479	37	20
EPS	**$1.68**	**$1.90**	**$6.77**	**$1.99**	**$2.12**	**$2.16**	**$2.57**	**$8.88**	**$10.06**	**$11.14**
y/y growth	−18.5%	−8.2%	−14.8%	18.9%	50.3%	28.4%	35.1%	31.3%	13.3%	10.7%

Source: Company Reports.

Table AIII.9 Long-Term Estimates

FY December	*FY*	*FY*	*FY*	*FY*	*FY*	*FY*	*FY*	*FY*	*FY*	*FY*	*FY*	*3 Years (CAGR)*	*5 Years (CAGR)*	*10 Years (CAGR)*
	2020E	*2021E*	*2022E*	*2023E*	*2024E*	*2025E*	*2026E*	*2027E*	*2028E*	*2029E*	*2030E*	*2020–2023*	*2020–2025*	*2020–2030*
Our Estimates														
Domestic assessments	**6,538**	**7,126**	**7,700**	**8,213**	**8,800**	**9,482**	**10,140**	**10,838**	**11,535**	**12,275**	**13,059**	**8%**	**8%**	**7%**
q/q growth	–	–	–	–	–	–	–	–	–	–	–			
y/y growth	−3.6%	9.0%	8.1%	6.7%	7.2%	7.7%	6.9%	6.9%	6.4%	6.4%	6.4%			
Cross-border volume fees	**3,504**	**4,175**	**4,500**	**5,000**	**5,500**	**6,000**	**6,500**	**7,000**	**7,500**	**8,000**	**8,500**	**13%**	**11%**	**9%**
q/q growth	–	–	–	–	–	–	–	–	–	–	–			
y/y growth	−37.5%	19.1%	7.8%	11.1%	10.0%	9.1%	8.3%	7.7%	7.1%	6.7%	6.3%			
Transaction processing fees	**8,692**	**9,785**	**10,818**	**11,745**	**12,753**	**13,847**	**15,036**	**16,328**	**17,521**	**18,783**	**20,114**	**11%**	**10%**	**9%**
q/q growth	–	–	–	–	–	–	–	–	–	–	–			
y/y growth	2.6%	12.6%	10.6%	8.6%	8.6%	8.6%	8.6%	8.6%	7.3%	7.2%	7.1%			
Other revenues	**4,811**	**5,597**	**6,269**	**7,021**	**7,863**	**8,807**	**9,864**	**11,047**	**12,373**	**13,858**	**15,521**	**13%**	**13%**	**12%**
q/q growth	–	–	–	–	–	–	–	–	–	–	–			
y/y growth	16.7%	16.3%	12.0%	12.0%	12.0%	12.0%	12.0%	12.0%	12.0%	12.0%	12.0%			
Rebates and incentives	**(8,487)**	**(9,049)**	**(9,682)**	**(10,457)**	**(11,293)**	**(12,197)**	**(13,172)**	**(14,226)**	**(15,364)**	**(16,594)**	**(17,921)**	**7%**	**8%**	**8%**
q/q growth	–	–	–	–	–	–	–	–	–	–	–			
y/y growth	4.8%	6.6%	7.0%	8.0%	8.0%	8.0%	8.0%	8.0%	8.0%	8.0%	8.0%			
Vocalink	**354.0**	**360.0**	**385.0**	**400.0**	**401.0**	**402.0**	**403.0**	**404.0**	**405.0**	**406.0**	**407.0**	**4%**	**3%**	**1%**
q/q growth	0.0%	0.0%	–	–	–	–	–	–	–	–	–			
y/y growth	1.5%	1.3%	1.3%	1.2%	1.1%	1.0%	1.0%	0.9%	0.8%	0.8%	0.7%			
Total operating revenues	**15,412**	**17,994**	**19,990**	**21,922**	**24,024**	**26,341**	**28,771**	**31,391**	**33,970**	**36,728**	**39,679**	**12%**	**11%**	**10%**
q/q growth	–	–	–	–	–	–	–	–	–	–	–			

(Continued)

Table AIII.9 (Continued)

FY December	*FY*	*FY*	*FY*	*FY*	*FY*	*FY*	*FY*	*FY*	*FY*	*FY*	*FY*	*3 Years (CAGR)*	*5 Years (CAGR)*	*10 Years (CAGR)*
	2020E	*2021E*	*2022E*	*2023E*	*2024E*	*2025E*	*2026E*	*2027E*	*2028E*	*2029E*	*2030E*	*2020–2023*	*2020–2025*	*2020–2030*
y/y growth	−9.8%	18.2%	11.1%	9.7%	9.6%	9.6%	9.2%	9.1%	8.2%	8.1%	8.0%			
Total operating expenses	**6,791**	**7,090**	**7,787**	**8,434**	**9,161**	**9,909**	**10,717**	**11,587**	**12,443**	**13,357**	**14,334**	**7%**	**8%**	**8%**
% of revenue	44.6%	39.4%	39.0%	38.5%	38.1%	37.6%	37.3%	36.9%	36.6%	36.4%	36.1%			
y/y growth	−5.9%	4.4%	9.8%	8.3%	8.6%	8.2%	8.2%	8.1%	7.4%	7.3%	7.3%			
Operating margin	**55.4%**	**60.6%**	**61.0%**	**61.5%**	**61.9%**	**62.4%**	**62.7%**	**63.1%**	**63.4%**	**63.6%**	**63.9%**	**4%**	**2%**	**1%**
bps y/y	−184	519	45	48	34	51	37	34	28	26	24			
Adjusted EBITDA margin	**59%**	**64%**	**64%**	**65%**	**65%**	**65%**	**65%**	**65%**	**66%**	**66%**	**66%**			
bps y/y	−119	479	37	20	19	36	23	21	17	16	15			
EPS	**$6.77**	**$8.88**	**$10.06**	**$11.14**	**$12.39**	**$13.79**	**$15.09**	**$16.77**	**$18.28**	**$20.04**	**$21.88**	**18%**	**15%**	**12%**
y/y growth	−14.8%	31.3%	13.3%	10.7%	11.2%	11.3%	9.4%	11.1%	9.0%	9.6%	9.2%			

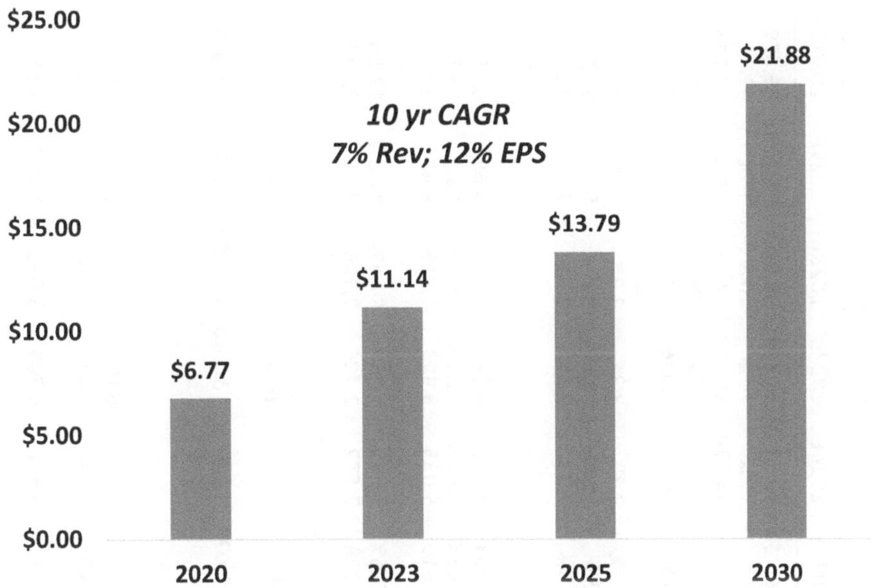

Figure AIII.14 Long-Term Earnings Forecast.

Source: Company Reports.

Table AIII.10 Balance Sheet and Cash Flow

FYE December	*Mar-19*	*Jun-19*	*Sep-19*	*Dec-18*	*FY*	*Mar-20*	*Jun-20*
	1Q 19	*2Q 19*	*3Q 19*	*4Q 18*	*2019*	*1Q 20*	*2Q 20*
Balance Sheet							
Cash and cash equivalents	5,857	5,691	5,101	6,988	6,988	10,207	11,137
q/q change	−12.3%	−2.8%	−10.4%	37.0%	–	46.1%	9.1%
% of total assets	24.9%	23.0%	19.6%	23.9%	23.9%	33.3%	34.7%
LT debt	5,799	7,806	7,735	8,527	8,527	12,466	12,498
% of total assets	24.7%	31.6%	29.8%	29.2%	29.2%	40.7%	38.9%
Cash Flow							
Operating income (EBIT)	2,213	2,397	2,655	2,399	9,664	2,211	1,707
Taxes	341	471	426	375	1,613	294	270
NOPAT	1,872	1,926	2,229	2,024	8,051	1,917	1,437
Depreciation and amortization	117	122	137	146	522	144	145
Capital expenditures	83	91	132	116	422	131	70
Unlevered free cash flow	1,229	1,445	2,223	2,581	7,768	1,728	1,388
% net income	66%	71%	105%	123%	97%	102%	98%
Overall cash balance per diluted share	$5.68	$5.55	$5.01	$6.90	$6.84	$10.11	$11.05

Table AIII.11 Cash Flow Estimates

Fiscal Year December	*FY 2018*	*FY 2019*	*FY 2020E*	*FY 2021E*	*FY 2022E*	*FY 2023E*	*FY 2024E*	*FY 2025E*	*FY 2026E*	*FY 2027E*	*FY 2028E*	*FY 2029E*	*FY 2030E*
Net revenues	14,950	16,883	15,228	17,994	19,990	21,922	24,024	26,341	28,771	31,391	33,970	36,728	39,679
y/y growth	*20%*	*13%*	*−10%*	*7%*	*32%*	*17%*	*20%*	*18%*	*11%*	*10%*	*10%*	*10%*	*9%*
Net income	5,859	8,118	6,783	8,682	9,713	10,732	11,825	13,078	14,374	15,777	17,157	18,637	20,225
y/y growth	*50%*	*39%*	*−16%*	*28%*	*12%*	*10%*	*10%*	*11%*	*10%*	*10%*	*9%*	*9%*	*9%*
Depreciation and amortization	459	522	623	630	660	723	793	869	949	1,036	1,121	1,212	1,309
% of revenue	3.1%	3.1%	4.1%	3.5%	3.3%	3.3%	3.3%	3.3%	3.3%	3.3%	3.3%	3.3%	3.3%
Capital expenditures	330	422	359	450	500	548	601	659	719	785	849	918	992
% of revenue	2.2%	2.5%	2.4%	2.5%	2.5%	2.5%	2.5%	2.5%	2.5%	2.5%	2.5%	2.5%	2.5%
Current Assets													
Accounts receivable	2,276	2,514	2,640	2,879	3,098	3,398	3,724	4,083	4,459	4,866	5,265	5,693	6,150
% of revenue	15.2%	14.9%	17.3%	16.0%	15.5%	15.5%	15.5%	15.5%	15.5%	15.5%	15.5%	15.5%	15.5%
Settlement due from customers	2,452	2,995	3,145	3,419	3,498	3,836	4,204	4,610	5,035	5,493	5,945	6,427	6,944
% of revenue	16.4%	17.7%	20.7%	19.0%	17.5%	17.5%	17.5%	17.5%	17.5%	17.5%	17.5%	17.5%	17.5%
Prepaid expenses and other current assets	1,432	1,763	1,851	1,914	1,869	2,024	2,199	2,378	2,572	2,781	2,986	3,206	3,440
% of operating expenses	18.7%	24.4%	27.3%	27.0%	24.0%	24.0%	24.0%	24.0%	24.0%	24.0%	24.0%	24.0%	24.0%
Total current assets	**6,160**	**7,272**	**7,636**	**8,212**	**8,465**	**9,258**	**10,127**	**11,071**	**12,066**	**13,140**	**14,196**	**15,326**	**16,534**
Current Liabilities													
Accounts payable	537	489	340	369	405	439	476	515	557	603	647	695	745
% of operating expenses	7.0%	6.8%	5.0%	5.2%	5.2%	5.2%	5.2%	5.2%	5.2%	5.2%	5.2%	5.2%	5.2%
Settlement due to customers	2,189	2,714	2,850	2,969	2,998	3,288	3,604	3,951	4,316	4,709	5,095	5,509	5,952
% of revenue	14.6%	16.1%	18.7%	16.5%	15.0%	15.0%	15.0%	15.0%	15.0%	15.0%	15.0%	15.0%	15.0%

(Continued)

Table AIII.11 (Continued)

Fiscal Year December	*FY 2018*	*FY 2019*	*FY 2020E*	*FY 2021E*	*FY 2022E*	*FY 2023E*	*FY 2024E*	*FY 2025E*	*FY 2026E*	*FY 2027E*	*FY 2028E*	*FY 2029E*	*FY 2030E*
Accrued expenses	4,747	5,489	5,763	5,318	5,684	5,904	6,413	6,936	7,502	8,111	8,710	9,350	10,034
% of operating expenses	61.9%	76.0%	84.9%	75.0%	73.0%	70.0%	70.0%	70.0%	70.0%	70.0%	70.0%	70.0%	70.0%
Other current liabilities	1,449	928	974	974	974	974	974	974	974	974	974	974	974
% of revenue	9.7%	5.5%	6.4%	5.4%	4.9%	4.4%	4.1%	3.7%	3.4%	3.1%	2.9%	2.7%	2.5%
Total current liabilities	**8,922**	**9,620**	**9,928**	**9,630**	**10,062**	**10,605**	**11,467**	**12,377**	**13,349**	**14,396**	**15,427**	**16,528**	**17,705**
Annual change in NWC	**(2,762)**	**(2,348)**	**(2,292)**	**(1,417)**	**(1,597)**	**(1,347)**	**(1,340)**	**(1,306)**	**(1,283)**	**(1,257)**	**(1,231)**	**(1,202)**	**(1,171)**
Change in debt	**(849)**	**(3,545)**	**(4,473)**	**(373)**	**(156)**	**(194)**	**0**	**0**	**0**	**0**	**0**	**0**	**0**

Valuation-*Discounted Cash Flow*

Mastercard has long-term upside potential, but limited upside over the short term. Our three-year intrinsic value is roughly $333, five-year $377, and ten-year $485. The stock is currently trading in the mid-$350 range. Investors would need to build in a reasonable *margin of safety* in order to feel comfortable with the purchase. The shorter the investment time horizon, the larger the *margin of safety* needed, given how restricted upside is based on our valuation analysis over the short term. If we use a five-year time horizon, we recommend a margin of safety of 50%, putting the purchase level in the $240 range. If you use a ten-year time horizon, then you could buy the stock at the $350 level or below. All things considered, you should think about initiating a position as close to $300 as possible, so look for a pullback in the market. **We have our FCFE valuation and our assumptions below** (Table AIII.12).

Valuation-*Relative*

Mastercard is expensive based on our three-point valuation (PE, EV/EBITDA, P/CF). Mastercard is trading at a mid to high 30×'s PE multiple (39× 2021). The 39× multiple is an 8% premium to Visa, which trades at 36× 2021. The premium in relation to the market is even larger. Mastercard trades at almost a 100% premium to the market with the S&P500 trading at 20× 2021. Historically, Mastercard has traded in a P/E range of 16× to 38× over the last ten years with a five-year average P/E of 34×.

Mastercard is trading at a low 30× EV/EBITDA multiple (31× 2021). The 31× multiple is a 10% premium to Visa, which trades at 29× 2021. Historically, Mastercard has traded in an EV/EBITDA range of 16× to 38× over the last five years on average P/E of 23×.

We have included our estimates for Mastercard. The company is trading in the mid 40× P/CF (44× 2021). The 44× multiple is an 18% premium to Visa, which trades at 36.7×. Historically, Mastercard has traded in a P/CF range of 23× to 55× over the last five-year average P/CF of 34×. All three of our relative valuation metric appear to be consistent, Mastercard is richly priced (Tables AIII.13 and AIII.14).

Multi-Point Valuation Analysis

Five-Year Valuation Outlook

Mastercard appears to be trading at a rich premium and fully valued when taking a five-year outlook. Mastercard is trading at roughly $350 at the beginning of September 2020. Our five-year DCF implies the company has an intrinsic value of roughly $360. If we want to buy stock using a 5-year time horizon, we will look for an entry point around $240, which builds in a 50%+ discount. There is a lot of flexibility on how close to the $240 level we would purchase the stock, but we would suggest at least a 20% margin of safety or discount on the intrinsic value. If we look at Mastercard on a relative valuation basis, we see it trades at a large premium to its peers and the market itself based on all our different relative valuation metrics-P/E, EV/EBITDA, and P/CF. The Company is trading at the upper end of its valuation range, implying a lack of opportunity in the name over the short term (Figure AIII.15).

Table AIII.12 Mastercard FCFE Intrinsic Valuation (Aug-20)

General Assumptions/Info			*Intrinsic Value*			
Ticker	MA					
Share price as of last close	$354.58			**Year**	**FCFE**	**NPV**
Latest closing share price date	9/01/20			2021	6,965	6,581
Market cap	$351.93	billion		2022	7,863	7,020
Debt	$12.60	billion		2023	8,859	7,474
% of equity	97%			2024	10,143	8,086
Dividend yield	0.4%			2025	11,646	8,773
Diluted shares	1,022			2026	12,454	8,865
Cost of Equity				2027	13,894	9,345
RFR	1.23%			2028	15,295	9,721
Beta	1.22			2029	17,252	10,360
ERP	5.00%			2030	18,735	10,631
k_e=	5.83%					
After Tax Cost of Debt						
RFR	1.23%			**Three-year**	**Five-year**	**Ten-year**
Default spread	0.63%		NPV	21,075	37,935	86,857
Marginal tax rate	17.5%		Terminal value	369,248	453,356	702,474
k_d=	1.53%		Discounted terminal value	319,003	347,143	409,258
WACC	5.69%		Total	340,079	385,078	496,115
Growth	3.00%		**Intrinsic value**	**$333**	**$377**	**$485**

Source: Company Reports; FactSet.

Table AIII.13 2021 Multi-Point Valuation

	P/E	*EV/EBITDA*	*EV/FCF*
Historical average (five year)	24–53×	16–38×	23–55×
FinTech Group*	38×	30×	41×
Forward (2021 forecast)	$8.88	$11,504	$8,095
Current multiples	40×	31×	44×
Target multiples	39×	31×	44×
Rough fair value (five year)	$350		

Opportunity Improves on the 10-year Valuation Outlook

Mastercard appears to be undervalued when taking a ten-year view of the name. Mastercard is trading at roughly $350 at the beginning of September 2020. Our 10-year DCF implies the company is worth roughly $485, which is our intrinsic value, a 35% premium. An investor taking this view could buy the stock right now, which should return a decent premium over a long period of time. If we want to buy the stock using a 10-year time horizon, we will buy it somewhere near the $360 level, which build's in a 35%+ discount. However, to be truly conservative, you could argue for a 50% discount, which would put the purchase price in the $320 range (Figure AIII.16).

Table AIII.14 FinTech Valuation Comparison

FINTECH															
	Closing Price Market Cap			*EPS*			*P/E*			*EV/EBITDA*			*P/FCF*		
Company Name	*Ticker*	*01-09-2020*	*(Millions)*	*CY 20E*	*CY 21E*	*CY 22E*	*CY 20E*	*CY 21E*	*CY 22E*	*CY 20E*	*CY 21E*	*CY 22E*	*CY 20E*	*CY 21E*	*CY 22E*
Card Networks:															
Mastercard	MA	$357	$354.5	$6.77	$8.88	$10.06	52.7 x	40.2 x	35.5 x	40.0 x	31.3 x	28.0 x	56.4 x	44.5 x	39.5 x
Visa	V	$213	$451.3	$5.01	$5.83	$8.99	42.6 x	36.6 x	23.7 x	32.4 x	28.6 x	24.7 x	47.9 x	36.7 x	33.0 x
Average							47.7 x	38.4 x	29.6 x	36.2 x	30.0 x	26.4 x	52.1 x	40.6 x	36.3 x
Bank Core Processors:															
FIS	FIS	$152	$94.6	$5.52	$6.73	$7.76	27.6 x	22.6 x	19.6 x	21.5 x	18.4 x	16.5 x	12.5 x	15.4x	13.5 x
Fiserv	FISV	$99	$66.5	$4.36	$5.36	$6.20	22.8 x	18.5 x	16.0 x	16.5 x	14.1 x	12.9 x	13.3 x	10.2x	8.2 x
Jack Henry	JKHY	$164	$12.6	$3.86	$3.74	$4.38	42.6 x	43.9 x	37.5 x	23.1 x	22.7 x	20.3 x	45.1 x	42.7x	35.7 x
Average							31.0 x	28.4 x	24.4 x	20.4 x	18.4 x	16.6 x	23.6 x	22.8 x	19.1 x
Gateways/ Payment Svcs:															
Adyen	ADYEN -NL	$1,758.51	$52.10	$9.51	$15.21	$21.82	184.9 x	115.6 x	80.6 x	123.5 x	84.7 x	58.8 x	123.0 x	114.2 x	72.1 x
Square	SQ	$162	$75.8	$0.53	$1.17	$1.70	306.5 x	138.8 x	95.5 x	235.0 x	105.5 x	70.2 x	558.8 x	110.0 x	91.1 x
Paypal	PYPL	$209	$244.7	$3.72	$4.55	$5.54	56.2 x	45.9 x	37.7 x	32.9 x	33.7 x	28.0 x	43.6 x	32.3 x	30.3 x
PagSeguro	PAGS	$44	$13.9	$0.87	$1.21	$1.62	50.3 x	36.2 x	27.0 x	38.0 x	27.8 x	12.1 x	223.1 x	138.1 x	53.5 x
MercadoLibre	MELI	$1,209	$60.3	$0.64	$1.73	$5.64	N/A	699.0 x	214.4 x	102.1 x	82.9 x	44.2 x	422.6 x	182.9 x	187.2 x
Average							53.3 x	41.1 x	32.4 x	35.5 x	30.8 x	20.1 x	133.4 x	85.2 x	41.9 x
Merchant Acq:															
Global Payments	GPN	$180	$53.1	$6.38	$7.95	$9.34	28.2 x	22.6 x	19.2 x	20.4 x	17.4 x	15.5 x	18.7 x	14.6x	12.9x
Total Average							40.4 x	33.3 x	27.0 x	28.1 x	24.3 x	19.8 x	57.6 x	41.8 x	28.3x
S&P 500 Index	SP50	$3,527	–	$130.44	$164.70	$189.18	27.0 x	21.4 x	18.6 x						

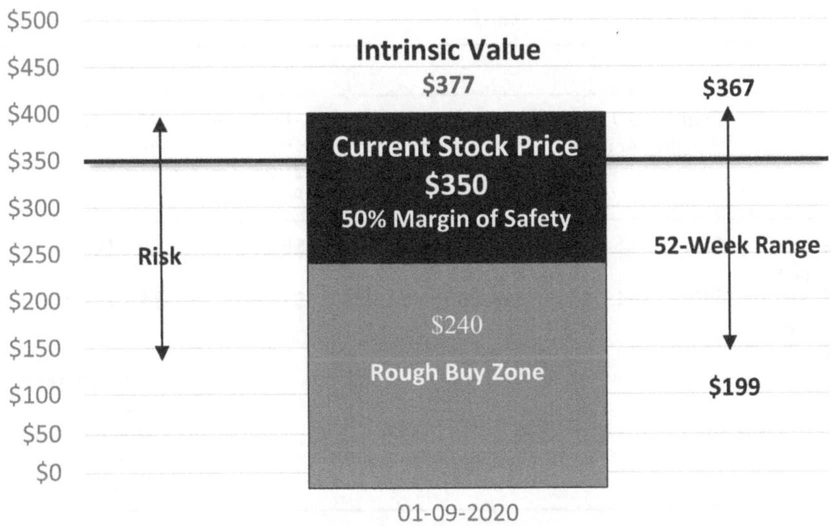

Figure AIII.15 Mastercard 5-Year Valuation Analysis (FCFE).

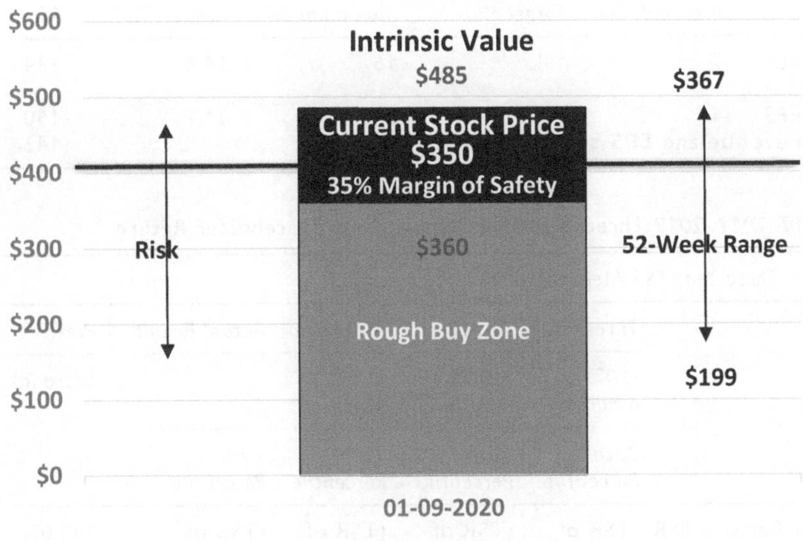

Figure AIII.16 Mastercard 10-Year Valuation Analysis (FCFE).

Management-Compensation

Mastercard has a corporate compensation scorecard known as their Senior Executive Annual Incentive Compensation Plan (SEAICP) based on their performance in the areas of adjusted net income and net revenues goals vs. strategic objectives. The company's 2020 executive compensation formula was:

Corporate score (0% – 200%) × individual performance (0% – 200%)
= bonus payout (0% – 250%) as % of target

Table AIII.15 2019 Management Scorecard

2019 SEAICP							
Metrics	*Goal Weight*	*2018 Adj Actuals*	*Threshold*	*Target*	*Maximum*	*2019 Adj Actuals*	*Score*
			50% Payout	*100 % Payout*	*200% Payout*		
Adjusted net income ($ mn)	67%	$6,713	$7,398	$7,885	$8,352	$8,044	134%
Adjusted net revenue ($ million)	33%	$14,931	$16,263	$16,861	$17,459	$16,980	120%
						Financial score	129%
						Strategic performance Ad	−4%
						Total	125%

Table AIII.16 2017–2019 Three Year Management Revenue and EPS Targets

2017–2019	*Three Year Measurements*				
	Threshold (%)	*Target (%)*	*Maximum (%)*	*Actual (%)*	*Score (%)*
Adjusted net revenue	7	11	16	14.4	134
Adjusted EPS	14	19	23	24.1	150
Avg net revenue and **EPS score (Pre-TSR score)**					142

Table AIII.17 2017–2019 Three Year Management Total Shareholder Return

2017–2019 Three Year TSR Measurements						
	Threshold	*Target*	*Maximum*	*Actual Result*	*Pre-TSR*	*Modifier*
	(50% Modifier)	*(100% Modifier*	*(150% Modifier*		*Score (a)*	*(b)*
	25th Percentile	*50th Percentile*	*75th Percentile*	*99th Percentile*		
Three Year Relative TSR	(TSR of 2.35%)	(TSR of 35.10%)	(TSR of 71.05%)	(TSR of 188.91%)	142.0%	150%
Avg net revenue and **EPS score (Pre-TSR score)**						200%

The corporate score is a two-step process: Step (1) measures the performance vs. adjusted net income (2/3) and net revenue (1/3) and Step (2) adjust for strategic performance, which in 2019 was based on three factors: Grow, diversify, and build, which allows you to adjust Step 1 measurements of +10 points up or down −20 percentage points. Here is how the corporate score worked in 2019 (Table AIII.15).

The 2019 long-term management compensation plan was 50% Performance Stock Units (PSUs) and 50% Options. The long-term (three-year) plan was for the years 2019 to 2021. The

PSU targets are evenly split between EPS and net revenue performance. Targets look to be aligned with shareholders. However, the targets are adjustable on a 1:1 basis if consumption falls outside the designated range, which favors management over shareholders. Mastercard does not reveal the actual numerical PSU targets for 2020 for competitive reasons. Below is the long-term PSU and TSR worked in 2017–2019: The 2019 stock option priced at $227 (Tables AIII.16 and AIII.17).

The compensation plan was changed in 2020 to 60% Performance Stock Units (PSUs), 20% Options, and 20% Restricted Stock Units (RSUs). The 2020 stock grants were generally made around a price of $290, which is an important number with the stock trading at roughly $360. The actual targets, which were made pre-COVID, were not disclosed. We do know management's original 2019 guidance called for low teens' net revenue growth, which implies guidance is set at 100% of the targets. We can only suppose the same methodology was used for the original 2020 guidance implying targets were set at low teens net revenue growth again implying a roughly $18,500 to $19,000, a 10%–13% increase. Over the long-term, Mastercard has provided the Street with targets of low teen net revenue CAGR, minimum 50% operating margins, and high teens EPS CAGR-2019-2021.

Management-Team

Michael Miebach, incoming CEO, January 2021. Michael has been a key person in helping Mastercard become a multi-rail company in his role as Chief Product Officer. He has 25 years of experience in payments, banking, and technology. He is involved in several charities.

Ajay Banga, President, outgoing CEO, and board member. Prior to Mastercard, Mr. Banga was CEO of Citigroup Asia Pacific. He began his career at Nestlé, India, where he worked for 13 years. He spent two years with PepsiCo as well. He is a graduate of Delhi University and the Indian Institute of Management, Ahmedabad.

Ann Cairns, Executive Vice Chairman. Ms. Cairns was formerly the president of international markets for Mastercard. Prior to joining Mastercard in August 2011, she was a managing director and head of the Financial Industry Services group for Europe with Alvarez & Marsal in London. Previously, Ms. Cairns was chief executive officer, Transaction Banking, at ABN-AMRO in London.

Michael Froman, Vice Chairman, President Strategic Growth. Prior to joining Mastercard, Michael was on the council of Foreign Relations and continues to serve as a distinguished fellows. He served as a trade representative in the Obama administration. Michael is a member of the Disney Board of Directors.

Sachin Mehra, CFO. His prior role was as chief financial operations officer. He joined Mastercard in 2010 as a group executive and treasurer.

Craig Vosburg, President, North America. Mr. Vosburg is president of North America for Mastercard. Prior to assuming this role, he served as the company's chief product officer. Mr. Vosburg spent a decade working in the Asia Pacific region with Mastercard, and earlier in his career, worked for Bain & Company and A.T. Kearney.

Investment Risks

Regulation. Regulation on interchange fees and the payments industry could pose a potential threat to core business operations. Governments have in the past and could look to regulate interchange in the future. Different governments may support other potentially domestic payment systems. Merchants may charge more for their products when using a Mastercard product, forcing consumers to use different means of payment. Mastercard must adhere to international regulations

Table AIII.18 Income Statement

FYE December	*FY*	*FY*	*Mar-20*	*Jun-20*	*Sep-20*	*Dec-20*	*FY*	*Mar-21*	*Jun-21*	*Sep-21*	*Dec-21*	*FY*	*FY*	*FY*	*FY*	*FY*
	2018	*2019*	*1Q 20*	*2Q 20*	*3Q 20E*	*4Q 20E*	*2020E*	*1Q 20E*	*2Q 20E*	*3Q 20E*	*4Q 20E*	*2021E*	*2022E*	*2023E*	*2025E*	*2030E*
Revenue	**14,950**	**16,883**	**4,009**	**3,335**	**3,795**	**4,089**	**15,228**	**4,295**	**4,390**	**4,422**	**4,887**	**17,994**	**19,990**	**21,922**	**26,341**	**39,679**
Q/Q growth	–	–	−9.2%	−16.8%	13.8%	7.8%	–	5.0%	2.2%	0.7%	10.5%	–	–	–	–	–
Y/Y growth	19.6%	12.9%	3.1%	−18.9%	−15.1%	−7.4%	−9.8%	7.1%	31.6%	16.5%	19.5%	18.2%	11.1%	9.7%	9.6%	8.0%
Y/Y cc growth		16.0%	5.0%	−17.0%												
General and administrative	5,085	5,763	1,494	1,368	1,350	1,400	5,612	1,500	1,450	1,450	1,450	5,850	6,437	7,059	8,482	12,777
% of revenue	34.0%	34.1%	37.3%	41.0%	35.6%	34.2%	36.9%	34.9%	33.0%	32.8%	29.7%	32.5%	32.2%	32.2%	32.2%	32.2%
Advertising and marketing	996	934	154	93	170	165	582	160	160	160	160	640	700	725	727	732
% of revenue	6.7%	5.5%	3.8%	2.8%	4.5%	4.0%	3.8%	3.7%	3.6%	3.6%	3.3%	3.6%	3.5%	3.3%	2.8%	1.8%
Depreciation and amortization	459	522	144	145	140	140	569	150	150	150	150	600	650	650	700	825
% of revenue	3.1%	3.1%	3.6%	4.3%	3.7%	3.4%	3.7%	3.5%	3.4%	3.4%	3.1%	3.3%	3.3%	3.0%	2.7%	2.1%
Provision for litigation settlement	1,128	0	6	22	0	0	28	0	0	0	0	0	0	0	0	0
% of revenue	7.5%	0.0%	0.1%	0.7%	0.0%	0.0%	0.2%	0.0%	0.0%	0.0%	0.0%	0.0%	0.0%	0.0%	0.0%	0.0%
Total operating expenses	**7,668**	**7,219**	**1,798**	**1,628**	**1,660**	**1,705**	**6,791**	**1,810**	**1,760**	**1,760**	**1,760**	**7,090**	**7,787**	**8,434**	**9,909**	**14,334**
% of revenue	51.3%	42.8%	44.8%	48.8%	43.7%	41.7%	44.6%	42.1%	40.1%	39.8%	36.0%	39.4%	39.0%	38.5%	37.6%	36.1%
y/y growth	30.5%	−5.9%	7.3%	−5.1%	−8.4%	−15.4%	−5.9%	0.7%	8.1%	6.0%	3.2%	4.4%	9.8%	8.3%	8.2%	7.3%
Operating income	**7,282**	**9,664**	**2,211**	**1,707**	**2,135**	**2,384**	**8,437**	**2,485**	**2,630**	**2,662**	**3,127**	**10,904**	**12,203**	**13,488**	**16,432**	**25,346**
Operating margin	48.7%	57.2%	55.2%	51.2%	56.3%	58.3%	55.4%	57.9%	59.9%	60.2%	64.0%	60.6%	61.0%	61.5%	62.4%	63.9%
Adjusted operating income	**8,410**	**9,664**	**2,211**	**1,707**	**2,135**	**2,384**	**8,437**	**2,485**	**2,630**	**2,662**	**3,127**	**10,904**	**12,203**	**13,489**	**16,435**	**25,354**
Adjusted operating margin	56.3%	57.2%	55.2%	51.2%	56.3%	58.3%	55.4%	57.9%	59.9%	60.2%	64.0%	60.6%	61.0%	61.5%	62.4%	63.9%
EBITDA	**7,741**	**10,186**	**2,355**	**1,852**	**2,275**	**2,524**	**9,006**	**2,635**	**2,780**	**2,812**	**3,277**	**11,504**	**12,853**	**14,138**	**17,132**	**26,171**

(Continued)

Table AIII.18 (Continued)

FYE December	*FY*	*FY*	*Mar-20*	*Jun-20*	*Sep-20*	*Dec-20*	*FY*	*Mar-21*	*Jun-21*	*Sep-21*	*Dec-21*	*FY*	*FY*	*FY*	*FY*	*FY*
	2018	*2019*	*1Q 20*	*2Q 20*	*3Q 20E*	*4Q 20E*	*2020E*	*1Q 20E*	*2Q 20E*	*3Q 20E*	*4Q 20E*	*2021E*	*2022E*	*2023E*	*2025E*	*2030E*
EBITDA margin	51.8%	60.3%	58.7%	55.5%	59.9%	61.7%	59.1%	61.4%	63.3%	63.6%	67.1%	63.9%	64.3%	64.5%	65.0%	66.0%
Adjusted EBITDA	**8,869**	**10,186**	**2,355**	**1,852**	**2,275**	**2,524**	**9,006**	**2,635**	**2,780**	**2,812**	**3,277**	**11,504**	**12,854**	**14,140**	**17,136**	**26,180**
Adjusted EBITDA margin	59.3%	60.3%	58.7%	55.5%	59.9%	61.7%	59.1%	61.4%	63.3%	63.6%	67.1%	63.9%	64.3%	64.5%	65.1%	66.0%
Total other income (expense)	**(78)**	**(52)**	**(224)**	**(17)**	**(95)**	**(95)**	**(332)**	**(95)**	**(95)**	**(95)**	**(95)**	**(380)**	**(430)**	**(480)**	**(580)**	**(830)**
Pretax income from continuing operations	**7,204**	**9,612**	**1,987**	**1,690**	**2,040**	**2,289**	**8,105**	**2,390**	**2,535**	**2,567**	**3,032**	**10,524**	**11,773**	**13,008**	**15,852**	**24,516**
Pretax margin	48.2%	56.9%	49.6%	50.7%	53.7%	56.0%	53.2%	55.6%	57.7%	58.0%	62.0%	58.5%	58.9%	59.3%	60.2%	61.8%
Income tax expense (benefit)	1,345	1,613	294	270	357	401	1,322	418	444	449	531	1,842	2,060	2,276	2,774	4,290
Tax rate	18.7%	16.8%	14.8%	16.0%	17.5%	17.5%	16.3%	17.5%	17.5%	17.5%	17.5%	17.5%	17.5%	17.5%	17.5%	17.5%
Net income	**5,859**	**7,999**	**1,693**	**1,420**	**1,683**	**1,889**	**6,783**	**1,972**	**2,091**	**2,118**	**2,501**	**8,682**	**9,713**	**10,732**	**13,078**	**20,225**
Net margin	39.2%	47.4%	42.2%	42.6%	44.3%	46.2%	44.5%	45.9%	47.6%	47.9%	51.2%	48.3%	48.6%	49.0%	49.6%	51.0%
Adjusted net income	**6,793**	**7,942**	**1,693**	**1,420**	**1,683**	**1,889**	**6,783**	**1,972**	**2,091**	**2,118**	**2,501**	**8682**	**$9,713**	**$10,733**	**$13,081**	**$20,233**
Adjusted net margin	45.4%	47.0%	42.2%	42.6%	44.3%	46.2%	44.5%	45.9%	47.6%	47.9%	51.2%	48.3%	48.6%	49.0%	49.7%	51.0%
EPS	**$5.60**	**$7.94**	**$1.68**	**$1.41**	**$1.68**	**$1.90**	**$6.77**	**$1.99**	**$2.12**	**$2.16**	**$2.57**	**$8.88**	**$10.06**	**$11.14**	**$13.79**	**$21.87**
Y/Y growth	53.3%	41.9%	−7.1%	−29.5%	−18.5%	−8.2%	−14.8%	18.9%	50.3%	28.4%	35.1%	31.3%	13.3%	10.7%	11.3%	9.2%
Adjusted EPS	**$6.49**	**$7.77**	**$1.68**	**$1.41**	**$1.68**	**$1.90**	**$6.77**	**$1.99**	**$2.12**	**$2.16**	**$2.57**	**$8.88**	**$10.06**	**$11.14**	**$13.79**	**$21.88**
Y/Y growth	41.8%	19.7%	−5.6%	−25.5%	−21.6%	−3.6%	−12.9%	18.9%	50.3%	28.4%	35.1%	31.3%	13.3%	10.7%	11.3%	9.2%
Diluted shares	1,047	1,022	1,010	1,008	999	993	1,002	990	988	979	973	977	965	963	949	925
Y/Y growth	−2.4%	−2.3%	−2.1%	−1.7%	−2.0%	−2.0%	−1.9%	−2.0%	−2.0%	−2.0%	−2.0%	−2.5%	−2.5%	−2.5%	−2.5%	−2.5%

and standards such as anti-money laundering, which expose them to risk and can change over time. Regulations like PSD2 are evolving and could pose a threat.

Privacy and **Security**. Mastercard processes secure payments. The company collects an increasing amount of data across these transactions. The processing and collection of the data needs to be secure. Governments are putting increased regulations on the collection of data. As a result, the costs of securing the data and compliance with regulations are expected to increase. Mastercard's processing system could potentially face outages.

Competitive Landscape. Mastercard faces competition from changes in the technological landscape, new (and old) products offered by incumbents, and new players in the payments space. Competition includes traditional payment methods such as cash, paper checks and ACH, debit and credit cards (Visa, etc.), digital wallets (Google Checkout, Amazon Payments, etc.), Mobile-based payments (Apple Pay, Android Pay, etc.), eCommerce (PayPal, Adyen, etc.) as well as money transfer offerings (Western Union, etc.). The company could be disintermediated by other players in the industry. There is the potential to lose large financial institutions. Competition could lead to pricing pressure.

Economic Risk. Mastercard is exposed to changes in consumer discretionary spending. Deterioration in the global macro environment could have a negative impact on consumer sentiment and spending conversely affecting revenues. Adverse macroeconomic conditions include, but are not limited to, recessions, inflation, high unemployment, currency fluctuations, actual or anticipated large-scale defaults or failures, or slowdown of global trade.

Cryptocurrencies. The advent of blockchain and other cryptocurrencies could have a significant impact on the entire payment ecosystem. Blockchain technologies are decentralized and eliminate many of the risks associated with hacking a centralized database. If Mastercard fails to adapt or keep pace with new technologies in the payments space in a timely manner, it could harm the company's ability to compete.

Share Class B. Mastercard has Class B shares, which are non-voting shares. The shares may be converted to voting shares in the future date, which may dilute the shareholder (Table AIII.18).

Bibliography

Capgemini. (2019, September 17). World payments report 2019. https://www.capgemini.com/news/press-releases/world-payments-report-2019/

Company, T. B. (2020, September 29). Global FinTech market segments. https://www.thebusinessresearchcompany.com/press-release/global-fintech-market-segments

eMarketer. (2020, June 22). Global Ecommerce 2020. https://www.emarketer.com/content/global-ecommerce-2020

ReportLinker. (2020, September 16). The global payment processing. *GlobeNewswire*.

Appendix IV

Equations (Financial Tool Set)

Economics

Real (Inflation Adjusted) GDP:

$$\text{Real GDP} = \text{consumption spending} + \text{investment} + \text{government spending} + \text{net exports} \left(\text{exports} - \text{imports}\right)$$

Ratios

Income Statement

Growth Rates:

$$\text{Growth rate} = \left({}^{\text{current}}\!/_{\text{prior}} - 1 \right) * 100$$

$$\text{Growth rate} = \text{RR} \times \text{ROE}$$

$$\text{Rentention rate} \left(\text{RR}\right) = 1 - \frac{\text{dividends declared}}{\text{operating income after taxes}}$$

$$\text{Basic EPS} = \frac{\text{net income} - \text{preferred dividends}}{\text{wtd. avg. no. of common shs. outstanding}}$$

$$\text{Diluted EPS} = \frac{\text{adjusted income avail. for common shares}}{\text{wtd. avg. no. of common shs. outstanding}}$$

Profitability:

$$\text{Gross profit margin} = \frac{\text{gross profit}}{\text{revenue}}$$

$$\text{Operating profit margin} = \frac{\text{operating profit}}{\text{revenue}} = \frac{\text{EBIT}}{\text{net sales}}$$

$$\text{Net profit margin} = \frac{\text{net income}}{\text{revenue}}$$

Balance Sheet

Return Ratios:

$$\text{Return on Equity}\left(\text{ROE}\right)=\frac{\text{EBIT}}{\text{average shareholder equity}}$$

DuPont Analysis:

$$\text{Return on Equity}\left(\text{ROE}\right)=\left(\frac{\text{net income}}{\text{sales}}\right)\left(\frac{\text{sales}}{\text{assets}}\right)\left(\frac{\text{assets}}{\text{equity}}\right)$$

Or

$$\text{Return on Equity}\left(\text{ROE}\right)=\left(\text{net profit margin}\right)\left(\text{asset turnover}\right)\left(\text{equity multiplier}\right)$$

$$\text{Return on Asset}\left(\text{ROA}\right)=\frac{\text{EBIT}}{\text{average total capital}}$$

Liquidity Ratios:

$$\text{Current ratio}=\frac{\text{current assets}}{\text{current liabilities}}$$

$$\text{Quick ratio}=\frac{\text{cash}+\text{marketable securities}+\text{receivables}}{\text{current liabilities}}$$

$$\text{Defensive interval}=\frac{\text{cash}+\text{mrkt. sec.}+\text{receivables}}{\text{daily cash expenditures}}$$

Cash Management:

$$\text{Receivables turnover}=\frac{\text{annual sales}}{\text{average receivables}}$$

$$\text{Inventory turnover}=\frac{\text{cost of goods sold}}{\text{average inventory}}$$

$$\text{Payables turnover}=\frac{\text{purchases}}{\text{average trade payables}}$$

$$\text{Days of Sales Outstanding}\left(\text{DSO}\right)=\frac{365}{\text{receivables turnover}}$$

$$\text{Days of inventory on hand}=\frac{365}{\text{inventory turnover}}$$

$$\text{Number of days payable}=\frac{365}{\text{payable turnover ratio}}$$

$$\text{Cash conversion cycle}=\left(\text{days of inventory}\right)+\left(\text{days of sales outstanding}\right)-\left(\text{number of days payable}\right)$$

Asset Turnover Ratios:

$$\text{Total asset turnover} = \frac{\text{revenue}}{\text{average total net asset}}$$

$$\text{Fixed asset turnover} = \frac{\text{revenue}}{\text{average net fixed asset}}$$

$$\text{Working capital turnover} = \frac{\text{revenue}}{\text{average working capital}}$$

Debt Ratios:

$$\text{Debt-to-equity ratio} = \frac{\text{total debt}}{\text{total equity}}$$

$$\text{Total-debt ratio} = \frac{\text{total debt}}{\text{total asset}}$$

Interest coverage:

$$\text{Interest coverage} = \frac{\text{EBIT}}{\text{interest}}$$

$$\text{Fixed charge coverage} = \frac{\text{EBIT} + \text{lease payments}}{\text{interest} + \text{leases payments}}$$

Cash Flow Statement

Cash Flow Ratios:

$$\text{Free Cash Flow}\left(\text{FCF}\right) = \text{operating cash flow} - \text{net capital expenditures}$$

Indirect Method:

Net Income
+/− Assets
+/− Liabilities
+/− Cash Flow from Financing & Investing
Net Change in Cash Flows

Direct Method:

Net Cash Inflows
− Net Cash Outflows
+ Cash Flow from Financing & Investing
Net Change in Cash Flows

FCF Yield:

$$\text{Free cash flow yield} = \frac{\text{free cash flow per share}}{\text{current share price}}$$

Dividend Yield:

$$\text{Dividend yield} = \frac{\text{annual dividends per share}}{\text{current share price}}$$

Valuation

Future Value Formula

Future Value:

$$\text{Future value} = \text{PV}\left(1+r\right)^{n}$$

Present Value Formula

Present Value:

$$\text{Present value} = \text{FV}\Big/\left(1+r\right)^{n}$$

Ordinary Annuity:

$$\text{Present value} = \text{PMT}\left(\frac{1-\dfrac{1}{\left(1+r\right)^{n}}}{r}\right)$$

Perpetuity:

$$\text{Present value} = \frac{\text{PMT}}{r}$$

Growth Perpetuity:

$$\text{Present value} = \frac{\text{PMT}\left(1\times g\right)}{\left(r-g\right)}$$

Capital Measurements

Cost of Equity

CAPM Formula:

$$\text{Expected return} = \text{risk free rate} + \text{beta} \times \text{risk premuim}\left(\text{market risk} - \text{risk free rate}\right)$$

Or

$$k_e = \text{RFR} + \beta\left(R_{\text{mkt}} - \text{RFR}\right)$$

Cost of Equity:

$$k_e = \frac{D_1}{P} + g$$

Cost of Debt

Weighted Average Cost of Capital:

$$\text{WACC} = \left(w_d\right)\left(k_d\left(1-t\right)\right) + \left(w_{ps}\right)\left(k_{ps}\right) + \left(w_{cc}\right)\left(k_s\right)$$

Capital Efficiency

Return on Equity:

$$\text{Return on equity}\left(\text{ROE}\right) = \frac{\text{net income}}{\text{shareholder's equity}}$$

Equity Reinvestment:

$$\text{Equity reinvestment} = \left(\text{CapEx} - \text{Dep}\right) + \Delta\text{WC} - \left(\text{new debt} - \text{debt repaid}\right)$$

Reinvestment Rate:

$$\text{Reinvestment rate} = \frac{\text{equity reinvested}}{\text{net income}}$$

Return on Capital:

$$\text{Return on capital}\left(\text{ROC}\right) = \frac{\text{net income}}{\text{total capital}}$$

Holding Period Return:

$$R_t = \frac{P_t - P_{t-1} + D_t}{P_{t-1}}$$

Growth

$$\text{Retention ratio} = (\text{net income} - \text{dividends})/\text{net income}$$

$$\text{Growth} = (\text{retention ratio}) * (\text{ROE})$$

$$\text{Growth} = (\text{reinvestment rate}) * (\text{ROC})$$

Intrinsic Value

Dividend Discount Model

One Period Valuation Model:

$$\text{Value of stock or } V_0 = \frac{D_1}{(1+k_e)} + \frac{P_1}{(1+k_e)}$$

V_0 = Value of Stock
D_1 = Dividend in Period 1
k_e = Cost of Equity or discount rate
P_1 = Price of Stock in Period 1

Constant Growth or Gordon Growth Model:

$$\text{Value of stock or } V_0 = \frac{D_1}{k_e - g_c} \text{ or } \frac{D_0(1+g_c)}{k_c + g_c}$$

g_c = Growth of Capital

Multi Stage Growth Model:

$$V_0 = \frac{D_n}{(1+k_e)^n} + \frac{P_n}{(1+k_e)^n}$$

Where:

$$P_n = \frac{D_{n+1}}{(k_e - g_c)}$$

Buffett's Owner's Earnings Formula:

+ Reported Earnings
+ Depreciation Amortization
± Other Noncash Charges
– Avg Annual Maintenance Capex
± Changes in Working Capital
Owner's Earnings

Free Cash Flow to Equity (FCFE) Formula's:

$$\text{FCFE}\left(\text{Free Cash Flow to Equity}\right) = \text{net income} - \left(\text{CapEx} - \text{depreciation}\right) - \text{change in non-cash WC} + \left(\text{debt repaid} - \text{new debt issued}\right)$$

Or

$$\text{FCFE}\left(\text{Free Cash Flow to Equity}\right) = \text{EBIT} - \text{interest} - \text{taxes} + \text{depreciation \& amortization} + \text{changes in working capital} + \text{Capex} + \text{net borrowings}$$

Or

$$\text{FCFE}\left(\text{Free Cash Flow to Equity}\right) = \text{FCFF} - (\text{interest} \times \left(1 - \text{tax}\right) + \text{net borrowings}$$

FCFE Constant Growth:

$$\text{Value of stock or } P_0 = \frac{\text{FCFE}}{k_e - g_c}$$

FCFE Multistage Growth Model:

$$V_0 = \frac{\text{FCFE}}{\left(1 + k_e\right)^n} + \frac{P_n}{\left(1 + k_e\right)^n}$$

Free Cash Flow Firm (FCFF) Formula's:

$$\text{FCFF}\left(\text{Free Cash Flow to Firm}\right) = \text{net income} + \text{depreciation} + \left[\text{interest} \times \left(1 - \text{tax rate}\right)\right] - \text{CapEx} - \text{change WC}$$

Or

$$\text{FCFF}\left(\text{Free Cash Flow to Firm}\right) = \left[\text{EBIT} \times \left(1 - \text{tax rate}\right)\right] + \text{depreciation} - \text{CapEx} - \text{change WC}$$

Or

$$\text{FCFE}\left(\text{Free Cash Flow to Firm}\right)=\left[\text{EBITDA}\times\left(1-\text{tax rate}\right)\right]+\left(\text{depreciation}\times\text{tax rate}\right)$$
$$-\text{CapEx}-\text{change WC}$$

Or

$$\text{FCFF}\left(\text{Free Cash Flow to Firm}\right)=\text{CFO}+\left[\text{interest}\times\left(1-\text{tax rate}\right)\right]-\text{change WC}$$

FCFF Constant Growth:

$$\text{Value of stock or } P_0=\frac{\text{FCFF}}{\text{WACC}-g_c}$$

FCFF Multi-Stage Growth Model:

$$V_0=\frac{\text{FCFF}}{\left(1+\text{WACC}\right)^n}+\frac{P_n}{\left(1+\text{WACC}\right)^n}$$

Relative Value

Price Multiples

Price/Earnings Formula's:

$$\frac{P}{E}=\frac{\text{price}}{\text{earnings}}$$

$$\text{Leading }\frac{P}{E}=\frac{\text{price per share}}{\text{forecast EPS next 12 months}}$$

$$\text{Trailing }\frac{P}{E}=\frac{\text{price per share}}{\text{EPS previous 12 months}}$$

Price/Book Value Multiples:

$$\frac{P}{B}=\frac{\text{price per share}}{\text{book value per share}}$$

$$\text{Book value}=\frac{\text{assets}-\text{liabilities}}{\text{shares}}$$

Price/Sales Value Multiples:

$$\frac{P}{S}=\frac{\text{price per share}}{\text{sales per share}}$$

Price/Cash Flow Value Multiples:

$$\frac{P}{\text{CF}} = \frac{\text{price per share}}{\text{cash flow per share}}$$

PEG PE/Earnings Growth Formula:

$$\text{PEG} = \frac{\text{PE}}{\text{earnings growth}}$$

Enterprise Value to Earnings before Interest, Taxes, Dep. & Amort. (EV/EBITDA):

$$\begin{aligned}\text{Enterprise value} &= \text{market cap} + \text{preferred Shs} + \text{market value of debt} \\ &\quad + \text{minority interest} - \text{cash \& equivalent}\end{aligned}$$

Or Shortened Version

$$\text{Enterprise value} = \text{market cap} + \text{total debt} - \text{total cash}$$

$$\frac{\text{Enterprise value}}{\text{Earnings before interest, taxes, \& Dep. \& Amort.}} = \frac{\text{EV}}{\text{EBITDA}}$$

Justified Multiples

Justified PE:

$$\frac{P_0}{E_1} = \frac{\text{payout ratio}}{k - g}$$

Justified Price to Earnings Multiple:

$$\text{Leading } P/E = \frac{(1-b)}{r-g}$$

$$\text{Trailing } P/E = \frac{(1-b)\,(1+g)}{r-g}$$

g = growth
b = retention rate
r = required rate of return

Justified Price to Sales:

$$\frac{P}{S} = \frac{\text{PM}_0 \times (1-b)(1+g)}{r-g}$$

PM_0 = Profit Margin or Earnings/Sales
g = growth
b = retention rate
r = required rate of return

Justified Price to Book Value (P/BV) Formula:

$$\text{Justified } \frac{P}{\text{BV}} = \frac{\text{ROE} - g}{r - g}$$

ROE = Return on Equity
g = growth
r = required rate of return

Modern Portfolio Theory

Random Walk Time Series Formula:

$$X_t = X_{t-1} + E_t$$

X_{t-1} is the observation at the previous time step
E_t is the white noise or random fluctuation in time

Expected Return Formulas:

$$\text{Expected return} = \sum P(x_i)x_n \text{ or } E(X) = P(x_1)x_1 + P(x_2)x_2 + \ldots + P(x_n)x_n$$

$P(x_i)$ = Probability or weighting
x_n = Expected Return

Expected Return, variance of 2-stock portfolio
Expected Return of Two Stock Portfolio

$$E(R_p) = w_A\, E(R_A) + w_B\, E(R_B)$$

w_A = percentage or weighting of stock A
w_B = percentage or weighting of stock B
$E(R_A)$ = expected return of stock A
$E(R_B)$ = expected return of stock B

Variance of 2-Stock Portfolio

$$\text{Var}\left(R_{\text{p}}\right)=w_{\text{A}}{}^{2}\sigma^{2}\left(R_{\text{A}}\right)+w_{\text{B}}{}^{2}\sigma^{2}\left(R_{\text{B}}\right)+2w_{\text{A}}w_{\text{B}}\sigma\left(R_{\text{A}}\right)\sigma\left(R_{\text{B}}\right)\rho\left(R_{\text{A}},R_{\text{B}}\right)$$

$w_{\text{A}}{}^{2}$ = the square root of the weighting of stock A
$w_{\text{B}}{}^{2}$ = the square root of the weighting of stock B
$\sigma^{2}\left(R_{\text{A}}\right)$ = variance of stock A
$\sigma^{2}\left(R_{\text{B}}\right)$ = variance of stock B
$2w_{\text{A}}w_{\text{B}}\sigma\left(R_{\text{A}}\right)\sigma\left(R_{\text{B}}\right)\rho\left(R_{\text{A}},R_{\text{B}}\right)$ = 2 × weighting of A × weighting of B × covariance of A & B

Covariance Formula (Reminder):

$$\text{Cov}\left(x,y\right)=\frac{\sum\left(x-\bar{x}\right)\left(y-\bar{y}\right)}{n-1}$$

Correlation Formula (Reminder):

$$\text{Corr}\left(x,y\right)=\frac{\text{Cov}\left(R_{i},R_{j}\right)}{\sigma\left(R_{i}\right)\sigma\left(R_{j}\right)}$$

Roy's Safety Formula:

$$\frac{\left(\bar{r}_{\text{p}}-r_{\text{target}}\right)}{\sigma_{\text{p}}}$$

$\bar{r}_{\text{p}}$ = expected return of the portfolio
r_{target} = minimum required return for the investor
σ_{p} = standard deviation, or risk, of the portfolio

Sharpe Ratio Formula:

$$\frac{R_{\text{p}}-R_{\text{f}}}{\sigma_{\text{P}}}$$

R_{p} = the portfolio return
R_{f} = the risk-free rate or the rate for 90-day T-bills or cash
σ_{P} = standard deviation of the portfolio's return

Three Factor Model Formula:

$$r = R_f + B(R_m - R_f) + b_s * \text{SMB} + b_v * \text{HML}$$

R_f = Risk Free Rate

B = Beta

R_m = Market Risk

$(R_m - R_f)$ = Market Risk Premium

$R_f + B(R_m - R_f)$ = CAPM

b_s = coefficient of SMB

SMB = Small (market cap) Minus Big

b_v = coefficient of HML

HML = High (Book-to Market Ratio) Minus Low

Five Factor Model Formula:

$$r = R_f + B(R_m - R_f) + b_s * \text{SMB} + b_v * \text{HML} + b_w * \text{RMW} + b_x * \text{CMA}$$

R_f = Risk Free Rate

B = Beta

R_m = Market Risk

$(R_m - R_f)$ = Market Risk Premium

$R_f + B(R_m - R_f)$ = CAPM

b_s = coefficient of SMB

SMB = Small (market cap) Minus Big

b_v = coefficient of HML

HML = High (Book-to Market Ratio) Minus Low

b_w = coefficient of RMW

RMW = Return of most profitable firms Minus Weakest profitable

b_x = coefficient of CMA

CMA = Return of firms who invest Conservatively Minus Aggressively

Appendix V

Examples (Analyst Workshop)

Holding Period Return Example

Let's assume you bought 1,000 shares of AT&T (Ticker: ATT) at \$10. Your cost is \$10,000. The company paid a \$1 dividend per share while you own the stock and you sell all your shares at \$12.

Calculating Holding Period Return:

$$R_t = \frac{P_t - P_{t-1} + D_t}{P_{t-1}}$$

P_{t-1} = original cost basis

P_t = current value

D_t = total dividend

Or

P_{t-1} = \$10,000

P_t = \$12,000

D_t = \$1,000

Your HPR is 30%.

Keynesian Multiplier Example

The Marginal Propensity to Consume (MPC) is 50% or 0.5 for an economy. The tax rate is 30% or 0.3. What will the fiscal multiplier be?

$$\frac{1}{1 - \text{MPC}\left(1 - t\right)}$$

MPC = Marginal Propensity to Consume

t = tax rate

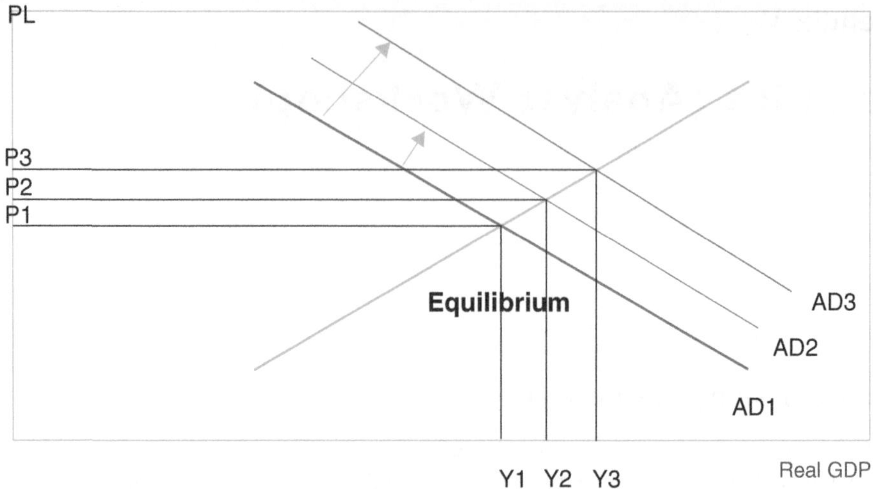

Figure AV.1 Keynesian Multiplier.

The fiscal multiplier would be 1.5×, which means every dollar of new income would generate about \$1.50 of extra income. We note there are money multipliers, which apply to monetary factors as well.

$$\frac{1}{\text{Reserve ratio}}$$

Reserve Ratio = Federal Reserve Ratio

Here is a graphic depiction of the Keynesian multiplier. The market begins at an equilibrium of P1 and Y1. The initial rise in aggregate demand moves the curve to AD2, but the multiplier moves the curve to AD3 (Figure AV.1).

GDP Example

The economy of Country A had \$7 trillion in consumer spending, \$10 trillion in gross investments, \$3 trillion in government spending, and exported \$1 trillion and imported \$2 trillion. What is the nominal GDP? What is the Real GDP assuming inflation of 25% or a price deflator of 1.25?

The nominal GDP is \$19 trillion, while the real GDP is \$15.2 trillion.

Present Value Example

An investor promised \$10,000 in 20 years with a 14% discount rate. What is the present value?

$$\text{Present value} = \text{FV} \Big/ (1+r)^n$$

FV = Future Value
r = Discount Rate
n = Periods
Ans. = \$727

Ordinary Annuity Example

An investor buys an annuity paying $1,000 per year at the end of each year for ten year, at a 10% discount rate. What is the present value of this annuity?

$$\text{Present value} = \text{PMT}\left(\frac{1-\frac{1}{(1+r)^n}}{r}\right)$$

PMT = Payment
r = Discount Rate
n = Periods
Ans. = $6,139

Perpetuity Example

An investor buys a console bond paying $1,000 per year at a 10% interest rate. What is the present value of this bond?

$$\text{Present value} = \frac{\text{PMT}}{r}$$

Ans. = $10,000

Growth Perpetuity Example

An investor buys a stock paying $10 dividend per year, expected to grow 2%, at a 6% discount rate. What is the present value?

$$\text{Present value} = \frac{\text{PMT}\,(1\times g)}{(r-g)}$$

PMT = Payment
g = growth rate
r = Discount Rate
n = Periods
Ans. = $255

Leading P/E Example

Mastercard is trading at roughly $350 on 8/25 the FactSet consensus Street estimates for 2021 are $8.72. What is the leading P/E?

$$\text{Leading } \frac{P}{E} = \frac{\text{price per share}}{\text{forecast EPS next 12 months}}$$

Ans. = $350/$8.72 or 40×

Justified P/E Example

Mastercard has a 5-yr payout ratio of 20.6%, cost of equity of 5.83%, and a constant growth rate of 3%. What is its justified P/E multiple?

$$\frac{P_0}{E_1} = \frac{\text{payout ratio}}{k - g}$$

Ans.-7×

EV/EBITDA Example

What is Mastercard's 2021 EV/EBITDA?

Step 1: Find Mastercard's Enterprise Value. The formula for Enterprise Value is:

$$\text{Enterprise value} = \text{market cap} + \text{preferred Shs} + \text{market value of debt} \\ + \text{minority interest} - \text{cash \& equivalent}$$

Or Shortened Version

$$\text{Enterprise value} = \text{market cap} + \text{total debt} - \text{total cash}$$

Mastercard has the following inputs for 2020 shortened Enterprise Value formula (Sept 2020):

Market Cap = \$361 billion
Preferred Shs = 0
Market Value of Debt = \$12.5 billion
Minority Interest = Insignificant
Cash and Equivalent = \$12.14 billion

We get an Enterprise Value of roughly \$361 billion. Can we then get our 2020 EV/EBITDA ratio by dividing the Enterprise Value by our 2020 EBITDA Estimate of \$9.0 billion?

The net result is a ratio of 40 × '20. If we use our '21 and '22 EBITDA estimates, we get 31× and 28×.

P/CF Example

What is Mastercard's 2021 P/CF?

Step 1: Find Mastercard's cash flow per share. The formula for CF per share is:

$$\text{Cash flow per share} : \frac{\text{cash flow}}{\text{share count}}$$

Mastercard's has the following inputs for 2021:

Our FCF estimate: \$8.095 billion
Share Count: 1.008 million
FCF per Share: \$8.03

Thus the Price to CF per shs is: \$357/\$8.03 or 44× for 2021. The P/CF for Mastercard for 2020 is 56× and 2022 is 39×.

Efficient Frontier Example

Find the **Estimated or Expected Return** and the **Efficient Frontier** for a two-stock portfolio AAPL and AMZN in 2019?

Step1: Expected Return

We begin by finding the monthly closing prices adjusted for dividends for AAPL and AMZN in 2019. We note we are using historical returns as opposed to estimating out the potential returns and applying the probabilities. We can find each monthly return by dividing the next month's price by the prior month and subtracting by one and converting to a percentage **(See Prior Holding Period Return Formula)**. We then take the mean or average of these returns for the individual stocks. We are constructing a portfolio of 50% AAPL and 50% AMZN for the purposes of learning how to first process the data. We can then calculate the expected return for each period weighing the return based on a 50/50 split (See Portfolio Returns column and expected returns formula below).

Formula for Expected Return

$$\text{Expected return} = \sum P(x_i)x_n \text{ or } E(X) = P(x_1)x_1 + P(x_2)x_2 + \cdots + P(x_n)x_n$$

$P(x_i)$ = Probability or weighting

x_n = Expected Return

We can proceed to finding additional metrics, which will be helpful in the construction of our Efficient Frontier. These metrics include the variance of returns, standard deviation (square root of variance), covariance, and correlation. We would suggest trying these calculations by hand for practice. Excel allows for quick computation of each metric (Table AV.1).

Expected Return, Variance of Two-Stock Portfolio

EXPECTED RETURN OF TWO-STOCK PORTFOLIO

$$E(R_p) = w_A\, E(R_A) + w_B\, E(R_B)$$

w_A = percentage or weighting of stock A

w_B = percentage or weighting of stock B

$E(R_A)$ = expected return of stock A

$E(R_B)$ = expected return of stock B

Table AV.1 Portfolio Returns Apple and Mastercard (50/50 Weighting)

2019	*AAPL Adj Close*	*MA Adj Close*	*50% AAPL Returns*	*50% MA Returns*	*Portfolio Returns*
Dec-18	$159	$1.502			
Jan-19	$168	$1,719	6%	14%	10%
Feb-19	$175	$1,640	4%	−5%	0%
Mar-19	$192	$1,781	10%	9%	9%
Apr-19	$203	$1,927	6%	8%	7%
May-19	$178	$1,775	−12%	−8%	−10%
Jun-19	$201	$1,894	13%	7%	10%
Jul-19	$216	$1,867	8%	−1%	3%
Aug-19	$213	$1,776	−2%	−5%	−3%
Sep-19	$228	$1,736	7%	−2%	3%
Oct-19	$254	$1,777	11%	2%	7%
Nov-19	$273	$1,801	8%	1%	5%
Dec-19	$300	$1,848	10%	3%	6%
		Mean	6%	2%	4%

Variance of Two-Stock Portfolio

$$\text{Var}\left(R_{\text{p}}\right) = w_{\text{A}}{}^{2}\sigma^{2}\left(R_{\text{A}}\right) + w_{\text{B}}{}^{2}\sigma^{2}\left(R_{\text{B}}\right) + 2w_{\text{A}}w_{\text{B}}\sigma\left(R_{\text{A}}\right)\sigma\left(R_{\text{B}}\right)\rho\left(R_{\text{A}}, R_{\text{B}}\right)$$

$w_{\text{A}}{}^{2}$ = the square root of the weighting of stock A

$w_{\text{B}}{}^{2}$ = the square root of the weighting of stock B

$\sigma^{2}\left(R_{\text{A}}\right)$ = variance of stock A

$\sigma^{2}\left(R_{\text{B}}\right)$ = variance of stock B

$2w_{\text{A}}w_{\text{B}}\sigma\left(R_{\text{A}}\right)\sigma\left(R_{\text{B}}\right)\rho\left(R_{\text{A}}, R_{\text{B}}\right)$ = 2 × weighting of A × weighting of B × covariance of A and B

Covariance Formula (Reminder)

$$\text{Cov}\left(x, y\right) = \frac{\sum\left(x - \bar{x}\right)\left(y - \bar{y}\right)}{n - 1}$$

Correlation Formula (Reminder)

$$\text{Corr}\left(x, y\right) = \frac{\text{COV}\left(R_i, R_j\right)}{\sigma\left(R_i\right)\sigma\left(R_j\right)}$$

Step 2: Efficient Frontier

We can then weigh the portfolio based on different contributions or weightings. We will then graph on the Efficient Market Frontier (Tables AV.2 and AV.3).

Finally, we can plot the results on a graph of the efficient frontier. The x-axis on the frontier is the standard deviation. The x-axis measures the amount of risk. The higher the standard deviation the higher the risk. The 5.66% return is 100% AAPL, so very risky. The y-axis measures the mean returns. The higher the mean returns the better. The graph would suggest a rough, even split would be the best balance (see Table AV.3 above for details). The *Northwest quadrant* or the area in the upper left-hand corner of the efficient frontier is where the optimal portfolio and asset allocation lies. Our section on asset allocation on previews the efficient frontier. The table and graph would suggest if you were going to use a 90/10 split you should do so weighted toward AAPL vs. AMZN (Figure AV.2).

Roy's Safety Example

Let's look at an example of **Roy's Safety** equation.

$$\frac{\left(\bar{r}_{\mathrm{p}} - r_{\mathrm{target}}\right)}{\sigma_{\mathrm{p}}}$$

$\bar{r}_{\mathrm{p}}$ = expected return of the portfolio

r_{target} = minimum required return for the investor

σ_{p} = standard deviation, or risk, of the portfolio

Table AV.2 Portfolio Return Apple and Mastercard Portfolio

2019	*AAPL Adj Close*	*MA Adj Close*	*50% AAPL Returns*	*50% MA Returns*	*Portfolio Returns*
Dec-18	$159	$1,502			
Jan-19	$168	$1,719	6%	14%	10%
Feb-19	$175	$1,640	4%	−5%	0%
Mar-19	$192	$1,781	10%	9%	9%
Apr-19	$203	$1,927	6%	8%	7%
May-19	$178	$1,775	−12%	−8%	−10%
Jun-19	$201	$1,894	13%	7%	10%
Jul-19	$216	$1,867	8%	−1%	3%
Aug-19	$213	$1,776	−2%	−5%	−3%
Sep-19	$228	$1,736	7%	−2%	3%
Oct-19	$254	$1,777	11%	2%	7%
Nov-19	$273	$1,801	8%	1%	5%
Dec-19	$300	$1,848	10%	3%	6%
		Mean	6%	2%	4%
		Variance	0.004255	0.003971	0.003243
		Std Dev	0.06813	0.06582	0.059482
		Covariance	0.002373		
		Correlation	0.577389		

Table AV.3 Apple vs. Amazon Returns Various Weighting

AAPL	*AMZN*	*Mean (%)*	*Variance*	*Std Dev (%)*
Weighting (%)				
0	100	1.93	0.003971	6
10	90	2.31	0.003686	6
20	80	2.68	0.003471	6
30	70	3.05	0.003326	6
40	60	3.43	0.003250	6
50	50	3.80	0.003243	6
60	40	4.17	0.003306	6
70	30	4.55	0.003439	6
80	20	4.92	0.003642	6
90	10	5.29	0.003913	6
100	0	5.66	0.004255	7

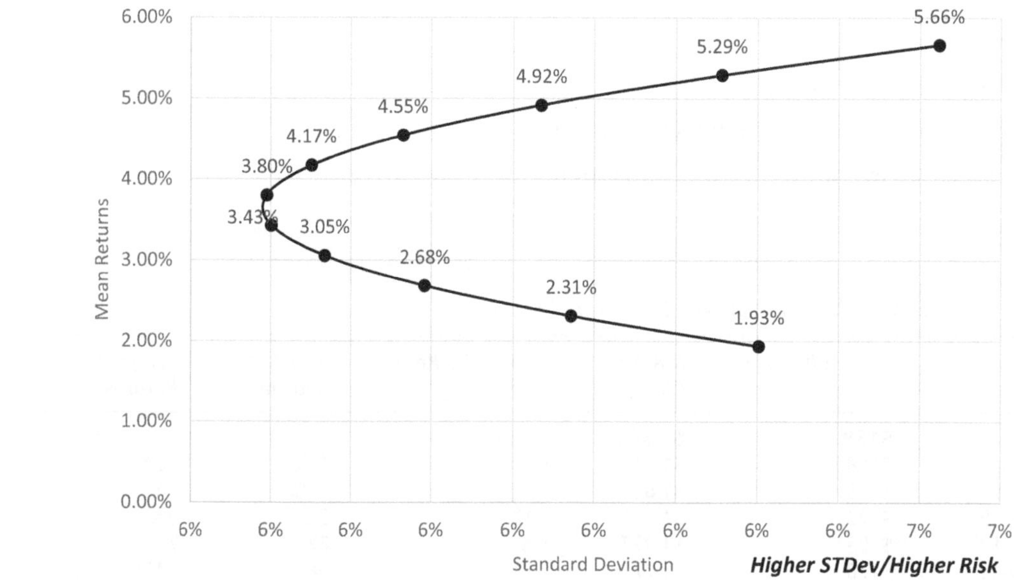

Figure AV.2 Efficient Frontier.

An investor is looking at three portfolios A, B, and C. The investor would like the optimal portfolio with the lowest amount of shortfall risk. The minimum return the investor is expecting is 5%.

Portfolio A has an expected return of 5% with 10% risk
Portfolio B has an expected return of 10% with 12% risk
Portfolio C has an expected return of 20% with 15% risk

Roy's Safety First Ratio would be:

Portfolio A = 0
Portfolio B = 0.42
Portfolio C = 1.0

The investor would choose portfolio C as it is the highest and 1 standard deviation below the mean.

Sharpe Ratio Example

A stock portfolio is expected to have a 10% annual return. The current risk-free rate is 7%, and the portfolio has a 1 standard deviation.

$$\frac{R_p - R_f}{\sigma_P}$$

R_p = the portfolio return

R_f = the risk-free rate or the rate for 90-day T-bills or cash

σ_P = standard deviation of the portfolio's return

The Sharpe ratio is 3.0, which means the portfolio carries 3.0 "units" of risk for each point of return. The higher the ratio the better. However, if the returns for the portfolio are generally the same, you would want the lower Sharpe ratio implying less risk per return. If there was a second portfolio with a 10% return and a 2.0 Sharpe ratio, you would prefer it to the 3.0.

CAPM Example

Let's look at an example of the CAPM. The market has an expected return of 10% and the risk-free rate is 7% and its Beta is 1.5.

$$k_e = \text{RFR} + \beta\left(R_{mkr} - \text{RFR}\right)$$

k_e = the cost of equity

RFR = risk-free rate

β = Beta

R_{mkr} = expected market return

The CAPM is 11.5%.

Security Market Line Example

The Security Market Line (SML) is a graphical representation of the CAPM. It represents the investment opportunity cost providing the combination of the risk-free rate and market portfolio. A zero-beta portfolio equals the risk-free rate. The slope of the line is the risk premium.

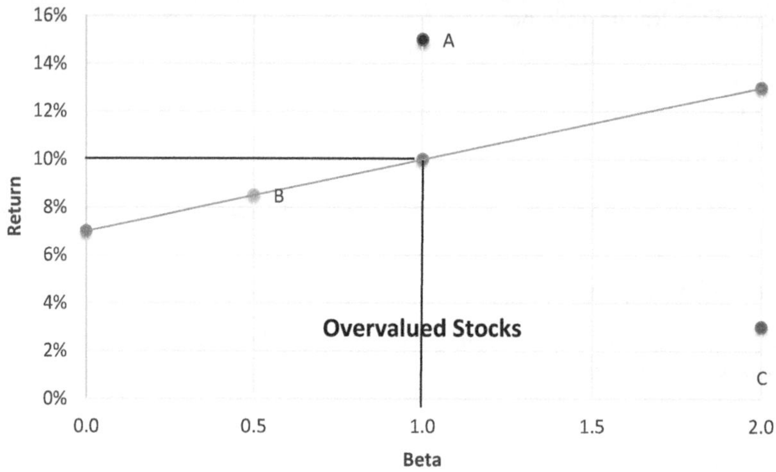

Figure AV.3 Security Market Line.

Correctly priced assets fall on the SML. The assets above the SML are undervalued those above are overvalued.

Let's look at an example of the SML. We begin by plotting the market information or portfolio on SML. We can then plot three different stocks to see if they are properly priced (Figure AV.3).

Security A has an expected return of 15% and a beta of 1.0
Security B has an expected return of 10% and a beta of 0.5
Security C has an expected return of 5% and a beta of 2.0
Security A has a CAPM of 15% and is *Undervalued*
Security B has a CAPM of 9% and is *Properly Valued*
Security C has a CAPM of 3% and is *Overvalued*

Appendix VI

Valuation Methods in Detail

Free Cash Flow to Equity (FCFE) Valuation Method for Mastercard (As of Mid-2020)

We can now value Mastercard as of roughly mid-2020. I have chosen the FCFE method. FCFE is the cash attributable to the **equity** shareholders of the company after investments and obligations debts, interests are satisfied. I include a look at Mastercard using a FCFF (Free Cash Flow to Firm) method solely for exemplary purposes.

Step 1-We estimated FCFE for Mastercard over the next ten years below. We included our FCF and FCFE calculations as well as points of reference. The FCF calculations are not necessary for our FCFE calculation (Table AVI.1).

Step 2-Figure out the inputs. You can do this by figuring out the: Cost of equity, debt, WACC, and growth rate. This can be tricky as the analyst has to make numerous assumptions (Table AVI.2).

Cost of Equity

The CAPM is essentially the cost of equity. There are three components to the CAPM: Risk-free rate (RFR), beta, and the equity risk premium. We used the 1.23% the rate for the 30-year bond for the risk-free rate. The beta for Mastercard is roughly 1.22. The historical risk premium of equities over other asset classes is roughly 5%. The net result is Mastercard's Cost of Equity (ke) comes out to about 5.83%. We note you may decide to make different assumptions regarding the various inputs for the cost of equity and debt over the long-term, but for the purposes of our calculation, we have left them the same (Table AVI.3).

Cost of Debt

We can calculate the after-tax cost of debt as well. There are a couple of components necessary: Risk-free rate, default spread, and marginal tax rate. We continue to use the 1.23% for the 30-year bond for the risk-free rate. The default spread can be found by looking at the quality of the debt or rating and interest coverage ratio. Mastercard has an AAA rating and a strong interest coverage ratio, putting it at very low risk. We use 0.63% here. The company's marginal tax rate is current 17.5%. The after-tax cost of debt is found by adding the risk-free rate to the default spread and multiplying it by one minus the marginal tax rate.

We can then find the WACC (Weighted Average Cost of Capital) by multiplying the percentage of equity for Mastercard 96% by the cost of equity and then adding it to the percentage of debt by the cost of debt. The WACC is thus roughly 5.69% (Table AVI.4).

Table AVI.1 Mastercard Ten-Year Free Cash Flow Estimates

FY Dec	*FY*	*FY*	*FY*	*FY*	*FY*	*FY*	*FY*	*FY*	*FY*	*FY*	*FY*	*FY*	*FY*
	2018	*2019*	*2020E*	*2021E*	*2022E*	*2023E*	*2024E*	*2025E*	*2026E*	*2027E*	*2028E*	*2029E*	*2030E*
Free Cash Flow													
Cash flow operations (CFO)	6,223	8,190	6,738	8,544	9,605	10,687	11,850	13,180	14,556	16,045	17,510	19,081	20,767
Capital expenditures (Capex)	*(330)*	*(422)*	*(355)*	*(450)*	*(500)*	*(548)*	*(601)*	*(659)*	*(719)*	*(785)*	*(849)*	*(918)*	*(992)*
FCF	**5,893**	**7,768**	**6,383**	**8,095**	**9,105**	**10,139**	**11,249**	**12,521**	**13,837**	**15,261**	**16,661**	**18,163**	**19,775**
Free Cash Flow Equity													
Net income	5,859	8,118	6,783	8,682	9,713	10,732	11,825	13,078	14,374	15,777	17,157	18,637	20,225
Net capital expenditures (+Dep-Capex)	129	100	265	180	160	175	192	211	230	251	272	294	317
Change in working capital (assets-liabilities)	(2,762)	(1,467)	(1,449)	(1,525)	(1,854)	(1,854)	(1,874)	(1,643)	(2,151)	(2,134)	(2,134)	(1,679)	(1,808)
Net debt issued	*849*	*(3,545)*	*(4,473)*	*(373)*	*(156)*	*(194)*	*0*	*0*	*0*	*0*	*0*	*0*	*0*
FCFE	**4,075**	**3,206**	**1,126**	**6,965**	**7,863**	**8,859**	**10,143**	**11,646**	**12,454**	**13,894**	**15,295**	**17,252**	**18,735**
Free Cash Flow Firm													
After tax operating income	5,922	8,042	7,061	8,996	10,067	11,128	12,262	13,557	14,894	16,338	17,759	19,280	20,910
Net capital expenditures (+Dep-Capex)	129	100	265	180	160	175	192	211	230	251	272	294	317
Change in working capital (assets-liabilities)	*(2,762)*	*(1,467)*	*(1,449)*	*(1,525)*	*(1,854)*	*(1,854)*	*(1,874)*	*(1,643)*	*(2,151)*	*(2,134)*	*(2,134)*	*(1,679)*	*(1,808)*
FCFF	**8,555**	**9,409**	**8,245**	**10,341**	**11,761**	**12,806**	**13,944**	**14,989**	**16,815**	**18,221**	**19,622**	**20,666**	**22,401**

Table AVI.2 Mastercard CAPM Inputs

General Assumptions/Info		
Ticker	MA	
Share price as of last close	$347.99	
Latest closing share price date	8/25/20	
Market cap	$345.32	billion
Debt	$12.60	billion
% of equity	96%	
Dividend yield	0.5%	
Diluted shares	1,022	

Table AVI.3 Mastercard Cost of Equity

Cost of Equity	
RFR	1.23%
Beta	1.22
ERP	5.00%
k_e=	5.83%

Table AVI.4 Mastercard after Tax Cost of Debt

After Tax Cost of Debt	
RFR	1.23%
Default spread	0.63%
Marginal tax rate	17.5%
k_d=	1.53%
WACC	5.69%

Growth

Our next step is to find a long-term growth rate. We know we need to find a growth rate below the 5.83% cost of equity or the equation will not work. Here is where things get tricky, as they so often do with valuation. If we turn to the financial formulas for help, we run into trouble.

Let's look at an example. Mastercard has the following five years statistics: ROE-90.2%, Retention Rate-79.4% (using 20.6% payout ratio), ROC-64.5%, and Reinvestment Rate-73.1%. What is the company's computed growth rate?

$$\text{Retention ratio} = (\text{net income} - \text{dividends})/\text{net income}$$

$$\text{Growth} = (\text{retention ratio}) * (\text{ROE})$$

$$\text{Growth} = (\text{reinvestment rate}) * (\text{ROC})$$

$$\text{Sustainable growth rate} = \text{beta} * (\text{ROE})$$

We can begin by trying the formula g = RR × ROE. The retention rate for Mastercard is roughly 79.4% and the ROE is 90.2% using a five-year average. If we multiply the two together, we get roughly a 71% growth rate, which would be much higher than the 5.83% cost of equity we are using and doesn't work.

Let's try the second formula g = Reinvestment Rate × ROC. The reinvestment rate is 73.1% and ROC is 64.5% for Mastercard. Here we get a growth rate of 47%, which still does not make sense. The sustainable formula presents problems as well as beta of 1.22 multiplied by ROE of 90.2% is 110%. None of these methods seems to work. Mastercard is currently in a hyper-growth phase with the metrics trending up over the next last couple of quarters, which contributes to our challenges. We believe Mastercard is a GDP or consumption plus annual growth rate business, thus we believe it would be fair to say the long-term growth rate is +3%, which although debatable is the rate we decide to use as none of the other options worked.

FCFE Intrinsic Valuation

We can now develop a three-, five-, and ten-year FCFE intrinsic values. We do this by using our key metrics to find the Net Present Value (NPV) for each FCFE estimate. We then add up those estimates for three, five, and ten years and add them to the discounted terminal value of the cash flow in the final year. The terminal value is found by using the formula below. We can then divide the total enterprise value by the outstanding share count.

$$\text{Terminal value} = \frac{\text{FCFE}_n\left(1+g_c\right)}{k_c - g_c}$$

Let's go through each calculation in detail, so we are clear on how the calculations are performed. The FCFE estimates are taken from the figure in p. 219.

Three-Year FCFE Intrinsic Valuation-$333

Terminal Value

$$\text{Terminal value} = \frac{10{,}143\left(1+0.03\right)}{0.0583-0.03} = 319{,}003$$

DCF

$$\frac{6{,}965}{\left(1+0.0583\right)} + \frac{7{,}863}{\left(1+0.0583\right)^2} + \frac{\left(8{,}859+319{,}003\right)}{\left(1+0.0583\right)^3}$$

Five-Year FCFE Intrinsic Valuation-$377

Terminal Value

$$\text{Terminal value} = \frac{12{,}454\left(1+0.03\right)}{0.0583-0.03} = 453{,}356$$

DCF

$$\frac{6{,}965}{(1+0.0583)}+\frac{7{,}863}{(1+0.0583)^2}+\frac{8{,}859}{(1+0.0583)^3}+\frac{10{,}143}{(1+0.0583)^4}+\frac{(11{,}646+453{,}356)}{(1+0.0583)^5}$$

Ten-Year FCFE Intrinsic Valuation-$485

Terminal Value

$$\text{Terminal value*} = \frac{19.297\,(1+0.03)}{0.0583-0.03} = 702{,}474$$

*19,297 derived from Year-10 FCFE (18,735*1.03) Using 3% growth rate

DCF

$$\frac{6{,}965}{(1+0.0583)}+\frac{7{,}863}{(1+0.0583)^2}+\frac{8{,}859}{(1+0.0583)^3}+\frac{10{,}143}{(1+0.0583)^4}+\frac{11{,}646}{(1+0.0583)^5}$$
$$+\frac{12{,}454}{(1+0.0583)^6}+\frac{13{,}894}{(1+0.0583)^7}+\frac{15{,}295}{(1+0.0583)^8}+\frac{17{,}252}{(1+0.0583)^9}$$
$$+\frac{(18{,}735+702{,}474)}{(1+0.0583)^{10}}$$

We have established three-, five-, and ten-year intrinsic value based on discounted cash flows. Our process began by making assumptions regarding the cost of equity, capital, and growth rates. After making these elaborate forecasts, we then discounted back the cash flows for each year and came up with a terminal value, which we also discounted back. We end up with a five-year DCF with an intrinsic value of $377 with the stock trading at roughly $350, a sub 10% premium. Not too much to get excited about.

The result of our efforts is that we believe Mastercard was fairly valued from an intrinsic value perspective, at least in the short term. However, if you take a longer-term view and use the ten-year intrinsic value of $485. It implies there is still +35% upside to the stock over the long term. We would most likely build in a margin of safety on the $485 intrinsic value putting the real buying opportunity somewhere in the roughly $300 range. We encourage investors to make their own assumption regarding the model once it is set up. There is a considerable amount of upside to the stock, especially if the long-term growth assumption is higher than expected! (Table AVI.5).

FCFF Valuation Method for Mastercard (As of Mid-2020)

We believe it makes sense to include an example of FCFF for comparison purposes. Remember the key difference between FCFE and FCFF is that FCFF is before debt. Let's try to use Mastercard as of August 2020 as an example, as we already have derived some of the key metrics necessary for the valuation calculation.

Table AVI.5 Mastercard's FCFE Valuation

MA Intrinsic/FCFE Valuation (Aug-20)						
General Assumptions/Info			*Intrinsic Value*			
Ticker	MA					
Share price as of last close	$354.58			**Year**	**FCFE**	**NPV**
Latest closing share price date	9/01/20			2021	6,965	6,581
Market cap	$351.93	billion		2022	7,863	7,020
Debt	$12.60	billion		2023	8,859	7,474
% of equity	97%			2024	10,143	8,086
Dividend yield	0.4%			2025	11,646	8,773
Diluted shares	1,022			2026	12,454	8,865
Cost of Equity				2027	13,894	9,345
RFR	1.23%			2028	15,295	9,721
Beta	1.22			2029	17,252	10,360
ERP	5.00%			2030	18,735	10,631
k_e=	5.83%					
After Tax Cost of Debt						
RFR	1.23%			**Three-year**	**Five-year**	**Ten-year**
Default spread	0.63%		NPV	21,075	37,935	86,857
Marginal tax rate	17.5%		Terminal value	369,248	453,356	702,474
k_d=	1.53%		Discounted terminal value	319,003	347,143	409,258
WACC	5.69%		Total	340,079	385,078	496,115
Growth	3.00%		**Intrinsic Value**	**$333**	**$377**	**$485**

Source: Company Reports; FactSet.

Step 1-We estimated FCFF for Mastercard over the next ten years below. We included our total FCF, FCFE, and FCFF estimates for comparisons (Tables AVI.6 and AVI.7).

Step 2-We had already previously established the inputs for Mastercard including cost of equity, debt, and WACC. It is very important to note we will be using the WACC instead (as a substitute for) the cost of equity when calculating FCFF.

FCFF Intrinsic Valuation

We can now develop a three-, five-, and ten-year FCFF intrinsic values. The process is similar to the FCFE calculation. We do this by using our inputs to find the NPV for each annual FCFF estimate. We then add up those estimates for three, five, and ten years and add them to the discounted terminal value of the cash flow in the final year. The Terminal Value formula can be found using the formula below.

$$\text{Terminal value} = \frac{\text{FCFF}_n\left(1+g_c\right)}{\text{WACC}_c - g_c}$$

Table AVI.6 Mastercard's Free Cash Flow to Firm

Cash Flow Estimates													*MasterCard (MA)*
FY Dec	*FY 2018*	*FY 2019*	*FY 2020E*	*FY 2021E*	*FY 2022E*	*FY 2023E*	*FY 2024E*	*FY 2025E*	*FY 2026E*	*FY 2027E*	*FY 2028E*	*FY 2029E*	*FY 2030E*
Free Cash Flow Firm													
After tax operating income	5,922	8,042	7,061	8,998	10,067	11,128	12,262	13,557	14,894	16,338	17,759	19,280	20,910
Net capital expenditures (+Dep-Cap Ex)	129	100	265	180	160	175	192	211	230	251	272	294	317
Change in working capital (assets-liabilities)	*(2,762)*	*(1,487)*	*(1,449)*	*(1,525)*	*(1,854)*	*(1,854)*	*(1,874)*	*(1,643)*	*(2,151)*	*(2,134)*	*(2,134)*	*(1,679)*	*(1,808)*
FCFF	8,555	9,409	8,245	10,341	11,761	12,806	13,944	14,989	16,815	18,221	19,622	20,666	22,401

Source: Company Report.

Table AVI.7 Mastercard's Free Cash Flow to Firm Estimates

Cash Flow Estimates													*MasterCard (MA)*
FY Dec	*FY*	*FY*	*FY*	*FY*	*FY*	*FY*	*FY*	*FY*	*FY*	*FY*	*FY*	*FY*	*FY*
	2018	*2019*	*2020E*	*2021E*	*2022E*	*2023E*	*2024E*	*2025E*	*2026E*	*2027E*	*2929E*	*2023E*	*2030E*
Free Cash Flow													
Cash flow operations (CFO)	6,223	8,190	6,738	8,544	9,605	10,687	11,850	13,180	14,556	16,045	17,510	19,081	20,767
Capital expenditures (CapEx)	*(330)*	*(422)*	*(355)*	*(450)*	*(500)*	*(548)*	*(601)*	*(659)*	*(719)*	*(785)*	*(849)*	*(918)*	*(992)*
FCF	5,893	7,768	6,383	8,095	9,105	10,139	11,249	12,521	13,837	15,261	16,661	16,163	19,775
Free Cash Flow Equity													
Net income	5,859	8,118	6,783	8,682	9,713	10,732	11,825	13,078	14,374	15,777	17,157	18,637	20,225
+Depreciation and amortization	459	522	623	630	660	723	793	869	949	1,036	1,121	1,212	1,309
-CapEx	(330)	(422)	(359)	(450)	(500)	(548)	(601)	(659)	(719)	(785)	(849)	(918)	(992)
Net capital expenditures (+Dep-CapEx)	129	100	265	180	160	175	192	211	230	251	272	294	317
Change in working capital (assets-liabilities)	(2,762)	(1,467)	(1,449)	(1,525)	(1,854)	(1,854)	(1,874)	(1,643)	(2,151)	(2,134)	(2,134)	(1,679)	(1,808)
Net debt issued	*849*	*(3,545)*	*(4,473)*	*(373)*	*(156)*	*(194)*	*0*	*0*	*0*	*0*	*0*	*0*	*0*
FCFE	4,075	3,206	1,126	6,965	7,863	8,859	10,143	11,646	12,454	13,894	15,295	17,252	18,735
Free Cash Flow Firm													
After tax operating income	5,922	8,042	7,061	8,996	10,067	11,128	12,262	13,557	14,894	16,338	17,759	19,280	20,910
Net capital expenditures (+Dep-CapEx)	129	100	265	180	160	175	192	211	230	251	272	294	317
Change in working capital (assets-liabilities)	*(2,762)*	*(1,467)*	*(1,449)*	*(1,525)*	*(1,854)*	*(1,854)*	*(1,874)*	*(1,643)*	*(2,151)*	*(2,134)*	*(2,134)*	*(1,679)*	*(1,808)*
FCFE	8,555	9,409	8,245	10,341	11,761	12,806	13,944	14,989	16,815	18,221	19,622	20,666	22,401

Source: Company Reports.

Let's go through each calculation in detail, so we are clear on how the calculations are performed. We present the total NPV (Net Present) calculation below. The FCFF estimates are taken from the figure in p. 219.

Three-Year FCFF Intrinsic Valuation-*NPV Calculation*

Terminal Value

$$\text{Terminal value} = \frac{13{,}944\,(1+0.03)}{0.0569-0.03} = 534{,}059$$

DCF

$$\frac{10{,}341}{(1+0.0569)} + \frac{11{,}761}{(1+0.0569)^2} + \frac{(12{,}806+534{,}059)}{(1+0.0569)^3}$$

Five-Year FCFF Intrinsic Valuation-*NPV Calculation*

Terminal Value

$$\text{Terminal value} = \frac{16{,}825\,(1+0.03)}{0.0569-0.03} = 644{,}019$$

DCF

$$\frac{10{,}341}{(1+0.0569)} + \frac{11{,}761}{(1+0.0569)^2} + \frac{12{,}806}{(1+0.0569)^3} + \frac{13{,}944}{(1+0.0569)^4} + \frac{(14{,}989+644{,}019)}{(1+0.0569)^5}$$

Ten-Year FCFF Intrinsic Valuation-*NPV Calculation*

Terminal Value

$$\text{Terminal value*} = \frac{23{,}072(1+0.03)}{0.0569-0.03} = 883{,}689$$

*23,072 derived from Year-10 FCFF (22,401*1.03) Using 3% growth rate

DCF

$$\frac{10{,}341}{(1+0.0569)} + \frac{11{,}761}{(1+0.0569)^2} + \frac{12{,}806}{(1+0.0569)^3} + \frac{13{,}944}{(1+0.0569)^4} + \frac{14{,}989}{(1+0.0569)^5}$$
$$+ \frac{16{,}815}{(1+0.0569)^6} + \frac{18{,}221}{(1+0.0569)^7} + \frac{19{,}622}{(1+0.0569)^8}$$
$$+ \frac{20{,}666}{(1+0.0569)^9} + \frac{(22{,}401+883{,}689)}{(1+0.0569)^{10}}$$

FCFF Additional Steps

There are four adjustments that need to be made to our calculations to find the value per share. The analyst should add back the cash balance and the minority interests, then subtract other potential liabilities and stock options. We have performed the function below. FCFF is typically higher than the FCFE (Table AVI.8).

Table AVI.8 Mastercard FCFF Valuation

MA Intrinsic/FCFF Valuation (Aug-20)						
General Assumptions/Info			*Intrinsic Value*			
Ticker	MA					
Share price as of last close	$354.58			**Year**	**FCFE**	**NPV**
Latest closing share price date	9/01/20			2021	10,341	9,784
Market cap	$351.93	billion		2022	11,761	10,529
Debt	$12.60	billion		2023	12,806	10,848
% of equity	97%			2024	13,944	11,175
Dividend yield	0.4%			2025	14,989	11,366
Diluted shares	1,022			2026	16,815	12,065
Cost of Equity				2027	18,221	12,370
RFR	1.23%			2028	19,622	12,603
Beta	1.22			2029	20,666	12,559
ERP	5.00%			2030	22,401	12,881
k_e=	5.83%					
After Tax Cost of Debt						
RFR	1.23%			**Three-year**	**Five-year**	**Ten-year**
Default spread	0.63%		NPV	20,314	42,337	116,181
Marginal tax rate	17.5%		Terminal value	534,059	644,019	883,689
k_d=	1.53%		Discounted terminal value	463,220	499,730	521,029
WACC	5.69%		+Cash balance	18,227	21,090	30,507
Growth	3.00%		+Minority interest	–	–	–
			−Potential liabilities	4,138	4,801	6,802
			−Management options	150	175	200
			Total	497,473	558,181	660,715
			Intrinsic value	**$487**	**$546**	**$646**

Source: Company Reports; FactSet.

Index

For Product Safety Concerns and Information please contact our EU representative GPSR@taylorandfrancis.com Taylor & Francis Verlag GmbH, Kaufingerstraße 24, 80331 München, Germany